D1714875

Out of This World

OUT OF THIS WORLD

Speculative Fiction in Translation
from the Cold War
to the New Millennium

RACHEL S. CORDASCO

**UNIVERSITY OF
ILLINOIS PRESS**
Urbana, Chicago, and Springfield

Library of Congress Cataloging-in-Publication Data
Names: Cordasco, Rachel S., author.
Title: Out of this world: speculative fiction in translation
    from the Cold War to the new millennium / Rachel S.
    Cordasco.
Description: Urbana: University of Illinois Press, [2021] |
    Includes bibliographical references and index.
Identifiers: LCCN 2021038170 (print) | LCCN 2021038171
    (ebook) | ISBN 9780252043987 (cloth ; acid-free paper) |
    ISBN 9780252052910 (ebook)
Subjects: LCSH: Speculative fiction—Translations into
    English—History and criticism. | LCGFT: Literary
    criticism.
Classification: LCC PN3448.S64 C67 2021 (print) | LCC
    PN3448.S64 (ebook) | DDC 809.3/876—dc23
LC record available at https://lccn.loc.gov/2021038170
LC ebook record available at https://lccn.loc.gov/2021038171

A casual observer should expect science fiction to be more international than other kinds of popular fiction, precisely as a result of this stress on change: for isn't it reasonable to assume that the hopes, fears and expectations of people will be different in different countries, their ways of looking at things unlike those in one's own country?

—Franz Rottensteiner, *View from Another Shore: European Science Fiction* (1999)

Contents

Introduction

The early twenty-first century has witnessed an explosion of speculative fiction in English translation (SFT). Whether these texts come to us as novels, collections, anthologies, or stand-alone stories published in online and print magazines, they both demonstrate and contribute to the ongoing process of globalization. And while globalization itself has its downsides, one positive result is the growing desire of Anglophone countries to move outside of their literary comfort zones and learn about how the non-Anglophone world thinks and writes about future technology, the supernatural, the uncanny, the horrifying, and the (im)possible.[1]

Speculative fiction is the literary vehicle with which writers explore such issues, and in many such texts Earth itself is united (for better or worse) due to events like alien invasions, pandemics, and the formation of utopian scientist-led governments. The "fantastic," as any study of the subgenre will argue, is universal, while horror, in the words of scholar and critic Jess Nevins, "needs no passport."[2] It follows, then, that some kind of reference text detailing non-Anglophone speculative fiction available in English translation should exist. And now, with *Out of This World: Speculative Fiction in Translation from the Cold War to the New Millennium*, it does.

Speculative fiction as a term has itself evolved over the past few decades, and at this point it generally refers to any work of science fiction, fantasy, horror, magical realism, surrealism, the Weird,[3] or a related subgenre (which I discuss in more detail below).[4] Ultimately, I agree with Gary K. Wolfe's view that *speculative fiction* "has been useful precisely because it allows the blurring of boundaries, which in turn permits a greater auctorial freedom from genre constraints and 'rules.'"[5] Along with its discussion of available SFT, *Out of This World* reveals how different subgenres have emerged and developed in different source languages since the mid-twentieth century and, most important for this volume, which subgenres have been translated into English and why.

This book focuses exclusively on speculative fiction that has been translated into *English* for several reasons. First, a book about SFT from and into any and all languages would run to several massive volumes, though such a project would be a worthy undertaking. Second, Anglophone speculative fiction (particularly science fiction) dominated world markets for decades during the twentieth century, such that many *science fiction* authors around the world were first introduced to the genre via translations of, for instance, Asimov, Clarke, Bradbury, and Dick. It's only in recent years that critics and fans have started asking why such associations as the World Science Fiction Society and the World Fantasy Convention include the word *world* in their titles but mostly hand out awards to Anglophone authors.[6] Third, this author is herself from the United States and is thus more aware of what is being translated into English.

This volume does not explore those texts written by people whose native language is not English but who choose to write in English. Given the dominance of Anglophone speculative fiction around the world, it makes sense for authors to choose to write in the language that will bring them the most readers. Since texts originally written in English often get more attention than SFT, I have decided to focus on the latter.

While the early twenty-first century is certainly a golden age of SFT, it isn't the first. A more modest but nonetheless significant golden age occurred in the 1970s. Following Japan's lead in launching the first International Symposium on Science Fiction in 1970,[7] which brought together Japanese, US, UK, and Soviet writers for the first time, a group of major Anglophone speculative fiction authors founded the international association known as "World SF" at the First World Science Fiction Writers' Conference in Dublin in 1976.[8] While its "stated aim was 'the general dissemination of creative sf, the furthering of scholarship, the interchange of ideas . . . the fostering of closer bonds between those who already hold such deep interests in common around the globe,'" a "major" unstated aim was "to provide opportunities for contact between sf writers in Western and Iron Curtain countries" via a professional organization. Major genre writers like Harry Harrison (US), Frederik Pohl (US), Brian Aldiss (UK), and Sam Lundwall (Sweden) served as some of World SF's presidents, with Pohl establishing the Karel Award for "excellence in sf translation."

Two anthologies emerged from the work of this association (both in 1986): *The Penguin World Omnibus of Science Fiction*, edited by Aldiss and Lundwall, and *Tales from the Planet Earth*, edited by Pohl and Elizabeth Anne Hull.[9] Yet they were far from the first. While non-Anglophone authors had been included in speculative fiction anthologies before, it had been as a minority bloc. Pohl's magazine *International Science Fiction* ran for just two issues (November 1967 and June 1968) but helped pave the way for Franz Rottensteiner's *View from Another Shore: European Science Fiction* (1974)—the first anthology featuring *only* SFT from multiple countries.[10] By the end of the decade, we had two more such anthologies: Donald A. Wollheim's (somewhat dismissively titled) *The Best from the Rest of the World* (1976) and Maxim Jakubowski's *Twenty Houses of the Zodiac* (1979). Just five years before *Best from the Rest*, Wollheim and his wife, Elsie B. Wollheim, had founded the major US science fiction and fantasy publisher DAW, through which they published a remarkable twenty-four works of SFT in the 1970s and '80s.

Multiple such anthologies followed over the next few decades, with eight in the 1980s, two in the 1990s, three in the 2000s, and nine in the 2010s. While some anthologies focused exclusively on what at the time was agreed upon as "science fiction," more and more eschewed that specific label, using only "SF" (which could mean either "science fiction" or "speculative fiction") or adding *fantasy* to their titles. These anthologies came from multiple publishers: Seabury, Doubleday, DAW, Tor Books, Apex Publications, Rosarium Publishing, Future Fiction, and more. Once again, World SF participants like Pohl and Aldiss were involved as editors, as well as Rottensteiner, David Hartwell, James Gunn, and James Morrow and Kathryn Morrow, and more recently Lavie Tidhar, Francesco Verso, Bill Campbell, and Ann VanderMeer and Jeff VanderMeer. Several source languages have also had SFT editor-champions over the years (see individual chapters).

The amount of available SFT from certain source languages changes over time, depending on geopolitical circumstances: for instance, Russian-language SFT dominated the market in translated speculative fiction during the Cold War, Japanese-language SFT increased following the post-world-war US occupation and during its economic expansion in the last third of the twentieth century, and Arabic-language SFT (specifically dystopias) leaped onto the scene in the early 2000s, following the US-led invasion of Iraq and nearly two-decades-long war in Afghanistan. Such peaks in particular source-language SFT will tell a story to future generations about how political, economic, and social shifts around the world influenced which speculative fiction was translated and why.

Readers of this volume may also notice the (sometimes startling) gender imbalances in certain source-language chapters. In some cases, this has to do with women's socioeconomic positions in their cultures and the opportunities to publish in what has traditionally been a male-dominated genre. Polish and Russian SFT, for instance, are almost all male until the turn of the twenty-first century, while the Japanese SFT chapter includes just four women writers. With SFT, the question is not just who is *writing* the text but who is being *translated*. Are translators and publishers missing or skipping over a whole segment of, for example, Japanese or Czech women writers? Based on the data that I've collected on these fourteen source languages, women SFT writers in translation account for a larger percentage of the whole post-2000. Whether that's due to a rise in the number of women getting published, in women writing SFT, in women being translated, or all of the above is outside the scope of this current study.

Terms and Definitions

Literary genre categories are notoriously slippery, coined in some instances by marketing departments to sell certain kinds of books in ways that make them more enticing to the general reading public. Nonetheless, we humans love categories, since they help us make sense of our chaotic world. Speculative fiction authors, critics, scholars, publishers, editors, and readers are no different in their attempt to pin down terms like *science fiction, fantasy, horror,* and *magical realism.*[11] In fact, entire books have been written about these terms. For the purposes of this book, which is more concerned with highlighting available SFT than anything else, I do not intend to reinvent the wheel, especially since so many veteran scholars in the field have already offered useful working definitions.

For the most part, I've turned to the print and online versions of *The Encyclopedia of Science Fiction* (*SFE*) and to Gary K. Wolfe's *Critical Terms for Science Fiction and Fantasy* (1986) for broad definitions of the various subgenres of speculative fiction.[12] And while different language traditions have some slightly different definitions of these subgenres, they generally tend to agree on the following.

Science fiction includes texts whose stories are based on agreed-upon scientific or historical premises and involve what Darko Suvin has called the "interaction of estrangement and cognition" in the face of a "novum" (new physical law, idea, and so forth). According to the *SFE*, the term has shifted since its inception in the 1920s by Hugo Gernsback ("By 'scientifiction' I mean the Jules Verne, H. G. Wells and Edgar Allan Poe type of story—a charming romance intermingled with scientific fact and prophetic vision") to Alvin Toffler's 1974 claim that science fiction, "by dealing with possibilities not ordinarily considered—alternative worlds, alternative visions—widens our repertoire of possible responses to change." Ultimately, as the *SFE* authors of this entry argue, calling "science fiction" a genre may not be entirely accurate, since, "historically, it grew from the merging of many distinct genres, from utopias to space adventures."[13] Since a book like this benefits from the use of genre and subgenre boundaries, I'm labeling "science fiction" any of those texts that include space travel, alien worlds, new technology, a dystopian or postapocalyptic Earth, and certain alternate-history stories.[14]

Fantasy includes texts that tell stories that are consistent within their own worlds but would be impossible in the "real" world; they often include supernatural or magical characters and events, and this subgenre can act as a vast umbrella term for epic fantasy, gothic fantasy, surrealism, magical realism, and the Weird. In its introduction, *The Encyclopedia of Fantasy* characterizes "fantasy" as those "tales involving Dreams and Visions, Allegory and Romance, Surrealism and Magic Realism, Satire and Wonderland, Supernatural Fiction, Dark Fantasy, Weird Fiction and Horror—all of these and more besides, sometimes expressing conflicting understandings of the nature of fantasy."[15] In this category I have placed everything from the surreal fantasy of Gustav Meyrink and Jean Ray and Andrzej Sapkowski's epic fantasy *Witcher* series to the magical realist dreamlike tales of Murakami Haruki.

Horror is usually all about a reader's emotional reaction—usually fear or intense disgust; these texts introduce a menacing Other that upends everyday reality. The *SFE* describes the evolution of "horror" over the past couple of centuries: "Horror itself, as a separate genre, has roots older than those of sf, and had begun to develop its distinctive patterns by the time of the Romantic movement in the very early nineteenth century—a little earlier than sf. Like sf it was by the 1930s widely if incorrectly considered as distinct from other literary genres. Horror did not, however, become a major genre in the mass market until the late 1970s and early 1980s—a boom that partly resulted from Stephen King's popularity."[16] "Horror" is often an *element* in science fiction and fantasy texts that elicits the reader's fear or dread. Those texts that take that emotion as their main thrust have been placed in the "horror" category in this book, including Suzuki Koji's *Ring* series, the gothic horror of Hanns Heinz Ewers, and Iginio Ugo Tarchetti.

Terms like *the fantastic* or *fantastika* generally function in the same way as *speculative fiction*, that is, as umbrella terms for the myriad speculative subgenres. In Italian and Korean speculative fiction, for instance, *science fiction* and *fantasy* are merged into a single term: *fantascienza17* and *gongsang gwahak soseol* (science fantasy fiction), respectively.[18] Though Italians first dubbed it *scienza fantastica* in 1952, *fantascienza* eventually became its "official" designation in the science fiction and fantasy community. As Italian speculative fiction scholar Arielle Saiber suggests, the reason *fantasy* precedes *science* may have "to do with the skepticism early twentieth-century Italy showed toward the sciences."[19] In South Korea, *science fiction* emerged as the preferred term by the start of the twenty-first century, since *science fantasy fiction* had become synonymous with material for younger readers.

Each chapter in *Out of This World* is divided into subgenre sections in order to make it easier for users to quickly locate the kinds of texts in which they're most interested. However, the order of these subgenre sections differs from one chapter to another, depending on which subgenres were translated into English when and the amount of each subgenre that exists in English. Certain fascinating patterns emerge when we compare source languages and the rise and fall of subgenres: for instance, by the early 1990s, both French- and Russian-language SFT shift from being mostly science fiction to mostly fantasy. These two source languages also happened to dominate in the 1960s and '70s, around the time when "fantasy" was only just starting to become popular in the United States and United Kingdom. Conversely, by the 2000s, translations of Japanese-language science fiction and fantasy gave way to more science fiction, while Spanish SFT moved from a mix of fantasy and science fiction to more of the latter. Of course, so many factors influence what gets translated and published and why, including which non-Anglophone editors, critics, and fans are promoting which particular subgenre.[20]

Finnish SFT stands out in that it skews significantly toward fantasy, with 76 percent of titles falling into such categories as magical realism, surrealism, and ecofantasy.[21] Also noteworthy is the seeming lack of horror fiction in Chinese, Finnish, Hebrew, Korean, or Polish SFT (though horror elements are mixed in with some fantasy). Perhaps the fact that the SFT from those first four languages on this list fall into the group of ten to thirty-nine titles has something to do with it. Then again, the SFT from those source languages with more than forty titles tends to have a more diverse subgenre offering. Japanese-, Spanish-, and Swedish-language SFT all boast a significant amount of horror, though the latter is mostly due to a single prolific author. Overall, the trend toward more fantasy and horror is clear across most of the source languages included here, perhaps signaling a global shift in readers' tastes and the influence of recent movies, streaming television, and video games.

How This Book Is Organized

Out of This World offers readers in-depth chapters on the SFT from fourteen different source languages: Arabic, Chinese, Czech, Finnish, French, German, Hebrew, Italian, Japanese, Korean, Polish, Russian, Spanish, and Swedish. These languages were chosen for inclusion because they each have at least ten texts (novels/collections/anthologies) in English translation (Korean is the exception with nine, though its recent sudden expansion made it important to include here). Though this is an arbitrary number, it was a necessary cutoff point to ensure that this volume didn't mushroom into multiple volumes or a truly massive tome. Of course, works of speculative fiction translated from such languages as Catalan, Croatian, Danish, Dutch, Greek, Icelandic, Portuguese, Romanian, Tamil, and Ukrainian (as well as many others) are available in English translation and deserve the attention due them. Perhaps they will fill a future volume.

Each chapter is generally organized chronologically in terms of when texts were translated into English, *not* when texts were published in their original source language. This is not because the book privileges Anglophone texts but because *Out of This World* is primarily a guide for Anglophone readers, critics, and scholars interested in learning more about what actually exists in translation. This, to me, seems more practical than the inclusion in the third edition of Neil Barron's *Anatomy of Wonder* of a section on speculative fiction that *hasn't* been translated. If, however, readers of this book can and want to read the texts listed here in their original source languages, they can of course do that, too.

I chose to focus just on texts published in English translation starting in the 1960s because it was that decade that brought Anglophone readers the first major wave of SFT from multiple source languages. Since then, some of the most well-known texts have even been retranslated: Chicago Review Press came out with the first of many Strugatsky retranslations in 2012, while Karel Čapek's books, originally translated into English in the 1920s and '30s, have been retranslated multiple times since then. Texts by Calvino, Borges, Levi, Saramago, and Bulgakov have also received new translations. Other titles have received their first direct-to-English translations only within the past two decades: one of Witold Gombrowicz's books was first brought into English via a combination of French, German, and Spanish translations but was translated directly from the Polish only in 2000; Stanisław Lem's *Solaris* was translated from the French version in 1964 and directly from Polish in 2011. It would be interesting to compare the direct and nondirect translations of these texts, but that is outside the scope of this volume.

SFT isn't confined, of course, to adult-level novels, collections, and anthologies, but because that describes the majority of what has been available to Anglophone readers since 1960, that is one of this volume's constraints. Many works of young-adult SFT exist and deserve their own in-depth study, including the entire subgenre of Japanese light novels that has soared in popularity both in Japan and in Anglophone countries since the 1990s. One exception to the prose rule was made in this volume for Harry Martinson's Swedish-language epic science fiction poem *Aniara*. Its centrality to Swedish speculative fiction, and adaptation into other media such as film and opera, necessitated its inclusion in the Swedish-language SFT chapter.

The wealth of short *stand-alone* SFT, especially since the spread of the Internet in the 1990s, demands a separate volume. Though appearing sporadically in print publications such as *Analog, Asimov's,* and the *Magazine of Fantasy and Science*

Fiction since the 1960s, SFT regularly appears in multiple online fiction magazines that sprang up around the turn of the twenty-first century. These publications either regularly include SFT in their story lineups (*Clarkesworld Magazine, Strange Horizons, World Literature Today, Words without Borders*,[22] *Latin American Literature Today,* the *Dark Magazine, Tor.com*) or devote themselves entirely to publishing and promoting SFT (*Samovar Magazine, Future Science Fiction Digest*). *Clarkesworld Magazine*, in particular, has partnered with Chinese and Korean organizations to publish at least one work of SFT in almost every issue for a specified period of time. *Locus Magazine*, too, keeps readers up to date on the latest published SFT in the US and UK. In terms of academic studies, volumes such as the essay collection *Lingua Cosmica: Science Fiction from around the World* (edited by Dale Knicker-bocker, University of Illinois Press) and Palgrave's *Studies in Global Science Fiction* series (edited by Anindita Banerjee, Rachel Haywood Ferreira, and Mark Bould) are leading the way in focusing the academy's attention on and legitimizing a literature that was often (and is still often) dismissed as not worthy of serious study.

Out of This World, then, is a resource for anyone interested in learning more about adult-level, book-length prose speculative fiction in English translation since 1960.[23] In order to contextualize each chapter, I invited translators, editors, scholars, and authors knowledgeable about each of these source languages' traditions of speculative fiction to write short introductions. Some focus on how speculative fiction has developed in the source language or country (or both) over a century and a half, while others explore questions of translation or the politics and economics of publishing translations in Anglophone countries. And while some discuss speculative fiction in general, others focus on particular sub-genres like science fiction. Their insights offer us thought-provoking ideas about the complicated and sometimes convoluted process by which non-Anglophone speculative fiction makes its way into English. I want to thank them here, as well, for reading and commenting on my chapter drafts.

Sources

In order to write this book, I've relied not just on my own wide reading of SFT (and related reviews) but also on the wealth of print and online reviews, critical analyses, and book-length studies (in English) that take on non-Anglophone speculative fiction.[24] *The Encyclopedia of Science Fiction* and its companion *The Encyclopedia of Fantasy* have been invaluable in my research, often bringing to my attention authors and texts of which I was wholly ignorant. Their contributors' analyses and overviews have certainly enriched this volume. The Internet Speculative Fiction Database, too, has been an important resource in my efforts to track down translated titles. International literature reviewer Michael A. Orthofer's reviews have provided consistent critical and in-depth analysis, while professional review sites such as *Kirkus Reviews* and *Publishers Weekly* have offered pithy overviews of sometimes obscure titles. For most of the texts, I have relied on publishers' summaries, Goodreads summaries, *Publishers Weekly* and *Kirkus* reviews, and the inexhaustible *Encyclopedia of Science Fiction* for my plot discussions. Those summaries that I gleaned from reviews or essays (both others' and my own) are cited in the chapter endnotes.

For most of the texts that I discuss in this book, I provide both the date of publication in the original source language and that of first publication in English (for example, *"Return from the Stars* [1961; 1980]"). However, some collections and anthologies *as collections and anthologies* exist only in English translation (that is, the stories were never published as a collection in their original source language). For those texts, I include only the date of publication in English.

Thanks to my affiliation with the University of Wisconsin–Madison, I've also had access to a massive amount of academic papers and dissertations on a wide variety of SFT authors. So, too, has this affiliation allowed me to check out many out-of-print and obscure titles that are available only via WorldCat. This highlights one of the major issues involving in getting SFT in Anglophone readers' hands: without access to a university library, some readers will simply not be able to borrow the SFT titles they seek. However, readers should consult with their local libraries to see what their options are. Of course, many readers will turn to the Internet to find obscure SFT, which is often available on various websites. Readers should also check publishers' backlists online to find lesser-known SFT. Finally, local independent bookstores are the perfect places to stumble across obscure or older SFT. I, for example, found some early Perry Rhodan and first edition Stanisław Lem novels at indie bookstores in the Madison, Wisconsin area, and it felt like I had struck gold. Science fiction and fantasy convention dealer rooms, library book sales, and garage sales are also great places to find SFT.

✳ ✳ ✳

Out of This World: Speculative Fiction in Translation from the Cold War to the New Millennium is the first of its kind to gather and analyze SFT available to Anglophone readers. However, it is not the first attempt by an individual to track and document these books generally. Buried in the *Anatomy of Wonder* volume are brief summaries of certain SFT titles, while Lavie Tidhar's *World SF Blog* (2009–13) and Cheryl Morgan's Science Fiction and Fantasy Translation Award (2009–14) brought renewed attention to SFT at the start of the twenty-first century. My own website, *SFinTranslation.com*, is the direct descendant of these earlier sites and grew out of my own increased interest in the SFT I was reviewing for John DeNardo's *SF Signal* (2003–16). As I write this, I am aware of several other projects involving critical analysis of non-Anglophone speculative fiction and SFT, which suggests that this field will only continue to grow.[25]

Notes

1. See Csicsery-Ronay, "What Do We Mean When We Say 'Global Science Fiction'?"

2. Nevins, *Horror Needs No Passport.*

3. See Langford, "New Weird"; and VanderMeer and VanderMeer, introduction to *The Weird.* According to Langford, "Complex, grimy urban-noir settings and a fondness for grotesquerie are characteristic but not necessarily defining qualities [of "New Weird"]. Perhaps more useful is the sense that New Weird stories freely mingle sf, dark Fantasy and Horror tropes without the disdain for genre sometimes seemingly exuded by writers of Slipstream fiction." I capitalize *Weird* in this book as Langford and VanderMeer and VanderMeer do.

4. As Gary Wolfe points out, "By the late 1960s . . . a number of younger writers returned to Heinlein's 1951 suggestion that 'speculative fiction' be adopted as a replacement term for 'science fiction,' or at least that science fiction be regarded as a subtype of speculative fiction rather than the other way around" (*Critical Terms,* 122).

5. Wolfe, *Critical Terms,* 122.

6. Though not focusing on any particular genre, translation theorist and critic Lawrence Venuti (who translated several works of Italian speculative fiction) has noted that "by routinely translating large numbers of the most varied English-language books, foreign publishers have exploited the global drift towards American political and economic hegemony since World War II, actively supporting the international expansion of British and American cultures" (*Translator's Invisibility,* 13).

7. Gardner, "1970 Osaka Expo and/as Science Fiction."

8. Hansen, Langford, and Walewski, "World SF."

9. As readers will note, many of these early international anthologies focus on science fiction to the exclusion of other subgenres, which reflects the dominance of Anglophone science fiction exportation to the rest of the world in the mid-twentieth century.

10. Seven anthologies of just Soviet science fiction, and one of French, were published in English between 1961 and 1970.

11. See Wolfe, *Evaporating Genres.*

12. Also notable are Farah Mendlesohn's *Rhetorics of Fantasy* (2008), Jess Nevins's *Horror Fiction in the 20th Century: Exploring Literature's Most Chilling Genre* (2020), Tzvetan Todorov's *The Fantastic: A Structural Approach to a Literary Genre* (1975), and Darko Suvin's *Metamorphoses of Science Fiction: On the Poetics and History of a Literary Genre* (1979).

13. Stableford, Clute, and Nicholls, "Definitions of SF."

14. See also Canavan and Link, *Cambridge History of Science Fiction.*

15. Introduction to *The Encyclopedia of Fantasy.*

16. Nicholls and Clute, "Horror in SF."

17. See Saiber, "Flying Saucers."

18. See Park, "Brief History of South Korean SF Fandom."

19. Saiber, "Flying Saucers," 4.

20. The Polish culture website Culture.pl suggests that one reason for a turn toward fantasy, at least in Poland, is that "on average fantasy books have considerably larger editions than science fiction or horror publications, following a worldwide trend for catering to the youth market. This group of readers values simplicity and expects literature to be entertaining and relaxing. That is not the case with science fiction and its tendency to challenge the reader" (Zwierzchowski, "Futurological Congress").

21. I calculate percentages by drawing on my spreadsheet of SFT, available here: https://docs.google.com/spreadsheets/d/1RyMOXmi1Zd4yvuTVHQcw5gka8YLZ1In42GJn6Rhh12E/edit#gid=67096027.

22. I had the honor of editing a special feature on Italian speculative microfiction in translation for *Words without Borders* in 2019: https://www.wordswithoutborders.org/article/may-2019-italian-speculative-microfiction-in-translation-three-writers.

23. See also the special issues of *Science Fiction Studies*: "On Global Science Fiction," pts. 1 and 2.

24. Due to space constraints, I do not discuss every single text that is listed in each chapter's "Primary Source" list, though I have made an effort to include the vast majority of them.

25. Arielle Saiber's course on World Science Fiction is a useful ongoing resource: https://courses.bowdoin.edu/ital-2500-spring-2015/.

Secondary Sources

Canavan, Gerry, and Eric Carl Link. *The Cambridge History of Science Fiction*. New York: Cambridge University Press, 2019.

Csicsery-Ronay, Istvan, Jr. "What Do We Mean When We Say 'Global Science Fiction'? Reflections on a New Nexus." *Science Fiction Studies* 39, no. 3 (2012): 478–93.

Gardner, William O. "The 1970 Osaka Expo and/as Science Fiction." *Review of Japanese Culture and Society* 28 (2011): 26–43.

Hansen, Rob, David Langford, and Konrad Walewski. "World SF." In *The Encyclopedia of Science Fiction*, edited by John Clute, David Langford, Peter Nicholls, and Graham Sleight. London: Gollancz, updated August 31, 2018. http://www.sf-encyclopedia.com/entry/world_sf.

Introduction to *The Encyclopedia of Fantasy*, edited by John Clute and John Grant. London: Orbit, 1997. http://sf-encyclopedia.uk/fe.php?id=0&nm=introduction.

Langford, David. "New Weird." In *The Encyclopedia of Science Fiction*, edited by John Clute, David Langford, Peter Nicholls, and Graham Sleight. London: Gollancz, updated April 19, 2012. http://www.sf-encyclopedia.com/entry/new_weird.

Nevins, Jess. *Horror Needs No Passport: 20th Century Horror Literature Outside the U.S. and U.K.* Independently published, 2018.

Nicholls, Peter, and John Clute. "Horror in SF." In *The Encyclopedia of Science Fiction*, edited by John Clute, David Langford, Peter Nicholls, and Graham Sleight. London: Gollancz, updated December 5, 2019. http://www.sf-encyclopedia.com/entry/horror_in_sf.

"On Global Science Fiction—Part 1." Special issue, *Science Fiction Studies* 26, pt. 3 (November 1999). https://www.depauw.edu/sfs/covers/cov79.htm.

"On Global Science Fiction—Part 2." Special issue, *Science Fiction Studies* 27, pt. 1 (March 2000). https://www.depauw.edu/sfs/covers/cov80.htm.

Park, Sang Joon. "A Brief History of South Korean SF Fandom." In *Readymade Bodhisattva: The Kaya Anthology of South Korean Science Fiction*, edited by Sunyoung Park and Sang Joon Park, 409–23. Los Angeles: Kaya Press, 2019.

Saiber, Arielle. "Flying Saucers Would Never Land in Lucca: The Fiction of Italian Science Fiction." *California Italian Studies* 2, no. 1 (2011). https://escholarship.org/uc/item/67b8j74s#main.

Stableford Brian, John Clute, and Peter Nicholls. "Definitions of SF." In *The Encyclopedia of Science Fiction*, edited by John Clute, David Langford, Peter Nicholls, and Graham Sleight. London: Gollancz, updated January 2, 2020. http://www.sf-encyclopedia.com/entry/definitions_of_sf.

VanderMeer, Ann, and Jeff VanderMeer. Introduction to *The Weird: A Compendium of Strange and Dark Stories*. New York: Tor Books, 2012.

Venuti, Lawrence. *The Translator's Invisibility: A History of Translation*. 2nd ed. London: Routledge, 2008.

Wolfe, Gary. *Critical Terms for Science Fiction and Fantasy*. New York: Greenwood Press, 1986.

———. *Evaporating Genres: Essays on Fantastic Literature*. Middletown, CT: Wesleyan University Press, 2011.

Zwierzchowski, Marcin. "Futurological Congress: Contemporary Polish Fantasy & Sci-Fi." *Culture.pl* (June 2012). https://culture.pl/en/article/futurological-congress-contemporary-polish-fantasy-and-sci-fi.

Out of This World

Arabic-Language SFT

Introduction[1]

Genre literature in translation—specifically Arabic science fiction in English—is a *very* underdeveloped field. To my knowledge, none of the classics of Egyptian SF have been translated into English: texts by Tawfik al-Hakim (1898–1987), Mustafa Mahmoud (1921–2009), and Nihad Sharif (1921–2011). In fact, at an SF event I once attended at the Egyptian Writers' Union, I bumped into a descendent of Sharif, only to hear an acquaintance of his complain that it was about time that some of his works be translated.

The situation is different with al-Hakim and Mahmoud, as al-Hakim was a distinguished playwright and literary critic, while Mahmoud was an Islamic thinker and celebrity across the Arab world. Nonetheless, even though much of their nongenre fiction has been translated, their science fiction has not, despite their status as pioneers of Egyptian SF in the 1950s and 1960s. Sharif is not nearly as well known internationally, although he was the first Arab author to specialize in SF, beginning in the 1970s, ushering in a whole new generation of authors.

The Maghreb (the western part of the Arab world) has fared better as far as translation is concerned because many of its authors write in French. The first Algerian SF authors—Mohammed Dib (1920–2003) and Safia Ketou (1944–89)—wrote in French, while other contemporary Maghrebi authors, such as Moussa Ould Ebnou (Mauritania) and Faycel Lahmeur (Algeria), often publish in French first, specifically to reach a wider audience (they're keen on moving

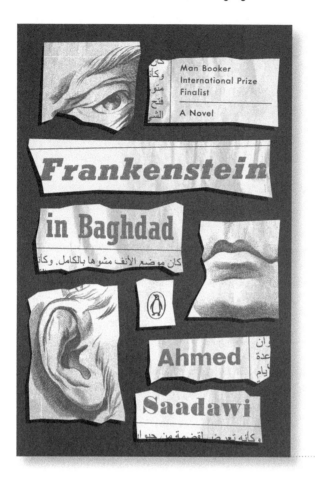

Frankenstein in Baghdad (2018)

into English, too).[2] We're a bit more isolated here in the eastern part of the Arab world, though, and it's our own fault. Egypt's National Centre for Translation and Publishing, for instance, is exclusively concerned with translation from other languages *into* Arabic, despite their commendable role in charging competitive translation rates and sorting out copyright issues. Most literary translation work in Egypt is done on a one-on-one basis, with individuals connecting translators with those interested in having their manuscript translated into English; acceptable rates are then agreed upon privately. Sometimes, translators struggle to track down an author online to get their permission to translate a beloved short story, with the promise to split the proceeds afterward, if the translator can find a buyer (for instance, online short-story contests or magazines that also deal with translated

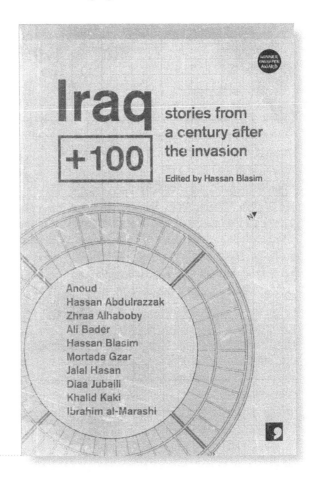

Iraq + 100 (2016)

texts). Then it's up to the translator *how* to translate it: relying on formal English that sounds like Arabic or on colloquial English that foreign readers will recognize.

It's a laborious and haphazard process. If publishers in the Arab world made a concerted effort to hire (or advertise for) translators and target specific authors, works, genres, and foreign audiences, the process would work much more smoothly and Arabic-language SF would have more of an impact on foreign perceptions of the genre from this source language. International publishing houses seem to be filling the breach, luckily, but even here there are problems. Arabic literature expert Marcia Lynx Qualey has explained that the West is now very interested in Arabic SF, especially since the Arab Spring, wanting to use it as a barometer for things to come.[3] Alas, some of the most famous translations have been of bleak dystopias: Ahmed Khaled Towfik's *Utopia* (2012), Mohammad Rabie's *Otared* (2016), and Basma Abdel Aziz's *The Queue* (2016).[4] Is it a coincidence that all three novels are dystopias and that Towfik's first novel, written originally in 2008, was translated only in 2012? The same goes for Ahmed Saadawi's *Frankenstein in Baghdad* (2013), originally written not after the Iraq War but following the Arab Spring, along with the equally depressing stories in the *Iraq + 100* anthology. This is a commendable first step, but the political focus offers a skewed image of Arab genre literature. Most SF writers in Egypt write horror, detective fiction, and dark fantasy, including Towfik and Rabie. This is either out of personal preference or to make ends meet. And even when they write SF, it's not necessarily dystopian. Themed anthologies of children's SF are quite popular, as well as other subgenres like postapocalypse, cyberpunk, alien invasion, first contact, conspiracy-theory SF, Sufi-themed SF, and resistance literature.

Another barrier for Arabic SFT is the focus on famous authors, regardless of subgenre.[5] Ahmed Salah al-Mahdi, a friend of mine, has been struggling to get English versions of his works (fantasy as well as SF) published, but to no avail, even with the help of enthusiastic and experienced foreigners. Several friends of mine from the Indian subcontinent and sub-Saharan Africa tell me that they face the same problem. Translations of younger and widely read authors would give Anglophone readers a much better picture of the true current state of Arabic speculative literature. It would also show the range of influences writers draw from that go beyond politics. They have access to a much wider and very different set of foreign SF works—classics, pulp sci-fi, comics, video games, cinema—while still being strongly influenced by folktales and legends. There's also the geographical dispersal, with a good many authors from the provinces, and their language skills, geared more to colloquial Arabic. Their writing methodology is also different, relying far more extensively on research (facilitated in part by the Internet) than previous generations.

Self-publishing, e-books, podcasts, blogs, and online translation and short fiction contests are filling this breach and bringing Arabic SFT to the Anglophone world despite everything.

Emad El-Din Aysha

The Texts

The majority of modern Arabic-language SFT has come to us within the past decade, mostly from Egyptian and Iraqi authors. Given the fraught relationship in the late twentieth and early twenty-first centuries between the Anglophone world and the Middle East (particularly since the first Gulf War, in 1990–91), it's not surprising that many of those Arabic texts translated into English are dystopias or works of dark fantasy (as Emad El-Din Aysha discusses in the chapter introduction). Because of translators like Elisabeth Jaquette, Jonathan Wright, Chip Rossetti, and others, Arabic-language SFT is gaining prominence in both genre-specific and general literary publications and presses.[6]

While many of the texts in this chapter fall into the overly broad "fantasy" category, together they reveal just how rich and diverse such stories can be. Some of these texts can be called "high fantasy" because they include magical creatures (like ghosts and jinns) or ancient gods, while others deal with mythology, magic-based time travel, fable, and unexplained disappearances. The four dystopian novels in this chapter (all translated and published in English between 2011 and 2017) imagine an apocalyptic, authoritarian future, while the horror and science fiction novels (totaling two) examine questions of immortality and the existence of the soul.

FANTASY

The first work of Arabic-language fantasy translated into English is Ibrahim al-Koni's *Anubis: A Desert Novel* (2002; 2005). A unique work of fantastic mythology based on Tuareg folklore about Anubis, the ancient Egyptian god of the underworld, this book takes readers on a kaleidoscopic journey through the Libyan desert. A young Tuareg boy goes on a quest to find the father he barely remembers from his childhood, but the spirit world seems to challenge him at every turn. An oasis that gradually deteriorates into a mundane human community, a lover who turns into a sibyl-like priestess, animal metamorphosis, human sacrifice: all of these pieces form the picture of a complex history and culture in which the ancient past and the troubled present confront one another.

Gamal al-Ghitani's *The Zafarani Files* (1976; 2009), a darkly comic fantasy from Egypt, is in keeping with his other books that critiqued what Ghitani saw as a resistance to innovation in his native country. *The Zafarani Files* explores the concept of surveillance from the perspective of an unnamed observer who watches the residents of Zafarani Alley, a small village located in a corner of Old Cairo. The highs and lows, betrayals, love affairs, and gossip play out as in any other close-knit community, only Zafarani Alley must also deal with the fallout from a spell cast on it by the mysterious Sheikh Atiya.

Like Ghitani's novel, Khairy Shalaby's *The Time-Travels of a Man Who Sold Pickles and Sweets* (1991; 2010) is a work of semihumorous fantasy. This is the story of Ibn Shalaby, who finds himself mysteriously able to travel through time, though he seems to have no control over when or where he goes. Jumping around randomly in Egypt's rich past—with his briefcase and Islamic-calendar wristwatch—Ibn Shalaby encounters poets, sultans, celebrities, politicians, and other notable Egyptians, including the Nobel Prize–winning author Naguib Mahfouz.

The spirit world is brought to the fore in Saudi author Ibraheem Abbas's *HJWN* (2013; 2014). A mix of fantasy, science fiction, and romance, *HJWN* is told from the perspective of a jinni whose life seems to parallel those of the humans among whom he's lived for so many years. As human populations have grown and their settlements have expanded, jinns have been unintentionally caught up in human affairs. Hawjan in particular, despite his best efforts, has fallen in love with a human woman (Sawsan), and while they can communicate only through a Ouija board, their relationship grows strong. Sawsan's terminal brain cancer, though, has driven her desperate father to seek the help of a sorcerer, who intends to drive out what he calls the devilish spirits who haunt her house. Hawjan, with the help of a human who has agreed to possession, intends to fight back to save Sawsan and her father.

In Amir Tag Elsir's and Ibtisam Azem's fantasy texts, supernatural beings, spells, and curses are nowhere to be found. Elsir's *Telepathy* (2015; 2015) is a psychological thriller about the tenuous relationship between imagination and reality.[7] When a Sudanese writer realizes that one of his recent characters (whom he condemned to an early death) strangely resembles a real person whom he's never met, he starts to wonder if he should warn that person about their fate. Set in two Khartoums (the rich, bustling city and the seedy, poverty-stricken one), *Telepathy* investigates the nature of narrative, sanity and insanity, and where we draw the line between fiction and reality. Azem's *The Book of Disappearance* (2014; 2019), the first work of Palestinian speculative fiction in English translation, is a work of fantastical alternate history. The novel's premise—the sudden disappearance of all Palestinians from Israel—asks readers to think more deeply about the ongoing conflict in that region and raises issues of memory, loss, guilt, friendship, and hope that make up the past and present of this fraught area of the world.

Thanks in large part to Iraqi-born author Hassan Blasim, who now lives in Finland, the recent but rich tradition of speculative Iraqi fiction has started its journey into English. Blasim's own surrealistic-fantastic collection, *The Iraqi Christ* (2013), is the first work of speculative fiction by an Iraqi author translated into English and includes stories that feature the ghosts of car-bomb victims, jinns, soldiers from various wars, and more.[8] Blasim's fiction draws on the brutality, violence, and absurdity of life in a country wracked by war and internal clashes to create a kind of art that forces readers to see Iraq differently than it's depicted in the American or UK media.

Rather than commenting outright on political or social issues, Syrian-born author Osama Alomar invites us to think more deeply about the creatures and things that surround us and construct our personal realities. His collection *The Teeth of the Comb, and Other Stories* (2017) takes the notion of a fluid boundary between fantasy and reality even further. A group of fables and tales of magical realism, Alomar's main characters are not people but personified animals, natural elements (swamps, rainbows), and artificial creations (trucks, numbers).[9] Some are just one line, like "Swamp": "I turned into a swamp of inactivity, and because of this no one was able to see the gems in my depths." *The Teeth of the Comb* is an invitation to step inside of ourselves to gain a new perspective on the objects and the world around us.

DYSTOPIA

The Arabic SFT coming out of Egypt since 2011 (when protests first erupted against Hosni Mubarak) has been unsurprisingly dark, given the unrest and anger that, to American news audiences, seemed to spread quickly throughout that country. Published in English between 2011 and 2017, such novels as *Utopia*, *The Queue*, *Otared*, and *Using Life* adopt a pessimistic view of what Egypt might become. Ahmed Khaled Towfik's **Utopia** (2009; 2011) offers us a grim view of Egypt in 2023, in which a young man and his girlfriend venture out of their wealthy gated community (named "Utopia") in order to see how the other half lives.[10] The poverty and despair that confront them profoundly shift their worldview, but one man whom they meet knows that he needs to get them back to their community before something terrible happens.

A near-future dystopia, Basma Abdel Aziz's **The Queue** (2012; 2016) focuses on the oppressive relationship between the government and the people, rather than economic disparities.[11] Set against a failed political uprising, *The Queue* offers readers a vision of the ultimate bureaucratic nightmare: a centralized authority known as "the Gate" has risen up after the crackdown on protesters, and people from all walks of life must line up outside of this nondescript building in order to get the authority to sign off on anything from permission to have surgery to remove a bullet to permission to change one's name. The Gate, however, never actually opens, and as the line grows longer the people in that line form an increasingly complex community that becomes tied to the pronouncements of the Gate and the hope that it might open one day.

It's not surprising that the Egyptian SF translated into English focuses on near-future failed revolutions, since the unrest in Egypt didn't immediately lead to some perfect, utopian society with a responsive, nonrepressive government. Indeed, this SFT reflects the complicated, messy outcome of political revolution and the clash between people's hopes and the realities of governmental and bureaucratic power. Mohammad Rabie's **Otared** (2015; 2016) starts, like *The Queue*, from a failed revolution, but here Egypt is subsequently invaded.[12] Set in 2025, Rabie's novel follows Ahmed Otared, a former police officer who joins up with other ex-cops to try to liberate Egypt through violence.

Less dystopian but tending toward the apocalyptic, Ahmed Naji's *Using Life* (2014; 2017) is set in modern-day Cairo and tells the story of a documentary filmmaker (Bassam Bahgat) hired by a secret society to create a series of films about the urban planning and architecture of the city.[13] Told through text and black-and-white illustrations (by Ayman Al Zorkany), *Using Life* charts Bahgat's horror as he discovers that this society has had a hand in shaping political regimes, geographical boundaries, and religions around the world. It manipulates urban architecture to achieve its ends, and its next plan involves wiping out and rebuilding Cairo.

HORROR

Ahmed Saadawi's *Frankenstein in Baghdad* (2013; 2018) combines horror and the absurd to comment on the American invasion of Iraq and the concepts of the soul and life after death.[14] Hadi, a scavenger in the rubble and blood that is US-occupied Baghdad, collects the body parts of bomb victims and sews them together into a single corpse, which he plans to bury and thus give some sort of peace to the victims' souls. What he doesn't expect is for a stray soul to inhabit the corpse and then rampage through the city bent on revenge on behalf of the victims of which it's composed. This revenge, though, soon turns into a bloodlust that overwhelms the criminal and the innocent alike.[15]

SCIENCE FICTION

Questions of aging and reproduction drive Jordanian author Fadi Zaghmout's *Heaven on Earth* (2014; 2017). Set in Jordan eighty years in the future, Zaghmout's novel imagines that advances in bioscience and nanotechnology can offer people eternal youth and the ability to create new life in a society in which reproduction is strictly regulated.[16] Both a personal look at one family's navigation of new technology and a general assessment of Jordanian society nearly a century from now, *Heaven on Earth* ensures that Arabic-language narratives are heard in the global debates about technological advances and societal shifts.

It is thanks to Iraqi author Blasim that we have *Iraq + 100: Stories from a Century after the Invasion* (2016). The contributing authors were asked to imagine what their home city might look like in 2103, many years after the end of the US- and British-led invasion.[17] A mix of stories originally written in Arabic and in English, these examples of science fiction, magical realism, fantasy, and horror include self-aware statues, alien invaders, tiger droids, and the ever-present Tigris. The pressure of the past is clear in these tales, as authors draw on old myths and stories as well as present scientific breakthroughs and potential future developments. An important collection that not only gives Anglophone readers an inside look at Iraqi culture and storytelling but also introduces those readers to a variety of Iraqi authors together for the first time, *Iraq + 100* is hopefully the first of many such anthologies.

While Iraq and Egypt are the main sources of Arabic speculative fiction in English translation, several other countries in the region have also contributed to the growing corpus of Arabic speculative fiction in English. It is hoped this trend in translated speculative fiction coming from Arabic-speaking countries will only continue.

Primary Sources

EGYPT

1976: Ghitani, Gamal al-. *The Zafarani Files.* Translated by Farouk Abdel Wahab. American University in Cairo Press, 2009.

1991: Shalaby, Khairy. *The Time-Travels of a Man Who Sold Pickles and Sweets.* Translated by Michael Cooperson. American University in Cairo Press, 2010.

2009: Towfik, Ahmed Khaled. *Utopia.* Translated by Chip Rossetti. Bloomsbury Qatar Foundation, 2011.

2012: Aziz, Basma Abdel. *The Queue.* Translated by Elisabeth Jaquette. Melville House, 2016.

2014: Naji, Ahmed. *Using Life.* Translated by Benjamin Koerber. University of Texas Press, 2017.

2015: Rabie, Mohammad. *Otared.* Translated by Robin Moger. Hoopoe, 2016.

IRAQ

2013: Blasim, Hassan. *The Iraqi Christ.* Translated by Jonathan Wright. Comma Press.
      Saadawi, Ahmed. *Frankenstein in Baghdad.* Translated by Jonathan Wright. Penguin Books, 2018.

2016: Blasim, Hassan, ed. *Iraq + 100: Stories from a Century after the Invasion.* Various translators. Comma Press.

JORDAN

2014: Zaghmout, Fadi. *Heaven on Earth.* Translated by Sawad Hussain. Signal 8 Press, 2017.

LIBYA

2002: Koni, Ibrahim al-. *Anubis: A Desert Novel.* Translated by William M. Hutchins. American University in Cairo Press, 2005.

PALESTINE

2014: Azem, Ibtisam. *The Book of Disappearance.* Translated by Sinan Antoon. Syracuse University Press, 2019.

SAUDI ARABIA

2013: Abbas, Ibraheem. *HJWN*. Translated by Yasser Bahjatt. Yatakhayaloon, 2014.

SUDAN

2015: Elsir, Amir Tag. *Telepathy*. Translated by William M. Hutchins. Bloomsbury Qatar Foundation, 2015.

SYRIA

2017: Alomar, Osama. *The Teeth of the Comb, and Other Stories*. Translated by the author and C. J. Collins. New Directions.

Notes

1. Special thanks to Layla, Zahraa, and the Egyptian Society for Science Fiction.

2. See the language experiences of an Algerian speculative author friend I interviewed: Aysha, "Islam Sci-Fi Interview of Algerian Fantasy Author Djamel Jiji," http://www.islamscifi.com/islam-sci-fi-interview-of-djamel-jiji/.

3. Qualey, "Arabic Literature in English."

4. Parenthetical dates refer to when the text was first translated into English.

5. See my review article: Aysha, "Double Trouble," https://the-levant.com/double-trouble-moataz-hassaniens-2063-charting-course-today-world-tomorrow/.

6. For a comprehensive discussion of Arabic science fiction, see Campbell, *Arabic Science Fiction*.

7. Carson review.

8. Tarbush and McGregor reviews.

9. Schnelbach review.

10. See Greenberg, "Ahmed Khaled Towfik." See also reviews by Samatar and Orthofer.

11. Cordasco and Dhaimish reviews.

12. See Mokrushina's "Reality and Fiction in Mohammad Rabie's Novel, *Otared*."

13. Pepe review.

14. See reviews by Cordasco and Murphy, as well as a critical essay by Botting ("Infinite Monstrosity").

15. *Frankenstein in Baghdad* won the 2014 International Prize for Arabic Fiction and France's Grand Prize for Fantasy and was a finalist for the 2018 Man Booker International Prize.

16. Fras review.

17. Cordasco and Khan reviews.

Secondary Sources

Aysha, Emad El-Din. "Double Trouble: Moataz Hassanien's *2063*, Charting a Course for Today, from the World of Tomorrow!" *Levant* (2019). https://the-levant.com/double-trouble-moataz-hassaniens-2063-charting-course-today-world-tomorrow/.

————. "Islam Sci-Fi Interview of Algerian Fantasy Author Djamel Jiji." *Islam and Science Fiction* (2018). http://www.islamscifi.com/islam-sci-fi-interview-of-djamel-jiji/.

Botting, Fred. "Infinite Monstrosity: Justice, Terror, and Trauma in *Frankenstein in Baghdad*." *Journal of the Fantastic in the Arts* 30, no. 1 (2019): 6–24.

Campbell, Ian. *Arabic Science Fiction*. Cham, Switzerland: Palgrave Macmillan, 2018.

Carson, Michael J. Review of *Telepathy*, by Amir Tag Elsir. *Reviewer's Bookwatch* (2016).

Cordasco, Rachel. Review of *Frankenstein in Baghdad*, by Ahmed Saadawi. *World Literature Today* (January 2018). https://www.worldliteraturetoday.org/2018/january/frankenstein-baghdad-ahmed-saadawi.

————. Review of *Iraq + 100*, edited by Hassan Blasim. *SFinTranslation.com* (2016). https://www.sfintranslation.com/?p=1185.

————. Review of *The Queue*, by Basma Abdel Aziz. *SFinTranslation.com* (2016). https://www.sfintranslation.com/?p=713.

Dhaimish, Sherif. "Basma Abdel Aziz: *The Queue*." *World Literature Today* 90, no. 5 (2016): 73–74.

Fras, Jona. "Fadi Zaghmout's *Paradise on Earth*: Family Dynamics in Futuristic Jordan." *ArabLit.org* (2015). https://arablit.org/2015/04/15/science-fiction-jordan/.

Greenberg, Nathaniel. "Ahmed Khaled Towfik: Days of Rage and Horror in Arabic Science Fiction." *Critique: Studies in Contemporary Fiction* 60, no. 2 (2019): 169–78.

Khan, Yasmin. "Hassan Blasim, ed. *Iraq + 100*." *Foundation: The International Review of Science Fiction* 46.2, no. 127 (2017): 114–15.

McGregor, Steven. "The Stuff of Nightmares." *Spectator* 322, no. 9639 (2013): 53–54.

Mokrushina, A. A. "Reality and Fiction in Mohammad Rabie's Novel, *Otared*." *Asian & African Studies* (Vestnik of Saint Petersburg University) 10, no. 1 (2018): 68–74.

Murphy, Sinéad. "*Frankenstein in Baghdad*: Human Conditions, or Conditions of Being Human." *Science Fiction Studies* 45, no. 2 (2018): 273–88.

Orthofer, M. A. Review of *Utopia*, by Ahmed Khaled Towfik. *Complete Review* (2011). http://www.complete-review.com/reviews/egypt/towfikak.htm.

Pepe, Teresa. Review of *Using Life*, by Ahmed Naji and Ayman Al Zorkany, translated by Benjamin Koerber. *Strange Horizons* (2019). http://strangehorizons.com/non-fiction/reviews/using-life-by-ahmed-naji-and-ayman-al-zorkany-translated-by-benjamin-koerber/.

Qualey, M. Lynx. "Arabic Literature in English: The Blog as Cross-cultural Salon." Talk delivered at the American University in Cairo, Tahrir campus, March 26, 2012.

Samatar, Sofia. Review of *Utopia*, by Ahmed Khaled Towfik. *Strange Horizons* (2011). http://strangehorizons.com/non-fiction/reviews/utopia-by-ahmed-khaled-towfik/.

Schnelbach, Leah. "Fables for the Modern Age: Osama Alomar's *The Teeth of the Comb, and Other Stories*." *Tor.com* (2017). https://www.tor.com/2017/08/09/fables-for-the-modern-age-osama-alomars-the-teeth-of-the-comb-and-other-stories/.

Tarbush, S. Review of *The Iraqi Christ*, by Hassan Blasim. *TLS—Times Literary Supplement* 5812 (August 2014): 34–35.

Chinese-Language SFT

Introduction

Science fiction has a long history in China, at least as long as most of the other modern genres that were introduced into Chinese literature at the end of the Qing dynasty, such as political fiction and detective fiction. When compared with the realist fiction that has dominated the Chinese literary scene since the May Fourth era (1917–21), though, science fiction has an even longer history. Its inception is traceable to the beginning of the twentieth century, when Liang Qichao (1873–1929), a leading reformer, called for a revolution in fiction in 1902 and named science fiction as one of the major new genres to promote. Known then as *kexue xiaoshuo* (literally "science fiction"), it was one of the most popular fiction genres of the late Qing. Through the efforts of Liang Qichao and such contemporaries as Wu Jianren and Xu Nianci, the genre was instituted as mainly a utopian narrative that projected the political desire for China's reform into an idealized, technologically more advanced world—as exemplified by the wondrous Civilized Realm portrayed in Wu Jianren's *New Story of the Stone* (1908).

Early Chinese science fiction manifested the cultural hybridity resulting from a combination of translated modernity and self-conscious yearning for the rejuvenation of the Chinese tradition. Most of the science fiction by the late Qing writers were under the obvious influence of Western authors, particularly Jules Verne, whose work was much translated at this time. The scientific "nova" that Verne foregrounded in his narratives made a major "point of difference" that has been recapitulated by Chinese authors in their depictions of the brave new worlds in a Chinese context. For example, in *New Story of the Stone*, Jia Baoyu's submarine adventure and airborne safari are both clearly modeled upon similar images in Jules Verne's novels. But at the same time, the Civilized Realm that Baoyu visits is shown as a utopian version of the revitalized Confucian world and has all its scientific inventions grounded in Chinese tradition and the merits of its political system rooted in Confucianism.

Despite a promising beginning, however, the history of Chinese science fiction has been sporadic. Only three short booms can be identified: the last decade of the Qing dynasty (1902–11), the first four years of the New Era (1978–82), and the beginning of the twenty-first century. These booms alternated with dormant periods that lasted so long that, each time the genre was revived, the new generation of science fiction writers had to invent their own tradition, giving Chinese science fiction multiple points of origin.

Early science fiction lost its momentum when mainstream modern Chinese literature was conceptualized almost completely as realism after the May Fourth movement. The genre was reinstated during the 1950s as a subgenre of children's literature, made possible by imitating the Soviet literary system. Its generic name also changed to *kexue huanxiang xiaoshuo* (science fantasy fiction), a translation of its Russian equivalent. Some science fiction writers who began to gain recognition in the 1950s, mostly scientists in their own right, survived the Cultural Revolution and contributed to a short-lived revival of the genre at the beginning of the New Era. Leading writers of the genre during this time period, including Zheng Wenguang, Tong Enzheng, and Ye Yonglie, through serious engagement with social criticism, lifted science fiction from being a subgenre of children's literature under the socialist literary system and turned it into a sophisticated literary form that enabled both reflections on China's recent past and the representation of hope for change.

This generation of science fiction authors was silenced by the government in the early 1980s. Because of their frustration in pursuit of science fiction, the above-mentioned three authors conferred upon the genre negative or, at best, ambiguous images: the bat that is neither beast nor bird, or the strange bird considered alien and monstrous, or simply Cinderella. This second boom came to an abrupt halt when the Communist Party's propaganda organs named science fiction as one of the sources of "spiritual pollution" in 1983 and shut down all science fiction magazines but one, the Chengdu-based *Kexue wenyi* (Science Literature), which later was renamed *Kehuan shijie* (Science Fiction World) and became the base for the genre's third revival.

The situation has changed only recently. Since the late 1990s when the Internet became a new platform for literary creation, new science fiction authors have

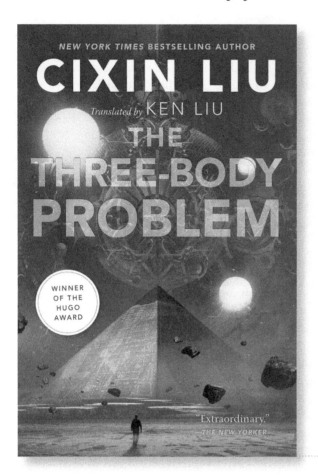

NEW YORK TIMES BESTSELLING AUTHOR

CIXIN LIU

Translated by KEN LIU

THE THREE-BODY PROBLEM

WINNER
OF THE
HUGO
AWARD

"Extraordinary."
—THE NEW YORKER

The Three-Body
Problem (2014)

emerged, first as online writers, creating an increasingly large fandom among young netizens. They have begun to gain recognition from mainstream media in mainland China over the past two years. This new wave of science fiction has led to a sudden boom of this genre for the third time—one that is still developing. The prominent authors emerging with this new wave include Liu Cixin, Wang Jinkang, and Han Song, as well as younger writers like Chi Hui, Fei Dao, Chen Qiufan, Xia Jia, Bao Shu, and Hao Jingfang. Like the two earlier generations, their literary imagination has matured less under the influence of earlier Chinese literature than from the contemporary West. In particular, postwar American and British new-wave SF, ranging from space opera to cyberpunk, has left its traces on Chinese new-wave SF. But like the earlier writers, the new generation has

"There's a new world master among us, and her name is Can Xue."
—Robert Coover

Frontier

Translated from the Chinese by Karen Gernant & Chen Zeping

Can Xue

Frontier (2017)

had to come to terms with their own questions about how to present China in science fiction.

Deeply entangled with the politics of a changing China, science fiction today both strengthens and complicates late-Qing utopian visions of a new, powerful nation: it mingles nationalism with self-reflective irony and parody, blurs the boundary between utopia and dystopia, sharpens social criticism with an acute awareness of China's potential for further reform as well as its limitations, and envelops political consciousness in scientific discourses on the power of technology or the technology of power. By 2010 science fiction in China was no longer a marginal phenomenon. Gaining national fame, the new wave in Chinese science fiction has formed a distinctive "selective tradition" within the literary field of contemporary China, speaking in a unique voice to evoke an array of sensations ranging from the grotesque to the sublime, from the apocalyptic to the transcendent, and from the human to the posthuman.

In a peculiar way, Chinese science fiction has entered its golden age as it simultaneously generates a new-wave subversion of the genre. Chinese science fiction enlivens the dream for the future of a new China, and the contemporary new wave also unleashes its nightmarish shadows. The new wave has a dark and subversive side: it dismantles utopianism by including dystopian anomalies and questions some of the key concepts of Chinese modernity, such as progress, development, nationalism, and scientism. At its most radical, the new wave embraces an avant-garde cultural spirit that encourages the reader to question reality and think beyond conventions.

Mingwei Song

The Texts

Since Chinese-language SFT burst onto the Anglophone scene in the first decade of the twenty-first century, two strands have emerged: those stories that tend toward the fantastic/magical realist mode and those that lean toward the science fictional/dystopian, both at times referencing the legacy of the Cultural Revolution of the 1960s. Most of the Chinese SF in English is in the form of short stories, a trend initiated by translator Ken Liu. Because of his efforts in the early 2010s, *Clarkesworld Magazine* has partnered with the Chinese media company Storycom to bring readers a new work of Chinese SFT each month, rendered into English by a host of accomplished translators.

Meanwhile, a large and vibrant online community of Chinese-to-English translators has for years been translating *wuxia* and *xanxia* stories, that is, stories focusing on martial arts with fantastical elements. Fantasy and martial arts are important to any understanding of Chinese speculative fiction, but the focus here is on novels and collections published by presses (mostly Tor Books, as well as various university presses) and available in print and in e-formats. These authors hail from China, Taiwan, and Hong Kong and demonstrate the varieties of style and historical perspective that that geographical diversity can bring. Thanks to translators like Liu, Joel Martinsen, Annelise Finegan Wasmoen, and several others, Anglophone readers can finally join the millions of Sinophone readers who have enjoyed these remarkable stories for decades.

FANTASY

Martial arts fantasy has been an extremely popular subgenre of Chinese-language speculative fiction for centuries, though modern *wuxia* emerged in the early twentieth century, with twenty-first-century authors continuing the tradition (mostly online) and translators bringing those works to Anglophone readers. The prolific and celebrated author Jin Yong (the pen name of Louis Cha), whose name is synonymous with *wuxia*, has multiple works in English (all originally published in Chinese in the 1950s). The books in the *Legends of the Condor Heroes* series have been sold to Anglophone readers as the "Chinese *Lord of the Rings*." In the first book to appear in English, *The Book and the Sword* (1955–56; 2005), Jin Yong draws on legend and fantasy to craft a story that's steeped in Chinese myth and history. Focusing on the eighteenth-century Manchu emperor Qian-long, and the legend that he was not a Manchu but rather Han Chinese because of a baby swap, Yong tells the stories of secret societies, kung-fu masters, a city guarded by wolves, and a mysterious princess.

A Hero Born (1957; 2018), set in AD 1200, tells the story of Guo Jing, who grows up with Genghis Khan's rising army in Mongolia.[1] His fate is to meet an opponent who is his polar opposite: privileged, cunning, and adept in the martial arts. Guo Jing learns that he has to return to China to fulfill his destiny, but the war raging between the Song Empire and the Jurchen will test his skill and bravery. In the following book, *A Bond Undone* (1959; 2019), Guo Jing is confronted by many multiple dilemmas simultaneously: dealing with his father's death, the fact that he's betrothed to two women (neither of whom is his beloved), and getting drawn into the struggle for the supreme martial text—the *Nine Yin Manual*. Meanwhile, he's being hunted by the widow of a man he accidentally killed long ago.[2]

A work of contemporary high fantasy from China is Tang Qi's *To the Sky Kingdom* (2009; 2016), a story about immortals and their complicated relationships with humans and one another. Immortal lovers threatened by old enemies, mortals and immortals whose love is thwarted by jealousy, and a war god whose spiritual energy is revived from the heart's blood of a devoted student: these are the stories that span time and worlds, mortal and immortal life, showing that love, loyalty, and revenge unite them nonetheless.

A kind of magical realist fantasy, too, has come to Anglophone audiences in recent years from China and Taiwan, including Dung Kai-cheung's *Atlas: The Archaeology of an Imaginary City* (1997; 2012). Set in a world similar to the author's native Hong Kong, *Atlas* is written from the perspectives of four future archaeologists who are attempting to rebuild the lost City of Victoria. The city comes to life via a mix of real-life scenarios and imaginary people. To enable the archaeologists to tell this story, Dung blends genres and styles in order to disrupt (scientific, historical) assumptions about how we can know the "true" history of a place.

Wu Ming-Yi's eco-fantasy *The Man with the Compound Eyes* (2011; 2013) offers readers two separate stories of loss and redemption that connect when an island boy who is determined not to be a sacrifice to the Sea God winds up crashing onto the shore in Taiwan, interrupting a woman (Alice) planning to commit suicide after the loss of her husband and son in a climbing accident. Together they retrace her husband's journey into the mountains, forming an unusual bond and learning secrets that undermine everything Alice knows. Su Wei's *The Invisible Valley* (2018) reveals what it was like for young people who were sent into rural China during the Cultural Revolution for "reeducation."[3] This is the story of one young man's transformation from uninterested Communist Party member used to modern comforts and technology into an individual at home in the natural world and the people who live there—people who are steeped in legends of fantastical creatures and what Westerners might call "superstitions."

The surrealist stories of Dorothy Tse and Can Xue (the pen name of Deng Xiaohua) invite readers to question human perception and the very nature of reality. Tse's collection *Snow and Shadow* (2014) features texts that begin realistically and then abruptly shift into dreamscapes and nightmares: logic breaks down, limbs are lopped off, and absurdity abounds.[4] Can Xue, too, doesn't hesitate to dive into the strangeness that is human life and love. Her novels *The Last Lover* (2005; 2014),[5] *Frontier* (2008; 2017),[6] and *Love in the New Millennium* (2013; 2018)[7] feature characters who, for instance, find themselves in absurdly complicated relationships and can step into one another's fantasies, with Can Xue exploring the nature of reality and the strangeness of human relationships.

SCIENCE FICTION

The first book-length work of Chinese speculative fiction to be translated into English is Lao She's 1930s dystopian science fantasy, *Cat Country* (1932; 1970).[8] When a Chinese space traveler crash-lands on Mars, he finds himself in a country entirely inhabited by Cat People.[9] While on the surface the story is about the wholesale corruption of Cat society (social, political, moral, economic), on another level it harshly criticizes pre–World War II Chinese society with what Lao She saw as its blind adulation of all things "foreign," its anemic education system, and its utterly corrupt government.

Nearly two decades later, Anglophone authors were then treated to more science fiction from China in the form of Wu Dingbo and Patrick Murphy's

anthology *Science Fiction from China* (1989). These eight stories (by six different authors), critical introduction, and chronological bibliography offer readers a
sample of the kind of contemporary science fiction that was being written around
the mid- to late twentieth century, despite years of censorship.

Only in 2014, however, did Chinese-language science fiction truly take the
Anglophone world by storm, thanks to the work of translator Ken Liu, himself an
award-winning Anglophone speculative fiction author. Though Liu started selling
translations of short Chinese science fiction in 2011 to Anglophone magazines, it
was his translation of Liu Cixin's hard science fiction *Three-Body* trilogy (known
in Chinese as "Remembrance of Earth's Past") that catapulted Chinese SFT into
the limelight.[10] A story about humanity's tragic and destructive first contact with
an alien race, the trilogy ultimately takes a uniquely grand perspective on the life
and death of the universe and the ways in which complex alien species might
destroy entire galaxies in order to preserve themselves. Liu's exploration of politics, memory, self-preservation, and theories of the cosmos has made him one
of the most important living science fiction authors.

The Three-Body trilogy has been such a success that related Chinese-language
fan fiction, written by Baoshu (the pen name of Li Jun), a respected science fiction
author in his own right, has also gained critical acclaim. *The Redemption of Time*
(2011; 2019), set in the Three-Body universe, imagines what happened to the brain
of Yun Tianming, which was launched into space in the path of the Trisolaran
fleet as part of humanity's plan for survival.[11] After being captured, tortured, and
turned into a traitor against humanity, Yan is ultimately given a clone body and a
chance to make up for what he was forced to do and ultimately save the human
race from an entity that threatens the entire universe.

The wild popularity of the Three-Body trilogy among Anglophone readers
has led to even more translations of Liu Cixin's novels, including *Ball Lightning*
(2005; 2018)[12] and *Supernova Era* (2003; 2019),[13] which were both published in
Chinese *before* the hit trilogy. The former tells the story of a boy who witnesses
his parents get incinerated by the mysterious phenomenon of ball lightning and
grows up intending to study it in order to understand its nature and how to protect
people from its destructive force. His quest takes him into the realm of weapons
research and geopolitical conflict, but also inspires him to look at atoms and mol-
ecules in a new way—a way that revolutionizes how humanity sees the universe.
More apocalyptic than *Ball Lightning*, *Supernova Era* concerns the fallout from a
supernova event that has showered Earth in deadly levels of radiation. Knowing
that everyone over the age of thirteen will die within a year, parents and care-
givers across the planet start trying to prepare their children to carry on human
civilization by apprenticing them and passing on knowledge. This last generation,

though, doesn't necessarily want to carry on what their parents are leaving behind, but this attempt at a new trajectory may result in humanity's destruction.

Tor Books has capitalized on Liu Cixin's success and the popularity of short works of Chinese SFT in Anglophone magazines by issuing two anthologies of stories translated and edited by Ken Liu: *Invisible Planets* (2016)[14] and *Broken Stars* (2019).[15] Though these include stories that some will have read before, having them together in two volumes offers readers a new way of conceptualizing the issues and interests of Chinese-language science fiction. Both anthologies include major Chinese authors like Chen Qiufan, Xia Jia, Liu Cixin, Hao Jingfang, and Ma Boyong. Columbia University Press, too, has published an anthology of Chinese SFT: *The Reincarnated Giant: An Anthology of Twenty-First-Century Chinese Science Fiction* (2018), which includes stories about supercomputers, dreams, intergalactic war, robots, and much more.[16] This intense wave of Chinese SFT underscores contemporary China's power on the world stage and its speculative authors' creative flexibility in writing about humanity's place in the universe.

The future of Chinese SFT looks bright, especially with the work of writers of the next generation, like Chen Qiufan and Xia Jia. Chen's *Waste Tide* (2013; 2019), a sweeping novel about the hazards of unchecked globalization and trade, the e-waste and recycling industry, and the plight of China's labor migrants, imagines what might happen if biohazardous e-waste (in the form of, for example, a helmet prosthetic or a discarded but still-functioning mecha) winds up infecting a human being and altering their brain chemistry to produce a strange new human-artificial hybrid.[17] Bringing together age-old issues in Chinese culture and new global concerns about humanity in an age of increasingly complex machines, *Waste Tide* promises a future filled with even more timely and sophisticated Chinese SFT.

Primary Sources

Unknown: Wei, Su. *The Invisible Valley*. Translated by Austin Woerner. Small Beer Press, 2018.

1932: Lao She. *Cat Country*. Translated by William A. Lyell. Ohio State University Press, 1970.

1955–56: Jin Yong [Louis Cha]. *The Book and the Sword*. Translated by Graham Earnshaw. Oxford University Press, 2005.

1957: Jin Yong [Louis Cha]. *A Hero Born (Legends of the Condor Heroes #1)*. Translated by Anna Holmwood. MacLehose Press, 2018.

1959: Jin Yong [Louis Cha]. *A Bond Undone (Legends of the Condor Heroes #2)*. Translated by Gigi Chang. MacLehose Press, 2019.

1989: Wu Dingbo, and Patrick D. Murphy, eds. *Science Fiction from China*. Praeger.

1997: Dung Kai-cheung. *Atlas: The Archaeology of an Imaginary City*. Translated by Anders Hansson, Bonnie S. McDougall, and the author. Columbia University Press, 2012.

2005: Can Xue. *The Last Lover*. Translated by Annelise Finegan Wasmoen. Yale University Press, 2014.

Liu Cixin. *Ball Lightning*. Translated by Joel Martinsen. Tor Books, 2018.

2006: Liu Cixin. *The Three-Body Problem*. Translated by Ken Liu. Tor Books, 2014.

2008: Can Xue. *Frontier*. Translated by Karen Gernant and Chen Zeping. Open Letter Books, 2017.

Liu Cixin. *The Dark Forest*. Translated by Ken Liu. Tor Books, 2015.

2009: Tang Qi. *To the Sky Kingdom*. Translated by Poppy Toland. AmazonCrossing, 2016.

2010: Liu Cixin. *Death's End*. Translated by Ken Liu. Tor Books, 2016.

2011: Baoshu. *The Redemption of Time*. Translated by Ken Liu. Tor Books, 2019.

Wu Ming-Yi. *The Man with the Compound Eyes*. Translated by Darryl Sterk. Harvill Secker, 2013.

2013: Can Xue. *Love in the New Millennium*. Translated by Annelise Finegan Wasmoen. Yale University Press, 2018.

Chen Qiufan. *Waste Tide*. Translated by Ken Liu. Tor Books, 2019.

Liu Cixin. *Supernova Era*. Translated by Joel Martinsen. Tor Books, 2019.

2014: Tse, Dorothy. *Snow and Shadow*. Translated by Nicky Harman. Muse/East Slope.

2016: Liu, Ken, ed. and trans. *Invisible Planets: Contemporary Chinese Science Fiction in Translation*. Tor Books.

2018: Song, Mingwei, and Theodore Huters, eds. *The Reincarnated Giant: An Anthology of Twenty-First Century Chinese Science Fiction*. Columbia University Press.

Su Wei. *The Invisible Valley*. Translated by Austin Woerner. Small Beer Press.

2019: Liu, Ken, ed. and trans. *Broken Stars: Contemporary Chinese Science Fiction in Translation*. Tor Books.

Notes

1. Møller-Olsen and Orthofer reviews.
2. Orthofer and Cordasco reviews.
3. Lantrip and Cordasco reviews.
4. Santos review.
5. Evans review.
6. James review.
7. Myles review.
8. See Wu and Hollinger, "Chinese Science Fiction."
9. Cordasco review.
10. First published in China in 2007, *The Three-Body Problem* (the first book in the trilogy) was a major success before it was ever taken on as a project by Tor Books. Numerous reviews have been written about each novel in the trilogy; for trilogy overviews, see Song, "Liu Cixin's Three-Body Trilogy"; Cordasco, "Remembrance of Earth's Past and Humanity's Future"; and Gaffric, "Chinese Dreams." See also "Special Section on Liu Cixin."
11. Cordasco and Morrison reviews.
12. Henriksen review.

13. Cordasco review.
14. Cordasco review.
15. Wolfe review.
16. Huang review.
17. Bhatia review.

Secondary Sources

Bhatia, Gautam. "*Waste Tide* by Chen Qiufan, Translated by Ken Liu." *Strange Horizons* (2019). http://strangehorizons.com/non-fiction/reviews/waste-tide-by-chen-qiufan -translated-by-ken-liu/.

Cordasco, Rachel. "A Bond Undone." *Strange Horizons* (2019). http://strangehorizons.com /non-fiction/reviews/a-bond-undone-by-jin-yong-translated-by-gigi-chang/.

———. "The Lyricism and Pathos of Chinese SF: *Invisible Planets*, Edited and Translated by Ken Liu." *Tor.com* (November 2016). https://www.tor.com/2016/11/03/the-lyricism -and-pathos-of-chinese-sf-invisible-planets-edited-and-translated-by-ken-liu/.

———. "Remembrance of Earth's Past and Humanity's Future: Reflections on the Three-Body Trilogy." *Tor.com* (2016). https://www.tor.com/2016/09/27/remembrance-of -earths-past-and-humanitys-future-reflections-on-the-three-body-trilogy/.

———. "Review: *Cat Country* by Lao She." *SFinTranslation.com* (2016). https://www .sfintranslation.com/?p=569/.

———. "Review: *The Invisible Valley* by Su Wei." *SFinTranslation.com* (2018). https://www. sfintranslation.com/?p=4206.

———. "Review: *The Redemption of Time* by Baoshu." *SFinTranslation.com* (2019). https:// www.sfintranslation.com/?p=6763.

———. "*Supernova Era* by Cixin Liu." *World Literature Today* (2020). https://www.world literaturetoday.org/2020/winter/supernova-era-cixin-liu.

Evans, David. "*The Last Lover*, by Can Xue, Translated by Annelise Finegan Wasmoen." *FT.com* (October 2014).

Gaffric, Gwennaël. "Chinese Dreams: (Self-)Orientalism and Post-Orientalism in the Reception and Translation of Liu Cixin's Three-Body Trilogy." *Journal of Translation Studies* 3, no. 1 (2019): 117–37.

Henriksen, Erik. "Science Pushes Open New Doors with Blood-Smeared Hands: Cixin Liu's *Ball Lightning*." *Tor.com* (2018). https://www.tor.com/2018/08/14/book-reviews -cixin-liu-ball-lightning/.

Huang, Yingying. Review of *The Reincarnated Giant: An Anthology of Twenty-First-Century Chinese Science Fiction*, edited by Mingwei Song and Theodore Huters. *Chinese Literature Today* 8, no. 1 (2019): 146–47.

James, Evan. "The Mysterious Frontiers of Can Xue." *New Yorker* (June 2017). https://www .newyorker.com/books/page-turner/the-mysterious-frontiers-of-can-xue.

Lantrip, Amy. "Su Wei: *The Invisible Valley*." *World Literature Today* 92, no. 2 (2018): 70.

Møller-Olsen, Astrid. "*A Hero Born* by Jin Yong." *Asian Review of Books* (March 2018). https://asianreviewofbooks.com/content/a-hero-born-by-jin-yong/.

Morrison, Michael A. "*The Redemption of Time: A Three-Body Problem Novel* by Baoshu." *World Literature Today* 93, no. 4 (2019). https://www.worldliteraturetoday.org/2019/autumn/redemption-time-three-body-problem-novel-baoshu.

Myles, Eileen. "Starvation and Suffering Also Get You High." *Paris Review* (November 2018). https://www.theparisreview.org/blog/2018/11/19/starvation-and-suffering-also-get-you-high/.

Orthofer, M. A. "*A Bond Undone.*" *Complete Review* (2020). http://www.complete-review.com/reviews/jin_yong/legends_condor_II.htm.

———. "*A Hero Born.*" *Complete Review* (2019). http://www.complete-review.com/reviews/jin_yong/legends_condor_I.htm.

Santos, Camila M. "Dorothy Tse's *Snow and Shadow.*" *Words without Borders* (July 2014). https://www.wordswithoutborders.org/book-review/dorothy-tses-snow-and-shadow.

Song, Mingwei. "Liu Cixin's Three-Body Trilogy: Between the Sublime Cosmos and the Micro Era." In *Lingua Cosmica: Science Fiction from around the World*, edited by Dale Knickerbocker, 107–28. Urbana: University of Illinois Press, 2018.

"Special Section on Liu Cixin." *Science Fiction Studies* 46, pt. 1 (2019). https://www.depauw.edu/sfs/covers/cov137.htm.

Wolfe, Gary. "Gary K. Wolfe Reviews *Broken Stars*, Edited by Ken Liu." *Locus Magazine* (June 2019). https://locusmag.com/2019/06/gary-k-wolfe-reviews-broken-stars-edited-by-ken-liu/.

Wu, Yan, and Veronica Hollinger, eds. "Chinese Science Fiction." Special issue, *Science Fiction Studies* 40, pt. 1 (2013). https://www.depauw.edu/sfs/covers/cov119.htm.

Czech-Language SFT

Introduction

The word "robot" is everywhere these days. We rarely think of its origins when we utter the word while watching a new video by Boston Dynamics, buying a Roomba, or reading a science fiction story. Yet it goes back a hundred years, first appearing in Karel Čapek's play *R.U.R. (Rossum's Universal Robots)* (1920). This is a widely known fact, and when you say "Czech science fiction," it is what usually comes first to people's minds. When you stray further away into the realm of fantasy and horror, there lurks another famous creature made by humans to toil for them: the golem. While more prominent in German-speaking Czech literature (Gustav Meyrink's novel *The Golem* is the most famous example), it's become one of the staples of the Czech Republic's capital, Prague. Both the robot and the golem have forced us to think about what it means to be a human, to do all those unnecessary but beautiful things that make us human.

Yet Czech speculative fiction is, and always has been, much more than robots and golems. Nowadays, it's as rich and diversified as anywhere in the world, in many ways mirroring developments in the English-speaking world. Approximately two-thirds of speculative fiction currently published in Czech are translations (compared to 40 percent for literature overall, including all nonfiction), the vast majority from English. It is therefore no surprise that this market has the greatest influence on the Czech market. Looking at long-term best-selling genre books, we can spot titles by widely read authors like David Weber, Larry Correia,

Stephen King, and G. R. R. Martin; less frequently, we find titles translated from non-English languages: Liu Cixin enjoys great popularity in the Czech Republic, just as in the United States, and Andrzej Sapkowski was extremely popular long before the game and TV adaptations of his *Witcher* series.

In Czech speculative literature, the best-selling titles usually fall within the subgenres of action fantasy or space opera, as in the English-speaking market. However, we can find various subgenres covered by current Czech authors, all the way from Weird fiction through historical or urban fantasy to hard SF. What is translated into English, though, doesn't exactly mirror the distribution of stories within different subgenres; it depends more on the people who do the selection and translation, and the process differs a lot for novels and short fiction. Novels tend to be handled by the original publishers and subsequently agents and foreign publishers (although there are notable exceptions—Jan Kotouč ran a very successful Indiegogo campaign for the translation of his novel). Short stories by Czech authors that appear in English are typically either written *in* English or translated by a few people—myself included—who choose the stories they like and think will be appreciated by English-speaking readers, which inevitably introduces some personal bias. For instance, although I like to read action fantasy once in a while, these stories don't seem unique or interesting enough to warrant a translation. On the other hand, I love the distinctive blend of hard SF and Weird speculation so typical of writers like Hanuš Seiner (though he writes new stories infrequently).

While translating between English and Czech in both directions is usually pretty straightforward, there are exceptions that can prove to be real "translators' nuts"[1] and explain why few Czech authors of speculative fiction have attempted to, for instance, challenge gender perceptions. To take one example from my own writing: an as-yet-unpublished story I wrote in English includes an augmented detective with an intersex body and two distinct personalities, one identifying as male and one as female. I used "they" as the pronoun for the hero, which sounded completely natural. Translating it into Czech, though, was quite difficult. Czech lacks both the singular "they" and the option to omit pronouns by saying, for example, "Inspector Gaillard knew there would be trouble. . . . Gaillard's experience was different." In English you can't tell the person's gender from these sentences, but in Czech the verb you use in a sentence flexes differently depending on the grammatical gender even if you leave out the pronoun, so the gender is *always* there. Even when you use a person's surname, failing to add the suffix "-ová" to a woman's surname can sound very strange in Czech, sometimes even to the point of disrupting the reading experience. There were no good solutions, only the task to choose the least wrong option.

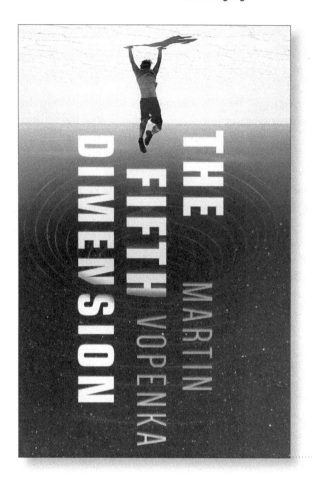

The Fifth Dimension
(2015)

There *is* a reason, then, why I enjoyed Ann Leckie's gender-bending Imperial Radch series much more in the original English, even though a very skilled and experienced translator is responsible for the Czech version. No wonder people so rarely conceive stories such as these in Czech. One is tempted to think of the Sapir-Whorf hypothesis.[2] While its strong form is untenable and can serve only as an interesting science fictional premise, the language we speak and think in does influence the way we act, to some extent. I usually find that I'm more open and sociable in English, which lacks social linguistic nuances, such as the formal "you" in Czech, German, and other languages.

The Czech- and English-speaking speculative markets have a lot in common subgenre- and theme-wise, but observations such as these illustrate that there will

MAREK ŠINDELKA

ABERRANT

Aberrant (2017)

perhaps always be differences, no matter how intermingled the shared popular culture becomes—and that is a good thing. It means we shall always be able to surprise one another.

Julie Nováková

The Texts

Any discussion of Czech-language speculative fiction in English must start with the works of Karel Čapek (1890–1938), one of the most radical, creative authors in any language.[3] The genre literally wouldn't be the same without his introduction of the word "robot," coined in his 1920 play *R.U.R. (Rossum's Universal Robots)* (translated into English in 1923), in which artificial people are made from synthetic organic matter. This idea of the robot as servant/slave who rises up in revolt against its masters is just a few years older than the term "science fiction" itself.

Čapek's speculative fiction was first translated into English in the 1920s and '30s, and all of these novels—*Krakatit* (1922), *The Absolute at Large* (1927), and *War with the Newts* (1935)—explore the same basic theme of how the combination of human greed and new technologies or scientific discoveries often results in apocalypse. Writing after the horrors of the first modern war and just before World War II, Čapek would have been understandably skeptical of humanity's ability or desire to use new weaponry or breakthroughs in chemistry for purely benevolent projects.

Czech SFT since the turn of the twenty-first century is excitingly varied in its themes and settings, from a twenty-third-century intergalactic empire to an alternate psychological dimension. Given that nine of the twelve works of Czech SFT were published after 2000, we have good reason to hope that much more is on its way.

SCIENCE FICTION

Of the six works of Czech-language science fiction available in English, two were published in the twentieth century and the other four in the twenty-first. And while the thirty-five years between Luděk Pešek's *Trap for* Perseus (1980) and Ondřej Neff's *The Fourth Day to Eternity, and Other Stories* (2015) offered Anglophone readers no Czech science fiction, since then we've had three such works in just four years. Thanks to dedicated authors, editors, and translators like Julie Nováková and Jaroslav Olša Jr., Czech-language SFT is taking its place as one of the most exciting sources for contemporary speculative fiction.

The first work of Czech-language science fiction to be published in English was Josef Nesvadba's collection ***In the Footsteps of the Abominable Snowman (The Lost Face)*** (1964; 1970), a Čapek-esque criticism of a naive, boundless faith in science, reason, and human ingenuity.[4] Here Nesvadba employs absurdist humor mixed with horror and devastation. Body-horror stories like "Doctor Moreau's Other Island" and "The Lost Face" explore the ways in which the human body's construction (its organs, features, and intangible aspects) combine to form what we think of as "personhood." Evolution, time travel, artificial intelligence, eugenics—Nesvadba tackles all of these to force readers to rethink our assumptions about the future of humanity and the assumption of civilization's forward progress.

Published in English just a decade later, Pešek's ***Trap for* Perseus** (1976; 1980) is a totalitarian dystopia set in the twenty-third century. When the Earth spacecraft *Perseus III* stumbles upon another ship that disappeared two hundred years before, it's up to the *Perseus*'s commander to find out just how the crew of 120,000 survived in deep space, why they have adopted alien ideologies, and how he can escape once he's taken prisoner. More than three decades after Pešek's book appeared in English, Neff's collection *The Fourth Day to Eternity, and Other Stories* was published in 2015 by Anvil Press in cooperation with the Czech Embassy, thanks to the efforts of diplomat and editor Jaroslav Olša Jr. Included are some of Neff's greatest stories from the 1980s. The title story was subsequently included in the 2007 *SFWA European Hall of Fame: Sixteen Contemporary Masterpieces of Science Fiction from the Continent*.

From Martin Vopěnka, a member of the most recent generation of Czech-language authors, we have *The Fifth Dimension* (2009; 2015), a story about murder and science in the Andes.[5] When physics student turned entrepreneur Jakub Dohnal submits himself to an isolating science experiment, he is left to mull over all that he left behind, including a potentially adulterous wife and his hold on "reality." Marek Šindelka's *Aberrant* (2008; 2017) also interrogates the line between reality and fantasy, mixing science fiction and fantasy tropes to create an intriguing plot about three childhood friends in a postapocalyptic Prague.[6] Here Šindelka offers us a window onto the world of rare-plant smuggling; in *Aberrant*, though, seemingly innocuous plants are dangerous and poisonous parasites, while anything appearing human could easily be occupied by an alien or demon.

Contemporary Czech-language space opera comes to us from Jan Kotouč, whose *Frontiers of the Imperium* (2018; 2019) (the first book in the Central Imperium series) explores the future of genetic engineering and a sprawling interstellar empire. When a member of the royal family working in naval intelligence barely escapes assassination, he relies on his genetic enhancements and intuition to discover the true reasons for the navy's upcoming mission to the Imperium's fringes and the existence of a new kind of communications ship. As he knows, the Imperium's enemies within and without are bent on tearing it apart, which he intends to stop.

FANTASY

In more recent years, Anglophone readers have had access to Michal Ajvaz's works of fantasy and magical realism, including *The Other City*, *The Golden Age*, and *Empty Streets*, all written around the turn of the twenty-first century and published in the early 2000s by Dalkey Archive. *The Other City* (1993; 2009), a kind of guidebook to the unseen Prague of ghosts, strange statues, and talking animals, tells the stories of libraries that can transform into jungles, sudden yawning secret passageways, and other events that seem to erupt into "reality."[7]

Ajvaz continues his interrogation of this alternate, unseen reality that exists simultaneously with our own in *The Golden Age* (2001; 2010), a travelogue narrated by a Gulliver-like figure. Upon encountering an island civilization in the Atlantic, the narrator at first believes that they just sit around observing the world and can make no distinction between reality and representation.[8] Then he discovers the mysterious Book at the heart of their civilization, a text filled with fantastical stories that anyone can add to by attaching small pouches of extra text. The stories within stories within stories spawned by this tangible product made out of words suggest that these people's stories are "real," while their quotidian lives are "imaginary"—an interesting twist to the dream-versus-reality debate.

Empty Streets (2004; 2016), too, is a novel about the instability of place (likely a nod to the upheavals that the Czech people experienced at the hands of other countries in the mid-twentieth century).[9] Here Ajvaz tells us of a writer who is searching for a story and comes up against numerous strange symbols and people as he wanders around the city. Paint and ink have magical properties, people wear disguises, and conversations all happen to occur in isolation (empty streets, stores, buildings). Ajvaz's obvious interest in metatextuality, the liminal space between "reality" and "fantasy," and the materiality of stories enables him to write magical realist, Borgesian novels that make us look beneath the surface of things.

Also published in English in 2016, though originally published in Czech in 1929, Jan Weiss's *The House of a Thousand Floors* depicts the feverish dreams of a soldier wounded in World War I. In these dreams, Petr Brok must rescue a princess who has been kidnapped by the man who rules the House of a Thousand Floors. Revolution is stirring throughout the house, but Petr keeps getting pulled into an alternate reality that might be a vision of the future or the reality of war from which his brain is trying to shield him.

This exciting mix of science fiction and fantasy in English by Czech speculative authors was highlighted in 2016 by author, translator, and editor Julie Nováková in her anthology *Dreams from Beyond: Anthology of Czech Speculative Fiction*.[10] Here Nováková features a diverse array of stories, including everything from space travel to dragons, alien viruses to worm holes that are actually *worms*, and much more. *Dreams from Beyond* also includes an introduction of each of the writers featured (including Jan Kotouč and Hanuš Seiner), plus a piece that Nováková previously published in *Clarkesworld*—"Small Markets, Big Wonders"—about the Czech speculative fiction market. Hopefully, this is just the first such anthology of Czech SFT.

Primary Sources

1929: Weiss, Jan. *The House of a Thousand Floors.* Translated by Alexandra Büchler. CEU Press Classics, 2016.

1964: Nesvadba, Josef. *In the Footsteps of the Abominable Snowman* (*The Lost Face*, US edition). Translated by Iris Irwin. Victor Gollancz, 1970.

1976: Pešek, Luděk. *Trap for* Perseus. Translated into German by Herbert Ungar and then translated from German into English by Anthea Bell. Bradbury Press, 1980.

1993: Ajvaz, Michal. *The Other City*. Translated by Gerald Turner. Dalkey Archive, 2009.

1994: Olša, Jaroslav. *Vampire and Other Science Stories from Czech Lands*. Star.

2001: Ajvaz, Michal. *The Golden Age*. Translated by Andrew Oakland. Dalkey Archive, 2010.

2004: Ajvaz, Michal. *Empty Streets*. Translated by Andrew Oakland. Dalkey Archive, 2016.

2008: Šindelka, Marek. *Aberrant*. Translated by Nathan Fields. Twisted Spoon Press, 2017.

2009: Vopěnka, Martin. *The Fifth Dimension*. Translated by Hana Sklenkova. Barbican Press, 2015.

2015: Neff, Ondřej. *The Fourth Day to Eternity, and Other Stories*. Various translators. Anvil.

2016: Nováková, Julie. *Dreams from Beyond: Anthology of Czech Speculative Fiction*. Various translators. Eurocon.

2018: Kotouč, Jan. *Frontiers of the Imperium* (*Central Imperium Book 1*). Translated by Isabel Stainsby. Arbiter Press, 2019.

Notes

1. A word-to-word translation of the charming Czech phrase *překladatelský oříšek*, meaning "a tough nut to crack." One can sometimes speak of translators' coconuts in jokes when alluding to something really difficult.

2. The strong version of the hypothesis claimed that a person's language determines their cognitive processes—essentially that, for instance, Czech-, English-, Spanish-, or Chinese-speaking people would each think differently from the others and their cognitive categories would never really meet.

3. See Philmus, "Karel Čapek's Can(n)on of Negation."

4. Boaz review.

5. Orthofer review.

6. Osborne review.

7. "The Other City—Michal Ajvaz."

8. Orthofer review.

9. Orthofer review.

10. Cordasco review.

Secondary Sources

Boaz, Joachim. "Short Book Reviews: Lloyd Biggle, Jr.'s *The World Menders* (1971), Pamela Sargent's *The Sudden Star* (Variant Title: *The White Death*) (1979), Josef Nesvadba's *In the Footsteps of the Abominable Snowman* (Variant Title: *The Lost Face*) (1964, trans. 1970)." *Science Fiction and Other Suspect Ruminations* (May 2019). https://science fictionruminations.com/2019/05/12/short-book-reviews-lloyd-biggle-jr-s-the-world

-menders-1971-pamela-sargents-the-sudden-star-variant-title-the-white-death-1979
-josef-nesvadbas-in-the-footsteps-of-the-abominable-snowm/#more-18012.

Cordasco, Rachel. "Review: *Dreams from Beyond: An Anthology of Czech Speculative Fiction*, Ed. Julie Nováková." *SFinTranslation.com* (2016). https://www.sfintranslation
.com/?p=944.

Orthofer, M. A. "*Empty Streets.*" *Complete Review* (2016). http://www.complete-review
.com/reviews/ceska/ajvazm3.htm.

———. "*The Fifth Dimension.*" *Complete Review* (2015). http://www.complete-review
.com/reviews/ceska/vopenkam.htm.

———. "*The Golden Age.*" *Complete Review* (2010). http://www.complete-review.com
/reviews/ceska/ajvazm2.htm.

Osborne, J. David. "*Aberrant* by Marek Šindelka." *World Literature Today* (September 2017).
https://www.worldliteraturetoday.org/2017/september/aberrant-marek-sindelka.

"The Other City—Michal Ajvaz." *Tongues of Speculation* (May 2017). https://tonguesof
speculation.wordpress.com/2017/05/22/the-other-city-michal-ajvaz/.

Philmus, Robert M. "Karel Čapek's Can(n)on of Negation." In *Visions and Re-visions: (Re)
constructing Science Fiction*, by Robert M. Philmus, 79–113. Liverpool: Liverpool University Press, 2005.

Finnish-Language SFT

When my first science fiction novel was published in 2004, the table was in many ways set for me. My name was already known to Finnish science fiction readers because I had translated several novels by Philip K. Dick and my publisher was well regarded by readers of Finnish speculative fiction.

Most important, however, was that Finland's science fiction readership was by no means made up of individual aficionados sitting patiently at home or next to the new-release shelf waiting for something interesting to appear. There existed a ready audience, an active fandom, and numerous associations, some in existence since the 1970s, publishing magazines and organizing events, more often than not as unpaid volunteers. The year my first novel was published, I went for the first time to Finncon, a gathering of thousands held every summer in one of four Finnish cities with science fiction readerships that are large enough to plan and organize the free event. Although the number of Finnish-language readers is small, a significant portion are active fans. Authors, and even translators, are thus not left to work alone, and Finnish fandom has been a delightfully free-thinking and safe place for men, women, young, old, hetero, gay, and trans.

This readership is also analytical and well informed. In a later visit to Finncon, I was invited to give a presentation in which I translated from the Dick novel I was working on in front of a live audience, with the original and the translation

The Rabbit Back
Literature Society
(2014)

projected on a screen. I could hardly get through half a line before someone in the audience would raise their hand and ask, "Why did you use that word?"

Writing fan translations is a decidedly common practice among Finnish science fiction readers, so they are acutely aware of the challenges, pitfalls, and problems of translation, more so than readers of so-called mainstream literature. The Finnish and English languages are very different in their structure, grammar, and means of expression; translating between Finnish and English is considerably more complicated than translating between English and its closer linguistic neighbors, such as German, French, or Spanish. For this reason, literary translation has long been a strong and well-respected profession in Finland. Finnish readers are downright spoiled when it comes to translations

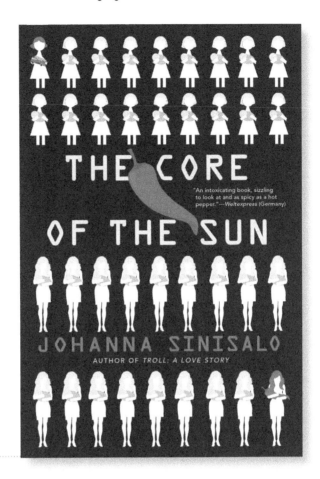

The Core of the Sun
(2016)

because publishers here have hired skilled professionals to translate foreign works, including science fiction and fantasy, ever since the days of Jules Verne. We've been able to enjoy our Stanisław Lem, J. R. R. Tolkien, Ursula Le Guin, J. K. Rowling, and Liu Cixin in first-rate Finnish translations.

Fan publications like *Tähtivaeltaja* and *Portti* and numerous science fiction short-story competitions offer writers an excellent way to publish short fiction that the largest publishing houses might shun. I am something of an exception among Finnish science fiction authors in that I've published several novels and a novel was my first published work.

I started out writing rather orthodox science fiction, but my newfound colleagues inspired me to step outside of strict genre categories, as Finnish authors such as Johanna Sinisalo and Leena Krohn had been doing for some time. Anne Leinonen, Pasi Ilmari Jääskeläinen, J. P. Koskinen, and I founded a *reaalifantasia* (realist-fantasy) writers' group, for which we created a manifesto declaring that we were free to use any ingredients in our stories that struck our fancy, whether they originally came from science fiction, fantasy, magic realism, crime fiction, or elsewhere.

The Finnish speculative fiction audience doesn't seem to have any problem with these leaps across styles and themes. When fantasy realism and *reaalifantasia*, alternative history, and even the "new plebian speculative fiction" (a group formed following the creation of the *reaalifantasia* writers) wanted to join the crowd, they too found a place there. The speculative fiction fandom of a language such as ours is inevitably so small that any subdivisions wouldn't really make sense, and speculative fiction readers haven't been upset when we writers defect once in a while for some other genre. Of the members of the *reaalifantasia* group, J. P. Koskinen has written numerous crime and historical novels, and my own Finlandia-nominated work, *Hunan,* is a historical novel with some slight magical realist elements.

The past couple of decades have also seen a gradual decrease in a suspicion of speculative fiction among the wider Finnish reading public. In a country where strict realism and realistic historical fiction have for decades been nearly the only respected literary genres, this development has happened surprisingly quickly. The awarding of the Finlandia Prize in 2000 to Johanna Sinisalo's *Not before Sundown* was the first public indication of the change; never before had Finland's most prestigious literary prize been given to a work of speculative fiction. Since then, works with speculative themes have found success in numerous contests and sales rankings not specifically restricted to speculative fiction. When I saw the list of works for the Finlandia for 2018, I noticed that in addition to *Hunan* there were at least two other novels that involved conversations with the dead, as well as a paranormal crime novel. Nonrealistic themes have also been an element in works by immigrant authors who have received much notice and been widely translated, such as Finlandia winner Pajtim Statovci, who was nominated for the 2019 National Book Award in the United States, and the internationally acclaimed Hassan Blasim, who is the first Finnish author to write in Arabic.

I have sometimes thought that if I have any literary mission, it is to blur the line between speculative and mainstream literature. Fortunately, in this aim I am not alone.

J. Pekka Mäkelä

The Texts

The Finnish speculative fiction that has been translated into English over the past two decades is dominated by novels and stories that draw heavily on magical realism, fantasy, and fairy tales. Yet because authors like Leena Krohn, Johanna Sinisalo, and Pasi Ilmari Jääskeläinen freely move between these subgenre "boundaries," some critics and authors have started calling this kind of literature "Finnish Weird."[2]

The history of Finnish speculative fiction in English is notable particularly because, in many cases, the number of years between original and translation publication dates is less than ten. All four of Sinisalo's novels were published in English three years after they came out in Finnish, while Risto Isomäki's and Jääskeläinen's novels have come out in English between eight and ten years after their Finnish publications. This rapid movement from Finnish to English speaks both to the vibrancy of the contemporary Finnish speculative fiction scene and to the dedicated work of the Finnish-to-English translators (mainly Lola Rogers, Owen Witesman, J. Robert Tupasela, and Hildi Hawkins), who also promote these works around the Internet and to Anglophone publishers. And while Finnish SFT has been booming since the beginning of the 2010s, 2013 was a particularly impressive year for these books, with a quarter of all Finnish SFT so far coming out that year.[3]

Furthermore, promotion by editors and authors Jeff VanderMeer and Ann VanderMeer, particularly of the works of Leena Krohn, has done much to put Finnish SFT on Anglophone readers' radar. The VanderMeers' micropress, Cheeky Frawg Books, is one of several indie presses publishing Finnish SFT; others include Peter Owen, Pushkin Press, Into Publishing, and Prime Books. The spread of the Internet and the popularity of the World Science Fiction Convention (Worldcon)—the first Finnish Worldcon took place in Helsinki in 2017—has also enabled Finnish editors and authors to promote Finnish SFT around the world.

FANTASY

One of Finland's most beloved living speculative fiction authors is Leena Krohn, whose works of magical realism, fantasy, and science fiction—written for both children and adults—explore questions of reality and illusion, artificial intelligence, and the power of the natural world. With Cheeky Frawg's release of her omnibus *Collected Fiction* in 2015, Krohn became better known in the Anglophone world for her bold, bizarre stories about sapient insects, plants that produce strange hallucinations, and talking pelicans. Yet three of her books had already come out in English before *Collected Fiction*. *Doña Quixote / Gold of Ophir* (two novels in one) was published in 1996, *Tainaron: Mail from Another City* in 2004, and, from Cheeky Frawg, *Datura; or, A Delusion We All See* in 2013.

Each of these novels (or novellas, in the case of *Doña Quixote / Gold of Ophir*) taps into the mystery of how we perceive the world around us, with reality functioning like a restless, turbulent ocean. Strange, unknowable cities form the backdrops of these tales, with characters often exploring a seemingly familiar place that becomes less so the closer they look. Both **Doña Quixote** and **Gold of Ophir** (1983; 1996) are, on one level, stories about cities on the verge of disaster. Set in a modern city that holds a strange secret, *Doña Quixote* follows the eponymous main character (who claims to be the female Don Quixote) whose inexplicable force draws the city's dispossessed to her. Krohn exchanges a modern city for one steeped in myth in *Gold of Ophir*, where alchemy, science, and biblical texts blend together to tell the story of the Tabernacle, watched over and maintained by a mysterious group of people called the Gold-Washers. Krohn's experimentation with form, time, and genre enables her to create stories that are both tantalizing and slightly out of focus.

Tainaron: Mail from Another City (1985; 2004 or 2006), probably Krohn's most well-known book in translation, continues exploring this theme of the unknowable city. According to author and editor Desirina Boskovich, who edited the Finnish SFT anthology *It Came from the North* (2013), *Tainaron* is "one of the most important works of post–World War II dark fantasy."[4] Through its title, the novella evokes the site of the ancient Greek Temple of Poseidon, with a nearby cave thought to be the entrance to the underworld. Krohn's story is told in a series of letters sent from a city populated by sapient insects, with the letter writer trying to adapt to and understand her new environment. Each letter offers readers increasingly surreal portraits of this city that seems to be many cities at once. Indeed, it may not actually be a *place* but rather an *idea*.

Krohn suggests in her work that altered states of mind could allow humans to perceive that which is hidden in a "normal" state, in which the brain is tethered tightly to reality. In **Datura; or, A Delusion We All See** (2001; 2013), we meet a narrator who is slowly poisoning herself through her obsessive consumption of datura seeds and working as an editor at a magazine that specializes in reporting on the strange and supernatural in the city.[5] While the datura seeds are giving her hallucinations, the Voynich Manuscript that she's trying to decipher (and who hasn't?) remains as opaque as ever, but perhaps Krohn is suggesting that only an altered brain state could allow a person to understand it.

Organic life, though, is not the only kind of life in which Krohn is interested. Among her stories and novels in **Collected Fiction** (2015) that explore plant, animal, and insect life are those that consider artificial life and biotechnology as worthy subjects to explore.[6] Her short story "Gorgonoids" explores one such creature, which she describes in great detail but then contradicts herself, acknowledging that "the gorgonoid appears to be only that which it appears to be." This constant referring back to that which humans can understand—kiosks, dreams, children—allows Krohn to put us face-to-face with the strange or unrecognizable and show us that, in fact, there's always a way in. Openness to the new and a defiance of strictures and boundaries, which Krohn practices in her own writing, allow humans to move outside of themselves to view an alternative everyday world—a practice that encourages compassion and an appreciation for all life on Earth.

This kind of cosmic tolerance powerfully informs Johanna Sinisalo's work.[7] Possibly the most well-known contemporary Finnish speculative author in English, Sinisalo has been called the "Queen of Finnish Weird" because of how she translates her deep interest in plants, folktales, and myth into stories about the animated natural world and the tension between it and human civilization. After all, as Boskovich writes in *It Came from the North*, "For Finns, nature is always near: a great presence, uncanny and powerful."[8] Like Boskovich, Sinisalo is a major advocate for Finnish SFT, having edited *The Dedalus Book of Finnish Fantasy*, coedited *Giants at the End of the World* with Toni Jerrman for Worldcon 75 in Helsinki, and written introductions and innumerable pieces for online magazines about the Finnish fantasy, science fiction, magical realism, and surrealism available in English.

Like Krohn, Sinisalo is eager to recognize artificial genre and subgenre boundaries within speculative fiction in order to disrupt them or use them as she sees fit. In an interview with the website *Books from Finland*, she explains that in her novel *Troll: A Love Story* (2000; 2003), she "deliberately aimed to close the rift between the Finnish realist tradition and speculative fiction."[9] The mythical past and mundane present collide in this novel where trolls exist alongside humans in contemporary Finland, although they are rarely spotted by humans and keep to themselves. When a photographer happens upon a young troll and decides to take it home with him, he soon finds that a relationship between a human and a troll is more complicated than he thought. Writing *Troll* allowed Sinisalo to explore the fraught position of creatures that we don't understand, whether they exist in our reality or not.

Sinisalo turns her attention from trolls to bees in *The Blood of Angels* (2011; 2014), weaving a work of dystopic eco-speculation in which the collapse of a single species signals the approaching end of human civilization. Drawing on the idea—attributed to Einstein—that if bees died off, humans would have four years left, Sinisalo tells the story of a Finnish funeral-home operator and beekeeper named Orvo who notices one day that his queen bee has died. Recognizing that the catastrophic bee disappearances affecting the United States have now hit

Europe, he sets out with his special knowledge of the bee species to try to save them, but his plan puts him into direct conflict with his animal-activist son. A story about humanity's mistreatment of animals and the environment, and the cost of that attitude, *The Blood of Angels* is Sinisalo's challenge to her readers to both recognize and reverse the damage that has already been done.

While *Troll* and *The Blood of Angels* are commentaries on humanity's environmental impact, **Birdbrain** (2008; 2011) is the story of how nature might fight back. Set in the most isolated regions of Tasmania, New Zealand, and Australia, the novel follows a young Finnish couple as they embark on a series of extreme hikes. While the powerful beauty of the scenery inspires them, the natural world around them takes on a sinister hue. The couple's only reading material, *Heart of Darkness*, serves as a metatextual signpost for this trip as their belongings start to disappear and a hyperintelligent parrot species (Kakapo) that is threatened with extinction seems to be playing with them like a cat with a captured mouse. Here, nature is not a passive victim but an active aggressor against the two humans who have, despite their good intentions, invaded this pristine area. Less overtly fantastical than Sinisalo's other works in English, *Birdbrain* occupies a powerful position at the forefront of a growing corpus of eco-horror being written around the world.

Finally, Sinisalo's most popular novel in English to date is **The Core of the Sun** (2013; 2016), a book that pays homage to Margaret Atwood's dystopian novel *The Handmaid's Tale* and H. G. Wells's pessimistic sci-fi novel *The Time Machine*.[10] Set in an alternative present in Finland, the novel imagines a society in which meek, submissive women ("eloi") are specially bred, while smart and independent women are sterilized and forced to work menial jobs. Vanna, who was raised as an eloi but is secretly intelligent, embarks on a quest to find her missing sister but veers off course when she partners up with a man named Jare to buy and sell chili peppers—an illegal stimulant in the Eusistocratic Republic of Finland. At one point, Jare discovers a strange religious cult that possesses the Core of the Sun, a chili pepper that is so hot it is claimed to cause hallucinations. *The Core of the Sun* is Sinisalo's examination of purely human relationships and the ways in which we try to control one another. As in Leena Krohn's work, it is through a natural hallucinogen that people can find alternative ways of viewing the world and their place in it.

In line with Sinisalo's warnings about humanity's impact on the natural world, Emmi Itäranta's **Memory of Water** (2012; 2014) and Antti Tuomainen's **The Healer** (2010; 2013) both use climate change as a symbol of environmental backlash. According to Itäranta's vision, global fighting over water has resulted in China's control of Europe and Scandinavia. Knowledge of the location of secret water sources resides in the minds of tea masters like Noria Kaitio and her father. When

Noria's father dies and water becomes scarce in her village, she's forced to choose between, on the one hand, staying home and dying along with her community or, on the other, setting off on a journey that might give her the answers she needs to save it. Itäranta's other novel in English, *The City of Woven Streets* (2015; 2016), also uses the threat of water (flooding this time) to signal coming catastrophe, but here it serves as the backdrop to a high fantasy story about a weaver who hides her birth defect so she isn't forced into exile.

Tuomainen's *The Healer*, too, imagines a dystopian future Helsinki crumbling under the pressures of climate change, with subway tunnels flooding and diseases like Ebola and the plague breaking out around the city. Unlike *Memory of Water*, though, with its classic fantasy tropes of secret knowledge and a desperate quest, *The Healer* is more of a thriller/sci-fi hybrid, with the main character (a poet still living in the rapidly deteriorating city) searching for his missing wife. This search uncovers information about a story she was investigating concerning "The Healer," a politically motivated serial killer who has claimed that he's punishing only those people he believes accelerated climate change and brought on the current social, economic, political, and environmental disasters.

SCIENCE FICTION

This kind of dystopian science fiction thriller can also be found in Risto Isomäki's novels, both of which differ significantly from the Finnish Weird discussed so far in this chapter. In *The Sands of Sarasvati* (2005; 2013), scientists discover vast underwater ruins off of India's west coast, prompting a marine archaeologist and submarine expert to investigate and decide whether this is the fabled island of Atlantis. The field of human skulls and skeletons that they uncover suggests that it is. Simultaneously, the world faces its own ecological catastrophe when a massive lake forms inside the Greenland ice sheet, threatening to submerge coastal cities.

Isomäki then turns his attention from devastating floods to the threat of nuclear war in *Lithium-6* (2007; 2015). Here terrorists steal lithium-6 from Japan and plutonium from France, suggesting to the US Nuclear Terrorism Unit that someone is trying to develop a doomsday weapon. The installation of breeder reactors around the world only aids these terrorists in hijacking the sensitive material, and it's up to two agents to stop them before the weapon is finished or before the world tears itself apart out of fear.

MAGICAL REALISM

Three Finnish Weird authors whose books and collections have come out mostly near the end of the 2010s hark back to the earlier Weird works in tone and perspective, but in general without the warnings about environmental catastrophe. Jyrki Vainonen's surrealist story collection, Pasi Ilmari Jääskeläinen's magical realist novels, and Laura Lindstedt's philosophical text explore romantic and familial relationships and questions about the afterlife as if to focus on what makes us human in terms of our "spirit" or consciousness, rather than in relation to our connection to the environment.

Vainonen's *The Explorer, and Other Stories* (2013) focuses on personal relationships and the ways in which jealousy, loneliness, and filial duty can, as author and editor Paul Di Filippo argues, "conjure up the most pedestrian scenarios in intimate detail, and then send those mundane worlds into surreal chaos. Or, if not chaos, then into otherwordly and oblique patterns of enigmatic events that resonate more on the subconscious level than the intellect."[11] Vainonen walks a fine line in many of these stories between the simply strange and the downright uncanny. While stories like "Blueberries" and "The Aquarium" aren't readily classifiable as "supernatural" tales, their depictions of madness and coincidence are unsettling in the extreme. "The Explorer," "The Garden," and "The Refrigerator," however, veer into sci-fi and horror: the titular explorer is out in search not of a distant land but of his own emotionally distant wife's body, which he finds a way to coinhabit; "The Garden" depicts a son caring for his parents as they suffer from strange transformations brought on by a mysterious plant; and "The Refrigerator" tells the story of Ahab, who rides the bus with his magical refrigerator without an apparent destination. With the exception of "Blueberries," each title is a singular noun, suggesting Vainonen's attempt to mystify that which we might find banal or uninteresting—refrigerators, aquariums, gardens. Like many of the other Finnish Weird authors, Vainonen seeks to change our perception of the world by nudging us out of our sensorial comfort zones.

Jääskeläinen's award-winning works of magical realism similarly play with our understanding of cause and effect and stable meanings. The mystery and metatextual layers in *The Rabbit Back Literature Society* (2006; 2015) make for a simultaneously fast-paced yet dreamlike plot, where highly contagious book viruses make words rearrange themselves on their pages and the town's cherished children's book author has disappeared in an unexpected snowstorm.[12] After Ella, a literature teacher, is invited to join "The Society," a highly selective and secretive group of authors in Rabbit Back, she discovers that its members are engaged in a potentially deadly ritual called "The Game" and that she is replacing a former member for unknown reasons. Jääskeläinen seems to take great pleasure in calling our attention to the materiality of his novel and the nondeterministic nature of language in the writing of fictional texts.

Jääskeläinen's other novel translated into English by Lola Rogers, *Secret Passages in a Hillside Town* (2010; 2018), is, like *Rabbit Back*, a magical realist novel set in a small (and weird) town.[13] Winner of the 2011 Kuvastaja Prize from Finland's Tolkien Society for best fantasy novel—which Jääskeläinen had previously won—*Secret Passages* invites us into the strange warrens of past and current romantic relationships and the brain's own neural pathways, within which lurk memories and realizations that were buried over time. Like the discontented and restless Ella of *Rabbit Back*, publisher Olli Suominen is trying to break out of his ennui by forming new relationships—in his case, joining a film club and communicating with an old girlfriend who added him on Facebook. Soon, nothing is as it once appeared to be and past mysteries return to haunt Olli, triggering memories about his childhood that had lain dormant for decades. *Secret Passages* overtly plays with pop culture through its references to social media, film, data analytics, and the current state of publishing, which both grounds the novel in its particular time and offers a contrast between our public and private lives.

Unlike Vainonen and Jääskeläinen, whose texts takes recognizable objects and spaces as their jumping-off points, Laura Lindstedt's only translated novel, *Oneiron* (2015; 2018), concerns itself with dreams and ideas about the afterlife.[14] Winner of the 2015 Finlandia Prize, the novel depicts seven women who have never met finding themselves in a blank, Swedenborgian space immediately after they've died. Without knowing what happened to them or how they arrived there, these women slowly begin to piece together what they remember of their lives. Realizing that they are dead, they begin sharing their stories, leading to sketchy but slowly developing memories of what killed them: an illness, for some; murder, for others. *Oneiron* is a philosophical exploration of what happens to us after death, particularly how women are remembered.

ANTHOLOGIES

Since 2006, Anglophone readers have had an opportunity to read a wide variety of Finnish speculative fiction authors like never before. The publication of such anthologies as *The Dedalus Book of Finnish Fantasy* (2006), *It Came from the North: An Anthology of Finnish Speculative Fiction* (2013), *Never Stop—Finnish Science Fiction and Fantasy Stories* (2017), and *Giants at the End of the World* (2017) (the first and third edited or coedited by Sinisalo) brought into English for the first time some of Finland's most exciting and experimental authors. Certain of these already discussed in this chapter appear in three of these volumes: Sinisalo, Vainonen, Krohn, and Jääskeläinen, all of whom have won awards for their work in Finnish and in English translation. To the editors' credit, none of these anthologies overlap, with the exception of selections from Leena Krohn's *Pereat Mundus* in the Dedalus book and *It Came from the North*. Thus, Anglophone readers are treated to new stories by recognizable names and previously unknown authors, enhancing our appreciation of the breadth and scope of the Finnish imagination.

In her introduction to *It Came from the North*, Boskovich notes that the included stories suggest "a uniquely Finnish surrealism" that is in the process of being created by the authors whose texts are included.[15] Despite the fact that they are all obsessed with the magical and the uncanny, certain authors are more interested in ideas about space and time, while others concern themselves with the isolation of the individual or the "strangeness of nature." Similarly, Sinisalo and Jerrman contextualize their anthology by observing that the stories within include "not spaceships, robots, planets or new universes—just humans. All of this is made richer and more intriguing by being Finnish, with authors being able to both plunge into the problems of the modern Finnish welfare state, and its ancient mythology of trolls, giants, goblins and magic."[16] The fact that *Giants at the End of the World* was put together specifically for Worldcon 75, in particular, attests to the strength of the Finnish SF scene, the growing worldwide recognition of Finnish SF authors, and the vibrant stories being translated into English now and in the future.

Primary Sources

1983: Krohn, Leena. *Doña Quixote / Gold of Ophir*. Translated by Hildi Hawkins. Carcanet Press, 1996.

1985: Krohn, Leena. *Tainaron: Mail from Another City*. Translated by Hildi Hawkins. Prime Books, 2004.

2000: Sinisalo, Johanna. *Troll: A Love Story* (UK title: *Not before Sundown*). Translated by Herbert Lomas. Peter Owen, 2003.

2001: Krohn, Leena. *Datura; or, A Delusion We All See*. Translated by Anna Volmari and Juha Tupasela. Cheeky Frawg Books, 2013.

2005: Isomäki, Risto. *The Sands of Sarasvati*. Translated by Owen F. Witesman. Into, 2013.

2006: Jääskeläinen, Pasi Ilmari. *The Rabbit Back Literature Society*. Translated by Lola M. Rogers. Thomas Dunne Books, 2015.

  Sinisalo, Johanna, ed. *The Dedalus Book of Finnish Fantasy*. Translated by David Hackston. Dedalus.

2007: Isomäki, Risto. *Lithium-6*. Translated by Owen F. Witesman. AmazonCrossing, 2015.

2008: Sinisalo, Johanna. *Birdbrain*. Translated by David Hackston. Peter Owen, 2011.

2010: Jääskeläinen, Pasi Ilmari. *Secret Passages in a Hillside Town*. Translated by Lola M. Rogers. Pushkin Press, 2018.

  Tuomainen, Antti. *The Healer*. Translated by Lola Rogers. Henry Holt, 2013.

2011: Sinisalo, Johanna. *The Blood of Angels*. Translated by Lola Rogers. Peter Owen, 2014.

2012: Itäranta, Emmi. *Memory of Water*. Translated by the author. Harper Voyager, 2014.

2013: Boskovich, Desirina, ed. *It Came from the North: An Anthology of Finnish Speculative Fiction*. Cheeky Frawg Books.

  Sinisalo, Johanna. *The Core of the Sun*. Translated by Lola Rogers. Grove Press, Black Cat, 2016.

Vainonen, Jyrki. *The Explorer, and Other Stories.* Translated by Juha Tupasela, Anna Volmari, and Hildi Hawkins. Cheeky Frawg Books.

2015: Itäranta, Emmi. *The City of Woven Streets* (US title: *The Weaver*). Translated by the author. Harper Voyager, 2016.

Lindstedt, Laura. *Oneiron.* Translated by Owen Witesman. Oneworld, 2018.

VanderMeer, Jeff, ed. *Leena Krohn: Collected Fiction.* Cheeky Frawg Books.

2017: Itäranta, Emmi, ed. *Never Stop—Finnish Science Fiction and Fantasy Stories.* Unknown translator. Osuuskumma-kustannus.

Sinisalo, Johanna., and Toni Jerrman, eds. *Giants at the End of the World.* Various translators. Worldcon 75.

Notes

1. Translated by Lola Rogers.

2. A website of that name offers Anglophone readers four issues of a magazine that includes SFT from Sinisalo, J. S. Meresmaa, Viivi Hyvönen, and many others. See also Roine and Samola, "Johanna Sinisalo and the New Weird."

3. Though Hannu Rajaniemi is a well-known Finnish author of science fiction, he writes directly in English.

4. VanderMeer and VanderMeer, *The Weird,* 657.

5. See Bebergal, "Cracking the Codes of Leena Krohn."

6. Hand review.

7. See Roine and Samola, "Johanna Sinisalo and the New Weird."

8. Boskovich, introduction to *It Came from the North.*

9. Sinisalo interview, http://www.booksfromfinland.fi/2011/09/weird-and-proud -of-it/.

10. Zutter review.

11. "Paul Di Filippo reviews Jyrki Vainonen and Leena Krohn."

12. Cordasco review.

13. Tankard review.

14. Orthofer review.

15. Boskovich, introduction to *It Came from the North.*

16. Sinisalo and Jerrman, introduction to *Giants at the End of the World.*

Secondary Sources

Bebergal, Peter. "Cracking the Codes of Leena Krohn." *New Yorker* (January 2016). https:// www.newyorker.com/books/page-turner/cracking-the-codes-of-leena-krohn.

Boskovich, Desirina. Introduction to *It Came from the North: An Anthology of Finnish Speculative Fiction,* edited by Desirina Boskovich. N.p.: Cheeky Frawg Books, 2013.

Cordasco, Rachel. "Review: *The Rabbit Back Literature Society* by Pasi Ilmari Jääskeläinen." *SFinTranslation.com* (2016). https://www.sfintranslation.com/?p=511.

Hand, Elizabeth. "Review: *Leena Krohn: Collected Fiction* Yields Writing of Strangeness and Beauty." *Los Angeles Times*, December 24, 2015. https://www.latimes.com/books/la-ca-jc-leena-krohn-20151227-story.html.

Orthofer, M. A. "*Oneiron*." *Complete Review* (2018). http://www.complete-review.com/reviews/suomi/lindstedtl.htm.

"Paul Di Filippo Reviews Jyrki Vainonen and Leena Krohn." *Locus Magazine* (December 2013). https://locusmag.com/2013/12/paul-di-filippo-reviews-jyrki-vainonen-and-leena-krohn/.

Roine, Hanna-Riikka, and Hanna Samola. "Johanna Sinisalo and the New Weird: Genres and Myths." In *Lingua Cosmica: Science Fiction from around the World*, edited by Dale Knickerbocker, 183–200. Urbana: University of Illinois Press, 2018.

Sinisalo, Johanna. Interview in *Books from Finland* (September 2011). http://www.booksfromfinland.fi/2011/09/weird-and-proud-of-it/.

Sinisalo, Johanna, and Toni Jerrman. Introduction to *Giants at the End of the World*, edited by Johanna Sinisalo and Toni Jerrman. N.p.: Worldcon 75, 2017.

Tankard, Lanie. "*Secret Passages in a Hillside Town* by Pasi Ilmari Jääskeläinen." *World Literature Today* (2019). https://www.worldliteraturetoday.org/2019/winter/secret-passages-hillside-town-pasi-ilmari-jaaskelainen.

VanderMeer, Ann, and Jeff VanderMeer, eds. *The Weird: A Compendium of Strange and Dark Stories*. N.p.: Tor Books, 2012.

Zutter, Natalie. "Replacing Handmaids with Elois: *The Core of the Sun* by Johanna Sinisalo." *Tor.com* (January 2016). https://www.tor.com/2016/01/04/book-reviews-the-core-of-the-sun-johanna-sinisalo/.

French-Language SFT

Introduction

Few would dispute America's dominance of twentieth-century science fiction, such that for a nation with so rich a literary history as France, the issue became how best to handle the alien invasion. There was the nomenclatural conundrum. The English label was met everywhere with distaste—"at once too exact and so ineloquent," sniffed genre writer Jacques Sternberg—even as what it labeled was widely embraced. Surely, then, the French had a word for it.

Or did they? Of the two words for "future" in French, it is telling that the more common, concrete, and imaginable *avenir*, contiguous with the present, lost out in science fictional contexts to the altogether woollier *futur*—as art historian Gavin Parkinson notes, "more removed, hypothetical, and perhaps metaphysical." Shifting from the Nazi occupation to the Marshall Plan, France went from shell shock to future shock. By the early fifties, there were three major science fiction imprints—Le Rayon Fantastique from the reputable houses Hachette and Gallimard, Anticipation from the lowbrow Fleuve Noir, and Denoël's Présence du futur—that gained the genre a foothold over the next decade. In the midfifties, it was fashionable for literati to say, "Science fiction is for simpletons, but I like that Bradbury fellow."

Buoyed by a booming industry, American science fiction insisted on its own newness, wielding "science" the way literature does realism—as a bid for legitimacy. Prediction would distinguish the genre from its imaginative brethren.

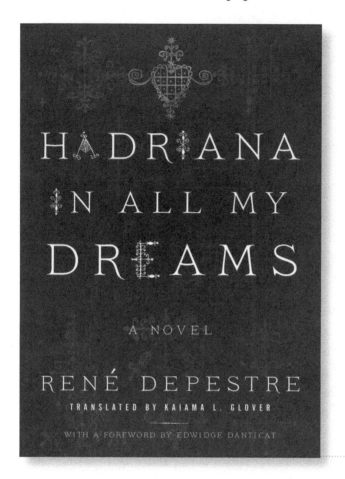

Hadriana in
All My Dreams
(2017)

To the morass of porous categories in any language can be added a transla-tion issue: the incongruity of concepts from culture to culture. In this light, Jules Verne's anointment as the genre's grandfather smacks of taxonomic retconning. Why, that kindly, bearded figure only penned adventure novels with a dash of "scientific vulgarization" that his publisher urged upon him. How could he have founded what in France was never its own grouping to begin with?

Small wonder, then, that the French were likely to dismiss futurology as Yan-kee hucksterism in favor of assimilating the import into existing traditions: the *merveilleux*, what we might call "fantasy," where magic abounded but was business as usual, and the *fantastique*, closer in our spectrum to horror, where a perfect surface of seeming realism was disturbed by some subtle, unsettling rift.

The Silent City (2002)

Thus, Sternberg was neither original nor alone among his countrymen in list-ing science fiction as the latest iteration of a long lineage whose age-old goal had always been *mystère*. The title of his chapbook essay on the topic is usually given as *A Branch of the Fantastique Called Science-Fiction,* but the word *"succursale"* is rather more specifically "branch office" or even "franchise." Such corporate jargon, from a writer famed for his mordant satires of modern bureaucracy, supplies surely deliberate critique of the postwar advance historian Victoria de Grazia famously credited to America's "irresistible empire."

For the generations after Sternberg's, the obvious and often global solution to American cultural imperialism has been fandom. Today the French, with a deft hyphen, have adopted *la science-fiction* as fully as they have *le week-end.* In such comics series as *Masked, Metropolis,* and *The Chimera Brigade,* contemporary author Serge Lehman proves he's internalized not only the methodology but the ambition of his Anglophone influences in his attempt to launch a subgenre he called "radiumpunk" with a clandestine master narrative weaving together characters from pan-European pulp, literature, and history—from Fantômas to Gregor Samsa to Marie Curie. Lehman saw the similarities between belle epoque France and midcentury America: both societies in full ebullition, as if feverishly tossing out fictional invention rooted in pulp adventure were an emergent property of rapid technological advance. This cribbing of a pastiche template popularized by Alan Moore and Philip José Farmer is ingenious—the empire's own tools turned against it, in a gambit to restore a lost French literature to its rightful place in genre history. But its originality may be circumscribed by the use of these very same tools.

Perhaps history offers us another submerged continuity. The belle epoque ended abruptly with the Great War, from whose ashes surrealism was born. But as Parkinson rightly observes, "The academic orthodoxy, prevalent in art history but present in every discipline . . . favours study of Surrealism of the 1920s and 1930s almost entirely at the expense of the one that followed the Second World War." In his introduction to a reissue of *The Incal,* another looming Gallic influence on American SF, comics writer Brian Michael Bendis asserts, "The question isn't who's ripped off Moebius, the question is who hasn't." We might similarly say, it's not about who was a surrealist—especially with despotic founder André Breton excommunicating movement members right and left—but who, in the French twentieth century, wasn't.

Surrealism's fascination with and influence on American speculative fiction has been well documented: Yves Tanguy's abstractions structuring a generation of Richard Powers's book covers, Dalí's "deliquescent watches" melting into William Sloane's novels, Max Ernst's landscapes bleeding into J. G. Ballard's. When critics Michel Carrouges, Roger Caillois, and Maurice Blanchot pondered the future of surrealism in the 1950s, they were also grappling with surrealism's relationship to futurity.

From the start, surrealism's crush on the pulps favored Lovecraft, but did not distinguish between Weird nightmares and science fictional stargazing. In SF surrealists saw not prophecy but mythology, not the news but dreams. What they sought were poetic images—whether set in a primordial past or an inconceivable future—with the imaginative power to remake society and alter humanity. Their predictors were dreams and the subconscious. Perhaps, then, the salient image for a generation of writers wasn't Alfred Barr's landmark 1939 Museum of Modern Art exhibition *Fantastic Art, Dada, Surrealism* but rather the coexistence, at the World's Fair that same year in Queens, of GM's Futurama and Salvador

Dalí's burlesque funhouse, the Dream of Venus: the virgin and the dynamo of the World of Tomorrow.

The book you hold in your hands brings back, under the umbrella "speculative," kinds of writing that, despite efforts since to segregate them, have more in common than most protest. Science fiction as it ages seems to gain in likeness to fantasy, as if Clarke's third law bent parabolically away from our present horizon toward future and past alike, making technologies either sufficiently advanced or antiquated both seem closer to magic.

"I believe that art and science will have merged by 2001," Dalí declared in the April 1956 issue of *Amazing Stories*. Bridging the energy of the belle epoque pulps and the American century, the single greatest French pan-artistic movement of the twentieth century, in its drawn-out decay, continues to irradiate our cultural exchanges.

Edward Gauvin

The Texts

Francophone speculative fiction comes to us from all over the world: France, Quebec, Algeria, Belgium, Haiti, Djibouti, Martinique, and the Republic of the Congo. While most still comes to Anglophone readers from France and Quebec, more is being translated into English from Caribbean and African countries with every passing year, contributing to the growing wealth and variety of this fiction. It is fitting, after all, that Francophone SFT is so numerous since readers all over the world tend to name a Frenchman, Jules Verne (1828–1905), as one of the first true "science fiction" authors.[1]

The flood of Verne translations into English around the turn of the twentieth century established the author of such well-known stories as *Journey to the Center of the Earth* (1864, trans. 1871) and *Twenty Thousand Leagues under the Sea* (1870, trans. 1872) as a pioneer of a new type of fiction that wove together scientific fact and entertainment in a way that lay readers could understand. Like H. G. Wells and Mary Shelley, Verne is credited with popularizing these kinds of stories in the Anglophone world on such a scale that by 1929, Hugo Gernsback had coined the term "science fiction" and speculative magazines started springing up by the dozens. Despite the fact that many of the early Verne translations were abridged and often censored by British and American translators,[2] his vision of a world filled with wonders to be explored and the technology to do that continues to inspire readers. As Verne scholar Arthur Evans points out, Verne was technically writing "scien*tific* fiction," not "science fiction," since the stories were meant to be mainly pedagogical vehicles, rather than sources of pure entertainment. To

Verne's contemporary Belgian-born J.-H. Rosny aîné, Evans credits "the world of SF proper."[3]

Verne's influence on speculative fiction is profound, but since most of his stories were translated in the late nineteenth and early twentieth centuries, they don't fall under the purview of this volume. However, recent efforts by Wesleyan University Press to publish new, more faithful translations of Verne's texts deserve mention here. Since 2007, six Verne novels have been retranslated and accompanied by scholarly introductions and explanatory notes, part of a larger effort to give Verne the serious attention he deserves as an innovative artist.

Wesleyan has also published a volume of novellas by the aforementioned J.-H. Rosny aîné, *Three Science Fiction Novellas: From Prehistory to the End of Mankind* (2012), bringing into English for the first time some of the earliest stories of alien life and alternative cosmic perspectives.[4] Joining Wesleyan in this endeavor to introduce Anglophone readers to the long speculative tradition in France is Black Coat Press, which publishes dozens of proto-SF, science fiction, fantasy, and mystery collections each year, the majority translated by prolific British science fiction author Brian Stableford. Because of the vast number of translations of these texts that have appeared within the past decade, I won't discuss them in detail but include a list on *SFinTranslation.com*.

Thus, while speculative fiction from France has found its way into English translation since before the term "science fiction" was coined, or before "fantasy" was seen as its own distinct subgenre, SFT from France and other Francophone countries doesn't seem nearly as ubiquitous today. Yet more than one hundred speculative novels, collections, and anthologies have been translated from French into English just since 1960 from authors as diverse as Stefan Wul, Nathalie Henneberg, Serge Brussolo, Marie Darrieussecq, Pierre Pevel, and Patrick Chamoiseau.

FRANCE

Science Fiction

While many different factors determine which novels, stories, collections, and anthologies get translated and then published in English, some of the key ones in relation to Francophone SFT have been strong author-publisher relationships and the historical shift from science fiction to fantasy and surrealism. The 1960s and '70s brought Anglophone readers a wealth of science fiction from France. The 1970s was a particularly fruitful decade for Franco-American literary relations, with nearly a quarter of all of the novels, collections, and anthologies listed in this chapter coming from France. Thanks to the efforts of translators such as Xan Fielding, C. J. Richards, and Patricia Wolf, as well as editor, author, and translator Damon Knight, French science fiction in particular was injected into the Anglophone consciousness like Verne had been a half century before.[5] The film version of Boulle's *The Planet of the Apes* released in the United States in 1968 further solidified this phenomenon.

Paul Berna (Jean-Marie-Edmond Sabran) initiated this second wave of French SFT with his novels *Threshold of the Stars* (1954) and its sequel, *Continent in the Sky* (1955). Like many of the French science fiction that followed, these novels imagine how nations will vie with one another to reach and then conquer space first. Berna's later translated work *The Last Dawn* (1974; 1977) focuses instead on Earth after a disastrous comet impact.

Pierre Boulle's science fiction novels quickly followed, with Vanguard Press releasing two novels and a collection between 1963 and 1966 and another three novels and a collection between 1971 and 1986. Already well known for his non-SF novel *The Bridge over the River Kwai* and its film adaptation in 1957, Boulle made a name for himself as a science fiction author with *The Planet of the Apes* (1963; 1963),[6] translated into English and Portuguese the same year as its initial publication in France and into a dozen other languages in subsequent years. An allegory about humanity's relentless geocentrism, the novel imagines what would happen if humans and simians eventually switched places evolutionarily, with the latter gaining in skills and intelligence as the former declined under the weight of inertia. A similar theme of evolution and domination appears several years after Boulle's novel in Christian Léourier's *The Mountains of the Sun* (1971; 1974), which imagines human expatriates on Mars returning to Earth after a devastating flood centuries before and finding humans who managed to survive in primitive conditions.

Boulle's next novel to be translated into English, *Garden on the Moon* (1964; 1965), once again deals with humanity's future spacefaring capabilities. Originally written five years before Neil Armstrong first set foot on the moon, this novel imagines an alternate reality in which Japan enters the space race between the United States and the Soviet Union. Beginning with early rocket tests in Hitler's Germany, *Garden on the Moon* follows various scientists as they flee the crumbling Reich and offer their services to the governments of their adopted countries. In this reality, Japan succeeds in reaching the moon first because its astronaut is willing to sacrifice himself for the success of the mission.

Between *The Planet of the Apes* and *Garden on the Moon*, on the one hand, and the three other Boulle novels translated into English in the 1970s and '80s, on the other, Vanguard Press published two collections of the author's stories: *Time Out of Mind* (1957; 1966) and *Because It Is Absurd (on Earth as in Heaven)* (1966; 1971). Among the tales in these collections are ruminations about time travelers trapping a person from the modern times in an endless present and scientists trying to "humanize" androids by creating deficiencies in their perception and judgment.

Boulle subsequently turned away from novels about spacefaring humans and distant futures to write about alternate Earth realities and the constants of human nature. In *Desperate Games* (1971; 1973), scientists overthrow governments across the globe and create one Scientific World Government that eliminates poverty, disease, and hunger, but also leaves people feeling worthless, hopeless, and suicidal. To counteract this malaise, the Department of Psychology begins staging violent gladiatorial-style battles and then, ironically, large-scale historical battle reenactments that involve chemical warfare and weapons of mass destruction.

The perils of unquestioned faith in science and extreme idealism also inform *The Good Leviathan* (1977; 1978) and *Mirrors of the Sun* (1982; 1986), with Boulle once again suggesting that the best intentions often either are misguided or have destructive consequences. When a giant nuclear-powered oil tanker takes to the seas in the former novel, a group of ecologists warns the world that this "monster" threatens humanity with both atomic and environmental catastrophe. These scientists are completely surprised when it turns out that both nuclear material and crude oil have almost magical healing properties. Scientists are also "proven" wrong in *Mirrors of the Sun*, with their claim that covering 10 percent of the arid land of Languedoc, Provence, and Corsica would generate 100 percent of the energy France requires and thus solve the problem of sustainability. When the "President Ecologist" attempts to push this agenda through, the subsequent environmental disasters demonstrate that there are actually no simple solutions to any crisis.

While Vanguard was publishing Boulle's novels throughout the 1960s and '70s, William Morrow, another American company, was introducing René Barjavel to Anglophone readers. Like Boulle, Barjavel used science fictional scenarios to comment on the rotten foundations of human civilization. His novel *Ashes, Ashes* (1943; 1967), set a century in the future, imagines what would happen if solar volatility wiped out electricity around the world. With the chaos unfolding around them, a small group of people sets out from Paris bound for Provence in order to set up a new society.[7] *The Ice People* (1968; 1970), too, offers readers a grim view of human nature. A best seller in France, this is the story of two people revived from a 900,000-year-old buried capsule beneath the Arctic ice and finding themselves in a highly advanced human society. As in Boulle's *Desperate Games*, scientists and politicians disagree about how best to address this scientific conundrum. Barjavel continues his exploration of time distortion in *The Immortals* (1973; 1974), in which the accidental discovery of an immortality virus in India leads to a government cover-up and forced exile to an island in the Aleutians for anyone who came into contact with it. All of the implications raised by the idea of life without death and how humans could (or could not) build a society around it are ultimately rendered moot when an atomic explosion destroys the island and its inhabitants.

Like Boulle and Barjavel, Algerian-born French author Robert Merle found American publishers for his science fiction novels *The Day of the Dolphin* (1967; 1969), *Malevil* (1972; 1973), and *The Virility Factor* (1974; 1977). Later made into a film starring George C. Scott, *The Day of the Dolphin* imagines what might happen if humans found a way to communicate with dolphins. Following government-sponsored experiments, Professor Sevilla breaks through the species barrier, but the knowledge that his discovery is going to be used for the purposes of warfare prompts him to try to hide the mammals. *Malevil*, like many other works of speculative fiction written in the 1960s and '70s, takes place in the aftermath of a nuclear holocaust. In this case, seven people who have taken shelter in a medieval castle form a new society, incorporating the survivors that straggle in and ultimately following the orders of a charismatic leader named Emmanuel Comte. Merle's last novel to be translated, *The Virility Factor* is a satirical take on second-wave feminism and its opposition. When a worldwide epidemic kills off all fertile men, women take the reins of power and proceed to act as foolishly and brutally as the men before them.

During the 1970s, DAW released seven Pierre Barbet novels in English—more than by any other single author writing in a language other than English. Two novels in his *Eridanus* trilogy (*The Napoleons of Eridanus* [1970; 1976] and *The Emperor of Eridanus* [1982; 1983]) tell the story of Napoleonic soldiers who, while retreating from Moscow, are kidnapped by aliens and put into service helping them build an empire. Barbet's Temporal Investigator Setni series (of which two were translated into English—*Games Psyborgs Play* [1971; 1973] and *The Enchanted Planet* [1973; 1975]) proffers the existence of a Galactic Federation ruled by the united Great Brains, which sends out Captain Setni to explore its realm. In *Games*, Setni travels to a planet that looks like ancient Earth back when Charlemagne ruled France in the eighth century, and it's up to him to figure out what is real and what is illusion. Setni is sent out once more in *Enchanted* to investigate the sudden appearance of a planet, which, like the world in *Games*, resembles ancient Earth, though this time with dragons and demons.

Barbet's *The Joan-of-Arc Replay* (1973; 1978) is a clear departure from these earlier novels in that it revolves around a computer simulation instead of planetary exploration. Here, two nonhuman "galactic historians" argue over whether similar planets will have similar histories, and they use a computer to determine if, say, the story of Joan of Arc on Earth would play out the same on Planet Noldaz of Sigma 32. *Replay* does share with *Games* an interest in medieval France and the relationship between Earth history and that of other potentially inhabited worlds. The last Barbet book to be published by DAW was *Cosmic Crusaders* (1980), which included the two novels ***Baphomet's Meteor*** (1971; previously published by DAW in 1972) and its sequel, ***Stellar Crusade***. Like Barbet's previous novels, these two texts take medieval history as their central themes. The alternate-history *Baphomet's Meteor* involves the eponymous alien attempting to take over the world via the Knights Templar during the Crusades. The Templars turn the tables on Baphomet in *Stellar Crusade* when they go into space and try to convert Baphomet's people to Christianity.[8]

The 1970s and early 1980s brought novels by French anthologist, editor, and author Gérard Klein into English via DAW and Doubleday. Editor of the prestigious SF imprint Ailleurs et Demain for four decades, Klein was influenced early on by golden-age American science fiction and wrote several space operas that focus on humans in the far future (four were translated into English). ***Starmasters' Gambit*** (1958) and ***The Overlords of War*** (1971), both of which came out in translation in 1973, tell stories about individual men encountering potentially alien species on distant planets. In the former, the main character, Jerg Algan, travels to a bizarre planet in which large black citadels (think Clarke and Kubrick's *2001: A Space Odyssey*) are placed like giant chess pieces on a massive board. As the title suggests, Algan must sacrifice something in order to gain an advantage over his extraterrestrial hosts.[9] Once again, one man (George Corson) is sent (via time travel) to a distant planet, but this time it's to end a lengthy war with the birdlike aliens of Uria. Corson's mission is hijacked when other powerful beings use him as a pawn in their own conflicts.

Like *Overlords*, ***The Mote in Time's Eye*** (1965; 1975) deals with (extreme) time travel and powerful alien intelligences. Twenty thousand years in the future, a ship from the human colonies of the Lesser Magellanic Clouds falls into a time trap set by feuding empires. The trap sends the human ship back millions of years into the past but also takes an unexpected toll on the powerful aliens, who hadn't counted on the accident in their cosmic plans. ***The Day before Tomorrow*** (1963; 1982), too, takes time travel as its central focus, with a technologically sophisticated federation guaranteeing its own stability by going back in time to tamper with the histories of worlds that might in the future threaten the federation. When a team is sent to Ygone, however, they encounter their own selves (from the past? the future?) and are ultimately thrown into an Escheresque time loop.

Another French SF author active in the late 1950s and translated into English in the 1970s was Stefan Wul (Pierre Pairault). In keeping with French science fiction's developing space-opera tradition during the mid-twentieth century, Wul wrote novels that depict humans who, while in impossible situations, nevertheless rise to the occasion and liberate themselves from alien domination. In ***The Temple of the Past*** (1957; 1973), a ship from Earth crashes onto a chlorine/silicone-based planet and is then swallowed by a whale. With the help of some telepathic lizards, the protagonist enters suspended animation, where he's discovered thousands of years later by another Earth expedition. These later humans conclude that the survivor of the earlier crash was actually from the lost city of Atlantis. *Fantastic Planet* (1957; 2010), written six years before *The Planet of the Apes*, tells a very similar story to Boulle's novel. Here the last humans on Earth are discovered by the Draags and taken to their home planet, where the humans are placed in zoos and used as servants. The human population is "culled" on a regular basis to keep down their population. When one human servant (named Terr) rebels against his alien masters and reconnects with some of the "wild" humans, he initiates a movement for liberty in the face of overwhelming oppression.

The 1970s also brought Anglophone readers two anthologies of science fiction from France: *Thirteen French Science-Fiction Stories* (1972)[10] and *Travelling towards Epsilon: An Anthology of French Science Fiction* (1977).[11] Both include stories by Claude-François Cheinisse, Nathalie Henneberg, Suzanne Malaval, and Gérard Klein, with Knight's anthology also including five stories by women (three of these are by Henneberg). The stories in these two anthologies range from science fiction to fantasy to horror, drawing on everything from folktales and myths to then current science and ideas about complicated alien technologies. *Travelling towards Epsilon* also includes stories by Daniel Walther and Belgian-born author Jacques Sternberg. While Sternberg already had a darkly pessimistic collection out in English from Seabury Press (*Future without Future* [1971; 1974]),[12] Walther would see two of his novels translated in the 1980s (see earlier discussion of Pierre Barbet).

While the Russian-born Henneberg has more stories in both Knight's and Jakubowski's anthologies than any other author, only one of her many novels has been translated into English.[13] Published by DAW in 1980, *The Green Gods* (1961) was the first science fiction novel by a French woman to be translated into English, as well as the first work of French SFT where both the author and the translator were women. Like her wildly creative and dark short stories, *The Green Gods* imagines that humans have colonized the galaxy and thus earned the enmity of an alien species, which surrounds Earth with a magnetic shield. Over the course of centuries, the shield creates a greenhouse effect that enables plants and insects to evolutionarily surpass humans. Supersentient and now with paranormal abilities, the former realize that the spaceships of humanity's descendants will soon arrive and prepare to wipe out Earth's last humans.

Later in the decade, DAW published two translations of Daniel Walther novels, both brought into English by science fiction author C. J. Cherryh. Walther, as the editor of Club du Livre d'Anticipation (a publication series from Éditions Opta), had published American high fantasy in French translation, including novels by Cherryh, who then translated the first two books in his Swa sequence for the American publisher. Set on a far-future postapocalyptic Earth (brought to that state because of political fanaticism, the tilting of the world's axis, and the shifting of the continents), *The Book of Shai* (1982; 1984) and *Shai's Destiny* (1983; 1985) tell the story of Swa and his heroic attempt to unite humanity after centuries of factional fighting.

The 1990s witnessed a shift in the French speculative fiction that was being translated into English. With stories about body swapping, perpetual-motion machines, ant empires, and cloning, French SFT turned away from aliens, space travel, and postapocalyptic wastelands. Instead, Anglophone readers were introduced to authors like René Belletto, Amin Maalouf, and Bernard Werber, whose novels are concerned more with earthly creatures and the body-soul dichotomy. In Belletto's *Machine* (1990; 1993), we learn about a special computer that allows people to exchange personalities. When a psychotherapist decides to test it on a psychopath under his care, the former winds up being trapped in the latter's body, with the psychopath free to abuse his doctor's family and colleagues. *Coda* (2005; 2011), which veers more toward fantasy than science fiction, is a kaleidoscopic romp through one character's increasingly bizarre life as he tries to figure out to whom the mysterious box of clams in his refrigerator belongs. Meanwhile, he winds up meeting Fate herself (who is disguised as a woman) and learns about the elimination of death from the world. Lebanese-born author Amin Maalouf's sci-fi dystopia *The First Century after Beatrice* (1992; 1994) imagines a near-future world in which a pharmaceutical company patents a drug they say can guarantee the birth of a male child. The resulting imbalance triggers a national disaster.

Bernard Werber's *Empire of the Ants* (1991; 1996) pulls the reader down into the literal depths of Earth to explore the hidden realms of Ant civilization.[14] The first novel in a trilogy (and the only one translated into English so far), *Empire* tells the story of a Paris-based American family living in an apartment that once belonged to an eccentric entomologist uncle. When their dog and then they themselves disappear, the narrative focus follows them down into a teeming, complex world in which ants work, fight, and survive together, in many ways as "human" as the family that disappeared into their realm.

While the 1980s and '90s saw a significant decrease in SFT from France, compared to the boom years of the 1960s and '70s, the start of the new millennium suggested that French SFT was making up lost ground. Novels and collections from writers like Michel Houellebecq, Jean-Claude Dunyach, and Serge Brussolo have pointed readers to contemporary themes like the dangers of cloning and memory manipulation. Houellebecq's *The Elementary Particles (Atomized)* (1998; 2000) is a near-future dystopia in which cloning has become a routine practice. Despite advances in the medical field that help stave off old age, however, human beings inevitably decay. Houellebecq continues to explore the human desire for immortality and its possible application in the near and far future in *The Possibility of an Island* (2005; 2006).[15] The novel's three characters are basically one: a man named Daniel (near future) and his two clones, who live in a postapocalyptic world (Daniel's world destroyed itself through nuclear war). Houellebecq explores ideas about the strength of the sex drive and the ultimate decay of every human against the backdrop of a wasted landscape with the ruins of tourist resorts and consumer goods scattered throughout like signposts of decline.

Whereas Houellebecq is considered a "literary" writer who uses speculative tropes in some of his work, Jean-Claude Dunyach has been recognized as one of France's best living science fiction authors. Two collections of his stories have been published in English by Black Coat Press, enabling Anglophone readers to sample a bit of Dunyach's much larger untranslated oeuvre. *The Night Orchid: Conan Doyle in Toulouse* (2004) includes fourteen stories, six of which are translations original to this volume. From Conan Doyle journeying to Toulouse with Professor Challenger to learn about an ancient horror to the "night life" of the dead and to memory wipes, *The Night Orchid* showcases Dunyach's talent and facility in moving among the subgenres of speculative fiction. *The Thieves of Silence* (2009) offers reader even more stories (sixteen this time). Here a group of scientists on a hostile planet must fight deadly vegetation in order to harvest a single bud that will give humans immortality, an astronaut acts as a shepherd to his artificial-intelligence (AI) sheep, and dinosaurs engage in bureaucratic shenanigans, among many other magical realist, space-opera, and horror tales.

The French speculative fiction that has been translated over the past decade reveals the exciting variety of stories and concerns as we head deeper into the century. Jean-Claude Carrière's playful *Please, Mr. Einstein* (2005; 2006) imagines Albert Einstein living in the early twenty -first century in a central European city, discussing his breakthrough discoveries about the nature of space-time and light with a physics student. Olivier Pauvert's dystopian *Noir* (2006; 2008) is deadly serious, following one man's nightmare journey through a future apartheid France. His journey to this world from the past brings with it large memory gaps and the fear that he has murdered someone. Black Coat Press's recent publications of P.-J. Hérault's *The Clone Rebellion* (2005; 2015) (about a clone's awareness that he and his army are nothing more than genetically engineered cannon fodder) and Oksana and Gil Prou's *Outre-blanc* (2016; 2018) (in which an astrophysicist is beheaded but subsequently finds a way to explore the powers of his own brain) point to interests in cloning and the continuing mystery of the human mind, which scientists are still just beginning to fathom.

Serge Brussolo's *The Deep Sea Diver's Syndrome* (1992; 2016) explores the materiality of dreams and the mysteries of the dream state that scientists continue to study.[16] In Brussolo's novel, lucid dreamers ("mediums") are able to harvest "ectoplasms" from their dreams—objects that function as art objects in the real world. When one of the most successful mediums realizes that his abilities are deteriorating with age, he embarks upon one last dive, which veers quickly into the realm of nightmare.

Hubert Hadad's *Desirable Body* (2015; 2018) is the story of a journalist who becomes paralyzed from the neck down following an accident. After receiving a full-body transplant, he must deal with the disorientation of his consciousness communicating with a literal "foreign body." A meditation on the mind-body duality, consciousness, and identity, *Desirable Body* is part of the twenty-first-century exploration by writers of the future relationship between the biological and the artificial.

The trajectory of translated science fiction from France since 1960 has largely been from alien worlds and galactic battles to the mysteries of the human mind and the consequences of human cloning, suggesting a shift away from the Other and toward the self. One major exception to this trend is Swiss author Laurence Suhner's Quantika tetralogy, of which only the first book, *Vestiges* (2012; 2019), has been translated into English.[17] Set in the twenty-fourth century on a frozen yet habitable extrasolar planet called Gemma in the binary Alta-Mira system, *Vestiges* is a complex story about a mysterious alien species that visited Gemma centuries before and the human factions currently fighting over how best to settle the planet for the foreseeable future.

Fantasy

While science fiction has outpaced fantasy in terms of English translations throughout the twentieth century, Anglophone readers nonetheless have a significant number of surrealist, decadent, magical realist, high fantasy, and Weird French SFT to choose from. The first French author of surrealistic texts to be translated into English was Raymond Roussel.[18] His influence on surrealism, Dadaism, the nouveau roman, and OuLiPo is extensive and can be classed with visual artists working in the 1920s such as Salvador Dalí and Joan Miró. Roussel's *Impressions of Africa* (1910; 1967) draws playfully on several kinds of narratives, including the Vernian fantastic voyage, the "Lost Race" tale, and stories of amazing inventions. The central story concerns a group of shipwreck survivors who stage theatrical performances for the emperor of the island on which they're trapped. Robotic creatures dance, sculpted slaves fly, and reality and illusion blend together seamlessly (a few decades later, Marcel Béalu would write *The Experience of the Night* [1945; 1997], which also explores the ways in which dreams and reality blend together). Roussel's *Locus Solus* (1914; 1970), published four years after *Impressions*, focuses on a group of visitors taking a tour of a wealthy scientist's estate. Written a couple of decades after Nikola Tesla's most famous inventions and discoveries, and around the same time as the beginnings of futurism in Italy, *Locus Solus* introduces readers to such bizarre inventions as a battery-driven hairless cat and a theater in which the dead are reanimated to act out the most important moments of their previous lives.

Contemporaneous with Roussel, symbolist Marcel Schwob drew on the kind of distorted yet vibrant imagery of Charles Beaudelaire's poetry. Schwob's collection *The King in the Golden Mask* (1891; 1984) includes twenty-one stories that blend fantastic and historical fiction to create a dizzying kaleidoscope of medieval witches, gambling noblemen, leprosy, murder, and suicide.[19] With *The Book of Monelle* (1894; 2012), Schwob explores the nature of his grief over the tuberculosis-related death of a woman with whom he'd been close for a couple of years. Fellow symbolists such as Stéphane Mallarmé and André Gide greatly admired this collection of fairy tales, aphorisms, and nihilistic musings, which highlighted the disturbing gulf between romance and fantasy, on the one hand, and harsh reality, on the other. And if the premise of *Monelle* sounds strangely similar to Giacomo Puccini's *La bohème*, that's because it is—*Monelle*, though, was written two years before the opera's debut in 1896.

Like Roussel, Lithuanian-born French author Romain Gary (Roman Kacew) infused his novels with humor, though of a much darker kind, influenced by the trauma of persecution and the horrors of World War II. Gary is the only author known to have won the Prix Goncourt (a French literature prize) twice under different names. Both *The Dance of Genghis Cohn* (1967; 1968) and the sequel, *The Guilty Head* (1968; 1969), were published in English just one year after their original French publications. In this duology, a former music-hall entertainer (Cohn), who was executed by a Nazi named Schatz during the Holocaust, comes back as a *dybbuk* to possess his murderer.[20] Gary's third novel in English, *The Enchanters* (1973; 1975), is a Roussel-like magical realist tale in which the narrator—the latest in a family of magicians, alchemists, and actors—tells the reader about his upbringing in Russia under Catherine the Great, which, since he's writing his story in the 1960s, makes him around 170 years old. A raucous tale of priceless but blank books, bloody final solutions, and immortality (complete with Jewish fiddlers), *The Enchanters* reads like a textual version of a Marc Chagall painting.

Since the 1990s, French fantasy in translation has tended toward magical realism and high fantasy, and even newer subgenres like Volodine's "post-exoticism." Marie Darrieussecq's novels, for instance, are intense blends of magical realism and science fiction, with women transforming into nonhuman creatures or splitting themselves into two. Her *Pig Tales: A Novel of Lust and Transformation* (1996; 1998), set in a near-future France, tells the story of a beauty-parlor employee who suddenly finds herself turning into a "werepig." Simultaneously, France itself is undergoing radical change with revolutions and counterrevolutions, famines, epidemics, and other apocalyptic trappings. With *Our Life in the Forest* (2017; 2018), though, Darrieussecq turns to the subject of cloning in order to talk about a near-future France in the throes of violence and the spread of a surveillance state. When a psychotherapist decides to flee the violence that has plagued her city, she travels to a "Rest Center," where her clone and many others lie in comas in order to supply their "other halves" with organs and body parts. These clones, though, revive and start behaving like wild teenagers, leaving the "original" people to question the benefits of basically cannibalizing themselves (even as France does the same to itself).

From Maurice Dantec, we have three fast-paced technothrillers that explore genetic modification, mass surveillance, and ruinous viruses (both artificial and biological). Dantec's cyberpunk novel *Babylon Babies* (1999; 2005) is set in a future France where Serbian mafiosi run underground cyborg communities.[21] One schizophrenic woman's unusual pregnancy sets off a series of events in which a battle-scarred man named Throop must smuggle her out of Russia and into Canada to deliver her to the American cult that created the genetically engineered babies she carries in her womb. Ultimately, the cult expects to use these babies as messiah figures in order to usher in a new kind of human.

Dantec's two other novels available in English, *Cosmos Incorporated* and *Grand Junction,* are set in the same universe but not considered a duology. Both draw on ideas first developed in *Babylon Babies*. In *Cosmos Incorporated* (2005; 2008), the human population that is left after decades of war and disease is under the control of UniWorld, a superstate that runs a massive computer program that catalogs everything about each individual, down to their genetic codes and dreams. *Grand Junction* (2006; 2009) focuses on the destruction of electronic devices around the world. The death and societal decay that result push humanity to the brink, but a few manage to keep civilization going in the spaceport. Another virus, this time biological, destroys individuals' language and ability to think, and it's up to survivors to fight a strange entity that seeks to sweep in and transform the world.

Meditations on transformation and self-obsession inform the short stories of Georges-Olivier Châteaureynaud, whose collection *A Life on Paper* (2010) won in the Long Form Category of the Science Fiction and Fantasy Translation Award in 2011. With stories previously published in such speculative fiction venues as *The Magazine of Fantasy and Science Fiction, Lady Churchill's Rosebud Wristlet,* and *Podcastle*, this collection offers us Châteaureynaud's take on the "fantastic," including a young husband struggling with his transformation into a winged creature ("Icarus Saved from the Skies") and a father's obsession with capturing in photographs every moment of his daughter's transformation from childhood to adulthood ("A Life on Paper").

It was around this time that the first French works of high fantasy were coming into English: specifically Pierre Pevel's *The Cardinal's Blades* trilogy (2007–10; 2009–11), and Pierre Grimbert's *The Secret of Ji* trilogy (1996–98; 2013–14). While Pevel uses an alternate seventeenth-century Paris to tell his story of dragons and political intrigue,[22] Grimbert creates a completely different kind of alternate world, filled with gods, magicians, merchants, warriors, and a mysterious legend. Grimbert's trilogy is less about royal machinations and knights than gods and unknown realms.[23] Dragons factor largely in Pevel's new series, High Kingdom, with *The Knight: A Tale from the High Kingdom* (2013; 2014) the only book of the series in English so far. Here a wrongfully imprisoned warrior is given royal authority to pacify the High Kingdom and also to take down those who oppose him. If he is victorious, he must then confront the lethal Black Dragon.

With the novels of Carole Martinez, Anglophone readers have access to an alternative kind of high fantasy, where swashbuckling knights are replaced with benevolent sorceresses and political intrigue is exchanged for mystical powers. Martinez's two novels in English, *The Threads of the Heart* (2007; 2012) and *The Castle of Whispers* (2011; 2014), are in reality an intriguing mix of high fantasy and magical realism, complete with sorceresses and mystical crossroads. In *The Threads of the Heart*, a sorceress named Frasquita is known to have healing powers and the ability, passed down to the women of each generation, to create garments that mask defects and give the wearer remarkable beauty. Her neighbors' jealousy, which spreads through their small village in Andalusia, and her husband's disastrous attempt to gamble on her honor lead to Frasquita's banishment and her attempt to find a better life for her and her daughters elsewhere. A strong and resilient woman is also at the center of *The Castle of Whispers*, set in the twelfth century, in which the teenage Esclarmonde refuses to marry the knight that the Lord of the Domain of Whispers (her father) has chosen for her husband. Instead, Esclarmonde dedicates herself to God, is imprisoned for her betrayal, and then encounters a mystical crossroads that connects the living and the dead. Her subsequent powers attract people from around the kingdom, who come to hear her saintly message.

Moroccan-born French author Muriel Barbery, known for her international best seller *The Elegance of the Hedgehog*, has one speculative novel in English, *The Life of Elves* (2015; 2016), in which two young girls are encouraged to cultivate their special talents in order to change history. In a village in Burgundy, Maria discovers her gift for clairvoyance, healing, and communing with nature, while Clara, in Italy, possesses an extraordinary musical gift. If a group of elves is able to bring the two girls together, the latter's combined gifts can shift the balance of power in a coming war between good and evil.

Neither "fantasy" nor "magical realism," but in a genre all their own, the "post-exotic" texts of Antoine Volodine offer a stark alternative to traditional fantasy and SF.[24] Volodine's oeuvre is a constellation of recurring heteronyms, characters, places, and themes that explore a kind of alternate world that is very close to this one. Whether they're set in a postapocalyptic wasteland (*Radiant Terminus*) or in the Tibetan afterlife or Bardo (*Bardo or Not Bardo*), Volodine's stories ask readers to consider the nature of dreams, the strength of the human survival instinct, and the possibility of an afterlife.

Often marked by sharp, sardonic wit, such Volodine novels as **Minor Angels** (1999; 2004) sometimes juxtapose hilarious scenarios with horrifying postapocalyptic landscapes. Here, a group of (potentially) immortal old women confined to a nursing home work together to create a boy who will crush any reviving capitalist forces in a world that had tried to stamp it out. **Post-exoticism in Ten Lessons, Lesson Eleven** (1998; 2015) brings together Volodine's heteronyms—all radical post-exotic authors—who are all dying off, with the last one approached by journalists interested in the inner workings of the movement, while **Bardo or Not Bardo** (2004; 2016) offers a piercingly witty and ironic take on the journey through the afterlife and reincarnation. **Radiant Terminus** (2014; 2017), however, gives readers a much darker perspective on human nature, with decrepit but sometimes (seemingly) immortal characters wandering around a desolate landscape scarred by radioactive waste after a series of nuclear meltdowns.[25] Once again, Volodine uses the trope of dream invasion to raise questions about power and morality.

Horror

While Volodine and other writers of speculative fiction in France incorporate elements of horror in their texts at times, the subgenre of horror is currently a shadow of what it once was. During the nineteenth century, the kind of horror written in France by Eugène Sue, Charles Baudelaire, Gérard de Nerval, and Guy de Maupassant drew upon the Terror of the French Revolution and the burgeoning field of scientific inquiry to explore the darkest places in the human psyche. Many of these stories have been translated into English, though few works of contemporary French horror have made it to Anglophone readers.[26] One that has is Roland Topor's **The Tenant** (1964; 1966), originally published in translation in the 1960s and then made into a film several years later. Here, an intensely shy and introverted man is psychologically sucked into the world of the previous tenant of his apartment who attempted to commit suicide. The main character's sanity deteriorates under the pressures of paranoia, obsession, and displaced feelings of guilt.

QUEBEC

Science Fiction

One of the major voices in science fiction from Quebec (SFQ) is undoubtedly Élisabeth Vonarburg.[27] An author, translator, and former editor of *Solaris* (the world's oldest established French-language science fiction magazine), Vonarburg has produced three series about the far future and planetary colonization, with a few finding their way into English (thanks to translators Howard Scott and Jane Brierley, as well as Vonarburg herself).

While Vonarburg has said that she may write a third novel in the Baïblanca/Mothers' Land universe, so far only *The Silent City* and *In the Mothers' Land* have been published, though the stories in *Slow Engines of Time* (2000) are also set in that universe.[28] Taking place centuries apart in the far future, these books tell a complex story about human adaptation in the face of catastrophe, future technological development, and the evolution of spiritual beliefs and myths. *The Silent City* (1981; 1988), which won the Grand Prix de l'Imaginaire and the Prix Rosny-Aîné in 1982, follows the protagonist, Elisa, from childhood into adulthood as she navigates the technologically sophisticated world in the underground City, which stands in stark contrast to the Outside/Surface, where environmental catastrophe has thrown humanity back into a kind of Stone Age.[29] Ultimately, it is up to Elisa, who is herself a product of genetic engineering, to create a new race of humans that will live on the Surface and merge back in with the people already there, forging a new civilization. The seeds of conflict that lie just under the surface here are fully developed in the next novel, *In the Mothers' Land* (1992; 1992), set a few centuries after *The Silent City*.[30] The winner of multiple awards in 1993, this novel is once again focalized through a young girl, Lisbeï, as she grows into adulthood and rebels against the rigid social structure that constitutes the religious matriarchal community of Betheley. She also discovers that a mutation in the population may signal yet another major shift in the course of human civilization on the planet.

Reluctant Voyagers (1994; 1995), written and translated between *In the Mothers' Land* and the first book in the Tyranaël series, is set in an alternate Montreal. When a professor/writer starts seeing strange things happening in the city (like streets shifting places), she starts questioning her sanity until she unintentionally gets involved in a secret revolutionary movement. Ultimately, this revelation leads her to question the basis of her reality, and it is her own writing that holds the key to the alternate worlds that she visits.

Vonarburg then takes us on an otherworldly journey in the **Tyranaël** series, of which only the first two, *Dreams of the Sea* (1996; 2003) and *A Game of Perfection*

(1996; 2006), have been translated into English. Here, the remaining human colonists on the planet Altair try to recover from a catastrophic flood. Taking refuge in the abandoned but intact cities left behind by an unknown alien civilization, the colonists start having mysterious dreams that may unlock the aliens' secrets and a way for the humans to survive on Altair (which they've named "Virginia"). The second book in the series continues the story of the colonists, but through the next generation. One of these children, Simon, is a telepath who can dream the ancient alien dreams but can also "read" their memory plates. It is this telepathic ability that allows this next generation to gain a better understanding of their home and its mysterious history.

The last book by Vonarburg to be translated is the collection ***Blood Out of a Stone*** (2009), which takes up questions of interstellar travel and translation. Vonarburg, who herself translates from French into English and vice versa, explores translation in its various guises throughout her work, whether in the form of Lisbeï deciphering ancient documents, or even in the sense of "mental translation" between humans and robots in the underground City, or telepathic interpretation on Altair/Virginia. With several more novels just waiting to be brought into English, Vonarburg offers us a wealth of SFQ that will be studied for years to come.

Another of the talented SFQ writers who emerged during the 1970s is Esther Rochon, also a winner of the Grand Prix de la science-fiction et du fantastique québecois, in both 1986 and 1987. Her Lovecraftian sci-fi horror novel *The Shell* (1985; 1990) explores cross-species sexuality and communication.[31] When several members of a family find themselves trapped on an island, they soon discover that they share it with a bizarre telepathic sea creature that seems more friendly than not. Eventually, several of the characters have sexual encounters with the creature, encounters that complicate our assumptions about the inability to ever truly connect with the Other/Alien.

The SFT coming out of Quebec since the turn of the twenty-first century has continued this focus on dystopias and off-world exploration. Joël Champetier's *The Dragon's Eye* (1991; 1999), set two centuries in the future, takes up the popular science fiction theme of Earth fighting with a rebellious colony planet. Here, Earth's government sends out spies to the planet New China to discover whether its government is planning to break away from the home planet. The colony's people are simultaneously struggling under the unblinking Dragon's Eye—one of the planet's suns that is so strong, the colonists have to completely cover themselves during daylight hours. Sylvie Bérard's *Of Wind and Sand* (2004; 2009) is also set on a hostile alien planet, though the accidental colonists must struggle not with their own species but with massive lizards that have developed their own sophisticated civilization. Despite attempts by both humans and lizards to establish a friendship, the planet's lack of resources necessary for human survival, coupled with the unexpectedness of the humans' arrival, eventually undercuts any chances that this friendship will blossom.

Serge Lamothe's *The Baldwins* and Karoline Georges's **Under the Stone**, both novellas, return us to Earth, albeit a dystopian one. *The Baldwins* (2006; 2006) is a metafictional critique of contemporary consumerism and an obsession over linguistic exactitude. Told as a series of vignettes set within the frame of an academic congress, after Lamothe's scholars discover evidence of the existence of a family called "the Baldwins" in a trash heap filled with historical artifacts, they attempt to extrapolate what people were like back when the Baldwins were alive. Also trying to piece together a view of the world based on little evidence is the main character in Karoline Georges's *Under the Stone* (2011; 2016). Since birth, he has been locked in cell #804, level 5969, of a massive structure that houses all remaining humanity. Tormented by abusive, fearful parents, he ultimately attempts to break through the concrete separating him from the Outside to learn about a wider, potentially different world.

Many of the authors discussed in the above section on Quebec have also been featured in a special anthology of translated Francophone science fiction: *Tesseracts*[Q] (2002), edited by Élisabeth Vonarburg and Jane Brierley. Part of the Tesseracts series begun by Judith Merril in the 1980s, *Tesseracts*[Q] includes such well-known Quebec-based authors as Yves Meynard, Jean-Louis Trudel, Rochon, Champetier, Brierley, and Vonarburg. In her foreword to the volume, Vonarburg discusses the position of SFQ in relation to the US market (physically closer) and the French market (linguistically closer).[32] Nonetheless, these authors stand at the crossroads of Anglophone and Francophone science fiction, and, as this section on science fiction from Quebec has shown, French-to-English and English-to-French translators, editors, and publishers have helped bring many novels and stories across the border in both directions.

Fantasy

A few works of Francophone fantasy have reached the Anglophone world from Quebec, including novels by Michel Tremblay, Christian Guay-Poliquin, and Pierre-Luc Landry. While Tremblay's **The City in the Egg** (1969; 1999) tells the story of a mysterious egg that appears depending on the phases of the moon and takes the protagonist on a bizarre journey through time and space, Landry's **Listening for Jupiter** (2015; 2017) is a surrealist meditation on what happens when two people living thousands of miles apart share the same dream.[33] What makes this English translation even more interesting is that the two very different main characters are each translated by different people.

Guay-Poliquin's two novels available in English are unique blends of magical realism and the postapocalyptic narrative. In **Running on Fumes** (2013; 2016), an unexplained nationwide power outage induces a young mechanic to drive across the country to be with his ailing father.[34] His journey, modeled on that of Theseus in the Labyrinth, leads him to differentiate between the necessities and those things that no longer matter and introduces him to other wandering souls with their own vague goals. *The Weight of Snow* (2016; 2019) follows up on *Running on Fumes* with the mechanic, injured in a terrible car accident, being taken care of by an old man amid devastatingly harsh winter weather. Ultimately, they must battle the difficult conditions and their own increasingly complicated relationship if they want a chance to escape from their deteriorating circumstances.

Horror

Internationally known horror and thriller writer Patrick Senécal has been called the Stephen King/Jo Nesbø of Quebec, and his two novels explore the monstrous that sleeps in each of us. In *Against God* (2010; 2012), Senécal explores questions of morality and purpose through a protagonist who has lost all reason for living or even caring about others. Might isolation and an individual's frayed relationship to their community drive them toward evil? *Seven Days* (2002; 2019), too, follows the psychological deterioration of a man experiencing intense grief. His coldly calculated plan to kidnap and torture the man who killed his daughter leads him down the path toward the monstrous, and it's up to a determined detective to stop him.

BELGIUM

All Francophone SFT from Belgium has come out over the past twenty years, with Wakefield Press in particular committed to publishing some of the most intriguing fantasy and horror from that country. With the science fiction of Jaqueline Harpman; the fantasy of Michel de Ghelderode, Paul Willems, and Peter Verhelst; and the horror of Jean Ray, Anglophone readers can gain a better perspective on the themes and concerns coming out of Belgium.

Harpman's disturbing sci-fi dystopia *I Who Have Never Known Men* (1995; 1997) tells the story of a young woman inexplicably kept in a cage with dozens of other women, with men as silent guards.[35] All she knows is that she is underground and has supposedly committed some kind of crime, though she can't imagine what it was. When this artificial, ahistorical world is unexpectedly broken open, Harpman's protagonist struggles with understanding her freedom and cultivating a life with meaning. Like Vonarburg's *The Silent City*, *Never Known Men* explores how female characters build their identities out of the scraps of history and the social structures imposed on them by men.

The works of fantasy by Verhelst, Willems, and Ghelderode come to us in English in the reverse order from when they were originally published in French, with

Ghelderode's *Spells* taking seventy-six years to be translated. Verhelst's ***Tonguecat*** (1999; 2003), a narrative journey across genres, time, and space, is the story of Prometheus returning to Earth centuries after he stole fire from the ancient gods and gave it to humans. Roaming around a (figurative and literal) cold city filled with the rejected and forgotten, Prometheus nonetheless witnesses the gathering rebellion against monarchy and oppression that spreads around the slums, especially through the tales of the "tonguecats" (storytelling prostitutes).

Unlike the mythic/visceral mashup that is *Tonguecat*, Willems's ***The Cathedral of Mist*** (1983; 2016) deals in the intangibility of the imagination and its influence on the mundane world. A collection of stories about strange architecture, dreamlike journeys, and the materials of memory, *Cathedral* asks us to imagine such structures as a church made entirely of warm air currents and fog, as well as a palace of emptiness. According to translator Edward Gauvin in his introduction to the volume, "[Willems] sought to create images whose power lay in the seamlessness, rather than the impossibility, of their union."[36] From dramatist and fiction writer Michel de Ghelderode we have ***Spells*** (1941; 2017), a collection of fantasy/Weird/horror that explores the grotesque and bizarre during a period of intense violence, terror, and world war.[37] Through the evocation of angels and demons, ghosts and gardens, mannequins and relics, Ghelderode disrupts our experience of the banalities of city life and the seemingly stable world around us.

Like Ghelderode, Flemish fantasist Jean Ray (Jean-Raymond-Marie De Kremer) (sometimes called the "Belgian Poe" or the "Flemish Lovecraft") sought to look beyond the veil of everyday life to reveal the inexplicable and the horrifying. Ray wrote some of his greatest stories while he was serving time in prison for embezzlement (1926–28). ***Malpertius*** (1943; 1998), Ray's first work to be translated into English, is a disturbing mix of gothic and cosmic horror. A manuscript stolen from a monastery and the remnants of the Inquisition in Belgium come together to create a story of unnerving resonance. His other four books in English are collections of stories that run the gamut from horror to fantasy and from the Weird to the supernatural. Often the stories in ***Ghouls in My Grave*** (1929; 1965), ***My Own Private Spectres*** (1999), ***The Horrifying Presence, and Other Tales*** (1925; 2009), and ***Whiskey Tales*** (1925; 2019) include an element of humor amid the horror (see, for example, "The Marlyweck Cemetery"), as if Ray were trying to jostle readers out of their generic comfort zones.[38] With titles like "The Pink Terror" and "The Great Nocturnal One," Ray was overtly tapping into the same ideas as those influencing Lovecraftian cosmic horror.[39] Several of Ray's stories are set at sea, in dark and dingy alleys, and atop mysterious mountain ranges. The latest collection out in English is notable particularly for the fact that some of the included stories first appeared in English in *Weird Tales* issues from the 1930s.

THE CARIBBEAN

Since the 1990s, Anglophone readers have had access to more magical realism and horror in translation from the Caribbean than ever before: specifically, from Martinique (still under French control) and Haiti (which broke away in 1803). Patrick Chamoiseau's internationally acclaimed historical novel *Texaco* (1992; 1997), while not explicitly "speculative," uses magical realist tropes in order to tell the story of Martinique more than a century and a half after slavery was outlawed.[40] The two novels from Haiti, René Depestre's *Hadriana in All My Dreams* (1988; 2017)[41] and Frankétienne's *Dézafi* (1975; 2018), are complex and disturbing "zombie" stories that rise far above pop culture's image of the undead creatures. In Depestre's story, a young French woman is on the cusp of marrying a Haitian man when she drinks a potion and collapses during the ceremony. Her burial, revival by an evil sorcerer, and eventual disappearance are explored in depth in the context of early-twentieth- and twenty-first-century ideas about race and sexuality. *Dézafi* moves in a different direction, using the zombie figure to tell a story about the history of slavery on the island. Here, a living plantation owner uses zombies to work his land, but when his daughter falls in love with one of these undead workers and helps bring him back to life, the rebellion that follows upends the seemingly stable balance of power.

AFRICA

The French colonial presence in Africa lingers on in the language that they left behind; thus, the SFT from Djibouti, Algeria, and the Republic of the Congo has all been translated from the French. Djiboutian author Abdourahman A. Waberi's *In the United States of Africa* (2006; 2009) asks us to imagine a world in which millions of people attempt to escape poverty, war, and despair by fleeing Europe and America in hopes of finding peace in the United States of Africa. Told through the perspective of a French-born woman who was adopted by an African doctor, *United States of Africa* disrupts Western assumptions about the trajectory of history.

Algerian SFT has a decidedly science fictional bent with Boualem Sansal's *2084: The End of the World* (2015; 2017). Sansal's novel, which won the Grand Prix du Roman from the Académie Française, imagines an Orwellian state in which religious fundamentalists, rather than Big Brother, control the population via fear and constant surveillance. It is only when the protagonist discovers that those who live on the fringes are immune from the authorities that he is able to open his mind to an alternative world.

From the Republic of Congo we have Emmanuel Dongala's collection of stories *Jazz and Palm Wine* (1981; 2017), which mixes witchcraft, American jazz, and colonial history to produce a powerful representation of postcolonial life. Dongala, who founded the National Association of Congolese Writers and the Congolese chapter of PEN, as well as the theater company Le Théâtre de l'Eclair, moves between Africa and the United States in these stories in order to examine questions of race and violence in the face of rapid technological development and government bureaucracy.

∗ ∗ ∗

Francophone speculative fiction is written around the world and is also one of the most popular source languages translated into English. Since the 1960s, Anglophone readers have had access to planetary romances from France, the Belgian Weird, future visions from Quebec, zombie novels from the Caribbean, and everything in between. Because of this, we can get a more nuanced and complex picture of the directions that Francophone SF is taking as we head deeper into the twenty-first century.

Primary Sources

ALGERIA

2015: Sansal, Boualem. *2084: The End of the World.* Translated by Alison Anderson. Europa Editions, 2017.

BELGIUM

1925: Ray, Jean. *The Horrifying Presence, and Other Tales.* Translated by António Monteiro. Ex Occidente Press, 2009.
———. *Whiskey Tales.* Translated by Scott Nicolay. Wakefield Press, 2019.
1929: Ray, Jean. *Ghouls in My Grave.* Translated by Lowell Bair. Berkley, 1965.
1931: Ray, Jean. *Cruise of Shadows: Haunted Stories of Land and Sea.* Translated by Scott Nicolay. Wakefield Press, 2019.
1941: Ghelderode, Michel de. *Spells.* Translated by George MacLennon. Wakefield Press, 2017.
1943: Ray, Jean. *Malpertius.* Translated by Iain White. Atlas Press, 1998.
1983: Willems, Paul. *The Cathedral of Mist.* Translated by Edward Gauvin. Wakefield Press, 2016.
1995: Harpman, Jacqueline. *I Who Have Never Known Men.* Translated by Ros Schwartz. Seven Stories Press, 1997.
1998: Connell, Kim, ed. *The Belgian School of the Bizarre: An Anthology of Short Stories.* Fairleigh Dickinson University Press.
1999: Ray, Jean. *My Own Private Spectres.* Translated by Hubert Van Calenbergh. Midnight House.
Verhelst, Peter. *Tonguecat.* Translated by Sherry Marx. Farrar, Straus & Giroux, 2003.

2012: Rosny aîné, J.-H. *Three Science Fiction Novellas: From Prehistory to the End of Mankind.* Translated by Danièle Chatelain and George Edgar Slusser. Middletown, CT: Wesleyan University Press.

DJIBOUTI

2006: Waberi, Abdourahman A. *In the United States of Africa.* Translated by David Ball and Nicole Ball. Bison Books, 2009.

FRANCE

Unknown: Salzman, Anne-Sylvie. *Darkscapes.* Translated by William Charlton. Tartarus Press, 2013.

1891: Schwob, Marcel. *The King in the Golden Mask, and Other Stories.* Translated by Iain White. Carcanet Press, 1984.

1894: Schwob, Marcel. *The Book of Monelle.* Translated by Kit Schluter. Wakefield Press, 2012.

1901: Lorrain, Jean. *Monsieur de Phocas.* Translated by Francis Amery. Dedalus Books, 1994.

1909: Marinetti, Filippo Tommaso. *Mafarka the Futurist: An African Novel.* Translated by Steve Cox and Carol Diethe. Middlesex University Press, 1998.

1910: Roussel, Raymond. *Impressions of Africa.* Translated by Rayner Heppenstall and Lindy Foord. Calder and Boyars, 1967.

1914: Roussel, Raymond. *Locus Solus.* Translated by Rupert Copeland Cunningham. Calder and Boyar, 1970.

1928: Breton, André. *Nadja.* Translated by Richard Howard. Grove Press, 1960.

1943: Barjavel, René. *Ashes, Ashes.* Translated by Damon Knight. Doubleday, 1967.

1945: Béalu, Marcel. *The Experience of the Night.* Translated by Christine Donougher. Dedalus, 1997.

1950: Ferry, Jean. *The Conductor, and Other Tales.* Translated by Edward Gauvin. Wakefield Press, 2013.

1957: Boulle, Pierre. *Time Out of Mind.* Translated by Xan Fielding. Vanguard, 1966.
Wul, Stefan. *Fantastic Planet.* Translated by Anthony Georges Whyte. Creation Oneiros, 2010.
———. *The Temple of the Past.* Translated by Ellen Cox. Seabury Press, 1973.

1958: Klein, Gérard. *Starmasters' Gambit.* Translated by C. J. Richards. DAW, 1973.

1961: Henneberg, N[athalie] C. *The Green Gods.* Translated by C. J. Cherryh. DAW, 1980.

1962–63: Bessière, Richard. *The Gardens of the Apocalypse / The Seven Rings of Rhea.* Translated by Brian Stableford. Black Coat Press, 2010.

1963: Boulle, Pierre. *The Planet of the Apes.* Translated by Xan Fielding. Vanguard.
Klein, Gérard. *The Day before Tomorrow.* Translated by P. J. Sokolowski. DAW, 1982.

1964: Boulle, Pierre. *Garden on the Moon.* Translated by Xan Fielding. Vanguard, 1965.
Topor, Roland. *The Tenant.* Translated by Francis K. Price. Doubleday, 1966.

1964–65: Caroff, André. *The Terror of Madame Atomos*. Translated by Brian Stableford. Black Coat Press, 2010.

1965: Klein, Gérard. *The Mote in Time's Eye*. Translated by C. J. Richards. DAW, 1975.

1966: Boulle, Pierre. *Because It Is Absurd (on Earth as in Heaven)*. Translated by Elisabeth Abbott. Vanguard Press, 1971.

1967: Gary, Romain. *The Dance of Genghis Cohn*. Translated by the author. World, 1968.

Merle, Robert. *The Day of the Dolphin*. Translated by Helen Weaver. Simon & Schuster, 1969.

1968: Barjavel, René. *The Ice People*. Translated by Charles Lam Markmann. William Morrow, 1970.

Gary, Romain. *The Guilty Head*. Translated by the author. World, 1969.

1970: Barbet, Pierre. *The Napoleons of Eridanus*. Translated by Stanley Hochman. DAW, 1976.

1971: Barbet, Pierre. *Baphomet's Meteor*. Translated by Bernard Kay. DAW, 1972.

———. *Games Psyborgs Play*. Translated by Wendayne Ackerman. DAW, 1973.

Boulle, Pierre. *Desperate Games*. Translated by Patricia Wolf. Vanguard Press, 1973.

Klein, Gérard. *The Overlords of War*. Translated by John Brunner. Doubleday, 1973.

Sternberg, Jacques. *Future without Future*. Translated by Frank Zero. Seabury Press, 1974.

1972: Knight, Damon, ed. and trans. *Thirteen French Science-Fiction Stories*. Bantam Books.

Léourier, Christian. *The Mountains of the Sun*. Unknown translator. Berkley Medallion, 1974.

Merle, Robert. *Malevil*. Translated by Derek Coltman. Simon & Schuster, 1973.

1973: Barbet, Pierre. *The Enchanted Planet*. Translated by C. J. Richards. DAW, 1975.

———. *The Joan-of-Arc Replay*. Translated by Stanley Hochman. DAW, 1978.

Barjavel, René. *The Immortals*. Translated by Eileen Finletter. Morrow, 1974.

Gary, Romain. *The Enchanters*. Translated by Helen Eustis. Putnam, 1975.

Jeury, Michel. *Chronolysis*. Translated by Maxim Jakubowski. Macmillan, 1980.

1974: Berna, Paul. *The Last Dawn*. Unknown translator. Angus and Robertson, 1977.

Merle, Robert. *The Virility Factor*. Translated by Martin Sokolinsky. McGraw-Hill, 1977.

1977: Boulle, Pierre. *The Good Leviathan*. Translated by Margaret Giovanelli. Vanguard Press, 1978.

Jakubowski, Maxim, ed. *Travelling towards Epsilon: An Anthology of French Science Fiction*. Translated by Maxim Jakubowski and Beth Blish. New English Library.

1980: Arnaud, G.-J. *The Ice Company*. Translated by J.-M. Lofficier and Randy Lofficier. Black Coat Press, 2010.

Barbet, Pierre. *Cosmic Crusaders* (includes *Baphomet's Meteor* and *Stellar Crusade*). Translated by C. J. Cherryh and Bernard Kay. DAW.

1982: Barbet, Pierre. *The Emperor of Eridanus.* Translated by Stanley Hochman. DAW, 1983.

Boulle, Pierre. *Mirrors of the Sun.* Translated by Patricia Wolf. Vanguard Press, 1986.

Walther, Daniel. *The Book of Shai.* Translated by C. J. Cherryh. DAW, 1984.

1983: Walther, Daniel. *Shai's Destiny.* Translated by C. J. Cherryh. DAW, 1985.

1986: Muno, Jean. *Glove of Passion, Voice of Blood.* Translated by Kim Connell. Owl Creek Press.

1990: Belletto, René. *Machine.* Translated by Lanie Goodman. Grove Press, 1993.

1991: Werber, Bernard. *Empire of the Ants (La Saga des Fourmis #1).* Translated by Margaret Rocques. Bantam, 1996.

1992: Brussolo, Serge. *The Deep Sea Diver's Syndrome.* Translated by Edward Gauvin. Melville House, 2016.

Maalouf, Amin. *The First Century after Beatrice.* Translated by Dorothy S. Blair. Abacus, 1994.

1996: Darrieussecq, Marie. *Pig Tales: A Novel of Lust and Transformation.* Translated by Linda Coverdale. New Press, 1998.

Grimbert, Pierre. *The Orphans' Promise (The Secret of Ji #2).* Translated by Eric Lamb and Matt Ross. AmazonCrossing, 2013.

———. *Shadow of the Ancients (The Secret of Ji #3).* Translated by Matt Ross. Amazon Crossing, 2014.

———. *Six Heirs (The Secret of Ji #1).* Translated by Matt Ross and Eric Lamb. AmazonCrossing, 2013.

Houellebecq, Michel. *The Elementary Particles (Atomized).* Translated by Frank Wynne. William Heinemann, 2000.

Volodine, Antoine. *Post-exoticism in Ten Lessons, Lesson Eleven.* Translated by J. T. Mahany. Open Letter, 2015.

1999: Dantec, Maurice G. *Babylon Babies.* Translated by Noura Wedell. Semiotext(e), 2005.

Volodine, Antoine. *Minor Angels.* Translated by Jordan Stump. University of Nebraska Press, 2004.

2001: Miller, Sylvie, and Philippe Ward. *The Song of Montségur.* Translated by Brian Stableford. Black Coat Press, 2010.

2004: Dunyach, Jean-Claude. *The Night Orchid: Conan Doyle in Toulouse.* Translated by Sheryl Curtis et al. Black Coat Press.

Volodine, Antoine. *Bardo or Not Bardo.* Translated by J. T. Mahany. Open Letter Books, 2016.

2005: Belletto, René. *Coda.* Translated by Alyson Waters. University of Nebraska Press, 2011.

Carrière, Jean-Claude. *Please, Mr. Einstein.* Translated by John Brownjohn. HMH, 2006.

Dantec, Maurice G. *Cosmos Incorporated.* Translated by Tina A. Kover. Del Ray, 2008.

Hérault, P.-J. *The Clone Rebellion.* Translated by Michael Shreve. Black Coat Press, 2015.

Houellebecq, Michel. *The Possibility of an Island*. Translated by Gavin Bowd. Weidenfeld and Nicolson, 2006.

2006: Dantec, Maurice G. *Grand Junction*. Translated by Tina A. Kover. Del Ray, 2009.

Pauvert, Olivier. *Noir*. Translated by Adriana Hunter. Counterpoint, 2008.

2007: Martinez, Carole. *The Threads of the Heart*. Translated by Howard Curtis. Europa Editions, 2012.

Pevel, Pierre. *The Cardinal's Blades (The Cardinal's Blades #1)*. Translated by Tom Clegg. Gollancz, 2009.

2009: Dunyach, Jean-Claude. *The Thieves of Silence*. Translated by Sheryl Curtis et al. Black Coat Press.

Pevel, Pierre. *The Alchemist in the Shadows (The Cardinal's Blades #2)*. Translated by Tom Clegg. Pyr, 2011.

2010: Châteaureynaud, Georges-Olivier. *A Life on Paper: Stories*. Translated by Edward Gauvin. Small Beer Press.

Pevel, Pierre. *The Dragon Arcana (The Cardinal's Blades #3)*. Translated by Tom Clegg. Gollancz, 2011.

2011: Martinez, Carole. *The Castle of Whispers*. Translated by Howard Curtis. Europa Editions, 2014.

2013: Pevel, Pierre. *The Knight: A Tale from the High Kingdom*. Translated by Tom Clegg. Gollancz, 2014.

2014: Volodine, Antoine. *Radiant Terminus*. Translated by Jeffrey Zuckerman. Open Letter Books, 2017.

2015: Barbery, Muriel. *The Life of Elves*. Translated by Alison Anderson. Text, 2016.

Haddad, Hubert. *Desirable Body*. Translated by Alyson Waters. Yale University Press, 2018.

2016: Oksana and Gil Prou. *Outre-blanc*. Translated by Sheryl Curtis. Black Coat Press, 2018.

2017: Darrieussecq, Marie. *Our Life in the Forest*. Translated by Penny Hueston. Text, 2018.

HAITI

1975: Frankétienne. *Dézafi*. Translated by Asselin Charles. University of Virginia Press, 2018.

1988: Depestre, René. *Hadriana in All My Dreams*. Translated by Kaiama L. Glover. Akashic Books, 2017.

MARTINIQUE

1992: Chamoiseau, Patrick. *Texaco*. Translated by Rose-Myriam Rejouis and Val Vinokurov. Pantheon, 1997.

QUEBEC

1969: Tremblay, Michel. *The City in the Egg*. Translated by Michael Bullock. Ronsdale, 1999.

1981: Vonarburg, Élisabeth. *The Silent City (Silent City #1)*. Translated by Jane Brierley. Porcépic, 1988.

1985: Massé, Johanne. *Beyond the Future.* Translated by Frances Morgan. Black Moss, 1990.
Rochon, Esther. *The Shell.* Translated by David Lobdell. Oberon Press, 1990.

1991: Champetier, Joël. *The Dragon's Eye.* Translated by Jean-Louis Trudel. Tor Books, 1999.

1992: Vonarburg, Élisabeth. *In the Mothers' Land / The Maerlande Chronicles (Silent City #2).* Translated by Jane Brierley. Bantam, 1992.

1994: Vonarburg, Élisabeth. *Reluctant Voyagers.* Translated by Jane Brierley. Bantam, 1995.

1996: Vonarburg, Élisabeth. *Dreams of the Sea (Tyranaël 1).* Translated by Howard Scott and Élisabeth Vonarburg. Tesseract Books, 2003.

———. *A Game of Perfection (Tyranaël 2).* Translated by Élisabeth Vonarburg and Howard Scott. Edge SF & F, 2006.

2000: Vonarburg, Élisabeth. *Slow Engines of Time.* Translated by the author and Jane Brierley. Tesseract Books.

2002: Senécal, Patrick. *Seven Days.* Translated by Howard Scott and Phyllis Aronoff. Simon & Schuster, 2019.

Vonarburg, Élisabeth, and Jane Brierley, eds. *Tesseracts*^Q. Edge SF & F.

2004: Bérard, Sylvie. *Of Wind and Sand.* Translated by Sheryl Curtis. Edge SF & F, 2009.

2006: Lamothe, Serge. *The Baldwins.* Translated by Fred A. Reed and David Homel. Talonbooks.

2009: Vonarburg, Élisabeth. *Blood Out of a Stone.* Various translators. Nanopress.

2010: Senécal, Patrick. *Against God.* Translated by Susan Ouriou and Christelle Morelli. Quattro Books, 2012.

2011: Georges, Karoline. *Under the Stone.* Translated by Jacob Hormel. Anvil Press, 2016.

2013: Guay-Poliquin, Christian. *Running on Fumes.* Translated by Jacob Homel. Talonbooks, 2016.

2015: Landry, Pierre-Luc. *Listening for Jupiter.* Translated by Arielle Aaronson and Madeleine Stratford. QC Fiction, 2017.

2016: Guay-Poliquin, Christian. *The Weight of Snow.* Translated by David Homel. Talonbooks, 2019.

REPUBLIC OF THE CONGO

1981: Dongala, Emmanuel. *Jazz and Palm Wine.* Translated by Dominic Thomas. Indiana University Press, 2017.

SWITZERLAND

2012: Suhner, Laurence. *Vestiges.* Translated by Sheryl Curtis. L'Atalante, 2019.

Notes

1. See Evans, "A Jules Verne Centenary."

2. Evans, "Jules Verne's English Translations," 80. According to Evans, "A number of Verne novels were rewritten to adhere to a pro-anglo political agenda and were methodically 'purged' of any perceived anti-British or anti-American content before being published."

3. Evans, "Science Fiction vs. Scientific Fiction in France," 8.

4. Ransom review.

5. See Slusser, "Science Fiction in France."

6. See Scott, "Aliens and Alienation."

7. See Clute, Nicholls, and Roberts, "Barjavel, René."

8. *Stellar Crusade* was translated by American science fiction writer C. J. Cherryh, who was beginning her own career as an award-winning speculative fiction author (also published by DAW). Cherryh went on to translate other works of French science fiction in the 1980s, including Nathalie Henneberg's *The Green Gods* (1980) and Daniel Walther's *The Book of Shai* (1984) and *Shai's Destiny* (1985).

9. *The Overlords of War* was translated by award-winning British science fiction author John Brunner (*Stand on Zanzibar*). Several of Brunner's novels were published, in turn, by Ailleurs et Demain under Klein's editorship.

10. Cordasco review.

11. Jakubowski went on to edit an international speculative fiction anthology in English: *Twenty Houses of the Zodiac: An Anthology of International Science Fiction* (1979).

12. In 1958 Sternberg published an essay titled "Une succursale du fantastique nommee science-fiction (A Branch of the Fantastic called Science Fiction)" in which he argued that science fiction was a subgenre of *fantastique*.

13. Nathalie wrote SF and fantasy with her husband, Charles Henneberg, until his death in 1959. Some of their joint stories were published just under Charles's name before then.

14. Jones review.

15. See Mul, "Possibility of an Island."

16. Osborne review.

17. Cordasco and Nicoll reviews.

18. See Hale and Hugill, "Science Is Fiction."

19. Foster review.

20. A *dybbuk* is, in Jewish folklore, a disembodied human spirit that, because of former sins, wanders restlessly until it finds a haven in the body of a living person (*Encyclopedia Britannica*).

21. See Morrey, "Natural and Anti-natural Evolution."

22. Pevel won the 2002 Grand Prix de L'Imaginaire and the 2005 Prix Imaginales.

23. Awarded the Prix Ozone for best French language fantasy novel and the Prix Julia Verlanger for best science fiction novel in any language.

24. See Mahany and Zuckerman's discussion with Volodine, "From Nowhere," https://www.theparisreview.org/blog/2015/07/08/from-nowhere-an-interview-with-antoine-volodine/. According to Volodine, post-exoticism can be described as "from nowhere, to nowhere. . . . Even in my first books, post-exoticism existed with its idiosyncrasies, its refusal to belong to the mainstream, its marginalized characters, its revolts, and its murky narrators. And behind this narration was a narrative background, a 'backfiction,' guided by exterior and manipulative voices."

25. Cordasco review.

26. One can look as well to the history of Le Théâtre du Grand-Guignol (1987–62), known for its naturalistic horror performances.

27. Vonarburg has received a lot of critical attention, and the special issue of *Femspec* 11, no. 2 (2011), edited by Amy Ransom, on her work is a good place to start.

28. See Santoro, "From Silence to Memory."

29. Cordasco review.

30. Cordasco review.

31. Ransom, "Lovecraft in Quebec."

32. Vonarburg, foreword to *Tesseracts*Q.

33. Cordasco review.

34. Cordasco review.

35. See Bainbrigge, "Jaqueline Harpman's Transgressive Dystopian Fantastic."

36. Gauvin, introduction to *The Cathedral of Mist*, xi.

37. Burke review.

38. Bilmes review.

39. According to Antonio Monteiro, there is no evidence "to prove (or to disprove) that Jean Ray was acquainted with Lovecraft's work, despite the fact that they were contemporaries. But, coincidental as they probably are . . . some similarities can be found. For instance, both authors seem to have been impressed by Einstein's theories that gave way to the consideration of parallel worlds" ("Ghosts, Fear, and Parallel Worlds").

40. See Woolward, "Patrick Chamoiseau's *Texaco*."

41. Takács review.

Secondary Sources

Bainbrigge, Susan. "Jaqueline Harpman's Transgressive Dystopian Fantastic in *Moi qui n'ai pas connu les hommes*: Between Familiar Territory and Unknown Worlds." *Modern Language Review* 105, no. 4 (2010): 1015–27.

Bilmes, Leonid. "More than the Belgian Poe: The Overdue Return of Jean Ray's *Whiskey Tales*." *Los Angeles Review of Books*, March 2, 2019. https://lareviewofbooks.org /article/more-than-the-belgian-poe-the-overdue-return-of-jean-rays-whiskey-tales/.

Burke, Christopher. "Review: *Spells* by Michel de Ghelderode." *Weird Fiction Review* (June 2017). https://weirdfictionreview.com/2017/06/review-spells-michel-de-ghelderode/.

Clute, John, Peter Nicholls, and Adam Roberts. "Barjavel, René." In *The Encyclopedia of Science Fiction*, edited by John Clute, David Langford, Peter Nicholls, and Graham Sleight. London: Gollancz, updated June 18, 2019. http://www.sf-encyclopedia.com /entry/barjavel_rene.

Cordasco, Rachel. "Guest Post: Three Short Stories by French Women SF Writers Pre-1969: 'The Devil's Goddaughter' (1960), Suzanne Malaval, 'Moon-Fishers' (1959), Nathalie Henneberg, 'The Chain of Love' (1955), Catherine Cliff." *Science Fiction Ruminations* (November 2016). https://sciencefictionruminations.com/2016/11/30 /guest-post-three-short-stories-by-french-women-sf-writers-pre-1969-the-devils -goddaughter-1960-by-suzanne-malaval-moon-fishers-1959-by-nathalie-henneberg -and-the-chain-of-love-1/.

———. "*Radiant Terminus* by Antoine Volodine." *World Literature Today* (March 2017). https://www.worldliteraturetoday.org/2017/march/radiant-terminus-antoine-volodine.

———. "Review: *In the Mothers' Land* by Élisabeth Vonarburg." *SFinTranslation.com* (July 2019). https://www.sfintranslation.com/?p=6967.

———. "Review: *Listening for Jupiter* by Pierre-Luc Landry." *SFinTranslation.com* (August 2017). https://www.sfintranslation.com/?p=2442.

———. "Review: *Running on Fumes* by Christian Guay-Poliquin." *SFinTranslation.com* (May 2017). https://www.sfintranslation.com/?p=2030.

———. "Review: *The Silent City* by Élisabeth Vonarburg." *SFinTranslation.com* (July 2019). https://www.sfintranslation.com/?p=7046.

———. "*Vestiges* (QuanTika, Book 1) by Laurence Suhner, Translated by Sheryl Curtis." *Strange Horizons* (July 2018). http://strangehorizons.com/non-fiction/reviews/vestiges-quantika-book-1-by-laurence-suhner-translated-by-sheryl-curtis/.

Evans, Arthur, ed. "A Jules Verne Centenary." Special issue, *Science Fiction Studies* 32, pt. 1 (2005). https://www.depauw.edu/sfs/covers/cov95.htm.

———. "Jules Verne's Translations." *Science Fiction Studies* 32 (2005): 80–104.

———. "Science Fiction vs. Scientific Fiction in France: From Jules Verne to J.-H. Rosny Aîné." *Science Fiction Studies* 15, no. 1 (1988): 8.

Foster, Tristan. "Marcel Schwob's *The King in the Golden Mask*." *Music and Literature* (August 2017). https://www.musicandliterature.org/reviews/2017/7/31/marcel-schwobs-the-king-in-the-golden-mask.

Gauvin, Edward. Introduction to *The Cathedral of Mist*, translated by Edward Gauvin. Cambridge, MA: Wakefield Press, 2016.

Hale, Terry, and Andrew Hugill. "The Science Is Fiction: Jules Verne, Raymond Roussel, and Surrealism." In *Jules Verne: Narratives of Modernity*, edited by Edmund J. Smyth. Liverpool: Liverpool University Press, 2000.

Jones, Gwyneth. "*Empire of the Ants* by Bernard Werber." *Foundation* (October 1996): 112.

Mahany, J. T., and Jeff Zuckerman. "From Nowhere: An Interview with Antoine Volodine." *Paris Review* (July 8, 2015). https://www.theparisreview.org/blog/2015/07/08/from-nowhere-an-interview-with-antoine-volodine/.

Monteiro, Antonio. "Ghosts, Fear, and Parallel Worlds: The Supernatural Fiction of Jean Ray." *Weird Fiction Review* (November 2011). http://weirdfictionreview.com/2011/11/ghosts-fear-and-parallel-worlds-the-supernatural-fiction-of-jean-ray/.

Morrey, Douglas. "Natural and Anti-natural Evolution: Genetics and Schizophrenia in Maurice G. Dantec's *Babylon Babies*." *Esprit Créateur* 52, no. 2 (2012): 114–26.

Mul, Jos de. "The Possibility of an Island: Michel Houellebecq's Tragic Humanism." *Journal of Aesthetics and Phenomenology* 1, no. 1 (2014): 91–110.

Nicoll, James. "Two Suns in the Sunset." *James Nicoll Reviews* (July 2018). https://jamesdavisnicoll.com/review/two-suns-in-the-sunset.

Osborne, J. David. "*The Deep Sea Diver's Syndrome* by Serge Brussolo." *World Literature Today* (May 2016). https://www.worldliteraturetoday.org/2016/may/deep-sea-divers-syndrome-serge-brussolo.

Ransom, Amy. "Lovecraft in Quebec: Transcultural Fertilization and Esther Rochon's Reevaluation of the Powers of Horror." *Journal of the Fantastic in the Arts* 26, no. 3 (2015): 450–68.

———. "Will the Real Rosny aîné Please Step Forward?" *Extrapolation* 54, no. 3 (2013): 291–300.

Santoro, Miléna. "From Silence to Memory: An Interview with Élisabeth Vonarburg." *Femspec* 11, no. 2 (2011): 29–67, 189–90.

Scott, Paul. "Aliens and Alienation in Pierre Boulle's *La Planète des Singes.*" *Romance Studies* 38, no. 1 (2020): 26–37.

Slusser, George, ed. "Science Fiction in France." Special issue, *Science Fiction Studies* 16, pt. 3 (1989). https://www.depauw.edu/sfs/covers/cov49.htm.

Takács, Bogi. "QUILTBAG+ Speculative Classics: *Hadriana in All My Dreams* by René Depestre." *Tor.com* (February 2019). https://www.tor.com/2019/02/14/quiltbag-speculative-classics-hadriana-in-all-my-dreams-by-rene-depestre/.

Vonarburg, Élisabeth. Foreword to *Tesseracts*^Q, edited by Jane Brierley and Élisabeth Vonarburg. N.p.: Edge SF & F, 2002.

Woolward, Keithley P. "Patrick Chamoiseau's *Texaco*; or, The Ecology of Caribbean Identity." *Journal of West Indian Literature* 24, no. 2 (2016): 63–73.

German-Language SFT

Introduction

As a lingua franca, English is perhaps *the* most important language of science fiction readership. Nonetheless, we should recognize that, at certain points in the history of German science fiction, the first language a story might have been translated into would have been Swedish, Danish, French, or Russian, with no English translation forthcoming or coming only much later.

This fact points to the existence of what my colleague Anindita Banerjee and I have termed the variety of "science fiction circuits" that are opened up or widened through the powerful act of translation. Put simply, these circuits represent the overlappings, intersections, convergences, divergences, waves, and ripple effects of the comings together of science fiction from cultures with different ways of knowing mediated through a second language.[1] Science fiction written in German was situated in other circuits that existed prior to its opening up to the Anglo-American world first in the early part of the twentieth century and then again beginning in the post–War World II period. For instance, a second science fiction circuit existed with France and a third between East Germany, Eastern Europe, and the Soviet Union from which few works were translated into English. Circuits too are porous and overlap, as this socialist one was continually in dialogue with publications and authors from the West in a variety of languages. Translation also influences the scholarly field of German studies, such as the recent turn to the works of Paul Scheerbart only after his works started to appear in English.

The Abolition of Species (2018)

As the following chapter points out, it was first in the sixties when translations of primarily West German science fiction began to appear in English as part of a general growth in translation of other major European writers. Still, German science fiction has a significant history dating back to the mid-nineteenth century. Its roots can be found in the scientific dreaming of the Enlightenment, Germany's significant role in the Industrial Revolution, and the fantastical and supernatural literature of German romanticism, which also collected, curated, and authored folktales and fairy tales. For instance, proto-robot automaton is present in E. T. A. Hoffmann's *The Sandman* (1816). As it is today, its authors and readers were very much aware and in dialogue with other contemporary science fiction authors across Europe, especially in France and the United Kingdom, as well as the significant traditions that were developing in Russia and later in the United States.

The Glass Bees (2000)

Interestingly, it was German author Karl May who was referred to as the "German Jules Verne," due to commonalities with May's adventures set in the American Old West rather than the science fiction story. Bertha von Suttner, founder of the German women's movement and winner of the 1905 Nobel Peace Prize, wrote one of the first major contributions to the genre called *The Machine Age* (1889). It remains untranslated, unlike her better-known autobiography, *Lay Down Your Arms*, of the same year. Kurd Lasswitz is perhaps the best-known early science fiction author from Germany, due in part to the translation of his "modern fairy tale," also with a message of peace about Mars, titled *Two Planets* (1897) into Danish and Swedish in 1898, English in 1971, and recently Russian in 2011.

The first international success from Germany was Bernhard Kellermann's novel *The Tunnel* (1913), which was translated into twenty-five languages, including

English, as well as the 1935 British film adaptation of the same name directed by Maurice Elvey. As such, for English speakers, notions of science fiction were primarily shaped by Germany's influential film industry up through 1933. Most well known was the first feature-length science fiction film, *Metropolis* (1927), directed by Austrian Fritz Lang, screenplay by Thea von Harbou. Lang also helped to shape the early science fiction–spy film with his *Dr. Mabuse* series starting in 1922. German cinema of the Weimar period also contributed to the science fiction–horror genre, along with a growing number of science fiction films in the past ten years such as Lars Kraume's *The Coming Days* (2010) and German Turkish director Özgür Yildirim's *Boy 7* (2015).

In general, since World War II, the German science fiction market has been dominated by translations of Anglo-American authors. Furthermore, science fiction has been a well-translated genre into the German language, in part because of the language's long-established printed book tradition and a strong interest in science, technology, and especially engineering. In fact, there are a number of translated titles available in German that are not available in English, in particular by authors from Russia and Europe. Today, there is a well-established market for science fiction in German-speaking countries that also includes a number of fan clubs, some of them dating back to the fifties and sixties. Even in East Germany, science fiction from socialist countries and approved nonsocialist titles were available. In several Eastern fan clubs, members typed up translated Western copies and maintained secret lending libraries for these titles. Fans traveled to international conventions to buy or share the latest publications. Historically and even today, some fans are also professional translators of science fiction into German. Unsurprisingly, the overwhelming number of titles translated from the United States and United Kingdom does make it more difficult to become established as a writer of the genre in German. Although from the beginning women have written German-language science fiction, it has been its male authors who have been able to publish regularly. Translation signifies an additional marker of quality or exposure, or both. Overall, despite high-quality contributions to the genre, science fiction does not enjoy a respected place in the German literary canon and often is referred to pejoratively in the public sphere as escapist entertainment. Still, there is a broad and dedicated following of German-language readers concentrated primarily in Germany, Austria, and Switzerland.

As is evident in the following pages, the richness that is this genre in the German original has opened up, particularly over the past forty years. Due to the multiple science fiction circuits of which German-language science fiction is a part, it is possible to find examples of almost every subgenre. Yet these titles differ from the Anglo-American versions and varieties because of the various social, cultural, and political differences across time and space that shape the identities of its authors and the texts they produce. Today these titles offer a wealth of perspectives that include, among other topics, climate change, the European Union, migration, colonialism and postcolonialism, and questions of gender, race, and ethnicity. Similar to examples of the genre from other countries, German-language science fiction offers that estrangement from the expected tropes and stereotypes in Anglo-American science fiction. It opens up the reader and their imagination to other worlds and knowledge that would have otherwise remained inaccessible but for translation.

Sonja Fritzsche

The Texts

The phrase "German-language SFT" will undoubtedly bring to mind the works of Kurd Lasswitz, Wolfgang Jeschke, and Andreas Eschbach, as well as the popular Perry Rhodan series, but the novels, short stories, collections, and anthologies listed here reveal that it is much more varied and interesting. Just under half (fifteen) of the thirty-one authors included in this chapter were born in Germany; ten came from Austria, one from the former Czechoslovakia, two from Poland, one from Switzerland, one from Italy, and one from Japan, suggesting that German-language SFT encompasses a multitude of perspectives and histories stretching across Central and Eastern Europe and beyond. Several of the authors not originally from Germany moved there before beginning their writing careers. From the fantastic surrealism of Gustav Meyrink and Paul Scheerbart to the high fantasy of Markus Heitz, to the quiet horror of Daniel Kehlmann and the hard science fiction of Ernst Jünger, German-language SFT offers Anglophone readers a rich trove of stories that explore everything from the depths of space to the darkest recesses of the human psyche.

Any discussion of German-language speculative fiction in English must also mention Franz Kafka and Herman Hesse, both of whom were published in German and then in English before 1960. While Kafka isn't usually classified as a writer of speculative fiction, his surreal, absurd tales offer readers an intentionally warped view of the world, as if we were looking at it in a funhouse mirror. With characters waking up as bugs and wandering endlessly through ridiculous bureaucracies, Kafka's stories ask us to consider that we live in a world on the brink of chaos. Many of his texts were translated into English during the 1930s, following his death in 1924, but several new translations have come out in the past two decades, suggesting that interest in Kafka shows no signs of waning. Like Kafka, Herman Hesse had a complicated relationship with German-language literature. Though born in Germany, Hesse eventually moved to Switzerland, where he wrote most of his books. Hesse's *The Glass Bead Game* (1943, trans. 1949, 1969)—for which he won the Nobel Prize for Literature in 1946—is his most overtly speculative work. A far-future utopia, *Glass Bead* follows the intellectually nurtured Joseph Knecht in his determination to win the incredibly difficult Glass Bead Game, which requires players to understand how aesthetics and the sciences complement each other and exist in harmony.

On the pulp side of German-language speculative fiction is the internationally popular Perry Rhodan series, created in 1961 by Walter Ernsting and Karl-Herbert Scheer and continuing to this day. With more than twenty-six hundred volumes, the series has spawned conventions and a dedicated fan base. Many of Rhodan's adventures occur in outer space, but some take on time travel, alternate realities, and cosmic mysteries. With a number of different writers and offshoot plots, the Perry Rhodan series has taken on a life of its own, proving that speculative fiction of the earlier "pulpy" kind can evolve while staying true to itself and still attract twenty-first-century readers. The series first appeared in the United States in 1969 courtesy of Forrest J. Ackerman and Ace Books, with Forrest's wife, Wendayne Ackerman, translating the texts into English. Perry's American sojourn lasted until 1977 and then from 1997 to 1998 by Vector Enterprises (edited by John Foyt).

Since 1960 American readers have had access to a wealth of science fiction, fantasy, and horror from German and Austrian writers, with Dedalus Books in particular emerging at the beginning of the twenty-first century as the major publisher of Austrian fantasy and science fiction in English. Thanks in large part to the work of translator Mike Mitchell, several Austrian authors can now be read in English. German science fiction, however, has followed, to some degree, the trend identified in the French-language SFT chapter, with the bulk of translations happening in the 1960s and '70s and then since 2000. No one publisher is responsible for bringing speculative fiction by German writers into English, though Jo Fletcher Books and Orbit Books have together published nine of high fantasy author Markus Heitz's novels, while Wakefield Press has committed to introducing Anglophone readers to the surrealist speculative fantasies of Paul Scheerbart.

GERMANY

Science Fiction

Mathematician, author, and philosopher Kurd Lasswitz is recognized by many in the field as the first major German science fiction author, comparable to and roughly contemporary with Jules Verne and H. G. Wells. While some of his stories were published in English in the *Magazine of Fantasy and Science Fiction* before 1960, his best-known novel from 1897, **Two Planets**, wasn't published in English until 1971. Because of his pioneering work as an early science fiction author, Lasswitz has a major prize named after him that is awarded to the best German science fiction from the previous year. According to author, editor, translator, and critic Franz Rottensteiner, to write *Two Planets* Lasswitz "carefully calculated the orbits of interplanetary spaceships, and he advanced the idea of an artificial satellite as a stepping-stone, a 'railway station' on the way to the planets."[2] Unlike Wells's *The War of the Worlds* (also published in 1897), in which Martians covet the flourishing Earth and attempt to take control of it by killing off humanity, Lasswitz's Martians are relatively benevolent, willing to offer humans their advanced knowledge in exchange for a share of Earth's natural resources. More than just a first-contact story, *Two Planets* explores the idea of relationships between Martians and humans, how an extended stay on Earth affects the Martians, what an alien life-form might look like, and how Earth might achieve a kind of utopian existence.

Lasswitz may have been the father of modern German science fiction, but his major novel was not the first of its kind to be published in English. That honor goes to Ernst Jünger's *The Glass Bees* (1957; 1960), a disturbing and prescient story about the clash of old modes of thinking and new technologies.[3] When a former military man named Captain Richard applies for a job at Zapparoni Works as chief of security, he's unprepared for the highly advanced robotics and information systems that he encounters there. Zapparoni, who rules over an entertainment and information empire, calls into question much that Captain Richard has believed about the world and his own existence. Jünger's description of Zapparoni's nano-bees functioning as a network is just one of the many impressively advanced ideas in a novel that was written years before the Internet we know was born. Another of Jünger's novels, *Eumeswil* (1977; 1993), took nearly twenty years to make its way into English. Set in a far-future dystopia in which a united world government has crumbled back into small enclaves, the novel follows the crafty steward of a tyrannical ruler. That steward, Martin Venator, imagines that he is a special person who exists outside of time, and he uses a kind of time machine or three-dimensional holographic projection to study those whom he thinks are like himself (that is, major figures such as Homer and Lenin).

Unlike Jünger, who used speculative fiction to explore human nature, Austrian-born author and cyberneticist Herbert Franke used it to imagine distant planets and alternative societies. His novels *The Orchid Cage* (1961; 1973) and *The Mind Net* (1961; 1974) were published in English as part of the DAW Collectors series and introduced a generation of Anglophone readers to his distinct style and perspective. Seabury Press, the major publisher of Stanisław Lem in English, picked up a third novel, *Zone Null* (1970), also in 1974. *The Orchid Cage* is not so much a story about exploring another planet as about the act of exploration itself. When humans discover an empty mechanized city on an Earthlike planet, they're tasked with uncovering clues as to who built it and why and then what happened to those creatures afterward. *The Mind Net*, too, seems like a story about explorers coming upon something of interest on an alien world, but it soon spirals out into a complicated nesting-doll tale that will make some readers think about the film *The Matrix*. Here, Franke investigates the ways in which the human mind can be manipulated and how computers will one day play a major part in shaping and directing perception and memory.

As in *The Mind Net*, Franke in *Zone Null* asks readers to question our assumptions about artificial intelligence and its relationship to humans and encourages us to interrogate our feelings of moral superiority. When scientists successfully break into the strange Zone Null and find a completely automated world running on computer time, the question becomes, which is the more repressive regime—the one that is predictable down to the second or the supposedly "Free World" that actually seems like a dictatorship?

Like Franke, Wolfgang Jeschke was not born in Germany but started his writing career there. Originally from the former Czechoslovakia, Jeschke is both a writer and an editor and won the 1987 Harrison Award for achievements in international science fiction. Of his three novels in English translation, two of them deal with environmental degradation or catastrophe, and all incorporate some kind of time travel. His first novel in English, and the winner of the 1982 Kurd Lasswitz Award, **The Last Day of Creation** (1981; 1982), involves a group of Americans trying to get their hands on Middle Eastern oil by sidestepping current political entanglements and problems through time travel, only to find themselves stuck in the past.

In *Midas* (1989; 1990), Jeschke tells the story of Earth in the near future, after severe ecological disaster. When scientists discover a matter-duplication system, they attempt to use it to produce humans, but what they create turns out to be too crude to survive for long. Like *Midas*, Jeschke's **The Cusanus Game** (2005; 2013) deals with a recognizable near-future Earth after environmental catastrophe due to climate change. In order to reintroduce various forms of plant and animal life and jump-start Earth's fertility once more, scientists attempt to travel back to the fifteenth century to gather samples. At one point, they try to convince philosopher and astronomer Nicholas of Cusa to change the future by founding a scientific academy. These efforts, however, are thwarted by the complicated nature of time and the "multiverse." This kind of hard science fiction involving ecological catastrophe presages the novels of late-twentieth-century German author Frank Schätzing.

While Jeschke is relatively well known in Anglophone science fiction circles because of the number of his novels and stories available in English, his compatriot Andreas Eschbach is perhaps even more recognizable due to the popularity of his first novel in English, **The Carpet Makers** (1995; 2005).[4] Eschbach, who trained as an aerospace engineer and has worked as a software engineer, is a well-established, award-winning SF author in his native Germany, with nine of his books having won the Kurd Lasswitz Award so far. One of Tor Books's earliest translated novels, *The Carpet Makers* imagines a multiplanet, centuries-old empire in which the inhabitants adhere to a strict system of carpet making passed down from generation to generation. When ships arrive with the news that the emperor is dead and the carpets are nowhere to be found, the weavers learn the absurd truth about the industry that has shaped their way of life.

Eschbach's *One Trillion Dollars* and *Lord of All Things*, though written a decade apart, both appeared in English in 2014. An updated rags-to-riches story, *One Trillion Dollars* (2001) follows the fortunes of a pizza delivery man when he discovers that he has become a trillionaire. The money, kept in trust for several generations by an Italian family, has a mysterious purpose that will influence the future course of humankind. Similarly, *Lord of All Things* (2011) explores the potentially catastrophic consequences of massive and sudden social change. Winner of the 2012 Kurd Lasswitz Award, Eschbach's latest novel in English tells the story of one man's efforts to eliminate poverty, work driven by his lifelong love of a single woman and his attempts to impress her. This attempt to push technology to its limits to achieve a kind of utopia winds up threatening the entire planet.

Eschbach's contemporary Frank Schätzing writes science fiction that combines Eschbach's interrogation of technology with Jeschke's environmental concerns. His first novel in English, *The Swarm* (2004; 2006), incorporates horror and thriller elements in a story about Earth's oceans and its inhabitants turning against humanity.[5] As whales sink ships and crabs poison the water, the American military attempts to fight back, but the water's power is a formidable foe. Eventually, scientists discover that an intelligent form of life is inhabiting the marine life and using it to punish humanity for the pollution and damage that it has caused for generations. As Gabriele Dürbeck argues in her paper on *The Swarm*, Schätzing "deploys disaster narratives to condense the temporal scale of global environmental decline and eco-thriller strategies to thematize human responsibility for the ecological health of planet Earth."[6]

Schätzing's only other novel in English so far, *Limit* (2009; 2013), set just a couple of generations in the future, focuses on the existence of a space elevator and the first-ever moon-based hotel. When a powerful and wealthy entrepreneur, Julian Orley, invites a couple dozen of the wealthiest people to visit this hotel and contribute to his efforts to build a second space elevator, the mission seems like a guaranteed success. All is not well, however, when a cybercop follows the trail of a young hacker who has information that might endanger the moon-bound millionaires.

The German science fiction that has been translated into English in the second decade of this century has focused not on interplanetary or time travel but on the future of the human species and the fundamentals of human nature. Dietmar Dath's *The Abolition of Species* (2008; 2012) explores the ways in which genetic engineering will change how we define who is or isn't "human." Spanning millennia, the story follows the development of highly evolved animal and plant life that nearly wipes out humanity, followed by a machine intelligence that has evolved in a different part of the world. Dath then jumps forward more than a thousand years to imagine a terraformed Venus and Mars and the next step in human-animal-machine fusion.

Also out in 2012 in English, Juli Zeh's novel *The Method* (2009) is more interested in questions about individuality in the face of an authoritarian state. Here citizens are expected to do everything they can to stay healthy and are required to submit their medical information each month to the governing authorities. When the protagonist, Mia, attempts to prove that her brother didn't commit the crime of which he was accused and for which he was murdered by the state, she comes up against a system that is so pathologically anti-illness that it will (ironically) kill anyone who doesn't conform to its unattainable ideals.

While these German authors have established German-language science fiction's contemporary focus on environmental disaster and future technologies, another German author, Paul Scheerbart, offers Anglophone readers a far different vision of the future.[7] An exact contemporary of Kurd Lasswitz, Scheerbart mixed scientific theories, the fantastic, architectural theories, and allegory to produce unique German expressionist texts about imaginary structures and alien architects. Scheerbart wrote about both Earthbound architectural pursuits and fantastical, quasi-science fictional tales of impossible structures built under nonterrestrial conditions. His novel *The Gray Cloth* (1914; 2001) and novella *Rakkóx the Billionaire* (1901; 2015) imagine powerful men trying to make a permanent mark on the landscape by either building astonishingly beautiful multicolored glass structures around the world (*Gray Cloth*) or reshaping Earth itself to turn a cliff into an architectural wonder (*Rakkóx*). With his masterpiece *Lesabéndio: An Asteroid Novel* (1913; 2012) (which Wakefield Press has called "an intergalactic utopian novel") and the novella *The Great Race* (1900; 2015), Scheerbart takes his visionary ideas into outer space, inviting us to imagine how alien intelligences might try to solve spatial problems with their own local materials and physical laws.[8]

The latest collection of Scheerbart texts to be published in English—the pair of novellas *The Stairway to the Sun* and *Dance of the Comets* (1903; 2016)—veer off into fairy tale and allegory. In the former, Scheerbart offers us four stories about the sun, the sea, animal life, and storms (set in star-based palaces or underwater glass lairs) that encourage us to see the world around us anew, while the latter was first written as the basis for a ballet to be scored by Richard Strauss in 1900, complete with directions for feather dusters, "violet moon hair," and planetary bodies.

Fantasy

Just a few works of German-language fantasy have been translated into English since the 1980s. Most notably, starting in 2009 with Markus Heitz's *The Dwarves*, Anglophone readers have had access to three different high fantasy series (two by Heitz and one by Bernhard Hennen). Those texts that aren't high fantasy are as diverse as any books can be that are classified in such a broad and elastic subgenre. Nonetheless, they each offer Anglophone readers insight into how German authors have been and still are moving works of fantasy in new and interesting directions.

One of the earliest authors writing surrealism in Germany during the Cold War was the Italian-born author, lawyer, judge, and composer Herbert Rosendorfer, whose dreamlike, fantastical takes on Nazi Germany, time travel, and "Last Man" narratives take readers on unexpected, kaleidoscopic journeys through time and space. Of his nearly two hundred books, only a handful have been published in English as of 2019. Two of Rosendorfer's absurdist stories about Nazi Germany, *German Suite* (1972; 1979) and *The Night of the Amazons* (1989; 1991), use black humor and alternate history to attempt to render in art the brutality and evil of that time. *German Suite* imagines a skewed version of our universe in which Germany continues to be ruled by the descendants of Ludwig II of Bavaria and the Nazis were just an annoying anomaly in the 1930s. In fact, the current heir to the throne is actually a human-gorilla hybrid. *The Night of the Amazons*, Rosendorfer's next novel about the Nazis, was written almost two decades later and included a character based on the real-life barroom bouncer turned Nazi officer Christian Weber, who helped Hitler come to power in Munich. Weber's staging of the propaganda event "Night of the Amazons" in the 1930s included women parading nude on horses, and Rosendorfer depicts the grotesque and hyperbolic nature of these "celebrations" of Aryan womanhood in his novel.

Rosendorfer's *The Architect of Ruins* (1969; 1992) is a nested story about what may or may not be a dream, involving, among other things, six hundred nuns on a train ride to Lourdes and four men who construct an underground Armageddon bunker. In an introduction to the translation, John Clute notes that this novel "contains the germ of all of Rosendorfer's work, like a dream. It is a tale of escape into story-land, a discourse about stories, a story about stories within stories: like an onion that makes one smile."[9] Like a twentieth-century German version of *The Decameron*, the men in *Architect* sit around and tell stories that grow beyond themselves, involving everyone from Faust to G. K. Chesterton.

Between *German Suite* and *The Night of the Amazons*, Rosendorfer wrote two time-travel novels: **Stephanie; or, A Previous Existence** (1987; 1995) and **Letters Back to Ancient China** (1983; 1997). In *Stephanie* a woman finds herself transferred into the body of an eighteenth-century Spanish duchess who has murdered her husband. Before she finally returns to her present day and the brother who saw her disappear, Stephanie writes letters to him that detail the isolation and strict social codes of the life she is forced to lead. Conversely, *Letters Back to Ancient China* involves someone who travels into the future (a thousand years, specifically, via a time machine) to modern Germany. There, he is overwhelmed by the noise and tumult of Munich and writes letters home about the strange people and practices that he encounters.

Of the five fantastic novels in this category that followed Rosendorfer's, two focus on animals, two draw on the art of the past, and one imagines multiple alternate scenarios. In **Cassandra** (1983; 1988), Christa Wolf (from the former East Germany) offers us a new perspective on the fall of Troy via Cassandra, the woman gifted or burdened with the ability to know the future but destined to never be believed.[10] Through her eyes, we see the effect that the Greek triumph had on the women of Troy and Cassandra's own bitterness about the course of her life. Written just six years before the fall of the Berlin Wall, *Cassandra* was itself a prescient work of art and stands now as a multivalent testimony to the violence and brutality of war in our own recent past.

Walter Moers's **A Wild Ride through the Night** (2001; 2003), too, draws on past works of art in order to explore a strange and fantastic world. A writer, cartoonist, and painter, Moers creates a larger-than-life story about a twelve-year-old boy named Gustav who must battle monsters and journey to the moon and back (among other things) before he can become the great artist that he knows he will be. Accompanied by the twenty-one woodcuts by nineteenth-century French illustrator Gustave Doré that inspired the book, *A Wild Ride* offers readers a surreal literary and visually captivating adventure.

The latter half of the 2010s saw the publication in English of two works of fantasy that revolve around either invisible or imaginary animals: Yoko Tawada's **Memoirs of a Polar Bear** (2011; 2016)[11] and Sibylle Lewitscharoff's **Blumenberg** (2011; 2017).[12] Told from the perspectives of three generations of polar bears who become famous for their circus performances and writings, *Memoirs* explore such issues as Cold War politics, ancestry, inheritance, entertainment, and consciousness. *Memoirs*, while an exquisite speculative study of the relationship between humans and polar bears and of polar bear consciousness, is ultimately a story about human relationships, exile, and cultural ignorance and discrimination. The animal in *Blumenberg*, however, functions more as a spectral presence than a living animal interacting with humans on equal terms. When a calm, stately lion appears one night to the real-life German philosopher Hans Blumenberg, who throughout his career explored the concept of metaphor and its relationship to reality, the philosopher takes it in stride, accepting the lion as a kind of guardian angel.

The high-fantasy boom in Germany, led by Heitz and Hennen, seems to be part of a global phenomenon in the second decade of the twenty-first century. Focusing on self-contained worlds that include dragons, dwarves, elves, and other fantastical creatures, rather than culturally specific events or histories, these kinds of novels are likely able to find more international readers. Markus Heitz's popular *Dwarves* (2003–15; 2009–18) and *Legends of the Älfar* (2009–14; 2014–19) series, published in large part by Orbit and Jo Fletcher Books, are filled with clashing armies, heroic dwarves, and dark powers. The five books in the *Dwarves* series tell the story of a blacksmith named Tungdil who lives as the only dwarf in the human kingdom of Girdlegard. When the kingdom is threatened, Tungdil must embrace his past and, together with other dwarves from other lands, fight the approaching evil. Among the dwarves' and humans' foes are the "älfar," with bloody reputations and a desire for the dwarves' homeland. Elves join the dwarves and humans in the four-book (so far) series to protect that land and the world itself.

Elves figure largely in Bernhard Hennen's work as well. His **Elven** series (2004–14; 2015–19) involves humans and elves joining forces to fight a bloodthirsty demon that has attacked their realms. When the Elven queen is the victim of an assassination attempt following the demon's defeat and a troll army invades the kingdom, it's up to a human who was raised by elves to help lead the resistance. With three of the original seven novels in English (thanks to Edwin Miles), Anglophone readers can reasonably expect more stories from Hennen in the near future. Hennen's other series, *Drachenelfen* and *Elfenritter*, remain untranslated as of 2019.

Horror

German-language horror, like fantasy, is difficult to find in English, though its impact on modern European horror (especially of the gothic kind) cannot be underestimated. With recent scholarship on the German gothic, in particular, introducing Anglophone readers to the vibrant genre of the eighteenth and nineteenth centuries, we are learning more about how authors like Carl Grosse, Friedrich Schiller, E. T. A. Hoffmann, and Jacob and Wilhelm Grimm contributed to the kinds of narratives of sublime horror that had wide popular appeal throughout Europe. According to one study of the subgenre, "German Gothic horror is a sublime horror, a physical perception of seeing that combines with the subjective imagination and as such is wrought with contingencies, uncertainty, and confused identity as experienced by the characters and by the reader who is drawn into the sublimity of horror through artfully crafted narratives."[13]

German horror advanced into the early twentieth century via the visceral novels and stories by Hanns Heinz Ewers. A spy in Mexico and the United States during World War I and then an early member of the Nazi Party (though he was later ejected), Ewers was obsessed with ideas of vampirism, eroticism, and depravity. His novels and collections were mostly written and then translated between the turn of the twentieth century and World War II. Only *Strange Tales* (1922; 2000) had to wait almost eighty years for its English publication.

Finding German horror post-1960, however, isn't easy, as Germans continue to grapple with the brutal legacy of World War II. Thus, the novels that could fall into the "horror" category are actually mixtures of subgenres. Both Patrick Süskind's *Perfume: The Story of a Murderer* (1985; 1987), which won the 1987 World Fantasy Award, and Daniel Kehlmann's *You Should Have Left* (2016; 2017) blend horror, surrealism, and even magical realism. *Perfume*, set in eighteenth-century France, is the story of Jean-Baptiste Grenouille, who was born with a perfect sense of smell.[14] While this inevitably leads him to apprentice himself to a perfumer and hone his natural-born gift, he eventually becomes obsessed with ever-newer and rarer scents: that of a young virgin, for instance. The horror of the story emerges as Grenouille descends into depravity and murder. Kehlmann's *You Should Have Left* evokes a more subtle kind of horror—the type that creeps in slowly and unexpectedly.[15] Reminiscent of the plot of Stephen King's *The Shining*, Kehlmann's novel follows the lives of a man, his wife, and their daughter as they settle into a rented house in the mountains of Germany. While attempting to write a screenplay to keep his reputation alive, the narrator slowly realizes that strange and unaccountable things are happening around him and eroding his confidence in his art. A work of psychological horror set in a potentially "haunted" house, *You Should Have Left* is one of Kehlmann's most unsettling works.

AUSTRIA

Science Fiction

Austrian SF critic, editor, and literary agent Franz Rottensteiner famously wrote in his introduction to *The Best of Austrian Science Fiction* in 2001 that "there is an Austrian SF insofar as there is SF being written by Austrian writers, but to try to find a specific Austrian quality in it would be a futile exercise."[16] Nonetheless, we can assume that, given Austria's twentieth-century transformation from empire to nation and its complex relationship with Germany, its literature grapples with problems and desires that Germany has not experienced, which would necessarily influence speculative fiction. While Rottensteiner argues that the science fiction isn't particularly "Austrian" because it is often first published in Germany anyway, Austrian fantasy might reveal inherent differences.

In the introduction to *The Dedalus/Ariadne Book of Austrian Fantasy: The Mey-rink Years, 1890–1930*, editor and translator Mike Mitchell argues that Austrian *fantasy* in general differs from Germany's version of the subgenre in a key way: "A culture which emphasizes the potential as much as the real, which has a taste for the humour of paradox, is one which does not take a too earnest view of itself. German literature takes itself, the world and the supernatural far more seriously. . . . But more characteristic Austrian fantasy tends to emphasize the puzzling coincidences, parallels and paradoxes of this world, revealing it as less solid than we would think."[17]

Of the six texts by Austrian authors that have been translated into English and that can be categorized as "science fiction," two are alternate histories, two are "Last Man/Woman" stories, and two are works of comic surrealism. As mentioned earlier in the "Germany" section of this chapter, the vast black cloud of World War II hung darkly over German-language speculative fiction for decades, and Austrian writers were necessarily influenced by this. Thus, we get novels like Otto Basil's *The Twilight Men* (1966; 1968) and Christoph Ransmayr's *The Dog King* (1995; 1997), both of which imagine alternative, and exceedingly dark, aftermaths of World War II. In Basil's novel, Hitler has won the war with atomic weapons but dies soon after, which leads to a bloody battle for power within his inner circle. The main character, a quack doctor and staunch Nazi, refuses to accept that the radiation unleashed by the bombs has created a new race of "subhumans," even as the Japanese then launch their own nuclear attack. Chaos, destruction, and despair reign as the Third Reich collapses in on itself. Ransmayr's novel, written nearly thirty years later, also imagines an alternate postwar Germany, only *The Dog King* doesn't involve Hitler's victory. Rather, it depicts a deindustrialized country across which countless small battles are continually being fought, drag-ging Germany down even further into decay.

The two "Last Man/Woman" stories by Austrian authors translated into Eng-lish since the 1960s are Marlen Haushofer's *The Wall* (1963; 1990) and Thomas Glavinic's *Night Work* (2006; 2008). While they both involve individuals who are suddenly and inexplicably left alone and must figure out how to psychologically adjust to the fact that it may not ever change, they differ in a few major respects: Haushofer's Last Woman is trapped inside a kind of transparent bubble or dome, through which she can see people and animals seemingly frozen in time, while Glavinic's Last Man is free to roam about the city of Vienna and beyond to Eng-land, seeing no signs of life but still feeling like he isn't completely alone. Whether these scenarios are the result of a botched military experiment or a technological or medical disaster, they highlight the ways in which individuals are part of the larger fabric of their communities. Marianne Gruber's *The Sphere of Glass* (1981; 1993) takes up a theme similar to Haushofer's regarding a person trapped in a transparent enclosure, though Gruber's characters *all* live in soundproof glass balls as an attempt to insulate themselves from the increasingly noisy and chaotic city around them.

Unlike these dark, almost brooding meditations on human psychology and behavior, Egon Friedell's *The Return of the Time Machine* (1946; 1972) and Gert Jonke's *Awakening to the Great Sleep War* (1982; 2012) are jocular, high-spirited takes on what seem like impossible scenarios. In *The Return of the Time Machine*, which has been called a "wry homage to H. G. Wells," Friedell's narrator takes up a correspondence with Wells's secretary and thereby gets his hands on a manuscript that describes the author-as-time-traveler's later journeys.[18] Via some complicated mathematical discussions, *The Return of the Time Machine* ultimately suggests that time travel is actually impossible. Ranging much wider than Friedell's Wells tale, Jonke's *Awakening to the Great Sleep War* takes on the texture of reality itself. In a funhouse-mirror version of Vienna, an "acoustical decorator" wanders around engaging in affairs with various women and manipulating the literally living and dynamic buildings and objects around him (for example, buildings sneeze and statues can fall asleep).[19] As a joke, he convinces the caryatids and telamones (male and female architectural supports) to try to fall asleep, and, unsurprisingly, chaos ensues. A story about the literal weight of history and culture in a city that was nearly destroyed during World War II, *Awakening* is considered one of Jonke's masterpieces.

Many other Austrian authors write science fiction, and some of their short stories can be found in Rottensteiner's anthology *The Best of Austrian Science Fiction* (2001). Included here are tales by writers discussed in this chapter, such as Franke (who was born in Austria but spent his career in Germany) and Gruber. Younger authors not yet known in the Anglophone world are also here and include physicist Peter Schattschneider and Barbara Neuwirth, who writes speculative fiction that sometimes fuses science fiction and fantasy.

Fantasy

In the introduction to *The Dedalus/Ariadne Book of Austrian Fantasy: The Meyrink Years, 1890–1930*, Mitchell offers us a cultural context for the surreal and fantastic stories that emerged from Austria around the turn of the twentieth century. Noting the rise of Sigmund Freud and psychoanalysis, on the one hand, and Ernst Mach's work in physics and the philosophy of science, on the other, Mitchell argues that "the literature which sprang from this background was one which casts doubt on the apparently solid surface of reality, which questions the meaningfulness of human activity, which is always ready to admit that the opposite might just as well be true. It is a literature that is a fertile ground for fantasy."[20] The surrealism of Alfred Kubin and Franz Kafka, the urban fantasy of Gustav Meyrink, and the postwar fantasy of Haushofer, Gruber, Jonke, and Neuwirth are a testament to the dynamic evolution of this subgenre in an Austrian context.

Known more for his illustrations than for his writings, Alfred Kubin contributed the striking images in Paul Scheerbart's science fiction and fantasy novel *Lesabéndio*. Kubin's own novel *The Other Side* (1909; 1967), written just after the turn of the twentieth century, is a deeply unsettling story about a quasi-utopian, almost reactionary "dream realm" called "Pearl" in which invitees live according to unspoken and unclear rules. Created by and presided over by the narrator's childhood friend, Pearl seems normal on the surface, but it actually deteriorates at an unbelievably fast rate after a wealthy American succeeds in discovering it and threatens the leader's rule. A disturbing mix of dream and reality, emerging from an era marked by decadent, expressionist, and gothic art, *The Other Side* interrogates what we mean by "utopia" and the ease with which communities can slide into chaos.

Writing around the same time as Kubin but exerting more influence on German-language literature was Gustav Meyrink (Gustav Meyer), who developed, through his portrayals of Prague, what would eventually become known as "urban fantasy."[21] Meyrink's experience translating Charles Dickens into German, along with his developing obsession with the occult, helped shape his unique style, in which nothing is as it seems and strange forces underlie even the most mundane events. In his introduction to *The Dedalus/Ariadne Book of Austrian Fantasy*, Mitchell explains that Prague ("with its brooding castle, crowded ghetto and mysterious atmosphere") and Meyrink have become synonymous with one another, especially in terms of the latter's short stories, in which "his fantasy has a sharp satirical edge, attacking all kinds of narrow-mindedness, especially military, religious, and scientific."[22] A contemporary of the Belgian fantasist Jean Ray, Meyrink shares with him an interest in the uncanny and unseen. With artistic movements like expressionism, Dadaism, surrealism, and others flourishing around the first quarter of the twentieth century when Meyrink was writing, it's not surprising that the Austrian ranged so wide in his explorations of the life beneath everyday life.

The first of Meyrink's novels to be translated since 1960 is *The Angel of the West Window* (1927; 1991), a story about the occult and its Elizabethan practitioner John Dee, who was also a British mathematician, astrologer, and cartographer. In Meyrink's vision, Dee's twentieth-century descendant Baron Mueller (who suspects that he is actually a reincarnated Dee) is led by the "Green Angel" into another dimension or universe in an attempt to vanquish those who seek to stop human spiritual progress. *The White Dominican* (1921; 1994), another of Meyrink's novels dealing with occult transcendence, relies on multiple mystical traditions and related imagery and follows one man's complicated spiritual journey with the end goal of "transfiguration" into a higher-level being, which exists beyond the material world.

Meyrink's *The Green Face* (1916; 1992) and *Walpurgisnacht* (1917; 1993), however, deal not with the occult so much as with the trauma of World War I. In *The Green Face*, a man enters a magician's shop and comes into contact with a horrifying old man, who turns out to be the Wandering Jew. A symbol of restlessness and despair, the Wandering Jew's appearance functions as a portent for the destruction of Amsterdam. Prague, though, serves as the setting for *Walpurgisnacht*, the title referring to the eve of the Christian feast day of Saint Walpurga (an eighth-century abbess who was celebrated for protecting people from evil spirits and witchcraft). In Meyrink's tale, the powerful German elite in the castle are in a standoff with the rebellious Czech people in the city below. Eventually, the people form a collective so strong that they are able to storm the castle and replace the German rulers with a poor violinist, whom they dub "Emperor of the World." This upending of the established order enabled Meyrink to more clearly demonstrate the unimaginable horror and destruction of World War I while it was happening.

Meyrink's virtuosic short stories and excerpts from his novels can be found in *The Opal, and Other Stories* (1902–7; 1994) and in *The Dedalus Meyrink Reader* (2010), both of which highlight the author's generic experimentation (across early science fiction, the gothic, ghost stories, satire, and more) and genuine interest in occult practices. Three of the stories in *Opal* also appear in the *Reader*: "Dr. Cinderella's Plants," "Blamol," and "The Ring of Saturn." The bizarre happenings in these stories—from miniature black holes to words that liquefy those who speak them—suggest that the reality we perceive is just a thin veneer under which exist horrors and wonders of which humans, caught up in their material existences, can't even dream.

In 1993 and then in 2003, Dedalus published two anthologies of Austrian fantasy, both translated by Mitchell: *The Dedalus/Ariadne Book of Austrian Fantasy: The Meyrink Years, 1890–1930* and *The Dedalus Book of Austrian Fantasy: 1890–2000*. The former includes several stories by Meyrink, of course, but also by Kubin, Kafka, Hans Strobl, Max Brod, and Rilke, offering us a revealing perspective on the development of the fantastic in Austria before World War II. And while the second anthology includes fifteen stories that were published in the first, it offers us a broader scope, bringing us stories written up to the end of the twentieth century. Alongside Meyrink, Kafka, Strobl, and von Hofmannsthal are Haushofer ("Cannibals" [1968]), Gruber ("The Epidemic" [1983]), Jonke ("My Day" [1970]), Neuwirth ("In the Sand" and "The Furnished Room" [both 1990]), and dozens of others. Here are stories about bureaucrats who shoot at ghosts, severed heads that think about their past lives, people turning cannibalistic in railway carriages, and more.

The wealth of science fiction, fantasy, and horror from German and Austrian authors suggests that a vibrant, diverse German-language speculative fiction scene not only exists but is indeed available to Anglophone readers. In an effort to highlight this fact, Wesleyan University Press published (in 2008) an anthology that includes science fiction from both Germany and Austria (as part of its Early Classics of Science Fiction series), titled *The Black Mirror, and Other Stories: An Anthology of Science Fiction from Germany and Austria*. Rottensteiner's lengthy introduction offers a sweeping overview of the literature beginning with Lasswitz in the 1870s and ending with Eschbach in the early 2000s. Noting the evolution of German-language SF from espousing nationalistic and militaristic themes (around World War I) to interrogating the social and ecological realities of the German Democratic Republic midcentury, to pursuing less ideologically driven ideas in the early decades of the twenty-first century, Rottensteiner explains that such an anthology is meant to represent not the "best" but the most "important" German-language stories and novels that have influenced the genre's direction across the decades. With stories by Scheerbart, Friedell, Franke, the Brauns, Jeschke, and Eschbach, *The Black Mirror* is required reading for anyone interested in learning more about the genre in Germany and Austria.

SWITZERLAND

Switzerland is an especially interesting case with its four official languages: German, French, Italian, and Romansh. While Swiss authors of speculative fiction are barely represented in Anglophone markets, a few have made it onto the radar. One author who has is the early-nineteenth-century pastor Jeremias Gotthelf (pen name of Albert Bitzius), whose work of horror *The Black Spider* (1842; 2013) was originally published in 1842. An allegorical tale about evil worming its way into individuals and the community at large, it is a chilling story told by an old man at an otherwise happy event (a christening). With its elements of mass hysteria and cosmic horror, *The Black Spider* has been seen as a warning, according to Thomas Mann, about the future threat of Nazism. As one reviewer put it upon its first English translation, "Gotthelf's talent is to make his horror credible by the simplicity of his style and the acuteness of his psychological perception, particularly of the herd instinct among the villagers."[23]

✳ ✳ ✳

Written by German-speaking authors from different countries, in different eras, and under the influences of war, privation, political unrest, and other social pressures, German-language speculative fiction offers Anglophone readers a rich tapestry of stories about otherworldly voyages, absurd government officials, advanced technology, social isolation, fantastic architecture, and much more.

And while these novels, collections, and anthologies may not appear on bookstore shelves or tables, they *are* available through publishers and libraries and can be ordered by local bookstores. Such a rich literature deserves to be read and discussed more widely in the Anglophone world.

Primary Sources

AUSTRIA

1902–7: Meyrink, Gustav. *The Opal, and Other Stories*. Translated by Maurice Raraty. Dedalus, 1994.

1909: Kubin, Alfred. *The Other Side*. Translated by Denver Lindley. Crown, 1967.

1916: Meyrink, Gustav. *The Green Face*. Translated by Mike Mitchell. Dedalus, 1992.

1917: Meyrink, Gustav. *Walpurgisnacht*. Translated by Mike Mitchell. Dedalus, 1993.

1921: Meyrink, Gustav. *The White Dominican*. Translated by Mike Mitchell. Dedalus, 1994.

1927: Meyrink, Gustav. *The Angel of the West Window*. Translated by Mike Mitchell. Dedalus, 1991.

1946: Friedell, Egon. *The Return of the Time Machine*. Translated by Eddy C. Bertin. DAW, 1972.

1963: Haushofer, Marlen. *The Wall*. Translated by Shaun Whiteside. Cleis Press, 1990.

1966: Basil, Otto. *The Twilight Men*. Translated by Thomas Weyr. Meredith Press, 1968.

1981: Gruber, Marianne. *The Sphere of Glass*. Translated by Alexandra Strelka. Ariadne Press, 1993.

1982: Jonke, Gert. *Awakening to the Great Sleep War*. Translated by Jean M. Snook. Dalkey Archive Press, 2012.

1993: Mitchell, Mike, ed. and trans. *The Dedalus/Ariadne Book of Austrian Fantasy: The Meyrink Years, 1890–1930*. Dedalus.

1995: Ransmayr, Christoph. *The Dog King*. Translated by John E. Woods. Chatto and Windus, 1997.

2001: Rottensteiner, Franz, ed. *The Best of Austrian Science Fiction*. Translated by Todd C. Hanlin. Ariadne Press.

2003: Mitchell, Mike, ed. and trans. *The Dedalus Book of Austrian Fantasy: 1890–2000*. Dedalus.

2006: Glavinic, Thomas. *Night Work*. Translated by John Brownjohn. Canongate, 2008.

2008: Rottensteiner, Franz. *The Black Mirror, and Other Stories: An Anthology of Science Fiction from Germany and Austria*. Translated by Mike Mitchell. Wesleyan University Press.

2010: Mitchell, Mike, ed. and trans. *The Dedalus Meyrink Reader*. Dedalus.

GERMANY

1897: Lasswitz, Kurd. *Two Planets*. Translated by Hans H. Rudnick. Southern Illinois University Press, 1971.

1901, 1990: Scheerbart, Paul. *Rakkóx the Billionaire / The Great Race*. Translated by W. C. Bamberger. Wakefield Press, 2015.

1903: Scheerbart, Paul. *The Stairway to the Sun / Dance of the Comets.* Translated by W. C. Bamberger. Wakefield Press, 2016.

1913: Scheerbart, Paul. *Lesabéndio: An Asteroid Novel.* Translated by Christina Svendsen. Wakefield Press, 2012.

1914: Scheerbart, Paul. *The Gray Cloth.* Translated by John A. Stuart. MIT Press, 2001.

1922: Ewers, Hanns Heinz. *Strange Tales.* Various translators. Runa-Raven Press, 2000.

1957: Jünger, Ernst. *The Glass Bees.* Translated by Louise Bogan and Elizabeth Mayer. Noonday Press/FSG, 1960.

1961: Franke, Herbert W. *The Mind Net.* Translated by Christine Priest. DAW, 1974.

———. *The Orchid Cage.* Translated by Christine Priest. DAW, 1973.

1969: Rosendorfer, Herbert. *The Architect of Ruins.* Translated by Mike Mitchell. Dedalus, 1992.

1970: Franke, Herbert W. *Zone Null.* Translated by Chris Herriman. Seabury Press, 1974.

1972: Rosendorfer, Herbert. *German Suite.* Translated by Arnold Pomerans. Quartet Books, 1979.

1976: Rosendorfer, Herbert. *Grand Solo for Anton.* Translated by Mike Mitchell. Dedalus, 1997.

1977: Jünger, Ernst. *Eumeswil.* Translated by Joachim Neugroschel. Eridanos Library, 1993.

1981: Jeschke, Wolfgang. *The Last Day of Creation.* Translated by Gertrud Mander. Century, 1982.

1983: Rosendorfer, Herbert. *Letters Back to Ancient China.* Translated by Mike Mitchell. Dedalus, 1997.

Wolf, Christa. *Cassandra.* Translated by Jan Van Heurk. Farrar, Straus & Giroux, 1988.

1985: Süskind, Patrick. *Perfume.* Translated by John E. Woods. Penguin, 1987.

1987: Fühmann, Franz. *Science Fiktion.* Translated by Andrew B. B. Hamilton and Claire van den Broek. Seagull Books, 2019.

Rosendorfer, Herbert. *Stephanie; or, A Previous Existence.* Translated by Mike Mitchell. Dedalus, 1995.

1989: Jeschke, Wolfgang. *Midas.* Translated by Sally Schiller. New English Library, 1990.

Rosendorfer, Herbert. *The Night of the Amazons.* Translated by Ian Mitchell. Secker and Warburg, 1991.

1995: Eschbach, Andreas. *The Carpet Makers.* Translated by Doryl Jensen. Tor Books, 2005.

2001: Eschbach, Andreas. *One Trillion Dollars.* Translated by Frank Keith. Bastei Entertainment, 2014.

Moers, Walter. *A Wild Ride through the Night.* Translated by John Brownjohn. Secker and Warburg, 2003.

2003: Heitz, Markus. *The Dwarves (Dwarves I).* Translated by Sally-Ann Spencer. Orbit, 2009.

2004: Heitz, Markus. *The War of the Dwarves (Dwarves II).* Translated by Sally-Ann Spencer. Hachette Digital, 2010.

Hennen, Bernhard, and James Sullivan. *The Elven (Saga of the Elven #1)*. Translated by Edwin Miles. AmazonCrossing, 2015.

Schätzing, Frank. *The Swarm*. Translated by Sally-Ann Spencer. Hodder & Stoughton, 2006.

2005: Heitz, Markus. *The Revenge of the Dwarves (Dwarves III)*. Translated by Sheelagh Alabaster. Orbit, 2011.

Jeschke, Wolfgang. *The Cusanus Game*. Translated by Ross Benjamin. Tor Books, 2013.

2006: Hennen, Bernhard. *Elven Winter (Saga of the Elven #2)*. Translated by Edwin Miles. AmazonCrossing, 2018.

2008: Dath, Dietmar. *The Abolition of Species*. Translated by Samuel P. Willcox. Seagull Books, 2012.

Heitz, Markus. *The Fate of the Dwarves (Dwarves IV)*. Translated by Sheelagh Alabaster. Orbit, 2012.

2009: Heitz, Markus. *Righteous Fury (The Legends of the Älfar I)*. Unknown translator. Jo Fletcher Books, 2014.

Schätzing, Frank. *Limit*. Translated by Shaun Whiteside, Jamie Searle, and Samuel Willcocks. Jo Fletcher Books, 2013.

Zeh, Juli. *The Method*. Translated by Sally-Ann Spencer. Harvill Secker, 2012.

2011: Eschbach, Andreas. *Lord of All Things*. Translated by Samuel Willcocks. AmazonCrossing, 2014.

Heitz, Markus. *Devastating Hate (The Legends of the Älfar II)*. Unknown translator. Jo Fletcher Books, 2015.

Lewitscharoff, Sybille. *Blumenberg*. Translated by Wieland Hoban. Seagull Books, 2017.

Tawada, Yoko. *Memoirs of a Polar Bear*. Translated by Susan Bernofsky. New Directions, 2016.

2012: Erpenbeck, Jenny. *The End of Days*. Translated by Susan Bernofsky. New Directions, 2014.

Heitz, Markus. *Dark Paths (The Legends of the Älfar III)*. Unknown translator. Jo Fletcher Books, 2016.

2014: Heitz, Markus. *Raging Storm (The Legends of the Älfar IV)*. Translated by Sorcha McDonagh. Orbit, 2019.

Hennen, Bernhard. *Elven Queen (Saga of the Elven #3)*. Translated by Edwin Miles. AmazonCrossing, 2019.

2015: Heitz, Markus. *The Triumph of the Dwarves (Dwarves V)*. Translated by Sheelagh Alabaster. Jo Fletcher Books, 2018.

2016: Kehlmann, Daniel. *You Should Have Left*. Translated by Ross Benjamin. Pantheon Books, 2017.

SWITZERLAND

1842: Gotthelf, Jeremias. *The Black Spider*. Translated by Susan Bernofsky. New York Review of Books, 2013.

Notes

1. Banerjee and Fritzsche, *Science Fiction Circuits of the South and East,* 5–7.
2. Rottensteiner, introduction to *The Black Mirror,* xv.
3. See Petteman, "Just Another Manic Monad."
4. See Petersen's "Andreas Eschbach's Futures and Germany's Past." *The Carpet Makers* won the 1996 Deutscher Science Fiction Preis and France's Grand Prix l'Imaginaire for foreign language novel in 2001.
5. McCalmont review.
6. Dürbeck, "Popular Science and Apocalyptic Narrative," 20.
7. See Partsch, "Paul Scheerbart and the Art of Science Fiction."
8. The illustrations that accompanied *Lesabéndio*'s original publication came with illustrations by the Austrian artist and author Alfred Kubin, who himself wrote a work of fantasy, *The Other Side.*
9. See Mitchell, "Introducing: Herbert Rosendorfer," 9.
10. For more on science fiction in East Germany, see Kiausch, "Orchids in a Cage."
11. Cordasco review.
12. Orthofer review.
13. Crawford and Worley, "The German Gothic: Introduction."
14. Krause, "In Search of the Maternal."
15. Orthofer review.
16. Rottensteiner, "Short History of Austrian Science Fiction," i.
17. Mitchell, introduction to *Dedalus/Ariadne Book of Austrian Fantasy,* 14.
18. Clute, "Friedell, Egon." While the Jewish Friedell wrote this story in the 1930s, he was forbidden from publishing it when the Nazis came to power, and he committed suicide rather than allow the Gestapo to arrest him. His novel was finally published in the original German in 1946.
19. Potts review.
20. Mitchell, introduction to *Dedalus/Ariadne Book of Austrian Fantasy,* 14.
21. The *SFE* defines it, in part, as "texts where fantasy and the mundane world intersect and interweave throughout a tale which is significantly *about* a real city."
22. Mitchell, introduction to *Dedalus/Ariadne Book of Austrian Fantasy,* 16.
23. Piers Paul Read, *Times* (London), quoted in publisher's copy.

Secondary Sources

Banerjee, Anindita, and Sonja Fritzsche, eds. *Science Fiction Circuits of the South and East.* Oxford: Peter Lang, 2018.
Clute, John. "Friedell, Egon." In *The Encyclopedia of Science Fiction,* edited by John Clute, David Langford, Peter Nicholls, and Graham Sleight. London: Gollancz, updated August 31, 2018. http://www.sf-encyclopedia.com/entry/friedell_egon.
Cordasco, Rachel. "Review: *Memoirs of a Polar Bear* by Yoko Tawada." *SFinTranslation.com* (November 2016). https://www.sfintranslation.com/?p=1198.

Crawford, Heide, and Linda Kraus Worley. "The German Gothic: Introduction." *Colloquia Germanica* 42, no. 1 (2009): 2–3.

Dürbeck, Gabriele. "Popular Science and Apocalyptic Narrative in Frank Schätzing's *The Swarm*." *Ecozon@* 3, no. 1 (2012).

Kiausch, Usch. "Orchids in a Cage: Political Myths and Social Reality in East German Science Fiction (1949–1989)." *Journal of the Fantastic in the Arts* 11, no. 4 (2001): 375–94.

Krause, Edith H. "In Search of the Maternal: Patrick Süskind's *Perfume*." *Germanic Review* 87, no. 4 (2012): 345–64.

McCalmont, Jonathan. "*The Swarm* by Frank Schätzing." *Strange Horizons* (September 2006). http://strangehorizons.com/non-fiction/reviews/the-swarm-by-frank-schatzing/.

Mitchell, Mike. "Introducing: Herbert Rosendorfer." In *The Architect of Ruins*, by Herbert Rosendorfer, translated by Mike Mitchell. Sawtry, Cambridgeshire: Dedalus, 1992.

———. Introduction to *The Dedalus/Ariadne Book of Austrian Fantasy: The Meyrink Years, 1890–1930*, edited and translated by Mike Mitchell. Sawtry, Cambridgeshire: Dedalus, 1993.

Orthofer, M. A. Review of *Blumenberg*, by Sibylle Lewitscharoff. *Complete Review* (June 2017). http://www.complete-review.com/reviews/moddeut/lewitscharoff2.htm.

———. Review of *You Should Have Left*, by Daniel Kehlmann. *Complete Review* (March 2017). http://www.complete-review.com/reviews/kehlmann/you_should.htm.

Partsch, Cornelius. "Paul Scheerbart and the Art of Science Fiction." *Science-Fiction Studies* 29 (July 2002): 202–20.

Petersen, Vibeke Rützou. "Andreas Eschbach's Futures and Germany's Past." In *Lingua Cosmica: Science Fiction from around the World*, edited by Dale Knickerbocker, 52–72. Urbana: University of Illinois Press, 2018.

Petteman, Dominic. "Just Another Manic Monad: Of Glass, Bees, and Glass Bees." *Discourse* 40, no. 1 (2018): 62–82.

Potts, George. "A Gallery of Mirrors (*Awakening to the Great Sleep War*)." *TLS* 5731 (February 2013): 21.

Rottensteiner, Franz. Introduction to *The Black Mirror, and Other Stories: An Anthology of Science Fiction from Germany and Austria*, edited by Franz Rottensteiner. Middletown, CT: Wesleyan University Press, 2008.

———. "A Short History of Austrian Science Fiction." In *The Best of Austrian Science Fiction*, edited by Franz Rottensteiner, translated by Todd C. Hanlin, i–iv. Riverside, CA: Ariadne Press, 2001.

Hebrew-Language SFT

Introduction

The story of Hebrew-language science fiction is an old-new story.[1] Much like the nation, much like the language, genre fiction in Hebrew has uncontested ancestry (as well as some contested ancestry!) while having completely reinvented itself. Indeed, even putting the smattering of precursors aside, the production of speculative fiction written in modern Hebrew has grown exponentially since the establishment of Israel in 1948. Numbering just under thirty full-length speculative novels in the 1940s, '50s, '60s, and '70s, *cumulatively* by the 1980s and '90s the production had doubled its pace, whereas today we've seen three times that number since 2010 alone (and this doesn't include speculative fiction aimed at young adults and children).[2] Adopting a broad definition of the genre, one arrives at a rough estimate of 250 titles in total—novels written in the mode of speculative fiction that were written originally in Hebrew.

This is not a large number, but, considering the age of the country and the size of the readership, it is no mean feat. Indeed, thinking of the specificities and idiosyncrasies of modern Hebrew, it seems a language that might be a natural medium for speculative fiction. Hebrew is an *abjad*—a writing system in which the vowels are implicit. Thus, any given sentence is rife with homonyms and homographs, leaving the reader to determine word function and meaning based on context or common sense. While native speakers are naturally adept at this, it becomes a powerful strategy for reference and allusion, direction and misdirection, that can

Muck (2018)

be so effective in SF. Furthermore, morphologically, like other Semitic languages, Hebrew is built on a pattern of triconsonant roots that then branch out, adding letters and variations to derive systems of word forms: nouns, verbs, adjectives, and so on, which are all linked to the root. The root structure grounds the language, lending it a concreteness and referentiality that more flexible languages arguably lack but, together with the context-based semantics of the language, can at the same time so often lead more to obfuscation or fabulation than to clarity. This tension between the familiar and knowable and the foreign or ambiguous is reflected in the name of the language itself: the very word "Hebrew" is linked etymologically to *eber* [Heb: e-v-er], roughly translated as "from the other side" (as in a riverbank) or "from beyond," *or*, conveniently for my argument, homographically, *a-v-a-r*, which means "the past." Modern Hebrew is a hybrid language

Dolly City (2015)

that weaves ancient past with recent pasts, insistently and meticulously renewing itself through incorporation, adaptation, and invention.

Thus, the impulse to estrange the familiar on which speculative fiction is premised is an inherent feature of this language *from beyond*, yet science fiction naturally works differently in Hebrew. Indeed, the very pace of SF changes. For example, the delicious ambiguity and postponed revelations in the original Le Guin or Ann Leckie, for example, are impossible in a Hebrew that must pronounce a gendered subject for every verb enacted.[3] Moreover, the kind of space spectacles and galactic operas of a Heinlein or a Bester or a Simmons, culturally based on traditions of empire and world domination, are near impossible, almost laughable, for a country so small and so young. Not to say that these haven't been tried! From the earliest days of Hebrew-language SF, writers have relied heavily on forms, tropes, and formulas of the Anglo-American traditions, including rocket ships, robots, and dystopian societies. And these are not all just cheap knockoffs. On the contrary, there are some delightful, sophisticated, and innovative writers whose novels enrich the genre and are almost coincidentally written in Hebrew. Language barrier aside, works by Ram Moav, Ofir Touché Gafla, and others could sit comfortably alongside many of the greats in the canon. This is no doubt at least partially thanks to Emmanuel Lottem—the most prominent and prolific translator of speculative fiction into Hebrew—who is almost single-handedly responsible for carving out a niche readership in Hebrew of English-language SF since as early as the 1970s. Lottem has translated Asimov, Herbert, Pohl, Tolkien, and many others who've had lasting influence on contemporary writers in Israel.

And then there are others who resist this impulse and write uncompromisingly and recognizably Israeli-Hebrew SF, with Israeli landscapes, Hebrew neologisms, and Israeli humor, but also Israeli realities that are reflected in the speculations. The inimitable enfant terrible of Israeli poets, David Avidan, is a key figure in this tale of the Israeliness of Hebrew SF, and his *Cryptograms from a Telestar* (1980) and other collections of SF poetry offer a unique experience that is rare in its explicit merging of the particularities of Hebrew, with speculative impulses, in poetic form. Growing numbers of contemporary writers, among them Yitzhak Ben-Ner, Keren Landsman, Efrat Roman-Asher, and Vered Tochterman, explore the boundaries of SF in contexts that are demonstrably Israeli. Moreover, Amos Kenan's *Road to Ein Harod* (1984), for example, a disturbing, surreal near future about Israeli's military realities; Shimon Adaf's *Sunburnt Faces* (2013), a metaleptic fantasy novel that incorporates Jewish mysticism into Israeli mundanities; or Orly Castel-Bloom's *Dolly City* (1992), a satirical and dystopian extrapolation of contemporary Israel and Jewish typologies—these are all texts that are insistently Israeli, and, curiously, they have all been translated into English. Indeed, while it is clear that a novel's successful translation will depend more on economics, politics, and some luck than on aesthetics and other literary considerations, a closer examination of the still-scant offerings of Hebrew SF available in English reveals a definite partiality to those novels that capture a recognizable snapshot of Israeli experience.

The turn of the twenty-first century has seen a dramatic growth in the publication of Hebrew SF, with some of the fastest-growing subgenres being fantasy, which blends Jewish mythologies with Israeli urbanity; alternate histories, which reimagine the country's origins in a variety of what-if scenarios; and near futures, in which political corruption, terror, and the growing scarcity for resources contend with the troubles and traumas of contemporary existence in Israel. What's more, the impact of this growth has become palpable: in 2003 the Geffen annual literary award for SF expanded its purview to include a category for Hebrew-language SF. This, together with the growing number of local scholars who work in the field, to say nothing of speculative film and TV, are gradually transforming the genre into a recognizable force in both high and popular cultural production in contemporary Israel and modern Hebrew.

Keren Omry

The Texts

The first anthology of Hebrew-language SFT, published in 2018, brought Anglophone readers an entirely new corpus of literature to absorb and explore. A labor of nearly a decade, *Zion's Fiction: A Treasury of Israeli Speculative Literature* sought to correct the Anglophone perception that Israeli authors don't write speculative fiction, and if they do they write it in English instead of Hebrew. As Sheldon Teitelbaum and Emmanuel Lottem have shown, however, Hebrew-language SFT does indeed exist. In fact, the intertwined and complicated histories of the State of Israel, the Jewish people, and the development of the modern Hebrew language have created a rich field of ideas and approaches for speculative fiction in the twenty-first century.

Discussing the relatively rapid development of Hebrew-language SFT in a nation that isn't even a century old yet, Teitelbaum notes that modern Israel as a concept was born out of the Bible and the ideas of late-nineteenth-century thinker and author Theodor Herzl, whose utopian novel *Old New Land* (*Altneuland* [1902]) was the first step in making Israel, once again, a homeland for the Jewish people. Nonetheless, the religious and political strife that has marked Israel's existence led the literary gatekeepers in the mid-twentieth century to deem speculative fiction a distraction from the supposedly more noble goal of creating a "realistic" literature that would firmly define the nation's values and goals.

Of the eleven book-length works of Hebrew-language SFT that have come out in English so far, five tend more toward science fiction, five tend toward fantasy, and the last is the anthology discussed above. As with much speculative fiction, genre boundaries here are quite fluid, but they also help us think through different authors' approaches to topics as wide ranging as the afterlife, revelation, finding one's homeland, and the role of fate in our lives. And while most of the authors discussed in this chapter were born and raised in Israel, a few moved there during childhood or early adulthood (from Egypt, Ukraine, Germany, and Russia). Two of these authors (Orly Castel-Bloom and Shimon Adaf) use their experiences as cultural outsiders (being born in or to immigrant families from North Africa) to comment on the social and political schisms in Israel, while several others (including Savyon Liebrecht and Nava Semel) use speculative fiction to explore their experiences as children of Holocaust survivors. In all of these stories,

Anglophone readers come face-to-face with questions of spiritual and cultural identity, nationhood, trauma, extremism, and hope for the future.

SCIENCE FICTION

The first novel-length work of Hebrew-language speculative fiction to be translated into English, Amos Kenan's *The Road to Ein Harod* (1983; 1988) is an alternate-history story of a fascist Israel in the wake of a military coup. When one Jewish opponent of the government tries to reach a legendary kibbutz in order to realize the socialist Zionist dream of coexistence with the Arabs, he must find a way to move past his own ideological barriers and work with an Arab outcast.

Far more dystopian and absurdist is Orly Castel-Bloom's *Dolly City* (1992; 1997). With its visceral imagery, scathing political and social critique, and unconventional language, this novel of a nightmarish Tel Aviv–like place called "Dolly City" deliberately assaults the reader's senses, provoking feelings of revulsion and horror.[4] That, in fact, is Castel-Bloom's goal in telling us about Doctor Dolly's chilling experiments on stray animals and on her own son, her intense paranoia, and the painful despair that infests the city like a colony of rats. The lifelessness of Dolly City and Doctor Dolly's violent proclivities are warped reflections of the atrocities of the Holocaust, Dolly's hyperprotectiveness of and obsession with her son is a twisted version of the "Yiddishe mama" stereotype, and her decision to carve a map of Israel onto her son's back suggests an extreme nationalism that literally results in blood and pain. Castel-Bloom's inclusion in this and other texts of slang, neologisms, foreign words, and biblical Hebrew suggests a deliberate and incisive experimentation that, like the tests Dolly performs on her lab subjects, exposes the raw nerves of a nation seeking to define itself in relation to the horrors of the past and the desire for a better future.

Trauma also informs Hillel Damron's novel *Sex War One* (1982; 2014), set in a technologically sophisticated, postapocalyptic underground colony. Damron, born on a kibbutz to Holocaust survivors, here imagines that a nuclear holocaust has killed off most of the human race. Those who remain have created a communal society and reproduce via a birth laboratory, with concepts like "love" and "familial devotion" no longer having any meaning. The accidental birth of a female baby who looks different from the other children upends the community's adherence to free love and spawns a war between the sexes that leads to a new matriarchal power structure.

The Holocaust lies at the heart of Nava Semel's partially alternate-history novel *Isra Isle* (2005; 2016), in which Jews from around the world moved to Ararat, New York, in the 1820s to escape persecution.[5] Semel raises issues of exile, belonging, the history of race and religion in the United States, and the question of Jewish assimilation in a Christian country, especially when one persecuted group replaces another on the same piece of land. Often compared to Michael Chabon's *The Yiddish Policeman's Union* (2007) for its exploration of a universe in which Jews settled somewhere other than Israel, *Isra Isle* brings together the world we know and the world as it could have been in an engaging mix of the detective and speculative genres.

Unlike Castel-Bloom, Damron, and Semel, who draw on specific historical events and trauma to craft speculative, often dystopic, narratives, Ofir Touché Gafla, in *The World of the End* (2004; 2013), writes about one man's attempt to reunite with his wife in the afterlife.[6] Gafla is, nevertheless, intensely interested in how the past erupts into the present and how our thoughts about the future influence it as well. When Ben Mendelssohn commits suicide following the unexpected death of his wife, he encounters the Other World, in which he meets those members of his family and friends who died before him. Yet he can't seem to find his wife, so Ben hires a detective to track her down. Along the way, Ben learns about the porousness of "reality" and the ways in which the dead speak to the living. A mix of fantasy, horror, science fiction, and mystery, *The World of the End* is at its heart an exploration of our understanding of immortality and relationships.

FANTASY

The five works of Hebrew-language fantasy that have been translated into English so far take up such diverse questions as spiritual revelation, coincidence, (the impossibility of) communication, and the acceptance of outsiders. Only one could be classified as "high fantasy" for its inclusion of sorcerers and magic, while the other four walk the blurry line of reality and fantasy. Shimon Adaf's **Sunburnt Faces** (2008; 2013), like *The World of the End*, is a mix of multiple genres—poetry, detective fiction, fantasy, and children's literature—that examines how a person's entire life can change after a single spiritual event.[7] Nonetheless, this is a novel preoccupied with fantasy and with exploring the concept of "Wonderland," children's books about fairies and magical places, and, above all, revelation. *Sunburnt Faces'* nested stories and its preoccupation with religious scripture and books that supposedly don't exist, combined with its exploration of the liminal space between childhood and adulthood, demonstrate a unique and lyrical take on human nature and consciousness.[8]

Offering us a different perspective on destiny and the choices we make is Yoav Blum's novel **The Coincidence Makers** (2011; 2018). Its three main characters, all official "coincidence makers" (having recently been promoted from "imaginary friends"), embark on their first attempts at shaping the future of humanity via carefully crafted situations.[9] Spilled cups of coffee, random meetings, traffic jams, and a million other seemingly small acts are the coincidence makers' tools, and they use them not only on unsuspecting mortals but on each other as well. Blum takes readers into this oddly bureaucratic world that lies just out of sight in order to ask us to think more deeply about how we make decisions, with whom we fall in love, and how everything we do just might just be the result of other beings pulling our strings.

This uncertainty about whether we have free will and if our actions will lead to the outcomes we desire informs Etgar Keret's collection of twenty-two short stories titled *Fly, Already* (2019).[10] While not every story could be considered "speculative," the contrast between those that could happen and those that probably wouldn't foregrounds the multiple ways in which human beings seek meaning in their lives. While some tales, like "Crumb Cake," explore familial relationships and the ways in which we fall into patterns of behavior that are difficult to break, others, like "Pineapple Crush," contrast meaningful relationships forged, say, on a beach between two strangers smoking joints and those relationships tenuously created on social media. (Possible) shape-shifters, clones, angels, apocalyptic youth armies—together these creatures and people make *Fly, Already* a many-layered investigation of our often bizarre, confusing world.

Dror Burstein imagines a strangely alternate world in *Muck* (2016; 2018), so perfectly encapsulated in the publisher's jacket copy: "Hipster kings and careerist prophets populate a fantastical Israel on the brink of destruction." Here, two poets (Jeremiah and Mattaniah, whose late father was the king of Judah) are locked in a bitter struggle for recognition in the literary world; this occurs in an Israel in which the First Temple and modern-day helicopters actually coexist. When Jeremiah has a vision that Mattaniah will eventually become king and see his people murdered and sent into exile, the former wonders if he should tell anyone, let alone his rival, of this terrible future. Torn between trusting in his own vision and sounding like a resentful literary failure, Jeremiah must figure out how to make his people believe him before it's too late.

Only Keren Landsman's *The Heart of the Circle* (2018; 2019) can be called "high fantasy," including as it does sorcerers whose powers are well known and feared by ordinary humans. Nonetheless, this novel anchors itself firmly in the contemporary world, depicting the persecution of those sorcerers by religious extremists to comment on the intolerance and violence of the early twenty-first century. Here, a sorcerer-led march for equal rights comes to a bloody end, and one sorcerer in particular must find a way to escape the same fate even as he is falling in love.

✳ ✳ ✳

With *Zion's Fiction: A Treasury of Israeli Speculative Literature*, Anglophone readers can finally learn more about the Israeli speculative fiction scene, which has been growing, albeit slowly, since the turn of the century.[11] Here we have

112

nine stories translated from the Hebrew, one translated from the Russian, and six originally written in English, imagining everything from dream teleportation and hyperintelligent mice to timeless libraries and everything in between. Two of the most powerful stories in the collection (Keren Landsman's "Burn Alexandria" and Savyon Liebrecht's "A Good Place for the Night") offer us visions of a fragile hope springing out of the ruins left behind by brutal alien invasion and an unexplained population-killing disaster, respectively. Mordechai Sasson's "The Stern-Gerlach Mice" and Nitay Peretz's "My Crappy Autumn" attack themes of hopelessness and devastation with the darkest kind of black humor. Magical realism and hard SF, too, populate *Zion's Fiction*, with stories of portal mirrors and disappearing stars, on the one hand, and accelerated evolution and spliced time lines, on the other. Visions of Jerusalem alleys, orange groves, the Mediterranean, the streets of Tel Aviv, and many others infuse these speculative stories with a uniquely Israeli personality, with references to Yiddish, Arabic, Hebrew, English, and Russian reminding us of the nation's cultural, religious, and linguistic diversity. Included as well are lyrical pieces by Shimon Adaf and Nava Semel.

With more Hebrew-language SFT coming out each year, Anglophone readers can expect to learn much more about the literary scene, as well as sociopolitical and cultural concerns and ideas, coming out of the tiny country of around nine million. Emerging out of this maelstrom of religions, nationalities, and languages is a literature being written in a modernized version of an ancient language. Combine this with modern Israel's formulation in an early speculative text, and you have the ingredients for a robust and inventive speculative fiction of the future.

Primary Sources

1982:   Damron, Hillel F. *Sex War One*. Translated by the author. HillelBridge, 2014.

1983:   Kenan, Amos. *The Road to Ein Harod*. Translated by Anselm Hollo. Grove Press, 1988.

1992:   Castel-Bloom, Orly. *Dolly City*. Translated by Dalya Bilu. Loki Books, 1997.

2004:   Gafla, Ofir Touché. *The World of the End*. Translated by Mitch Ginsberg. Tor Books, 2013.

2005:   Semel, Nava. *Isra Isle*. Translated by Jessica Cohen. Mandel Vilar Press, 2016.

2008:   Adaf, Shimon. *Sunburnt Faces*. Translated by Margalit Rodgers and Anthony Berris. PS, 2013.

2011:   Blum, Yoav. *The Coincidence Makers*. Translated by Ira Moskowitz. St. Martin's Press, 2018.

2016:   Burstein, Dror. *Muck*. Translated by Gabriel Levin. FSG, 2018.

2018:   Landsman, Keren. *The Heart of the Circle*. Translated by Daniella Zamir. Angry Robot Books, 2019.

Teitelbaum, Sheldon, and Emanuel Lottem, eds. *Zion's Fiction: A Treasury of Israeli Speculative Literature*. Mandel Vilar Press.

2019: Keret, Etgar. *Fly Already*. Translated by Sondra Silverston, Nathan Englander, Jessica Cohen, Miriam Shlesinger, and Yardenne Greenspan. Riverhead.

Notes

1. See Omry, "Israeli SF 101."
2. Estimated numbers are based on combined resources, including listings from the Geffen Awards, publisher catalogs, and research forums.
3. Leckie's translator includes his dilemmas and correspondence with the author, as an invaluable appendix to the Hebrew translation of *Ancillary Justice*.
4. Cordasco review. See also Ofengenden, "Language, Body, Dystopia."
5. Cordasco review.
6. Hebblethwaite review.
7. Cordasco review.
8. For further discussion of *Sunburnt Faces*, see Dekel's "The Place, *Makom*, Nonplace."
9. Di Filippo review.
10. The title story first appeared in English in the *New Yorker*, May 15, 2017.
11. Cordasco review.

Secondary Sources

Cordasco, Rachel. "Review: *Dolly City* by Orly Castel-Bloom." *SFinTranslation.com* (September 2016). https://www.sfintranslation.com/?p=1026/.

———. "Review: *Isra Isle* by Nava Semel." *SFinTranslation.com* (November 2016). https://www.sfintranslation.com/?p=1127.

———. "Review: *Sunburnt Faces* by Shimon Adaf." *SFinTranslation.com* (April 2017). https://www.sfintranslation.com/?p=1957.

———. "*Zion's Fiction: A Treasury of Israeli Speculative Literature*." *World Literature Today* (September 2018). https://www.worldliteraturetoday.org/2018/september/zions-fiction-treasury-israeli-speculative-literature.

Dekel, Yael. "The Place, *Makom*, Nonplace: Between Netivot and Tel Aviv in Shimon Adaf's *Panim zeruvei hamah* (*Sunburnt Faces*)." *Shofar* 36, no. 6 (2018): 60–77.

Di Filippo, Paul. "Paul Di Filippo Reviews *The Coincidence Makers* by Yoav Blum." *Locus Magazine* (March 2018). https://locusmag.com/2018/03/paul-di-filippo-reviews-the-coincidence-makers-by-yoav-blum/.

Hebblethwaite, David. "*The World of the End* by Ofir Touché Gafla." *Strange Horizons* (September 2013). http://strangehorizons.com/non-fiction/reviews/the-world-of-the-end-by-ofir-touche-gafla/.

Ofengenden, Ari. "Language, Body, Dystopia: The Passion for the Real in Orly Castel-Bloom's *Dolly City*." *Comparatist* 38 (October 2014): 250–65.

Omry, Keren. "Israeli SF 101." *SFRA Review* 306 (2013): 8–11.

Italian-Language SFT

Introduction

Italy has always been a major center of history, culture, and art, so it's no surprise that Italian literature and fiction reflect this ambition and limitation, that is, the idea that science and rational thinking have to bow to the necessities of aesthetics and philosophy. Since the Renaissance, Italian writers have speculated about an ideal society (see Tommaso Campanella's *The City of the Sun*) or its opposite dystopic scenario (see Machiavelli's *The Prince*) without using technology as a prominent feature and preferring the use of imagination and purely fantastic tropes. Nevertheless, Italy is also the country of Leonardo da Vinci, Galileo Galilei, Guglielmo Marconi, and Enrico Fermi, whose influences will return in the subtext of many science fiction stories once science and technology are no longer perceived in Italy as something "alien" to literature.

Today, in fact, even though many writers such as Tullio Avoledo, Valerio Evangelisti, and the group of writers called Wu Ming set their stories in alternative realities and uchronic secondary worlds, one of the most interesting movements arising in Italian science fiction is "Connettivismo" (Nexialism), which considers many scientific disciplines—from quantum physics to biotechnology and from astronomy to artificial intelligence—as the necessary mix of features upon which to build a plot. Giovanni De Matteo's novel *Sezione π^2* is one such work. Here De Matteo creates special police officers, known as "necromancers," as the cybernetic implant they are equipped with allows them to conduct their investigations by

Imago Mortis (2014)

starting from the recovery of the victims' memories. The story is set in Naples, rebuilt after a future eruption of Vesuvius and the catastrophic consequences of a third world war. The metropolis, flooded by refugees, has reached six million inhabitants and is besieged by an ecological threat of uncertain origins: an entropic mass able to regenerate itself by assimilating waste and invading areas abandoned by human activity.

Another example of this science fiction development in Italy (not related to Nexialism but particularly interesting as a mixture of SF and literary tropes) is represented by the stories of Clelia Farris, whose fiction beautifully blends regional traditions and the Sardinian language with contemporary science fiction themes such as climate change, biotechnology, and liquid identities. Her first collection of short stories, *La consistenza delle idee* (Future fiction, 2018),

Nexhuman (2018)

was published in English in 2020 by Rosarium Publishing with the title *Creative Surgery*.

My own contribution to Italian science fiction has covered many issues related to the genre from posthuman themes, the spread of AI, and postcyberpunk in the novels *e-Doll* and *Nexhuman* (Apex Books, 2018) to the latest developments in nanotechnology, solarpunk philosophy, and three-dimensional printing with *The Walkers* (consisting of *The Pulldogs* and *No/Mad/Land*, still unpublished in English). This story, in particular, tries to imagine a possible, viable exit strategy to the "No Future" present advocated by contemporary postmodernism and the postapocalyptic approach presented in too many mainstream genre books. These books offer a vision of community resilience, neo-nomadism, and off-grid renewable energy supply as a way to overcome the Anthropocene (the geological era caused by human behavior) and the Capitalocene (its economic deviation).

At the moment, Italian science fiction is experiencing a new golden age, with some excellent stories published on the national market. However, with few being translated into English, it's difficult to make them as visible internationally as they deserve.

Francesco Verso

The Texts

Italian speculative fiction in English is dominated by four of the major Italian authors of the twentieth century: Dino Buzzati, Tommaso Landolfi, Italo Calvino, and Primo Levi.[1] While the first three wrote the kind of literature that we would classify as "fantastic," Levi tended more toward an almost mystical science fiction. Each of these authors, though, has been classified as mainstream because Italy has only recently begun to embrace the role that speculative fiction plays in its national literature.[2] Indeed, because of this split between the literary and scientific modes of thought, according to *The Encyclopedia of Science Fiction*, "Fantastic Voyages and Utopian landscapes are the most effective contributions of Italian literature to the development of a genre that would eventually merge into sf, as in the Renaissance poem *Orlando Furioso*."[3] Thus, we have Calvino's intense interest in folktales and fables, Landolfi's and Buzzati's tendency toward allegory, and Levi's fusion of the mythic and historical in his science fiction stories. After all, the Italian term for "science fiction"—*fantascienza*—reflects this binary within which Italian speculative fiction authors have and continue to work. As Italian speculative fiction scholar Arielle Saiber notes, *fantascienza* "is one of the few translations of 'science fiction' that puts the 'fantasy/fantastic fiction' before the 'science.'"[4]

It's not surprising, then, that fantastic texts have dominated Italian SFT; since 1960 Anglophone readers have had access to nearly two dozen works of Italian fantasy, while science fiction has made its way into English only since the 1980s, and that only sporadically. In fact, collections and novels by Buzzati, Landolfi, Calvino, and Levi have almost exclusively come to us via mainstream publishers such as Random House, Liveright, and Harcourt Brace Jovanovich. Science fiction, on the other hand, has come from a variety of small or micro publishers, and much of it is available only electronically. Italian publisher Acheron Books took advantage of the rise of the Internet and electronic texts to publish several works of fantasy, science fiction, and horror in English between 2014 and 2017. Francesco Verso's Future Fiction is an exciting project that publishes international science fiction in translation. Perhaps more such publishers will appear in the future to bring Italian speculative fiction to Anglophone readers.

LITERARY FANTASY

An intriguing mix of surrealism, magical realism, and fabulation characterizes Italian fantasy in English. Some scholars have pointed to major shifts in Italian politics and in the arts since the turn of the twentieth century to account for this particular mixture. The two-decade struggle for unification ending in 1861, the rise of fascism via Mussolini during World War I, the devastation of World War II, and the social and economic chaos of the 1970s led writers such as Massimo Bontempelli, Landolfi, and Calvino to explore the absurd and bizarre erupting from the seemingly mundane events of daily life. Indeed, Buzzati and Landolfi turned to surrealism and magical realism as vehicles of social critique in a nation gripped by authoritarianism and militarism. Jorge Luis Borges's brand of magical realism, too, influenced Italian writers, particularly Calvino, who was fascinated by language and its structures.

Bontempelli, widely thought to be the first author to employ what we now think of as magical realism, was translated into English only during the twenty-first century. *Separations: Two Novels of Mothers and Children* (1929, 1930; 2004) and *On a Locomotive, and Other Runaway Tales* (?; 2013) are chilling, strange tales of a child being born twice to two different mothers, a mother so cold and distant that she becomes dangerous, technology that slips beyond human control, and more. Though head of the National Fascist Writers' Union in the mid- to late 1920s, Bontempelli officially broke with fascism by the 1930s. As scholar Wissia Fiorucci argues, Bontempelli critiqued the regime earlier than previously thought precisely through his "deconstruction of mimetic writing"—magical realism.[5]

Kafka's influence, as well, has become part of the fabric of Italian fantastic literature, particularly that of Dino Buzzati. While Buzzati wrote between the 1930s and 1970s, his work has only sporadically trickled into the Anglophone market. This is perhaps the reason that Buzzati isn't better known in the Anglophone world, even as his allegorical, fable-like stories remind us of tales such as Kafka's "The Metamorphosis." Buzzati's novel *Larger than Life* (1960; 1962), translated by the famous British World War II poet Henry Reed, is a dreamlike story about a top-secret military project, the purpose of which is revealed only long after the scientist recruited to work on it has started demanding answers.[6] Eventually, he learns that the project's overseer is attempting to re-create his lost lover via an entire city. Buzzati's other novel in English, *The Tartar Steppe* (1940; 1995), further explores this concept of place as a site of the fantastic. A critique of militarism and fear of the Other, *The Tartar Steppe* is the story of a young soldier named Giovanni Drogo who is sent to a distant fort on the eponymous steppe to await what he's told is an immanent invasion. Like Mann's protagonist in *The Magic Mountain*, Drogo doesn't feel the passage of time until he suddenly realizes that he's been at the fort for several years. Eventually, his quest for glory and excitement over the invasion wanes as the enemy fails to show up . . . until it actually does begin massing on the frontier.

Unlike these very site-specific novels, Buzzati's collection *Catastrophe, and Other Stories* (1965; 1982) offers us more allegorical stories about the absurdities of village life and the herd mentality.[7] Anglophone readers will find notes of Stephen Crane and Guy de Maupassant throughout the collection. And while some of these pieces have science fictional or fantastic elements, those elements are not the point of the stories but merely the vehicles by which Buzzati can explore such questions as "Can a government create a disease that singles out its critics?" ("The Epidemic") or "What would really happen if humans were confronted with an actual dragon?" ("The Slaying of the Dragon"). The perniciousness of the herd mentality is a major theme in *Catastrophe*, with Buzzati returning to it in several stories as if running an experiment multiple times in hopes of a different result. Buzzati's other collections, *Restless Nights* (1983) and *The Siren* (1984), continue to explore the fantastical themes for which he is known.

While Buzzati is interested in the violence and intolerance that lie beneath the veneer of civilized life, Landolfi goes further with this idea in his stories, veering at times toward the sadistic.[8] His work has been compared to that of Kafka and Borges, Poe, and especially Gogol, since Landolfi received a degree in Russian literature and translated several Russian texts. Through his three collections and one novel in English, Landolfi explores the threshold between the natural and supernatural via stories of, for instance, an animate inflatable doll ("Gogol's Wife"), an organic (and vengeful) spaceship ("Cancerqueen"), and the kiss of a (real? imaginary?) vampire. His collection *Gogol's Wife, and Other Stories* (1963) includes not only the chilling title story but also tales of languages that don't exist, a king with strange obsessions and phobias, and more.

The stories in *Cancerqueen* (1971)[9] and *Words in Commotion* (1986) are equally bizarre and perplexing, inviting us to accept the existence of creatures and scenarios that can burst through into reality at any minute. The eponymous story in the *Cancerqueen* collection is about a mad scientist and an equally mad writer who fly to the moon on the spaceship of the same name. As one goes slowly (more) insane and then jumps out of the vessel into space (becoming a satellite to the ship), the other realizes that he, too, is losing his grip on reality. Perhaps it is because the organic ship that he's piloting has turned against him and is doing everything she can to purge herself of him as well. Landolfi's exploration of (the threat inherent in) female power shows up multiple times in both collections, especially in "The Kiss" and "The Woman's Breast," in which the feminine becomes ever more monstrous.[10] Landolfi explores this further in *An Autumn Story* (1946; 1989), his only novel to be translated into English, which mixes the gothic and fantastic to produce a story much like Poe's "The Fall of the House of Usher." *Autumn* recalls the brief flowering of the Italian gothic in the mid-nineteenth century.

Like Landolfi, Italo Calvino was fascinated by language and the ways in which it could manipulate and be manipulated. A champion of Landolfi, Levi, and other Italian authors who moved easily between "mainstream" and "fantastic" fiction, Calvino himself experimented with the fairy tale, the meta-novel, surrealism, and the place where myth and science meet. Indeed, as scholar Alan Tinkler argues, "Fantasy, for Calvino, is not removed from reality; fantasy simply represents another performance of reality."[11] In his so-called Italian trilogy—*The Baron in the Trees* (1957; 1959), *The Nonexistent Knight* (1959; 1962), and *The Cloven Viscount* (1952; 1962)—Calvino draws upon his extensive knowledge of the Italian folktale tradition to explore questions of literal and metaphorical perspective, (self-)identity, and the nature of good and evil. His *Invisible Cities* (1972; 1974), however, is more concerned with our understanding of place and how it is perceived differently according to one's mood, for instance, or one's past. As Calvino's Marco Polo describes city after fantastic city to his host, Kublai Khan, the reader begins to wonder if these are truly different cities or his native Venice from a multitude of perspectives.

With the collections *t zero* (1967; 1969) and the well-known *Cosmicomics* (1965; 1968),[12] Calvino switches gears once again, this time mixing together the mythic form and scientific theory to produce stories that are at once enthralling and destabilizing. Through the seemingly immortal creature Qfwfq, we learn about the time when the moon was so close to Earth that one could leap from one to the other or the time before multicellular organisms when Qfwfq had only hydrogen atoms to play with. The story "t zero" is itself a contradiction, since it uses the vehicle of a story (which unfolds through time) to analyze a single crucial moment: When a lion is in midair, about to leap onto the narrator, and the narrator has a poison arrow directed at the lion, which one of the infinite possibilities will become reality?

Calvino explores the nature of narrative itself in his "hypernovel"[13] *If on a winter's night a traveler* (1979; 1981). Beginning like a normal novel, with a plot and characters, *If on a winter's night* quickly veers off course, turning into a completely different kind of text. Here, the Reader steps in as a character, taking the book back to the store from which it came to complain about its continual narrative reboots and in the meantime running into another person who has experienced the same problem. In the new copy of the book, the Reader discovers yet *another* novel, and this one is written in a dead (and invented) language. Each novel leads deeper into itself and to yet another novel, with one genre giving up its place to another. Questions of translation, authenticity, authorship, and narrative structure make *If on a winter's night* a text so obsessed with itself that it invites us to look at other texts with a new eye.

Writing around the same time as Calvino, Anna Maria Ortese and Guido Morselli explored the limits of magical realism and alternate history, respectively. In *The Iguana* (1965; 1987), which won the Fiuggi Prize when it was originally published in 1965, Ortese imagines a deserted island of lost noblemen, the iguana that they use (and abuse) as their servant, and the love that springs up between that iguana and a Milanese count who happens upon the island by accident. In such a community, cut off from the outside world, love between an iguana and a nobleman suddenly doesn't seem so outlandish, and Ortese's lyrical prose makes the reader forget about species and caste and more about the universals, like love and companionship. Morselli's *Past Conditional* (1973; 1991), in contrast, takes the entire world as its setting, only here the First World War ended in such a way that the second never even happened. Morselli uses actual historical figures (including Hitler) but rearranges their destinies according to this alternate version of the first modern war, inviting us to imagine (à la Calvino) the infinite number of possibilities that could have led to an infinite number of different outcomes. A more recent example of Italian magical realism is Alessandro Baricco's *Ocean Sea* (1993; 2000), in which characters write love letters to as-yet-unknown lovers, seek cures for mysterious illnesses, paint pictures of the sea with its own water, and connect with one another in strange and seductive ways.

GOTHIC AND MODERN HORROR

Italy's gothic and horror tradition is as old as its literary fantasy tradition, though the latter has not produced as many major texts. Nonetheless, Anglophone readers have access to the short stories of two of Italy's greatest gothic writers: Iginio Ugo Tarchetti and Camillo Boito. Their operatic tales of passion and murder written against the backdrop of the political frenzy of Italian unification (1848–71) can be seen as the precursors to later gothic and horror texts by authors from a century later. The late-twentieth-century version of gothic horror as developed by Giorgio De Maria and Nicola Pugliese reflects, once more, a time of political and social upheaval in Italy. The more contemporary horror of Samuel Marolla and Alessandro Manzetti, in contrast, falls into the tradition of the internationally known horror by authors such as America's Stephen King and Sweden's John Ajvide Lindqvist.

The gothic fantasy and horror that developed in Italy were influenced by the rise of nineteenth-century French bohemianism and even earlier romantic sensibilities.[14] As Tarchetti's translator—translation theorist Lawrence Venuti—explains, the movement "saw style as revolt, both in deviant behavior intended to shock bourgeois respectability and in outré experiments that opposed the Italian cultural establishment."[15] Compared by early critics to Edgar Allan Poe, Tarchetti used his own experiences in the army and his disgust with the nobility to craft stories about dreams, madness, reincarnation, resurrection, obsession, and bizarre phobias. In *Fantastic Tales* (1977; 1992), Tarchetti experiments with stories about, for example, metempsychosis and a nobleman's bizarre ordeal ("A Spirit in a Raspberry"), one man's phobia of the letter *U* ("The Letter U"), and a dream of reincarnation that may actually be a vision of the future ("The Legends of the Black Castle").

Boito, too, drew upon the bizarre and supernatural, as well as the image of the femme fatale, in the tales that make up *Senso, and Other Stories* (1882; 1993). And while his brother Arrigo was more visible in the *scapigliatura* movement, Camillo (an architect and architectural theorist) made important contributions to the developing Italian gothic genre. Boito's story "Christmas Eve" is about a man's obsession with his dead twin sister and his subsequent passion for a slovenly woman who looks like that sister. In "The Body," an artist and an anatomist project their own visions of life and death onto a woman with whom they are both obsessed, while "Buddha's Collar" involves a man fearing that he has contracted rabies due to a bite by a prostitute. This focus on the shocking, the depraved, and the horrific contrasted sharply with the realism in vogue in Italian literature in the nineteenth century.

In the two works of twentieth-century Italian gothic horror in English by Giorgio De Maria and Nicola Pugliese, we see how the concerns and imagery influenced by the politics of the mid-nineteenth century have been transformed by new social and political pressures. The economic and social unrest in Italy in the late 1960s and '70s, driven by student protests, terrorism, and the rise of neofascism, is reflected in the dark, apocalyptic pages of De Maria's *The Twenty Days of Turin* and Pugliese's *Malacqua*, both originally published in Italian in 1977 and then in English exactly forty years later. In *Twenty Days*, De Maria blends gothic and cosmic horror by telling the story of a series of bizarre murders involving strange "metallic" screams, statues switching places, and what appears to be a kind of collective psychosis.[16] Pugliese, meanwhile, draws on the decadelong political unrest to imagine a city's struggle with an endless rainstorm. Along with the deluge come dolls that scream, pocket change that makes musical sounds, and a thick silence that leads the citizens of Naples to begin questioning everything they believe about reality.

The horror fiction that has come out of Italy in the early twenty-first century was born in Milan (appropriately) and Rome. Less politically charged than the books by De Maria, Pugliese, and their predecessors, the novels and collections

123

by Samuel Marolla and Alessandro Manzetti suck in the reader with a supernatural horror that seems timeless. Marolla's novel *Imago Mortis* (2014; 2014) and collection *Black Tea, and Other Tales* (2014)[17] introduced the Italian author to Anglophone fans of contemporary international horror. His collection's title story, like the other two stories in the collection, unsettles precisely because it undermines the reader's own sense of reality. Here an electrician and his assistants arrive at an old woman's house to do repair work, but what they find is a nauseatingly shape-shifting house in which hallucinations seem only too real and the old woman turns out to be an evil creature bent on sucking the life out of each of the trapped men. In *Imago Mortis*, Marolla creates a junkie, Augusto, who gets high on the ashes of the dead. In order to make money to get his fix, Augusto works as a private investigator, but this time, when he inhales ashes and interacts with ghosts, he gets pulled into a truly horrifying situation.

Like Marolla, Manzetti has helped put Italian horror on the map. The winner of the 2015 Bram Stoker Award for poetry, Manzetti works in a variety of styles to tell his stories of cosmic horror and monsters. The six stories that make up *The Shaman, and Other Shadows* (2014) range from tales of human-devouring sacred mountain creatures ("The Mount Meru") and shamans who can identify the dead via bone fragments ("The Shaman") to wolves that drag their victims to the Reaper ("The Wolf Gate"). Manzetti's only novel in English, *Naraka: The Ultimate Human Breeding* (2018), is a version of *The Island of Doctor Moreau* but set in space. Walking the line between horror and science fiction, *Naraka* imagines the consequences of a meteorite slamming into Earth and setting off a chain of horrific events—martial law, cannibalism, and mutations. To ease the pressure on Earth, a megacorporation builds a prison on the moon where they house and then slaughter the inmates, package them in cans, and send them to the restaurants patronized by the ultrawealthy back on Earth.

MODERN HIGH FANTASY

The Italian contribution to high fantasy in English translation comes exclusively by way of Samuel Marolla's micropress Acheron Books (2014–17), through which he published his own novel and collection. Through these translations, Anglophone readers can learn more about how the subgenre—with its fairies, dwarves, elves, and spirits—is evolving in a uniquely Italian and twenty-first-century context. Luca Tarenzi's *Demon Hunter Severian—Lady of the Night Gates* (2014) and *The Landfill War (Poison Fairies #1)* (2014) revolve entirely around the lives and struggles of supernatural creatures like ancient deities and landfill fairies. *Demon Hunter* is set during the Roman Empire, just as Christianity was becoming more widespread. With this rise of one religion, the deities of earlier religions have returned to spread chaos and terror, a situation that only a demon hunter can handle. *The Landfill War*, however, is set in a version of modern times, with fairy tribes fighting over territory and the trash (car batteries, discarded food, and so forth) that they can use as energy (apparently the acid from car batteries is particularly nutritious for fairies). Strange magic, war, and a deadly mission together make *The Landfill War* a heady mix of fantasy, mystery, and thriller.

Alessio Lanterna's *Lieutenant Arkham: Elves and Bullets* (2014), described by Acheron as "*The Lord of the Rings* meets *Blade Runner*," is set in the fictional city of Nictropis, where the eponymous protagonist must investigate the murder of a powerful elf. Over the course of his investigation, Arkham must dodge the magic and bullets flying at him from ogres, trolls, hit men, and assorted other enemies. The fantasy by Livio Gambarini and Andrea Atzori, however, is firmly set in the past. Gambarini's *Eternal War: Armies of Saints* (2015; 2015), which takes place in thirteenth-century Florence, focuses on long-standing family feuds and the spirits that guide and assist each faction.[18] With their squabbles and resentments, the spirits are at times more tangible than the humans to whom they are attached. Atzori's *ŠRDN—From Bronze and Darkness* (2017) goes even further into the past, back to the time of the Bronze Age warriors on Sardinia.[19] A native of the island himself, Atzori draws on the myths of ancient Sardinia to tell the story of Incubi that have begun to pour out of the netherworld and destroy the villages in their path. It's ultimately up to the Shardans (the gatekeepers of hell and guardians of the ancient *nuraghe* structures) to lead the demons back into the depths.

Davide Mana's *The Ministry of Thunder* (2014), set just before the outbreak of World War II, tells the story of an Italian mechanic working on aircraft in China. Before he realizes it, Sabatini is drawn into a conspiracy around an ancient artifact and its mystical power—an object coveted by China, Japan, and Germany. Sabatini must inevitably face immortals, fox women, ninjas, dragons, and the mysterious Ministry of Thunder before he can escape the menace pursuing him.

SCIENCE FICTION

Modern science fiction has been dismissed in Italy as a nonserious genre, or one only for children, as well as a threat to traditional religious and political thought. Nonetheless, its emergence, starting in the early twentieth century, reveals the ways in which Italian speculative fiction in general has adopted and adapted to the Anglophone and Francophone version of the subgenre, turning it into something distinctively Italian.[20] Both mainstream authors such as Primo Levi and science fiction authors like Francesco Verso have, since their translations into English, shown Anglophone readers what Italian science fiction can contribute to the global evolution of the subgenre.

Like his friend and champion Italo Calvino, Levi is usually known in the Anglophone world as a mainstream author who sometimes includes fantastic or science fiction elements in his novels and stories. A chemist and Holocaust survivor, Levi wrote several memoirs of his time in Auschwitz, including *If This Is a Man* (1947; 1958) and *The Truce* (1963), documenting the atrocities he witnessed and his own determination to remember and record. Even before these memoirs, however, Levi was combining his passion for chemistry with his skills as a storyteller to write short works of science fiction. Calvino, upon reading a collection of stories that Levi sent to him, wrote the author, "The science fiction, or rather biological fiction, ones, always appeal to me. Your fantasy mechanism, which takes off from a scientific-genetic starting point, as a power of suggestion that's intellectual but also poetic, just like the genetic and morphological digressions of Jean Rostand. . . . You move in a dimension of intelligent digression on the edges of a cultural-ethical-scientific panorama that reflects the Europe we live in."[21] Beginning in 1989, Anglophone readers have had the opportunity to read Levi's speculative texts, which often begin with a scientific premise and then veer off into the mystical or vaguely fantastic.

The Mirror Maker: Stories and Essays (1986; 1989) brings together short fable-like pieces and essays that Levi wrote for the newspaper *La Stampa* over the course of two decades.[22] In the title story, a man invents a special kind of mirror that reflects how others actually perceive a person—a kind of updated analogue to Oscar Wilde's *The Picture of Dorian Gray*. Levi's next collection in English, *The Sixth Day, and Other Tales* (1971; 1990),[23] includes stories that probe our enthusiasm for new technology and suggest that scientific "progress" is not always positive. In some instances, these stories are based on actual Nazi scientists' experiments on camp prisoners. Levi's "Order on the Cheap" (and several connected stories) involves a "matter duplication" device that anticipates the three-dimensional printer and explores how one man's use of the machine leads to increasingly complicated and worrisome ethical and moral questions. In "Excellent Is the Water," an Italian river gradually increases in viscosity and spreads to the rest of the world, reflecting both ecological catastrophe and a metaphorical comment on humanity's sluggishness in the face of evil. The tales in *A Tranquil Star: Unpublished Stories* (2007) further reveal Levi's creative range, with paint that can ward off evil and an astronomer's obsession with a long-dormant star that might explode and take Earth along with it.

The 1980s also brought science fiction by Stefano Benni into English, specifically his wild and humorous novel *Terra!* (1983; 1985). Set during a nuclear winter brought on by six world wars (during which the surviving humans live underground), *Terra!* is about the discovery of a potentially habitable planet and the three remaining superpowers (the Arab-US coalition, the Japanese, and the Sino-Europeans) launching a last-ditch attempt to reach this potential Eden. Their massive table-tennis- and swimming-pool-carrying spaceships, microships with Samurai mice, and giant flying Mickey Mouse ears, respectively, embark on an adventure through a strange kind of space—one that sometimes has breathable air, gravity, shipwrecks, and whirlpools. Benni's novel is often compared to Douglas Adams's Hitchhiker books in its spoofing of science fiction tropes.

Not until 2010 did the Anglophone world have the chance to read Italian anthropologist Paolo Mantegazza's 1897 novel *The Year 3000: A Dream*, which imagines a futuristic utopia on another planet. A story of two lovers who travel from Rome to the capital of the United Planetary States to celebrate a "mating union," *The Year 3000* is ultimately a reader's journey through Mantegazza's imaginary future, which includes airplanes, artificial intelligence, and CAT scans. Mantegazza also uses this novel to explore turn-of-the-twentieth-century issues such as divorce and euthanasia in the context of the thirty-first century.

The rise during the 1980s of subgenres like "steampunk" and "cyberpunk" informs three works of Italian science fiction published in English between 2011 and 2014: Dario Tonani's *Cardanica* (2010; 2011), Sandro Battisti's *The Map Is a Contraction* (2011; 2012), and Fabio Casto's *Burn Slowly* (2014). Tonani, who has won several European and international speculative fiction awards, creates a steampunk story in *Cardanica*, where truck-like ships plow through poisonous and dangerous sands in a world without electricity. Battisti's cyberpunk story about techno grave robbers leads back to two citizens of imperial Rome, suggesting that time and space are more malleable than we think. Meanwhile, Casto's *Burn Slowly* takes up the financial crises of the early twenty-first century through the story of an economic "weed killer": a man who eliminates microeconomic enterprises that might threaten the global market. When he realizes that a major financial and social collapse is imminent, he arranges the construction of a small spaceship referred to in ancient Indian texts as a means of escape.

Publication in 2014 of Francesco Verso's cyberpunk novel *Nexhuman* (2013) signaled a new era in Italian speculative fiction in English.[24] Verso, who started the global science fiction–focused press Future Fiction, champions international science fiction and has forged editorial alliances with like-minded people in the United States, China, and elsewhere. Himself a winner of the prestigious Urania Award and other science fiction prizes, Verso explores issues of transhumanism and human evolution in his texts. In *Nexhuman*, Shelley's *Frankenstein* meets classic cyberpunk when a young man named Peter Payne, living in a world literally filled with trash, falls in love with an android. Determined to piece her back together after she is torn apart by a ruthless gang, Peter must rise above his physical and psychological limitations. Questions of identity, love, human evolution, the nature of consciousness, environmental degradation, and reality itself merge in this book to create a terrifying yet plausible portrait of what our world might yet become.

Other recent works of Italian SFT also point toward the bright future of the genre as conceived by Italian speculative authors. Paolo Aresi's **Beyond the Planet of the Wind** (2016) conceptually recalls Calvino's *Invisible Cities* in the former's story about the starship *Leonardo da Vinci* and its exploration of a fantastic galaxy. From planets with rocks shaped into spears and pinnacles by the powerful winds to those that harbor artifacts that may be gateways to another universe, Aresi's novel invites us to think more broadly about what we know of our place in the cosmos. Daniel Frisano's **Impermanence** (2017) explores what a future life underground (due to ecological catastrophe) might be like, especially when women discover the secret to immortality and allow the men to die off. Finally, Niccolò Ammaniti's **Anna** (2015; 2017) uses the trope of global catastrophe—a lethal virus that kills adults and the subsequent collapse of society through famine and fire—to tell the story of one young girl and her brother trying to survive in a brutal, terrifying world.

The variety of subject matter and style in the Italian speculative fiction available in English, as well as the Anglophone world's growing interest in it, suggests that we will continue to see more Italian SFT in the years to come. With Verso set to have another novel out in English soon, and collections by rising Italian science fiction authors such as Clelia Farris due out in English as well, we can expect great things.

Primary Sources

Unknown: Bontempelli, Massimo. *On a Locomotive, and Other Runaway Tales.* Translated by Gilbert Alter-Gilbert. Xenos Books, 2013.

1882: Boito, Camillo. *Senso, and Other Stories.* Translated by Christine Donougher. Dedalus, 1993.

1897: Mantegazza, Paolo. *The Year 3000: A Dream.* Translated by David Jacobson. Bison Books, 2010.

1929, 1930: Bontempelli, Massimo. *Separations: Two Novels of Mothers and Children.* Translated by Estelle Gilson. McPherson, 2004.

1940: Buzzati, Dino. *The Tartar Steppe.* Translated by Stuart C. Hood. David R. Godine, 1995.

1946: Landolfi, Tommaso. *An Autumn Story.* Translated by Joachim Neugroschel. Eridanos Press, 1989.

1957: Calvino, Italo. *The Baron in the Trees.* Translated by Archibald Colquhoun. Random House, 1959.

1959, 1952: Calvino, Italo. *The Nonexistent Knight and The Cloven Viscount.* Translated by Archibald Colquhoun. Random House, 1962.

1960: Buzzati, Dino. *Larger than Life.* Translated by Henry Reed. Secker and Warburg, 1962.

1963: Landolfi, Tommaso. *Gogol's Wife, and Other Stories.* Translated by Raymond Rosenthal, John Longriff, and Wayland Young. New Directions.

1965: Buzzati, Dino. *Catastrophe, and Other Stories.* Translated by Judith Landry and Cynthia Jolly. Riverrun, 1982.

Calvino, Italo. *Cosmicomics.* Translated by William Weaver. Harcourt, Brace & World, 1968.

Ortese, Anna Maria. *The Iguana.* Translated by Henry Martin. McPherson, 1987.

1967: Calvino, Italo. *t zero.* Translated by William Weaver. Harcourt, Brace & World, 1969.

1971: Landolfi, Tommaso. *Cancerqueen, and Other Stories.* Translated by Raymond Rosenthal. Dial Press.

Levi, Primo. *The Sixth Day, and Other Tales.* Translated by Raymond Rosenthal. Penguin, 1990.

1972: Calvino, Italo. *Invisible Cities.* Translated by William Weaver. Harcourt Brace Jovanovich, 1974.

1973: Morselli, Guido. *Past Conditional.* Translated by Hugh Shankland. Chatto and Windus, 1991.

1977: De Maria, Giorgio. *The Twenty Days of Turin.* Translated by Ramon Glazov. Liveright, 2017.

Pugliese, Nicola. *Malacqua: Four Days of Rain in the City of Naples, Waiting for the Occurrence of an Extraordinary Event.* Translated by Shaun Whiteside. And Other Stories, 2017.

Tarchetti, Iginio Ugo. *Fantastic Tales* (originally written 1860s?). Translated by Lawrence Venuti. Mercury House, 1992.

1979: Calvino, Italo. *If on a winter's night a traveler.* Translated by William Weaver. Harcourt Brace Jovanovich, 1981.

1983: Benni, Stefano. *Terra!* Translated by Annapaola Cancogni. Pantheon, 1985.

Buzzati, Dino. *Restless Nights: Selected Stories of Dino Buzzati.* Translated by Lawrence Venuti. North Point Press.

1984: Buzzati, Dino. *The Siren: A Selection from Dino Buzzati.* Translated by Lawrence Venuti. North Point Press.

1986: Landolfi, Tommaso. *Words in Commotion, and Other Stories.* Translated by Kathrine Jason. Viking.

Levi, Primo. *The Mirror Maker.* Translated by Stuart Rosenthal. Schocken Books, 1989. This and *The Sixth Day* combine stories from *Natural Histories* (1966) and *Flaw of Form* (1971). Translated by Jenny McPhee for *The Complete Works of Primo Levi.* Liveright, 2015.

1993: Baricco, Alessandro. *Ocean Sea.* Translated by Alastair McEwen. Vintage, 2000.

2007: Levi, Primo. *A Tranquil Star: Unpublished Stories.* Translated by Ann Goldstein and Alessandra Bastagli. W. W. Norton.

2010: Tonani, Dario. *Cardanica.* Translated by Caroline Smart. 40k, 2011.

2011: Battisti, Sandro. *The Map Is a Contraction.* Translated by Carlo Santulli. Graphe, 2012.

2013: Verso, Francesco. *Nexhuman* (Australian title: *Livid*). Translated by Sally McCorry. Xoum Fantastica Science Fiction, 2014.

2014: Casto, Fabio. *Burn Slowly.* Translated by Sarah Jane Webb. CreateSpace Independent Publishing Platform.

Lanterna, Alessio. *Lieutenant Arkham: Elves and Bullets.* Translated by Kate Mitchell. Acheron Books.

Mana, Davide. *The Ministry of Thunder.* Unknown translator. Acheron Books.

Manzetti, Alessandro. *The Shaman, and Other Shadows.* Translated by the author, Sanda Jelcic, and Sergio Altieri. Self-published.

Marolla, Samuel. *Black Tea, and Other Tales.* Translated by Andrew Tanzi. Acheron Books.

———. *Imago Mortis.* Unknown translator. Acheron Books.

Tarenzi, Luca [as Giovanni Anastasi]. *Demon Hunter Severian—Lady of the Night Gates.* Translated by Nigel Ross. Acheron Books.

Tarenzi, Luca. *The Landfill War (Poison Fairies #1).* Translated by Kieren Bailey. Acheron Books.

2015: Ammaniti, Niccolò. *Anna.* Translated by Jonathan Hunt. Cannongate, 2017.

Gambarini, Livio. *Eternal War: Armies of Saints.* Translated by Kieren Bailey. Acheron Books.

2016: Aresi, Paolo. *Beyond the Planet of the Wind.* Translated by Jessica Wehr. Delos Digital.

2017: Atzori, Andrea. *ŠRDN—From Bronze and Darkness.* Translated by Nigel Ross. Acheron Books.

Frisano, Daniel. *Impermanence.* Translated by Sarah Jane Webb. Independently published.

2018: Manzetti, Alessandro. *Naraka: The Ultimate Human Breeding.* Translated by Daniele Bonfanti. Independent Legions.

Notes

1. While some scholars and readers would include Umberto Eco in this list, he isn't discussed in this chapter because Eco's fiction is less concerned with the fantastic as with historical and linguistic puzzles.

2. See Saiber, "Flying Saucers Would Never Land in Luca."

3. Pagetti and Iannuzzi, "Italy."

4. Saiber and Rossi, "Italian SF." Professor Saiber's anthology of early classics of Italian SF is forthcoming from Wesleyan University Press.

5. Fiorucci, "Self-Censorship in Massimo Bontempelli's Magical Realism."

6. Boaz review.

7. Cordasco review.

8. Reza, "'Noi siamo uni.'"

9. Gathercole, "Tommaso Landolfi."

10. "The Kiss," according to Reza, "represents the process of the manifestation of a vampire—the metamorphosis and development of the supernatural being—and portrays D's internal desire as an external manifestation, where the vampire grows stronger as D grows weaker. . . . While Landolfi's contribution may not be as significant when compared to other national vampire traditions, within its Italian context and compared to its peers, *Il bacio* is both innovative and noteworthy as a contribution to Italian vampire literature" ("'Noi siamo uni,'" 86).

11. Tinkler, "Italo Calvino," 60.

12. See Philmus, " 'Elsewhere Elsewhen Otherwise.'"

13. Tinkler, "Italo Calvino," 84.

14. Venuti, introduction to *Fantastic Tales*, 10.

15. Venuti, introduction to *Fantastic Tales*, 7.

16. Zinos-Amaro, "Another Dimension."

17. Cordasco review.

18. Cordasco review.

19. Cordasco review.

20. See Rossi, Saiber, and Proietti, "Italian Science Fiction."

21. Quoted in Goldstein, *Complete Works of Primo Levi*, 2838.

22. Kapp, "*The Mirror Maker: Stories and Essays.*"

23. Drawn from the Italian collection *Storie naturali* (1966).

24. Cordasco and Proietti reviews.

Secondary Sources

Bioni, Simone, and Daniele Comberiati. *Italian Science Fiction*. Palgrave Macmillan, 2019. E-book.

Boaz, Joachim. "Book Review: *Larger than Life*, Dino Buzzati (1960, Trans. 1962)." *Science Fiction and Other Suspect Ruminations* (June 2017). https://sciencefictionruminations .com/2017/06/20/book-review-larger-than-life-dino-buzzati-1960-trans-henry-reed/.

Cordasco, Rachel. "*Nexhuman* by Francesco Verso, Translated by Sally McCorry." *Strange Horizons* (March 2017). http://strangehorizons.com/non-fiction/reviews/nexhuman -by-francesco-verso-translated-by-sally-mccorry/.

———. "Review: *Black Tea, and Other Tales* by Samuel Marolla." *SFinTranslation.com* (August 2016). https://www.sfintranslation.com/?p=825.

———. "Review: *Catastrophe* by Dino Buzzati." *SFinTranslation.com* (July 2018). https:// www.sfintranslation.com/?p=5000.

———. "Review: *Eternal War: Armies of Saints* by Livio Gambarini." *SFinTranslation.com* (June 2016). https://www.sfintranslation.com/?p=532.

———. "Review: *ŠRDN—From Bronze and Darkness* by Andrea Atzori." *SFinTranslation. com* (March 2017). https://www.sfintranslation.com/?p=1769.

Fiorucci, Wissia. "Self-Censorship in Massimo Bontempelli's Magical Realism." *Between: Journal of the Italian Association for the Theory and Comparative History of Literature* 5, no. 9 (2015): 1–23.

Gathercole, Patricia. "Tommaso Landolfi: *Cancerqueen, and Other Stories*." *Studies in Short Fiction* 10, no. 1 (1973): 113.

Goldstein, Ann. *The Complete Works of Primo Levi*. New York: Liveright, 2015.

Kapp, I. "*The Mirror Maker: Stories and Essays*." *New York Times Book Review* (February 1990): 15.

Pagetti, Carlo, and Giulia Iannuzzi. "Italy." In *The Encyclopedia of Science Fiction*, edited by John Clute, David Langford, Peter Nicholls, and Graham Sleight. London: Gollancz, updated March 27, 2020. http://www.sf-encyclopedia.com/entry/italy.

Philmus, Robert M. "'Elsewhere Elsewhen Otherwise': Italo Calvino's 'Cosmicomic' Tales." In *Visions and Re-visions: (Re)constructing Science Fiction*, by Robert M. Philmus, 190–223. Liverpool: Liverpool University Press, 2005.

Proietti, Salvatore. "Francesco Verso's *Livid*." *Foundation* 45.2, no. 124 (2016): 129–30.

Reza, Matthew. "'Noi siamo uni': Paradox in Tommaso Landolfi's Fantastic Literature." *Italianist* 35, no. 1 (2015): 78.

Rossi, Umberto, Arielle Saiber, and Salvatore Proietti, eds. "Italian Science Fiction." Special issue, *Science Fiction Studies* 42, pt. 2 (2015). https://www.depauw.edu/sfs/covers/cov126.htm.

Saiber, Arielle. "Flying Saucers Would Never Land in Lucca: The Fiction of Italian Science Fiction." *California Italian Studies* 2, no. 1 (2011). https://escholarship.org/uc/item/67b8j74s#main.

Saiber, Arielle, and Umberto Rossi. "Italian SF: Dark Matter or Black Hole?" *Science-Fiction Studies* 42, no. 2 (2015): 7–8.

Tinkler, Alan. "Italo Calvino." *Review of Contemporary Fiction* 22, no. 1 (2002): 59–94.

Venuti, Lawrence. Introduction to *Fantastic Tales*, by I. U. Tarchetti, translated by Lawrence Venuti. San Francisco: Mercury House, 1992.

Zinos-Amaro, Alvaro. "Another Dimension." *Orson Scott Card's Intergalactic Medicine Show* (March 2017). http://www.intergalacticmedicineshow.com/cgi-bin/mag.cgi?do=columns&vol=alvaro_zinos-amaro&article=018.

Japanese-Language SFT

Introduction

It is not difficult to discover the literary origin of science fiction in myths and legends. Yet it is more natural for us to locate the beginning of the genre in the moment someone established its market. Therefore, as Anglo-American science fiction started with Hugo Gernsback's *Amazing Stories* in 1926, Japanese science fiction began with Hayakawa Publisher's *Science Fiction Magazine*, edited by Masami Fukushima in 1959. Feeling uncomfortable with the kitsch taste of American pulp magazines, Fukushima selected as cover illustrator the distinguished surrealist Seikan Nakajima, whose work recalls the images of Salvador Dalí, Max Ernst, and Giorgio de Chirico. This choice emphasized that, just like the surrealist movement, science fiction would potentially transgress the border between high culture and popular culture, reinventing the frontier of modern literature.

Fukushima's dream came true. The three pillars of Japanese science fiction he discovered and cultivated in the 1960s—Hoshi Shinichi, Komatsu Sakyo (Komatsu Minoru), and Tsutsui Yasutaka—had a tremendous impact on Japanese literature. Hoshi established the "short short" story, whose popularity made him a national author comparable with Natsume Soseki, the father of modern Japanese fiction. Komatsu published quite a few best-selling novels meditating upon the future of the Japanese archipelago, such as *Japan Sinks* (1973). Tsutsui became well known for his black-humor metafiction, similar to that of science fictionists such as Robert Sheckley and Brian Aldiss but also

Sisyphean (2018)

postmodern fabulators like Kurt Vonnegut and John Barth. These texts won him not only science fiction awards but also a number of mainstream literary prizes. Following Fukushima's suggestions, the three pillars and their friends established the Science Fiction and Fantasy Writers of Japan (SFWJ) in 1963 (two years before the Science Fiction Writers of America) and the Japan Science Fiction Grand Prize in 1980 as the Japanese version of the Nebula Award.

Now in the early twenty-first century, postcyberpunk author EnJoe Toh has received the Akutagawa Prize, the most prestigious award for mainstream literature (established in 1935) with his post-Nobokovian speculative metafiction *Harlequin's Butterfly* (2011). Given that half of the present members of the Akutagawa Award selection committee (Murakami Ryu, Okuizumi Hikaru, Shimada Masahiko, Yamada Eimi, and Kawakami Hiromi) have published works of science

Dendera (2015)

fiction or speculative fiction, today's Japanese literature is more generous toward generic transgression and literary cross-fertilization.

However, whenever we meditate upon the history of modern Japanese science fiction, it is hard to ignore the influence of Abe Kōbō. What made Abe unique in world literature is not so much how he led an existentialist life as how he constructed his Janus-like face as both a literatus and a scientist. Without Abe's *Inter Ice Age 4* (1959), the first work of hard-core science fiction in Japan, postwar Japanese literature would not have enjoyed the flowering of fantastic and slipstream writing by the likes of Komatsu, whose influential literary manifesto, "Dear Comrade Ivan Antonovich Yefremov" (1963), proposed the necessity of establishing a "Science of Literature." Komatsu's recent memoir, *Autobiography of Komatsu Sakyo* (2008), tells us that when Abe received the Akutagawa Ryunosuke

Literary Prize in 1951 for his Kafkaesque story "The Wall: The Crime of S. Karma," an exhilarated Komatsu felt convinced that "science fiction is not trash but a branch of serious literature."[1]

Abe's most important contribution to Japanese science fiction is *Inter Ice Age 4*, which narrativizes the way in which a radical change in climate can cause the apocalyptic end of Japan and invites major scientists to come up with the bio-technological strategy for helping human beings survive the disaster. When I first read the novel in 1968 as a junior high school student, I had difficulty grasping how a computer might commit homicide; in the wake of cyberpunk in the 1980s, however, which made imaginable a variety of dangerous cyber beings, we have become more familiar with the concept of an impeccable digital copy that can betray, entrap, and menace its "original." Furthermore, Abe's vivid representation of the biotech aquans, constructed to survive the submersion of Tokyo, calls to mind the new species Arthur C. Clarke created in *Childhood's End* (1953), written only six years before *Inter Ice Age 4*, pointing forward to the deep-sea civilization envisioned in Miyazaki Hayao's popular anime *Ponyo on the Cliff by the Sea* (2008). Thus, today's posthumanist perspective, which makes us consider the possibility of symbiosis with artificial intelligence as well as with animals and chimeras, can lead to a reevaluation of Abe as one of the key prophets of contemporary science fiction.

What is more, we should not forget that Abe was one of the early members of the selection committee of Hayakawa's Science Fiction Contest, established in 1961. During his tenure (1961–63), Abe, along with his fellow members (film producer Tanaka Tomoyuki and SFX director Tsuburaya Eiji, who joined forces to create *Godzilla* in 1954), discovered the talents of Komatsu, Tsutsui, Mitsuse Ryu, Toyota Aritsune, Hirai Kazumasa, and Hanmura Ryo, most of whom became major writers in the first generation of Japanese science fiction. Indeed, Hanmura Ryo, the first secretary-general of the SFWJ, won the Naoki Award in 1975—another prestigious mainstream literature award comparable to the Akutagawa Award. It is the insight of Abe, who kept hovering between existentialist serious fiction and hard-core science fiction, who discovered these first-generation writers. This prehistory of Japanese science fiction helps us envision the slipstream potentiality of these writers, who all excel at transgressing generic boundaries.

Indeed, we can read Abe's masterpiece *The Face of Another* (1964) not only as a gothic doppelgänger fiction in the manner of Edgar Allan Poe and Oscar Wilde but also as a nuclear-age fiction predicting the advent of Komatsu's *Virus: The Day of Resurrection* (1963), Tim O'Brien's *The Nuclear Age* (1985), and director Sunao Katabuchi's *In This Corner of the World* (2016). As scholar Christopher Bolton argues, the Cuban Missile Crisis in 1962 coincided with the dawn of Japan's own nuclear era, concluding, "The heroine of the film described at the end of the novel is a survivor of Hiroshima, so through her the narrator's fate is connected explicitly with the nuclear threat. In *The Face of Another*, the [eponymous] mask represents a technology like this, where the excess freedom and power imparted by science threatens to spillover into violence or dangerous unpredictability.[2] Reading *The Face of Another* as a crypto-nuclear fiction makes it easier to understand Abe's science fictional route from *Inter Ice Age 4* to *The Ark Sakura* (1984), a text more obviously engaged with the phenomenology of nuclear panic that was published the very year that the Strategic Defense Initiative Organization was established within the US Department of Defense. In this sense, Abe Kobe could well be redefined as the true pioneer of Japanese science fiction and the genuine prophet of the literature of the future.

Takayuki Tatsumi

The Texts

Of all of the SFT available to Anglophone readers in the early twenty-first century, the most prominent and well known—especially through its connections to new media—is Japanese. Riding the wave of economic prosperity and global connectivity beginning in the 1970s, Japanese SFT went from a trickle in Anglophone publications like the *Magazine of Fantasy and Science Fiction* to more than 130 unique novels, collections, and anthologies by 2019. Japan's geographical proximity to Australia allowed its speculative fiction to find English-language markets there, and its strong post–World War II connection to the United States enabled its importation, along with American interest in Japanese ideas about education, corporate culture, and advanced technology. Above all, cultural ambassadors such as Judith Merril and English-Japanese translator teams in the last quarter of the twentieth century brought high-quality, incisive, and stylistically experimental Japanese science fiction, surrealism, and horror to Anglophone audiences interested in another culture's take on issues involving, for example, human-AI interaction and environmental catastrophe. The tendency of Japanese speculative fiction authors to move easily between and experiment with genres makes it difficult to pigeonhole them in categories like "science fiction" or "horror." As the editors explain in *Robot Ghosts and Wired Dreams: Japanese Science Fiction from Origins to Anime*, "The line between [science fiction and mainstream fiction] remains more fluid in Japan than in North America," necessitating our own open-mindedness when it comes to accepting these texts on their own terms.[3]

Also important to note is the rapid pace by which, according to scholar Tatsumi Takayuki, Japanese science fiction "ran through the great paradigm shift between outer space and inner space"—within a single decade (1960–70), compared to Anglo-American science fiction's three.[4]

While science fiction makes up the bulk of Japanese SFT since 1960, works of surrealism, magical realism, and horror have begun catching up, especially with the explosion of translated novels and stories by Murakami Haruki (since the 1980s) and Suzuki Koji (since the early 2000s). Five publishers in particular—Alfred A. Knopf, Kodansha, Haikasoru, Kurodahan, and Vertical—are responsible for the majority of the Japanese SFT that we have today, with the University of Minnesota Press also starting to publish classic Japanese SFT.

The massive community of Japanese-to-English translators who have made it possible for Anglophone fans to get their Japanese SFT fix over the past several decades also deserves our thanks. Beginning with the teams of translators that Merril helped organize in the 1970s down to the present-day dedicated individuals such as Dana (David) Lewis, Daniel Huddleston, Tyran Grillo, Ginny Tapley-Takemori, Jim Hubbert, Jocelyne Allen, Matt Treyvaud, and Kazuko Behrens, translators have been crucial cultural ambassadors, not only bringing fascinating Japanese stories to Anglophone audiences but doing it with style, wit, and grace. Editors such as Merril, Gene Van Troyer, Grania Davis, Tatsumi Takayuki, Edward Lipsett, Nick Mamatas, and Masumi Washington championed these translations and made them available to the Anglophone public.

Despite the impressive numbers, however, out of the thirty-plus Japanese writers working in the speculative genre, just four are women, which raises the question of whether Japanese women are getting published in their native language or if translation tends to skew male. The numbers may not be as skewed, however, in the realms of manga and light novels. Speaking of which, some Anglophone readers will be surprised to see that I haven't included those subgenres in my discussion of Japanese SFT. Because manga are Japanese comic books, and this book doesn't cover that kind of speculative text, the thousands of manga titles in English translation have been left for other scholars to tackle. Light novels, which are usually directed at juvenile audiences and may or may not be works of speculative fiction, have been left off because this book discusses only works of speculative fiction written for adult audiences.

SCIENCE FICTION

The three pillars of Japanese science fiction—Komatsu Sakyo (Komatsu Minoru), Hoshi Shinichi, and Tsutsui Yasutaka—were all translated into English beginning in the 1970s, and their diverse styles and choice of topics underscore the breadth of postwar speculative texts.[5] Komatsu, who won numerous literary prizes and conducted the 1970 International SF Symposium in Tokyo, wrote the first work of Japanese science fiction to be translated into English: the apocalyptic novel *Japan Sinks* (1973; 1976). Highly acclaimed in Japan and America, it won the 1974 Seiun Award, sold millions of copies in the original Japanese, and was made into films in both countries during the 1970s. A story about the Japanese archipelago sliding into the Japan Trench, Komatsu's novel is based on the history of Japan's birth from the shifting of tectonic plates millions of years before. Here the physical threat of the islands being pulled under the sea functions also as an allegory of Japan's delicate perch on the wave of economic recovery and expansion. Komatsu's other apocalyptic story in English, *Virus: The Day of Resurrection* (1964; 2012), was originally published in Japanese nearly a decade before *Japan Sinks*. Here, American astronauts bring a strange virus back to Earth, rogue scientists turn it into a killer flu, and most of humanity is wiped out. The only surviving humans live in research stations in Antarctica, but they must find a way to reach the United States and stop a potential nuclear disaster brought on by a major earthquake.[6]

Komatsu's contemporary and fellow science fiction heavyweight Hoshi Shinichi became Japan's first full-time science fiction writer with his unique "short short" stories and sharply satirical style. In describing Hoshi's approach to speculative fiction, especially those stories critical of television and radio, Robert Matthew (who translated five Hoshi collections) notes that the author "has managed with many-faceted approaches to remind us that behind the undoubted power of the media lie the human beings who with all their foibles and weaknesses determine what the media are going to do."[7] The eleven collections by Hoshi in English so far bring together his huge cache of short "Aesopic-type fables,"[8] with topics that range from advertising and subliminal messaging, to child rearing and discipline, and to the future of robotics and human-machine interactions. "Bokko-chan" (*The Spiteful Planet* [1978]), one of the first works of Japanese science fiction to be translated and published in English,[9] is a disturbing tale of an artificial feminized (and realistic) robot bartender and the suicidal customer who, through her, kills everyone in the bar. Long-term mental conditioning by corporations is the subject of "The Grand Design" (*The God of Television* [1989]), where devices called "Universal Child Rearers" raise an entire generation to become mindless consumers. The stories in *The God of Fortune* (1991) further explore the uses to which technology is put (an oath-commissioning machine in "The Oath"), the lengths to which people go to satisfy their greed ("The God of Fortune"), and humanity's deep-seated destructive impulses ("The Mirror").

The third major Japanese science fiction author, Tsutsui Yasutaka, continued Hoshi's tradition of satirizing the media and pointing out the absurdities of everyday life.[10] One of the first postmodernist writers in Japan, Tsutsui is connected to the new wave of the 1960s and '70s and to such satirists as Robert Sheckley, Norman Spinrad, and Kurt Vonnegut.[11] The two novels and four collections of Tsutsui's work in English constitute a fraction of his total oeuvre, but what Anglophone readers do have is a window into Tsutsui's unique and uncompromising perspective on Japanese society. His provocatively titled collection *Salmonella Men on Planet Porno* (2005; 2006) includes stories about erotic dreams caused by a phallus-shaped planet ("The Dabba Dabba Tree"), the media's hyperobsession with an ordinary office drone ("Rumours about Me"), and a "Household Economy Consultant" that destroys a marriage ("Hello, Hello, Hello!").[12] A more recent collection, *Bullseye!* (2017), draws on more than forty years of Tsutsui stories, in which the author imagines, for example, a weapon that lulls people to sleep and then kills them ("Sleepy Summer Afternoon") and "Zarathustra on Mars," which might as well have been written in the 2000s, with its on-point send-up of media hysteria, obsessive fandom, and mass culture.[13] In his two translated novels, Tsutsui images what "hell" might be like (*Hell* [2003; 2007]) and what might happen if scientists could extract and manipulate people's dreams (*Paprika* [1993; 2009].

The publication of nearly twenty Japanese speculative novels and collections in English by 1989 led to the first anthology of this literature in English: *The Best Japanese Science Fiction Stories* (1989). With stories by Abe, Hoshi, Komatsu, and Tsutsui, this anthology reveals the wide range of Japanese SFT available to Anglophone readers at the time, and highlights the group translation work that Judith Merril, Grania Davis and Stephen Davis, and Gene Van Troyer had done with their Japanese counterparts in the 1970s. Here are stories that have subsequently been widely anthologized, including Hoshi's "Bokko-chan" and Tensei Kono's "Triceratops."

Because such a large number of Japanese science fiction novels and collections are available in English, it seems fitting to discuss them according to the major themes that they explore. Thus, the following texts are grouped under eight subsections: "AI, Androids, and Cyborgs," "Aliens and Monsters," "Utopia and Dystopia," "Genetic Manipulation," "The Boundaries of Science," "Humans in Space," "Language and Communication," and "War and Terrorism." All of these texts were first written between 1980 and the early 2010s and translated since the 2000s, underscoring the magnitude of the Japanese SFT explosion since the turn of the twentieth century.

AI, Androids, and Cyborgs

Several Japanese science fiction authors have explored the role that artificial creatures might play in relation to humans in the near and far future. Ranging from a tale about a ship's self-aware android saving her captain's life to one about a virtual-reality war between androids and spiders, these stories by Ogawa Issui,

Kitano Yusaku, Moriyama Tomohito, Ubukata Tow, Ōhara Mariko, and Tobi Hirotaka demonstrate the diverse range of approaches that Japanese authors take to an issue that all nations must eventually face.

In Ogawa's *The Lord of the Sands of Time* (2007; 2009), Kitano's *Mr. Turtle* (2001; 2016), and Moriyama's *Two of Six: A Captain's Dilemma* (2018), androids not only are friendly toward humans but actively assist them at the androids' own peril. Ogawa's novel is reminiscent of the *Terminator* films in its depiction of an AI who travels back into the past to prepare humanity to fight the aliens that will destroy Earth in the future. Despite knowing that its actions will in turn destroy its own time line, Messenger O travels back to World War II, ancient Japan, and even the beginnings of humanity to achieve its purpose. In Kitano's *Mr. Turtle*, a cyborg turtle named Kame-kun realizes over time that he has been engineered to help fight a war on Jupiter against bioengineered Super Crayfish.[14] These crayfish were originally developed by a film company that was making a movie about Jupiter after humans figured out how to open wormholes to that planet. Finally, Moriyama's novella *Two of Six* depicts an AI that puts the safety of its captain before itself.[15] As in Ogawa's and Kitano's novels, the android in Moriyama's novella has a name (Elise), which further complicates the line (in the human mind) between person and machine.

The three novels by Ubukata, Ōhara, and Tobi, however, explore androids (and a cyborg, in one case) on their own terms. Ubukata's *Mardock Scramble* (2003; 2011) is the story of a young prostitute named Balot whose death at the hands of a brutal gambler was stopped only by a self-aware "Universal Tool" named Oeufcoque. The fusion of Balot and Oeufcoque produces a cyborg that chases down the gambler, his associates, and all manner of villains in this fast-paced work of cyberpunk noir. Ōhara's *Hybrid Child* (1990; 2018) is similarly dark, but in an even more disturbing way.[16] Ōhara, one of the few Japanese women whose science fiction has been published in either Japanese or English, creates a complex story about an alien machine civilization and a child murdered by her mother becoming the spirit of an AI-controlled house where a rogue cyborg takes refuge. Humans are nowhere to be found, however, in Tobi's *The Thousand Year Beach* (2002; 2018), which imagines a virtual world sealed off from a ruined Earth.[17] Created as an imitation European vacation spot, the Realm of Summer hasn't seen a single human for a thousand years, but the AIs that continue to live there are woken from their torpor by an invasion of mysterious Spiders that are "eating" the town.

Aliens and Monsters

Aliens fill the pages of Japanese SFT, with some aliens more openly hostile to humans than others. In the stories by Nojiri Housuke and Hayashi Jyouji, aliens linger on the outskirts of the respective narratives, leaving their purposes largely unclear (and perhaps more ominous). Mysterious alien builders threaten Earth's ecology in Nojiri's *Usurper of the Sun* (2002; 2009), though it's unclear whether they realize or care about this. It's ultimately up to the high school student who was one of the few humans to witness the tower construction on Mercury to figure out the aliens' intentions and convince them to alter their plans. Similarly, the alien intelligences alluded to in Hayashi's *The Ouroboros Wave* (2002; 2010) hover on the edge of the narrative.[18] When humans in the near future detect a black hole in Earth's neighborhood, they begin a generations-long project to harness its energy and start colonies on the other planets in the solar system. A collection of linked stories, each tale in *Ouroboros* features a different set of characters and a unique mystery centered around alien intelligence or advanced AI, but all of them are concerned with the profound questions of consciousness and *how* humans could ever know if they were receiving signals from an alien intelligence.

Sakurazaka Hiroshi's *All You Need Is Kill* (2004; 2009) and Kambayashi Chōhei (Kiyoshi Takayanagi)'s *Yukikaze* duology (1984, 1999; 2010, 2011) both explore human and android responses to alien invasion. In Sakurazaka's novel, aliens called the "Gitai" invade Earth, and their only opposition comes in the form of human recruits who die and are reborn to fight again. Only after his 158th iteration does the soldier Keiji Kiriya notice the presence of a different kind of soldier, who might either help him escape the torturous cycle or end the war once and for all. Kambayashi's military SF series also imagines that aliens have invaded Earth, though this time it's via a hyperspace egress at Earth's pole. In *Yukikaze*, humanity unites to repel the invaders and chase them back through hyperspace to their planet, which the humans have nicknamed "Fairy." One soldier from a unit of the Special Air Force is tasked with taking his fighter plane, the sentient FFR-31 Super Sylph (whose call sign is "Yukikaze") to the skies of Fairy for surveillance purposes. The struggle becomes much more complicated in *Good Luck, Yukikaze* as the sentient plane ejects its human pilot and ventures into Fairy on its own, raising the question of its loyalty to humanity and if it's been manipulated over the past thirty years by Earth's AI systems.

In Mitsuse Ryu's *Ten Billion Days and One Hundred Billion Nights* (1967; 2011), aliens have been on Earth all along, starting with Atlantis, which they built and on which they are plotting to suppress competition in the galaxy.[19] Buddha then encounters the aliens in India, and then Jesus Christ is saved by them to become their tool. The shifts in this novel from Earth to Andromeda and then beyond (to transcendence) track with the vast sweep of history and alternate explanations that Ryu gives us for a world that has been controlled by aliens from its earliest days. For Yamamoto Hiroshi, though, monsters, not aliens, are the answer to humanity's questions about itself and its world. In the skewed universe of *MM9* (2007; 2012), it's *kaiju* (massive monsters—think Godzilla), not earthquakes or tsunamis, that have caused Japan's worst natural disasters. It's up to the Japan Meteorological Agency in charge of *kaijus*, the Monsterological Measures Department (MMD), to assess monster threats and suggest how the Japanese Self-Defense Forces should deal with them.

Utopia and Dystopia

Several works of Japanese SFT interrogate the concepts of "utopia" and "dystopia" and how the former often deteriorates into the latter. In Yamada Masaki's *Aphrodite* (1987; 2004) and Project Itoh's *Harmony* (2008; 2010), what at first glance seems like a perfect society quickly reveals the rot and decay at its core. When the young Yuichi in *Aphrodite* escapes a claustrophobic Japanese society for the freedom of a floating city, he soon realizes that sinking global economy pulls Aphrodite down along with it until the once-majestic city has become a floating ruin and only Yuichi can save it. Another seemingly perfect society shows its cracks in *Harmony*, where three young women refuse to accept a world that is made *too* perfect by an authoritarian government. Medical nanotechnology has eradicated disease and an ethic of social welfare guarantees that no one falls through the cracks, but this mandated kindness and health also breed discontent and resentment.

Kyogoku Natsuhiko's ***Loups-Garous*** (2001; 2010) and Project Itoh's ***Genocidal Organ*** (2007; 2012) are set from the beginning in dystopian worlds. In Kyogoku's near-future cyberpunk thriller, a strict surveillance state oversees an extensive system of online networks by which people communicate. Despite rarely coming into contact with other people, though, several students are found murdered and the serial killer's identity is a mystery. It's then up to three teenage girls to stop the murders and in doing so disrupt the sterilized, almost inhuman structures of their world. *Genocidal Organ* also interrogates connections between murder and authoritarianism, only here the tragedy is on a much larger scale. After a homemade nuclear device destroys Sarajevo, the most powerful countries turn into totalitarian states, while the developing countries descend into chaos and genocide. All signs point to a single American man as the source of this global collapse, and one intelligence agent sets out to hunt down and stop him.

From Unno Jūza, one of the founding figures of Japanese science fiction (alongside Sakyo, Hoshi, and Tsutsui), comes a dystopian novella about a mechanized, obedient world à la Yevgeny Zamyatin's *We* (1920–21). In *Science: Hopes and Fears (Volume 2: Eighteen O'Clock Music Bath)* (1937; 2018), people can live as long as they like and do whatever they want . . . except during that one hour when they perform their necessary tasks with unprecedented productivity. They can do this thanks to the government-mandated half-hour "music bath," which uses subliminal messaging to keep the listening citizens obedient and easily controlled.

Tawada Yoko's dystopia, however, focuses more on individuals and their familial relationships against a disastrous backdrop. In *The Emissary* (2014; 2018), an unspecified disaster leaves Japan's children frail and sickly, while the elderly become more lively and energetic.[20] Cut off from the rest of the world after the disaster, the Japanese people begin to adapt to this strange reversal, as the old now look to the young for wisdom and hope.

Genetic Manipulation

Genetic manipulation, and its consequences for humanity, lies at the heart of Ueda Sayuri's *The Cage of Zeus* (2004; 2011), Torishima Dempow's *Sisyphean* (2013; 2018), and Fujii Taiyo's *Gene Mapper* (2012; 2015). In *The Cage of Zeus*, artificially created hermaphrodites (called "rounds") that were meant to test the human body's limits in space have become the target of a terrorist group that intends to wipe them out. Though they've taken refuge on a space station orbiting Jupiter and developed an alternative society based around their own ideas about gender, they are still not safe from terrorist attacks, one of which threatens the entire station and the rounds' existence. Like *Cage*, Torishima's *Sisyphean* is interested in how the human body can be manipulated for various purposes, though Torishima's novel goes a step further and considers how evolution impacts these changes.[21] Described as "bio-horror," "New Weird," and "post-apocalyptic horror," *Sisyphean* begins with a seed ship, launched from a potentially dying world, that is picked up by aliens, who study it. The four sections or stories that follow imply that these aliens have planted the seeds on new worlds to see what will grow, and perhaps humans are the result of these experiments.

Gene Mapper is less interested in genetic manipulation of humans and more concerned with how it has been and is currently being used on our food supply.[22] A technothriller for the twenty-first century, *Gene Mapper* raises several issues that Fujii explores throughout his oeuvre, specifically the "joys and sorrows of Internet connectivity: the potential it offers for communication, education, and betterment, versus the risks of integral accidents and viral catastrophes, both inadvertent and deliberate."[23]

The Boundaries of Science

Unno's *Science: Hopes and Fears (Volume 1: Selected Stories)* (2018) and Ishiguro Tatsuaki's *Biogenesis* (2015) offer readers a more generalized exploration of how far humans might go in manipulating and understanding the natural world. Originally written in the 1930s and '40s, Unno's stories offer a window into Japanese ideas about breakthroughs in chemistry, physics, and astronomy just before World War II. In "The World in One Thousand Years," a scientist emerges from cryogenic sleep to find a radically different world in which humans are immortal thanks to artificial organs, while "Mysterious Spacial Rift" suggests a strange connection between one man's dreams and his reality. Further stories about planetary colonization, a four-dimensional man, and a "living intestine" testify to Unno's grasp of the science that was capturing the Japanese imagination. Writing a half century later, Ishiguro offers us four stories in *Biogenesis* that interrogate certain strange scientific or medical problems.[24] Written in the form of official reports, these stories show us the ways in which life persists and even flourishes under bizarre circumstances and those times when death comes seemingly out of nowhere.

Humans in Space

While many works of Japanese science fiction in translation either take place in space or theorize about it, Aramaki's *The Sacred Era* (1978; 2017), Ogawa's *The Next Continent* (2003; 2010), and Tani's *The Erinys Incident* (1983; 2018) are specifically interested in how humans will live in and travel through space in the future. Though each of these novels was originally written in a different decade (Aramaki's in 1978, Tani's in 1983, and Ogawa's in 2003), they share a commitment to imagining human adaptation to a radically different environment and the consequences of that adaptation. Aramaki's *The Sacred Era* has been described as a masterpiece of new-wave science fiction, blending surrealism, post-Christian dogma, reincarnation, and spaceships fueled by human consciousness, taking on nothing less than the meaning of the universe and humanity's place in it.[25]

Ogawa's *The Next Continent* focuses on Japanese efforts in the near future to turn a Chinese moon base into a tourist destination.[26] When Gotoba General Construction starts moving forward with its plans to develop the base, its chairman sends his granddaughter to oversee the work and the people involved. Space opera meets hard science fiction in Tani's *The Erinys Incident*, which looks even further into the future and to a dying colony on one of Uranus's moons. Nearly forgotten after the Outer Planet Revolt of 2099, Erinys ultimately becomes the perfect hiding place for the remaining Outer Planets Alliance members as they attempt to rebuild their forces. With detailed discussions of questions in astrophysics and orbital dynamics, *The Erinys Incident* is just one part of Tani's larger universe of stories and novels about humanity's future in space.

Language and Communication

Three works of Japanese SFT published since 2010 explore the complexities and limits of language and communication: Kawamata Chaiki's *Death Sentences* (1984; 2012), Furukawa Hideo's *Belka, Why Don't You Bark?* (2005; 2012), and EnJoe Toh's *Self-Reference ENGINE* (2007; 2013).[27] Kawamata's novel jumps around in time and space, from 1980s Japan to post–World War II Paris and from Earth to Mars and beyond. Centering on a strange surrealist poem that kills its readers, *Death Sentences* mixes the hard-boiled detective story, science fiction, and horror to explore how one text can hold such power and how it could be stopped. *Self-Reference ENGINE*, too, asks us to attend more to the act of reading itself and how language, time, and human consciousness work together to create what we know as stories. Apparently, some catastrophic event in the past altered space-time, leaving us with a world in which the past and the future can be altered.

Unlike *Death Sentences* and *Self-Reference ENGINE*, *Belka, Why Don't You Bark?* is about communication *between* species, specifically between a girl and a military dog. When a KGB military dog handler kidnaps the daughter of a Japanese yakuza, the girl finds herself with a mysterious psychic connection to dogs. Focalized through several generations of dogs, Furukawa's novel invites us into the mind of a creature that, despite living with us for centuries, remains a mystery.

War and Terrorism

While several works of Japanese SFT explore the future of war and terrorism both on Earth and in space, Tanaka Yoshiki's *Legend of the Galactic Heroes* series (1982–87; 2016–19) and Fujii Taiyo's *Orbital Cloud* (2014; 2017) make these issues a central focus. The ten novels that make up Tanaka's series, originally published in Japanese between 1982 and 1987,[28] tell the story of a galactic war in the thirty-sixth century between a massive, centuries-old Empire (modeled on Prussia) and the democratic Free Planets Alliance.[29] Highly detailed space battles (inspired by the Napoleonic Wars and other nineteenth-century European conflicts) and the efforts of the respective leaders to conceptualize their goals and desires for the future of human civilization, *LoGH* is a unique meditation on the never-ending clash between autocracy and democracy and the act of writing history. In contrast to this space saga about the fate of humanity, *Orbital Cloud* focuses on the very near future to imagine a dangerous and believable scenario. In Fujii's technothriller, the Japan Aerospace Exploration Agency, the North American Air Defense Command, and the Central Intelligence Agency work together, and with the help of an Iranian scientist, to foil a high-tech terrorist plot.

This diverse array of science fiction from Japan was further showcased in Haikasoru's mini anthology *Saiensu Fikushon, 2016* (2016), which includes stories by three highly acclaimed contemporary Japanese science fiction writers. EnJoe Toh's story "Overdrive" asks us to consider the speed of thought, Tobi Hirotaka's "Sea Fingers" imagines the "Deep" consuming Earth and leaving just a few surviving humans, and Fujii Taiyo's "A Fair War" looks forward to the future of war and drone technology . . . and beyond. This "narrative software of tomorrow," as Haikasoru calls the anthology, highlights the kinds of issues that Japanese science fiction writers are interested in now and points to the future shape of Japanese SFT.

MAGICAL REALISM AND SURREALISM

The majority of the Japanese-language magical realism and surrealism that has been translated into English comes from Abe and one of his most successful literary successors, Murakami Haruki.[30] And while the unstable realities and confusing situations that characterize Abe's and Murakami's work dominate the Japanese SFT fantasy scene, other types of fantasy have slowly come into English from authors such as Sakuraba Kazuki and Sato Yuya.

Abe's slipstream novels and collections, which move freely between science fiction, surrealism, and magical realism, share a fascination with the absurd and bewildering. Influenced by the work of Franz Kafka and Samuel Beckett, Abe sets his characters in bizarre situations (a town at the bottom of a sandpit, a confusing and nightmarish hospital), as if conducting an experiment on how humans function under extreme circumstances. His first novel published in Japanese, however, is a work of apocalyptic science fiction. In *Inter Ice Age 4* (1958–59; 1970), a secret group of Japanese scientists plans to confront the impending worldwide flooding due to melting polar ice caps by genetically manipulating the next generation. When an information scientist who came up with the ice-cap prediction refuses to accept that his unborn child will be turned into a water breather, or "aquan," his resistance foregrounds the extent to which humans should use scientific predictions to influence how they live their lives.

The other seven novels by Abe in English, however, are more in the surrealist or magical realist mode. His *Woman in the Dunes* (1962; 1964) tells the story of an amateur entomologist who, after missing his tour bus, is forced to stay overnight at the bottom of a large sandpit. Eventually, he realizes that the locals who live there won't let him leave until he helps shovel back the sand that threatens to engulf the village. *The Ark Sakura* (1984; 1988), written more than two decades later, flips this situation on its head with its description of a man obsessed with walling himself in—specifically into a bomb shelter, though no actual nuclear disaster has occurred.

Abe takes the bizarre to a whole new level in *Secret Rendezvous* (1977; 1979), which follows one man's nightmarish journey through a sadistic hospital. When his wife is taken by an ambulance in the middle of the night for no apparent reason, the protagonist follows her to the hospital, where he finds a surveillance network, strange sex experiments, and violent patients. Deranged hospitals appear again in *Kangaroo Notebook* (1991; 1996), where a man notices one day that his legs are growing edible radish sprouts. The hospital sends him to hot-spring therapy in "Hell Valley," which turns out to be a literal door to the underside of the city's streets. In *The Ruined Map* (1967; 1969), Abe merges the tropes of detective fiction with surrealist imagery to tell the story of a salesman who mysteriously disappears and his wife's belated efforts to find him. When the detective who takes her case attempts to locate the salesman in Tokyo's underworld, he finds himself in dreamlike situations that make him doubt his own identity.

Two of Abe's novels from the 1960s and '70s focus specifically on questions of identity and transformation: *The Face of Another* (1964; 1966) and *The Box Man* (1973; 1974). When a laboratory accident leaves a scientist with disfiguring scars on his face, he begins to understand what a literal "loss of face" means. Not only do his relationships begin to suffer, but so does his own personal sense of identity. With the lifelike mask that he creates in his lab, the scientist then wonders about the broader consequences of the ability to change one's face on a whim: What would it do to social and romantic relationships? How might it radically change human society in general? Conversely, *The Box Man* explores what happens when someone willingly gives up their identity and wanders the streets of Tokyo with a cardboard box over his head.

Abe's influence is overt in Murakami Haruki's texts. Known internationally for his surrealistic texts that examine memory, isolation, libraries, cats, and Japanese history, Murakami has been inspired by such authors as Richard Brautigan and Kurt Vonnegut.[31] Many of his novels have just the slightest tinge of surrealism, yet even that small amount colors his narratives enough to make them seem speculative. His *Rat* series, which includes *Hear the Wind Sing* (1979; 1987), *Pinball, 1973* (1980; 1985), *A Wild Sheep Chase* (1982; 1989), and *Dance Dance Dance* (1988; 1994),[32] follows various characters' meandering thoughts and obsessions about everything from pinball to sheep. Appearing throughout these novels are, for example, one-armed beachcombing poets, psychic teenagers, and twins who seem to appear out of nowhere. Murakami's *Hard-Boiled Wonderland and the End of the World* (1985; 1991) seems to leave "reality" as we know it far behind. This is two narratives in one: a work of cyberpunk (the odd-numbered chapters) and a work of fantasy (even-numbered chapters). The "Hard-Boiled Wonderland" chapters revolve around two systems fighting over data and a human data processor who uses his subconscious as an encryption key, while the "End of the World" section focuses on a newcomer to a Town whose residents do not have shadows or even minds. The newcomer, who is also the narrator, reads dreams from unicorn skulls in order to help with the process of purging "mind" from the Town; eventually, we learn that the Town is actually the world inside of the Hard-Boiled Wonderland narrator's subconscious.

Murakami's magical-realist novel *The Wind-Up Bird Chronicle* (1994–95; 1997) is reminiscent of Abe's *Secret Rendezvous* in that both become stories about husbands desperately searching for their wives and falling into alternate realities along the way. *Kafka on the Shore* (2002; 2005), like *Hard-Boiled Wonderland*, tells a story through alternating chapters, this time about an Oedipal curse and a murder. Both *Sputnik Sweetheart* (1999; 2001) and *After Dark* (2004; 2007) explore how sexual desire and dreams can lead characters onto unexpected paths, with the speculative aspects lingering on the margins of each text. Murakami's *1Q84* (2009–10; 2011), structured like *Hard-Boiled Wonderland* and *Kafka on the Shore*, also highlights how easily we can shift from one version of our lives to another. As one reviewer explains, "*1Q84* offers itself as a kind of revision to 1984, not a parallel universe but a rewritten one, one that erases the prior universe and writes over it, right on top, over what was there before."[33]

Murakami's latest novel in English, *Killing Commendatore* (2017; 2018), takes up questions about the power of art and how stories are told. When a portrait painter in his thirties is abandoned by his wife, he flees to the home of a famous artist and finds a mysterious painting of a scene from Mozart's opera *Don Giovanni*. The discovery of mysterious ringing bells underground near the artist's house leads to the portrait painter's further discovery of a two-foot-tall manifestation of Commendatore from the painting. As in several other Murakami novels, the existence of a pit, references to the underworld and adventures through it, and skewed relationships combine to form a mazelike story just as mysterious as the two-foot-tall Commendatore himself.

Three collections of Murakami stories have also been translated into English since 1993: *The Elephant Vanishes* (2005; 1993),[34] *after the quake* (2000; 2002),[35] and *Blind Willow, Sleeping Woman* (2006). In these stories, Murakami focuses on a single incident or idea: elephants suddenly vanish into thin air, little green monsters literally emerge from the ground, and giant talking frogs help save Tokyo from destruction. The stories in *after the quake*, specifically, deal with the fallout from the 1995 Kobe earthquake. Despite these fantastical and grotesque elements, or perhaps because of them, Murakami has been embraced by genre and nongenre readers around the world. Indeed, his slightly skewed realities offer interesting windows on our own view of "reality."

Several other Japanese authors who write about the surreality of modern life have been translated into English since 2010. The novels and stories of Hoshino Tomoyuki, Sakuraba Kazuki, Sato Yuya, Kawakami Hiromi, and Yū Miri reveal the breadth of styles and themes that contribute to a new understanding of global fantasy and the subgenres associated with it. While Hoshino, Sato, Kawakami, and Yū write magical-realist novels and stories that reveal an unseen dimension to everyday life, Sakuraba veers further into a kind of high fantasy and even horror.

Sakuraba Kazuki's two novels in English—*Red Girls: The Legend of the Akakuchibas* (2006; 2015) and *A Small Charred Face* (2014; 2017)—demonstrate the author's literary versatility. The former focuses on three women in the Akakuchiba family and links the passing of each generation to Japan's quickly changing postwar society, asking us to consider how each matriarch deals with the expectations and hardships of her particular cultural moment.[36] The matriarch of the family, Manyo Tada is clairvoyant, and many random images prove to be flashes of future events and people. *Red Girls* is especially noteworthy because it was written and translated by women and explores three generations of a family through its female members. Sakuraba's *A Small Charred Face* walks the (blurry) line between fantasy and horror in its depiction of vampires and their relationship to humans.

Through the magical realism of the collection *We, the Children of Cats* (2012) and the surrealism of the novel *Me* (2010; 2017), Hoshino Tomoyuki is able to bring together such disparate elements as modern technology, traditional Japanese folklore, and Latin American literature. The stories in his collection are themselves attempts to make meaning out of the incomprehensible: people suddenly sprout new body parts; investigations lead to the criminal underworld, secret societies, and ghosts; and characters, like Hoshino himself, travel to Latin America and encounter a radically different culture to which they must adapt. In *Me*, a young man named Hitoshi Nagano employs a popular telephone scam to trick a woman into sending him money (since she believes he is her son). To his astonishment, Hitoshi soon finds that the woman he scammed continues to believe that he is her son, and Hitoshi's real parents no longer recognize him (they have a "new" son). As in Abe's *The Face of Another* and *The Box Man*, Hoshino explores the malleability of identity and its relation to changing technology and familial relations.

Family dynamics and the relationship of the individual to her community are at the heart of Sato Yuya's intense and magnetic novel *Dendera* (2009; 2015).[37] Here old women who are left to die on a mountaintop (as per village tradition) have set up a small hardscrabble community on the other side of the mountain, eking out an existence in the face of brutal cold and hungry wild animals. Throughout *Dendera*, Kayu and the other women debate the nature of "Paradise," whether it exists or not, and if being rescued forever bars a woman from entering it when she does die. Ultimately, discussions about mortality, custom, and the afterlife bring to the surface all of the seething tensions in the community and each woman's individual goals—destroy the village, continue to build up Dendera, or wait for death.

Kawakami Hiromi's *Record of a Night Too Brief* (1996; 2017) and Yū Miri's *Tokyo Ueno Station* (2014; 2019) both posit a ghost world that exists within our own. In Kawakami's collection of three stories, a woman goes on a dreamlike journey with companions of porcelain and mist, another woman mourns her brother who is invisible to everyone but her, and a shopgirl discovers that people throughout the city are hiding snake families for some unknown reason. Yū's novel tells the story of one man who, through a series of strange coincidences, finds his life tied to that of Japan's imperial family and a single spot in Tokyo—a park near Ueno Station. A laborer in the construction for the 1964 Olympics in Tokyo, Kazu eventually lives with other homeless people in the park, haunting the place after he dies. Traumatized by the 2011 tsunami and angered by the announcement of the 2020 Olympics, Kazu's is ultimately a story about the divide between rich and poor in Japan and the major events and disasters that marked the nation in the twentieth century.

HORROR

In terms of numbers, Japanese horror in translation is second only to its science fiction counterpart. Indeed, Suzuki Koji, Japanese horror's most well-known author in the Anglophone world, has ten books in English, four of which form an internationally acclaimed tetralogy. Like Suzuki, several of Japan's other horror writers (including Murakami Ryu, Nonami Asa, and Ogawa Yoko) move easily between subgenres, often mixing horror with science fiction or surrealism.[38]

Thanks to the numerous film adaptations of his novels and stories, Suzuki is already well known in the Anglosphere. Winner of numerous awards, Suzuki often focuses on the idea that "modernity brings the means to replicate viruses of all kinds—genes or memes, good or bad—on a truly, and often terrifyingly global, scale."[39] This is the major theme in the four books that make up the Ring series—a horror/science fiction hybrid about a psychic virus that spreads through various media, including film, video, and television. We are first introduced to the deadly virus in *Ring (Ring #1)* (1991; 2003), where a haunted bit of film kills whoever views it unless that viewer shows it to someone else. *Spiral (Ring #2)* (1995; 2004), which can be read as a stand-alone novel or as part of the *Ring* universe, reveals that the virus began with the murder of a psychic named Sadako Yamamura, who is able to resurrect herself through one of the virus's victims. We also learn the virus comes in two forms: an active one that is highly lethal and a dormant one that can be triggered by Sadako. Suzuki destabilizes the reader's understanding of the *Ring* stories in *Loop (Ring #3)* (1998; 2005), suggesting that the first two books in the series actually took place in a virtual-reality (VR) simulation, whose observers have now contracted the very same virus. The stories in *Birthday (Ring #4)* (1999; 2006) return readers to the *Ring* universe but at different points in time and examine different characters more closely. Suzuki's other horror collection, *Dark Water* (1996; 2006), was originally published in Japanese while Suzuki was publishing the *Ring* books, though it isn't set in that universe. Each story centers on water in one way or another, with characters abandoning other characters at sea, fishermen experiencing strange headaches, mysterious abandoned ships, and more.

As happens with other non-Anglophone authors whose later work is translated into English and becomes popular, making way for translations of their earlier work, Suzuki's first published novel in Japanese came out in English only after the *Ring* stories had become immensely popular. *Paradise* (1990; 2006) focuses on two prehistoric lovers who find themselves separated by the Bering Strait.[40] Their love is so strong, however, that their descendants in the nineteenth and twentieth centuries find themselves mysteriously attracted to one another across vast distances, guided by a spirit that wants them to be together. *Promenade of the Gods* (2003; 2008), written after the *Ring* novels, does refer to them here and there, though the novel isn't set in the same universe. *Promenade* does, however, share the *Ring* books' interest in mysterious disappearances. Here, a woman goes in search of her husband, who disappeared after watching a particular television show. Eventually, the wife, along with one of her husband's friends, realizes that the famous female personality on that show disappeared after the broadcast, too. Their search leads them ultimately to a bizarre religious cult.

Suzuki's latest two novels in English—*Edge* (2008; 2012) and *S (Es)* (2012; 2017)—draw once again on tropes developed in the *Ring* books: disappearances and a mysterious global threat. In *Edge*, the shifting of the San Andreas fault destroys California, but this catastrophe only highlights a much more menacing threat: the fact that, for some reason, the world at the quantum level is no longer stable. Like Komatsu's *Japan Sinks*, *Edge* examines how the Japanese people at a particular point in history might react to a massive natural disaster. Unlike *Edge*, *S (Es)* is connected to the *Ring* books, since its protagonist, Takanori Ando, is the son of *Spiral*'s main character, Mitsuo. Once more, a video clip (this time of a suicide) takes center stage, mutating each time Ando watches it and revealing the strange connections between Ando's fiancée, the psychic Sadako, and the philosophy professor Ryuji Takayama.

Though Murakami Ryu's four novels available in English translation are not all works of horror, three of them are gruesome enough to classify Murakami often as a horror writer. His *Coin Locker Babies* (1980; 1995), the first in translation, is more of a cyberpunk thriller in which two children orphaned at a train station grow up vowing to find and kill the women who rejected them. Along the way, these two boys become drawn to a shady area of Tokyo known as "Toxitown," and one unfolds a plan in prison to murder the people of Tokyo with an experimental chemical agent. It is with *In the Miso Soup* (1997; 2003) that Murakami explores in more depth the possibilities of the horror genre.[41] Here an American tourist (Frank) hires a Japanese guide (Kenji) to take him on a tour of Tokyo's sleazy nightlife. Though Kenji does this sort of thing often, there's something about Frank that makes him suspect that the American is actually the serial killer who is currently terrorizing Tokyo.

Murakami's *Audition* (1997; 2009) tells the story of a widower and documentary filmmaker (Aoyama) who is eager to remarry and his best friend who suggests that he hold fake auditions in order to find the woman of his dreams. Aoyama thinks he has found that woman in Asami, even when he learns of her troubled past. And though she disappears for a while, Asami returns to brutally torture the unsuspecting Aoyama. *From the Fatherland with Love* (2005; 2013), Murakami's latest work in translation, is a work of dystopian horror in which Japan's economy has collapsed and North Korea decides to invade the island. At the news of the invasion, the terrorist Ishihara and his group turn their attention away from the Japanese government and toward stopping the North Koreans. As usual, Murakami doesn't shy away from violence and gore in describing the terrorist group's clash with the enemy.

Nonami Asa's two books available in English are straightforward horror: *Now You're One of Us* (1993; 2007) is a work of domestic horror, while *Body* (1999; 2009) is a collection of stories devoted to people's perceptions of their own bodies. In Nonami's novel, a young woman named Noriko marries into a close-knit family, of which her husband is the eldest son. At first, Noriko just finds the eight members (multiple generations) somewhat quirky, but then she begins to suspect everything from murderous intent to incest. *Now You're One of Us* explores the strong bonds of kinship in Japanese culture while infusing it all with a creeping, surreal horror. The horror in *Body* is more of a physical kind, not surprisingly. Each story ("Buttocks," "Blood," "Face," "Hair," and "Chin") explores the consequences of everything from vanity to low self-esteem, and each title comes from the body part with which its main character is obsessed. The outcomes of these stories are chilling not just because of what happens but also because these characters are trying to improve their lives and end up doing the opposite.

A less physical but perhaps more sinister kind of horror informs the work of Ogawa Yoko. With a collection of three novellas, another collection of eleven stories, and a novel, Ogawa has become better known in the Anglophone world within the past decade. Her novellas in *The Diving Pool* (2008) are not so much works of horror as of sinister surrealism, with hallucinations, infatuations, and mysterious relationships causing the characters to question their own sanity. Whether lonely, jealous, or gripped by nostalgia, the women at the center of these novellas find that they have desires and fears they'd never recognized before. *Revenge: Eleven Dark Tales* (1998; 2013) includes stories with such titles as "Welcome to the Museum of Torture" and "Sewing for the Heart," revealing Ogawa's skill in unmasking the grotesque and terrifying that pulsate beneath everyday reality.[42] Characters are connected to one another across stories, making this collection what one reviewer called "a beautiful, lethal web."[43] In one story, a surgeon's lover threatens to kill him if he doesn't leave his wife. In the following story, the same surgeon meets a woman whose heart beats *outside* of her body.

This woman's request of a bag maker to design her a purse that will hold her heart becomes the subject of the next story, and so on.

Ogawa turns to psychological horror and the craft of writing itself in her novel *The Memory Police* (1994; 2019).[44] Set on an unnamed island, this is a story of disappearances and the rare ability to *remember* that which has disappeared. It is up to the eponymous police to make sure that what disappears stays lost *and* forgotten. Ultimately, a novelist who realizes that her editor might be arrested by the Memory Police decides to hide him under her floor, with her writing as the only way to make sure that the past is not completely forgotten.

In contrast to Ogawa's surrealistic and psychological horror, the work of Asamatsu Ken is firmly in the Lovecraftian cosmic-horror mode. Heavily influenced by this subgenre, Asamatsu has not only written many of his own novels and stories exploring the visceral horror of monsters and evil spirits, but also edited several collections of such stories for Kurodahan Press. In *Queen of K'n-Yan* (1993; 2008), Asamatsu imagines what would happen if archaeologists discovered a mummy from China's Shang dynasty that contained reptilian DNA.[45] Transferred to a Japanese lab, the mummy begins to reveal its secrets, sending one researcher into strange hallucinations of another time and place, suggesting that some kind of prehuman intelligence inhabited Earth aeons before. Cosmic horror meets alternate reality in Asamatsu's most recent collection in English. A group of stories written on the theme of evil as manifested in Nazism and the monstrous creatures created and developed by H. P. Lovecraft as part of his Cthulhu mythos, *Kthulhu Reich* (1999; 2019) offers readers a unique perspective on this mashup.[46] And while some nonfiction has been written about the Nazis' interest in black magic and ancient monsters, Asamatsu asks us what might have happened had their involvement in the occult actually yielded results.

The horror that we get from Otsuichi (who is also known for his dark fantasy) comes to us exclusively in the form of short stories and novellas. Both *Zoo* (2003; 2009) and *Goth* (2015) are collections of short fiction about everything from slow-working death traps, haunted parks, and refrigerators filled with hands to people buried alive and pits filled with dead dogs. Otsuichi's *Summer, Fireworks, and My Corpse* (2000; 2010) includes two short novels and an extra short story. In the title story, a group of children kills a nine-year-old girl, and it is she who tells us how she was murdered and how the children try to get away with their crime. "Yuko" involves a young housemaid who works for an aging couple, though she never sees the wife—that is, until she walks into one of the rooms and finds the wife surrounded by dolls, looking like a doll herself. Finally, "The Black Fairy" is a three-part fairy-tale meditation on vision and memory, involving a young girl who receives an eye transplant but can then "see" the experiences of the eye's previous dead owner.

Alongside the various kinds of horror in English discussed above, Vertical and Haikasoru have also brought us the work of Takami Koushun, Kishi Yusuke, Sena Hideaki, Kyogoku Natsuhiko, and Maijō Ōtarō. Takami's **Battle Royale** (1999; 2003), a novel about high school students forced to fight one another to the death by an authoritarian government, quickly became a best seller in Japan and was adapted into a manga series and a feature film, as well as a sequel. We find a similar scenario in Kishi's **The Crimson Labyrinth** (1999; 2006), only instead of students in a fascist alternate Japan we have characters from the socioeconomic periphery getting dropped into a desolate area of Australia to play an obscure game for no apparent reason. At one point, the players have access to a book (also called *The Crimson Labyrinth*) that is set on Mars and is supposed to function as a guide.

Sena's science fiction horror novel **Parasite Eve** (1995; 2008) brings together issues surrounding human evolution, reincarnation, and consciousness.[47] Here Sena imagines a world in which mitochondria, which are inherited through female lines of descent, are part of a larger consciousness named "Eve" that has been waiting throughout human evolution to achieve its potential and cause the birth of a child that can control its own genetic code. Alternately, Kyogoku's work of fantastic horror **The Summer of the Ubume** (1994; 2009) draws on Japanese folklore concerning the ghost that arises from the burial of a pregnant woman. In Kyogoku's novel (which is part of a larger, and so far untranslated, series), an exorcist named Kyogokudo who doesn't believe in spirits learns about a woman who has been pregnant for nearly two years and whose husband has mysteriously disappeared. Over the course of the investigation, Kyogokudo learns more than he ever wanted to know about the *ubume* legend.

Maijo's horror thriller **Asura Girl** (2003; 2014) focuses on the teenage Aiko, who lives in a brutal, violent area of town. When she learns that a recent fling has been kidnapped and that a serial killer is going around killing children, Aiko realizes that something terrible is stalking the streets. Furthering the chaos is an Internet bulletin board known as "the Voice from Heaven" that is encouraging young people to riot. Aiko posts a demand for her own murder on the board in order to draw out the individual who is responsible for the reign of terror.

Rounding out the rich and vibrant corpus of Japanese horror fiction in English are the four Kurodahan anthologies (edited by Asamatsu Ken) that collect the best horror stories from some of Japan's greatest genre writers. Collectively titled **Lairs of the Hidden Gods**, the individual volumes are: *Night Voices, Night Journeys* (2005), *Inverted Kingdom* (2005), *Straight to Darkness* (2006), and *The Dreaming God* (2007). Included in these anthologies are stories about madness-inducing creatures looking for hosts in post–World War II Japan, sacrificial cults, Kabuki horror writers, strange scars, the Old Ones, and much more. With introductions to each story by Robert Price and essays about modern occultism and Lovecraft, the *Lairs of the Hidden Gods* anthologies are crucial volumes to any understanding of modern and contemporary Japanese horror.

Kurodahan's most recent anthology of Japanese horror focuses on the figure of the vampire. In *Vampiric: Tales of Blood and Roses* (2019), we learn about how Japan has blended its own vampire tradition with that of the West over the course of the centuries to produce terrifying and sensual hybrids. Here we read about the complicated literary tradition of *kyūketsuki* ("blood-sucking monster") and how it's evolved over time and generally just how malleable the vampire subgenre continues to be.

ANTHOLOGIES

Several anthologies of Japanese speculative fiction in translation have been published since 2000, with the bulk of them coming from Kurodahan Press in the form of the *Speculative Japan* series. Others focus on speculative fiction but include both translated and Anglophone texts, while one (creatively titled *Monkey Brain Sushi*) showcases Japanese speculative fiction alongside other genres.

In 2002, both Kodansha International (*Monkey Brain Sushi* and Dalkey Archive's *Review of Contemporary Fiction* showcased work by Ōhara Mariko and Murakami Haruki, introducing audiences otherwise unfamiliar with their stories to two writers whose visions and styles are quite different. The *Review of Contemporary Fiction* also offered Anglophone readers stories by Aramaki ("Soft Clocks"), Takahashi Genichiro ("Ghostbusters—an Adventure Story"), and Tsutsui ("Just a Nobody"). Edited by Tatsumi Takayuki and Larry McCaffrey, this sampling of texts highlights the range of contemporary Japanese SFT for a mostly non-genre-reading audience.

Just a few years later, Kurodahan Press launched its *Speculative Japan* series— the culmination of decades of work by Judith Merril, Gene van Troyer, Grania Davis, and the many Japanese translators they worked with in the 1970s. In a preface to the first volume, David Brin champions this volume by arguing that "in much the same way that Hokusai offered us thirty-six views of Mount Fuji, the stories that you'll find collected here will broaden your view of what is possible or imaginable, provoking unusual—and sometimes uncomfortable—thoughts. That is as it should be."[48] Here Van Troyer and Davis include stories—overwhelmingly in the science fiction subgenre—by Komatsu Sakyo ("The Savage Mouth"), Kono Tensei ("Hikari"), Ohara Mariko ("Girl"—her most anthologized translated story), Tsutsui Yasutaka ("Standing Woman"), and several others. With *Speculative Japan 2* (2011) and the arrival of editor Edward Lipsett to Kurodahan, the range of stories expanded to include surrealism, magical realism, and fantasy. The publication of *Speculative Japan 3*[49] in 2012 and then *Speculative Japan 4* in 2018 gave Anglophone readers the chance to read more Asamatsu Ken, Ogawa

Issui, Ueda Sayuri, and Kaijo Shinji. Here we have stories about, for instance, friendship and love transcending space, time, and the human body (Masaya's "Angel French") and the end of evolution (Yuri's "The Finish Line"). These two anthologies continued Lipsett's efforts to showcase the diversity and richness of Japanese science fiction, fantasy, horror, surrealism, and more.

Haikasoru came out with its own anthology of Japanese stories in 2012, though the editors' approach was to blend translated tales by Japanese writers with Anglophone stories about or set in Japan. In *The Future Is Japanese*, Ken Liu's "Mono no Aware" rubs shoulders with Ogawa Issui's "The Golden Bread," and stories by EnJoe Toh and Project Itoh share space with those by well-known Anglophone authors such as Catherynne M. Valente and Bruce Sterling. Just three years later, Haikasoru brought out a themed anthology titled *Hanzai Japan: Futuristic Stories of Crime from and about Japan* (2015), again with a mix of translated and Anglophone stories.[50] Here are stories about, for example, vampires living in a near-future Japan, a talking map, a morphing tattoo, and a high school girl who brings down Japan's technological infrastructure. *Hanzai Japan* is a space where East and West collide and commingle, where speculative fiction authors write mysteries and crime stories and crime writers delve into the fantastical and supernatural.

Japanese culture itself has embraced speculative fiction in its various forms, and Japan's robust fandom and professional publications continue to encourage young writers inspired by their predecessors of the previous century. For all of these reasons and others, Japanese SFT has a bright future and Anglophone audiences can expect many more brilliant and mind-bending works from the most innovative Japanese authors.

Primary Sources

1937: Unno Jūza. *Science: Hopes and Fears (Volume 2: Eighteen O'Clock Music Bath)*. Translated by J. D. Wisgo. Independently published, 2018.

1958–59: Abe Kōbō. *Inter Ice Age 4*. Translated by E. Dale Saunders. Alfred A. Knopf, 1970.

1962: Abe Kōbō. *Woman in the Dunes*. Translated by E. Dale Saunders. Alfred A. Knopf, 1964.

1964: Abe Kōbō. *The Face of Another.* Translated by E. Dale Saunders. Alfred A. Knopf, 1966. Komatsu Sakyo. *Virus: The Day of Resurrection*. Translated by Daniel Huddleston. Haikasoru, 2012.

1966: Hoshi Shinichi. *The Capricious Robot*. Translated by Robert Matthew. Kodansha International, 1986.

1967: Abe Kōbō. *The Ruined Map.* Translated by E. Dale Saunders. Alfred A. Knopf, 1969.

Mitsuse Ryu. *Ten Billion Days and One Hundred Billion Nights.* Translated by Alexander O. Smith with Elye J. Alexander. Haikasoru, 2011.

1968: Tsutsui Yasutaka. *The African Bomb, and Other Stories.* Translated by David Lewis. Kodansha English Library, 1986.

1972: Tsutsui Yasutaka. *What the Maid Saw: Eight Psychic Tales.* Translated by Adam Kabat. Kodansha International, 1990.

1973: Abe Kōbō. *The Box Man.* Translated by E. Dale Saunders. Alfred A. Knopf, 1974.

Komatsu Sakyo. *Japan Sinks.* Translated by Michael Gallagher. Harper & Row, 1976.

1977: Abe Kōbō. *Secret Rendezvous.* Translated by Juliet Winters Carpenter. Alfred A. Knopf, 1979.

1978: Aramaki Yoshio. *The Sacred Era.* Translated by Baryon Tensor Posadas. University of Minnesota Press, 2017.

Hoshi Shinichi. *The Spiteful Planet, and Other Stories.* Translated by Bernard Susser and Tomoyoshi Genkawa. Japan Times.

1979: Murakami Haruki. *Hear the Wind Sing (Rat #1).* Translated by Alfred Birnbaum. Kodansha English Library, 1987. Released only in Japan.

1980: Murakami Haruki. *Pinball, 1973 (Rat #2).* Translated by Alfred Birnbaum. Kodansha English Library, 1985. Released only in Japan; retranslated and released in UK later.

Murakami Ryu. *Coin Locker Babies.* Translated by Stephen Snyder. Kodansha International, 1995.

1982: Murakami Haruki. *A Wild Sheep Chase (Rat #3).* Translated by Alfred Birnbaum. Kodansha English Library, 1989. Released only in Japan.

Tanaka Yoshiki. *Legend of the Galactic Heroes (Volume 1: Dawn).* Translated by Daniel Huddleston. Haikasoru, 2016.

1983: Tanaka Yoshiki. *Legend of the Galactic Heroes (Volume 2: Ambition).* Translated by Daniel Huddleston. Haikasoru, 2016.

Tani Kōshū. *The Erinys Incident.* Translated by Simon Varnam. Kurodahan Press, 2018.

1984: Abe Kobo. *The Ark Sakura.* Translated by Juliet Winters Carpenter. Alfred A. Knopf, 1988.

Chōhei Kambayashi. *Yukikaze.* Translated by Neil Nadelman. Haikasoru, 2010.

Hoshi Shinichi. *The God with the Laughing Face.* Translated by Robert Matthew. University of Queensland.

———. *The Leisure Club.* Translated by Robert Matthew. University of Queensland.

———. *There Was a Knock.* Translated by Stanleigh H. Jones. Kodansha International.

———. *The Visitor from Space.* Translated by Robert Matthew. University of Queensland.

Kawamata Chiaki. *Death Sentences.* Translated by Thomas Lamarre and Kazuko Y. Behrens. University of Minnesota Press, 2012.

Tanaka Yoshiki. *Legend of the Galactic Heroes (Volume 3: Endurance).* Translated by Daniel Huddleston. Haikasoru, 2016.

———. *Legend of the Galactic Heroes (Volume 4: Stratagem).* Translated by Tyran Grillo. Haikasoru, 2017.

1985: Hoshi Shinichi. *The Cost of Kindness, and Other Fabulous Tales.* Translated by
       Marianne MacDonald and Torajiro Mori. C and P.
       Murakami Haruki. Hard-Boiled Wonderland and the End of the World. Translated
       by Alfred Birnbaum. Kodansha International, 1991.
       Tanaka Yoshiki. *Legend of the Galactic Heroes (Volume 5: Mobilization).* Translated
       by Tyran Grillo. Haikasoru, 2017.
       ———. *Legend of the Galactic Heroes (Volume 6: Flight).* Translated by Tyran Grillo.
       Haikasoru, 2018.
1986: Tanaka Yoshiki. *Legend of the Galactic Heroes (Volume 7: Tempest).* Translated by
       Daniel Huddleston. Haikasoru, 2018.
1987: Tanaka Yoshiki. *Legend of the Galactic Heroes (Volume 8: Desolation).* Translated by
       Matt Treyvaud. Haikasoru, 2018.
       ———. *Legend of the Galactic Heroes (Volume 9: Upheaval).* Translated by Matt
       Treyvaud. Haikasoru, 2019.
       ———. *Legend of the Galactic Heroes (Volume 10: Sunset).* Translated by Matt
       Treyvaud. Haikasoru, 2019.
       Yamada Masaki. *Aphrodite.* Translated by Daniel Jackson. Kurodahan Press,
       2004.
1988: Murakami Haruki. *Dance Dance Dance (Rat #4).* Translated by Alfred Birnbaum.
       Kodansha International, 1994.
1989: Apostolou, John L., and Martin Harry Greenberg, eds. *The Best Japanese Science
       Fiction Stories.* Dembner Books.
       Hoshi Shinichi. *The Bag of Surprises.* Translated by Stanleigh H. Jones. Kodansha
       International.
       ———. *The God of Television: Twenty Short Stories.* Translated by Robert Matthew.
       Asiapac.
       ———. *Tales of Japanese Science Fiction and Fantasy.* Selected and translated by
       Robert Matthew. University of Queensland Press.
1990: Ogawa Yōko. *The Diving Pool.* Translated by Stephen Snyder. Picador USA, 2008.
       Ōhara Mariko. *Hybrid Child.* Translated by Jodie Beck. University of Minnesota
       Press, 2018.
       Suzuki Kōji. *Paradise.* Translated by Tyran Grillo. Vertical, 2006.
1991: Abe Kōbō. *Beyond the Curve.* Translated by Juliet Winters Carpenter. Kodansha
       International.
       ———. *Kangaroo Notebook.* Translated by Maryellen Toman Mori. Alfred A. Knopf,
       1996.
       Birnbaum, Alfred, ed. *Monkey Brain Sushi: New Tastes in Japanese Fiction.* Kodansha
       International.
       Hoshi Shinichi. *The God of Fortune.* Translated by Robert Matthew. Asiapac.
       Suzuki Kōji. *Ring (Ring #1).* Translated by Robert B. Rohmer and Glynne Walley.
       Vertical, 2003.

1993: Asamatsu Ken. *Queen of K'n-Yan*. Translated by Kathleen Taji. Kurodahan Press, 2008.

Nonami Asa. *Now You're One of Us*. Translated by Michael Volek and Mitsuko Volek. Vertical, 2007.

Tsutsui Yasutaka. *Paprika*. Translated by Andrew Driver. Alma Books, 2009.

1994: Kyogoku Natsuhiko. *The Summer of the Ubume*. Translated by Alexander O. Smith. Vertical, 2009.

Ogawa Yōko. *The Memory Police*. Translated by Stephen Snyder. Pantheon Books, 2019.

1994–95: Murakami Haruki. *The Wind-Up Bird Chronicle*. Translated by Jay Rubin. Alfred A. Knopf, 1997.

1995: Sena Hideaki. *Parasite Eve*. Translated by Tyran Grillo. Vertical, 2008.

Suzuki Kōji. *Spiral (Ring #2)*. Translated by Glynne Walley. Vertical, 2004.

1996: Kawakami Hiromi. *Record of a Night Too Brief*. Translated by Lucy North. Pushkin Press, 2017.

Suzuki Kōji. *Dark Water*. Translated by Glynne Walley. Vertical, 2006.

1997: Murakami Ryu. *Audition*. Translated by Ralph McCarthy. Bloomsbury, 2009.

———. *In the Miso Soup*. Translated by Ralph McCarthy. Kodansha International, 2003.

1998: Ogawa Yōko. *Revenge: Eleven Dark Tales*. Translated by Stephen Snyder. Picador USA, 2013.

Suzuki Kōji. *Loop (Ring #3)*. Translated by Glynne Walley. Vertical, 2005.

1999: Asamatsu Ken. *Kthulhu Reich*. Translated by Jim Rion. Kurodahan Press, 2019.

Chōhei Kambayashi. *Good Luck, Yukikaze*. Translated by Neil Nadelman. Haikasoru, 2011.

Kishi Yusuke. *The Crimson Labyrinth*. Translated by Masami Isetani and Camellia Nieh. Vertical, 2006.

Murakami Haruki. *Sputnik Sweetheart*. Translated by Philip Gabriel. Alfred A. Knopf, 2001.

Nonami Asa. *Bødy*. Translated by Takami Nieda. Vertical, 2009.

Suzuki Kōji. *Birthday (Ring #4)*. Translated by Glynne Walley. Vertical, 2006.

Takami Koushun. *Battle Royale*. Translated by Yuji Oniki. Viz Media, 2003.

2000: Murakami Haruki. *after the quake*. Translated by Jay Rubin. Alfred A. Knopf, 2002.

Otsuichi. *Summer, Fireworks, and My Corpse*. Translated by Nathan Collins. Haikasoru, 2010.

2001: Kitano Yusaku. *Mr. Turtle*. Translated by Tyran Grillo. Kurodahan Press, 2016.

Kyogoku Natsuhiko. *Loups-Garous*. Translated by Anne Ishii. Haikasoru, 2010.

2002: Hayashi Jyouji. *The Ouroboros Wave*. Translated by Jim Hubbert. Haikasoru, 2010.

Murakami Haruki. *Kafka on the Shore*. Translated by Philip Gabriel. Harvill Secker, 2005.

Nojiri Housuke. *Usurper of the Sun*. Translated by Joseph Reeder. Haikasoru, 2009.

Tatsumi Takayuki, and Larry McCaffery, eds. *The Review of Contemporary Fiction: XXII, #2: New Japanese Fiction*. Dalkey Archive Press.

Tobi Hirotaka. *The Thousand Year Beach*. Translated by Matt Treyvaud. Haikasoru, 2018.

2003: Maijō Ōtarō. *Asura Girl*. Translated by Stephen Snyder. Haikasoru, 2014.

Ogawa Issui. *The Next Continent*. Translated by Jim Hubbert. Haikasoru, 2010.

Otsuichi. *Zoo*. Translated by Terry Gallagher. Haikasoru, 2009.

Suzuki Kōji. *Promenade of the Gods*. Translated by Takami Nieda. Vertical, 2008.

Tsutsui Yasutaka. *Hell*. Translated by Evan Emswiler. Alma Books, 2007.

Ubukata Tow. *Mardock Scramble*. Translated by Edwin Hawkes. Haikasoru, 2011.

2004: Murakami Haruki. *After Dark*. Translated by Jay Rubin. Alfred A. Knopf, 2007.

Sazurazaka Hiroshi. *All You Need Is Kill*. Translated by Alexander O. Smith. Haikasoru, 2009.

Ueda Sayuri. *The Cage of Zeus*. Translated by Takami Nieda. Haikasoru, 2011.

2005: Asamatsu Ken, ed. *Inverted Kingdom (Lairs of the Hidden Gods #2)*. Kurodahan Press.

———, ed. *Night Voices, Night Journeys (Lairs of the Hidden Gods #1)*. Kurodahan Press.

Furukawa Hideo. *Belka, Why Don't You Bark?* Translated by Michael Emmerich. Haikasoru, 2012.

Murakami Haruki. *The Elephant Vanishes*. Translated by Jay Rubin and Alfred Birnbaum. Alfred A. Knopf, 1993.

Murakami Ryu. *From the Fatherland with Love*. Translated by Ralph McCarthy, Charles De Wolf, and Ginny Tapley Takemori. Pushkin Press, 2013.

Tsutsui Yasutaka. *Salmonella Men on Planet Porno*. Translated by Andrew Driver. Alma Books, 2006.

2006: Asamatsu Ken, ed. *Straight to Darkness (Lairs of the Hidden Gods #3)*. Kurodahan Press.

Sakuraba Kazuki. *Red Girls: The Legend of the Akakuchibas*. Translated by Jocelyn Allen. Haikasoru, 2015.

2007: Asamatsu Ken, ed. *The Dreaming God (Lairs of the Hidden Gods #4)*. Kurodahan Press.

EnJoe Toh. *Self-Reference ENGINE*. Translated by Terry Gallagher. Haikasoru, 2013.

Ogawa Issui. *The Lord of the Sands of Time*. Translated by Jim Hubbert. Haikasoru, 2009.

Project Itoh. *Genocidal Organ*. Translated by Edwin Hawkes. Haikasoru, 2012.

Troyer, Gene van, and Grania Davis, eds. *Speculative Japan*. Kurodahan Press.

Yamamoto Hiroshi. *MM9*. Translated by Nathan Collins. Haikasoru, 2012.

2008: Project Itoh. *Harmony*. Translated by Alexander O. Smith. Haikasoru, 2010.

Suzuki Kōji. *Edge*. Translated by Jonathan Lloyd-Davies and Camellia Nieh. Vertical, 2012.

2009: Sato Yuya. *Dendera*. Translated by Nathan Collins and Edwin Hawkes. Haikasoru, 2015.

2009–10: Murakami Haruki. *1Q84*. Translated by Jay Rubin. Harvill Secker, 2011.

2010: Hoshino Tomoyuki. *Me*. Translated by Charles De Wolf. Akashic Books, 2017.

2011: Kobayashi Yasumi, and Ogawa Issui, eds. *Speculative Japan 2: "The Man Who Watched the Sea," and Other Tales of Japanese Science Fiction and Fantasy*. Kurodahan Press.

2012: Fujii Taiyo. *Gene Mapper*. Translated by Jim Hubbert. Haikasoru, 2015.

Hoshino Tomoyuki. *We, the Children of Cats*. Translated by Brian Bergstrom. PM Press.

Lipsett, Edward, ed. *Speculative Japan 3: "Silver Bullet," and Other Tales of Japanese Science Fiction and Fantasy*. Kurodahan Press.

Mamatas, Nick, and Masumi Washington, eds. *The Future Is Japanese*. Haikasoru.

Suzuki Kōji. *S (Es)*. Translated by Greg Gencarello. Vertical, 2017.

2013: Torishima Dempow. *Sisyphean*. Translated by Daniel Huddleston. Haikasoru, 2018.

2014: Fujii Taiyo. *Orbital Cloud*. Translated by Timothy Silver. Haikasoru, 2017.

Sakuraba Kazuki. *A Small Charred Face*. Translated by Jocelyne Allen. Haikasoru, 2017.

Tawada Yōko. *The Emissary* (alternate title: *The Last Children of Tokyo*). Translated by Margaret Mitsutani. New Directions, 2018.

Yū Miri. *Tokyo Ueno Station*. Translated by Morgan Giles. Tilted Axis, 2019.

2015: Ishiguro Tatsuaki. *Biogenesis*. Translated by Brian Watson and James Balzer. Vertical.

Mamatas, Nick, and Masumi Washington, eds. *Hanzai Japan: Fantastical, Futuristic Stories of Crime from and about Japan*. Haikasoru.

Otsuichi. *Goth*. Translated by Andrew Cunningham. Haikasoru.

2016: Mamatas, Nick, ed. *Saiensu Fikushon, 2016*. Haikasoru.

Murakami Haruki. *Blind Willow, Sleeping Woman*. Translated by Philip Gabriel and Jay Rubin. Harvill Secker.

2017: Murakami Haruki. *Killing Commendatore*. Translated by Philip Gabriel and Ted Goossen. Alfred A. Knopf, 2018.

Tsutsui Yasutaka. *Bullseye!* Translated by Andrew Driver. Kurodahan Press.

2018: Lipsett, Edward, ed. *Speculative Japan 4: "Pearls for Mia," and Other Tales*. Kurodahan Press.

Moriyama Tomohito. *Two of Six: A Captain's Dilemma*. Translated by J. D. Wisgo. Amazon Digital Services.

Unno Jūza [Shōichi Sano]. *Science: Hopes and Fears (Volume 1: Selected Stories)*. Translated by J. D. Wisgo. Independently published.

2019: Dubnick, Heather, ed. *Vampiric: Tales of Blood and Roses from Japan*. Kurodahan Press.

Notes

1. Bolton, *Sublime Voices*, 46.

2. Bolton, *Sublime Voices*, 161.

3. Bolton, Csicsery-Ronay, and Tatsumi, *Robot Ghosts and Wired Dreams*, xiii. For an extensive discussion of the development of Japanese SF, see also Yamano's "Japanese SF, Its Originality and Orientation." See also Takayuki, Bolton, and Csicsery-Ronay, "Japanese Science Fiction."

4. Tatsumi, "Generations and Controversies."

5. Both Unno Jūza and Oshikawa Shunrō are considered the "founding fathers" of Japanese science fiction; nonetheless, Anglophone readers haven't had access to their stories. While one collection and one novella of Unno's has been translated into English and published in 2018, Oshikawa remains untranslated as of this printing.

6. See Tatsumi, "Sakyo Komatsu's Planetary Imagination."

7. Matthew, *Japanese Science Fiction*, 66.

8. See Carnes, "Japanese Face of Aesop."

9. Published in the November 1978 issue of the *Magazine of Fantasy and Science Fiction*.

10. See McCaffery and Tatsumi, "Keeping Not Writing."

11. Clements, "Tsutsui Yasutaka."

12. Orthofer review.

13. Cordasco review.

14. Cordasco review.

15. Cordasco review.

16. Hill review.

17. Nicoll review.

18. Cordasco review.

19. Orthofer review.

20. Hungate review.

21. Cordasco review.

22. Cordasco review.

23. Clements, "Fujii, Taiyo."

24. Cordasco review.

25. Cordasco review.

26. Ogawa's *The Next Continent* won the Seiun Award for Best Novel in 2004.

27. *Death Sentence* won the fifth Nihon SF Taishō Award in 1984.

28. The series won the Seiun Award in 1987.

29. See Cordasco, "Guest Post."

30. For more on the connections between Abe and Murakami's texts, see Tensor Posadas's *Double Visions, Double Fictions*. See also Dovale's "Postwar Japan's Hybrid Modernity."

31. Murakami is also a translator, of Truman Capote, Raymond Carver, F. Scott Fitzgerald, John Irving, and Ursula Le Guin into Japanese. For more on Murakami and translation, see Hamada, "Domesticating Wild Sheep."

32. *Hear the Wind Sing* and *A Wild Sheep Chase* were released in English only in Japan.

33. Yu, "World-Shifting."

34. According to the Internet Speculative Fiction Database, this collection was *first* published in Japanese in 2005, *after* its English publication in 1993.

35. Translator Jay Rubin notes in *Haruki Murakami and the Music of Words* that Murakami insisted the title should be all lowercase (255).

36. Cordasco review.

37. Cordasco review.

38. A major Japanese cyberpunk horror film is *Tetsuo: The Iron Man* (1989).

39. Clements, "Suzuki Kōji."

40. *Paradise* won the Japan Fantasy Novel Award.

41. *In the Miso Soup* won Murakami the Yomiuri Prize for fiction in 1997.

42. Alexander review.

43. Rao review.

44. Hebblethwaite review.

45. Dumas, "Monstrous Motherhood."

46. Cordasco review.

47. Orthofer review.

48. Brin, preface to *Speculative Japan*, 5.

49. Cordasco review.

50. Cordasco review.

Secondary Sources

Alexander, Niall. "Best Served Cold: *Revenge* by Yoko Ogawa." *Tor.com* (February 2013). https://www.tor.com/2013/02/04/review-revenge-yoko-ogawa/.

Bolton, Christopher. *Sublime Voices: The Fictional Science and Scientific Fiction of Abe Kobo.* Cambridge, MA: Harvard University Press, 2009.

Bolton, Christopher, Istvan Csicsery-Ronay Jr., and Takayuki Tatsumi, eds. *Robot Ghosts and Wired Dreams*. Minneapolis: University of Minnesota Press, 2007.

Brin, David. Preface to *Speculative Japan*, edited by Gene van Troyer and Grania Davis, 5–6. Kuma-gun, Kumamoto, Japan: Kurodahan Press, 2007.

Carnes, Pack. "The Japanese Face of Aesop: Hoshi Shin'ichi and the Modern Fable Tradition." *Journal of Folklore Research* 29, no. 1 (1992): 1–22.

Clements, Jonathan. "Fujii Taiyō." In *The Encyclopedia of Science Fiction*, edited by John Clute, David Langford, Peter Nicholls, and Graham Sleight. London: Gollancz, updated February 25, 2020. http://www.sf-encyclopedia.com/entry/fujii_taiyo.

———. "Suzuki Kōji." In *The Encyclopedia of Science Fiction*, edited by John Clute, David Langford, Peter Nicholls, and Graham Sleight. London: Gollancz, updated October 21, 2018. http://www.sf-encyclopedia.com/entry/suzuki_koji.

———. "Tsutsui Yasutaka." In *The Encyclopedia of Science Fiction*, edited by John Clute, David Langford, Peter Nicholls, and Graham Sleight. London: Gollancz, updated January 9, 2020. http://www.sf-encyclopedia.com/entry/tsutsui_yasutaka.

Cordasco, Rachel. "Guest Post—*Legend of the Galactic Heroes*." *Locus Magazine* (March 2020). https://locusmag.com/2020/03/rachel-s-cordasco-guest-post-legend-of-the-galactic-heroes/.

———. "Review: *Biogenesis* by Tatsuaki Ishiguro." *SfinTranslation.com* (May 2016). https://www.sfintranslation.com/?p=267.

———. "Review: *Bullseye!* by Yasutaka Tsutsui." *SFinTranslation.com* (August 2017). https://www.sfintranslation.com/?p=2643.

———. "Review: *Dendera* by Yuya Sato." *SFinTranslation.com* (May 2016). https://www.sfintranslation.com/?p=154.

———. "Review: *Gene Mapper* by Taiyo Fujii." *SFinTranslation.com* (May 2016). https://www.sfintranslation.com/?p=232.

———. "Review: *Hanzai Japan: Fantastical, Futuristic Stories of Crime from and about Japan*." *SFinTranslation.com* (May 2016). https://www.sfintranslation.com/?p=215.

———. "Review: *Kthulhu Reich* by Asamatsu Ken." *SFinTranslation.com* (July 2019). https://www.sfintranslation.com/?p=7085.

———. "Review: *Mr. Turtle* by Yusaku Kitano." *SFinTranslation.com* (August 2016). https://www.sfintranslation.com/?p=790.

———. "Review: *The Ouroboros Wave* by Jyouji Hayashi." *SFinTranslation.com* (February 2019). https://www.sfintranslation.com/?p=6344.

———. "Review: *Red Girls: The Legend of the Akakuchibas* by Kazuki Sakuraba." *SFinTranslation.com* (May 2016). https://www.sfintranslation.com/?p=218.

———. "Review: *Sisyphean* by Dempow Torishima." *SFinTranslation.com* (February 2018). https://www.sfintranslation.com/?p=3809.

———. "Review: *Speculative Japan 3* Edited by Edward Lipsett." *SFinTranslation.com* (August 2016). https://www.sfintranslation.com/?p=907.

———. "Review: *Two of Six: A Captain's Dilemma* by Tomohito Moriyama." *SFinTranslation.com* (September 2018). https://www.sfintranslation.com/?p=5379.

———. "*The Sacred Era* by Yoshio Aramaki." *World Literature Today* (September 2017). https://www.worldliteraturetoday.org/2017/september/sacred-era-yoshio-aramaki.

Dovale, Madeline. "Postwar Japan's Hybrid Modernity of In-Betweenness: Historical, Literary, and Social Perspectives." PhD diss., California State University, Long Beach, 2013.

Dumas, Raechel. "Monstrous Motherhood and Evolutionary Horror in Contemporary Japanese Science Fiction." *Science-Fiction Studies* 45, no. 1 (2018): 24–47.

Hamada, Kay S. "Domesticating Wild Sheep: Sociolinguistic Functions and Style in Translations of Haruki Murakami's Fiction." *Journal of Popular Culture* 45, no. 1 (2012): 41–55.

Hebblethwaite, David. "*The Memory Police* by Yōko Ogawa, Translated by Stephen Snyder." *Strange Horizons* (March 2020). http://strangehorizons.com/non-fiction/the-memory-police-by-yoko-ogawa-translated-by-stephen-snyder/.

Hill, Rachel. "*Hybrid Child* by Mariko Ōhara." *Strange Horizons* (October 2018). http://strangehorizons.com/non-fiction/reviews/hybrid-child-by-mariko-ohara/.

Hungate, Andrew. "Yoko Tawada's Dystopian Novel *The Emissary* Delivers a Bitingly Smart Satire of Present-Day Japan." *Words without Borders* (February 2018). https://www.wordswithoutborders.org/book-review/yoko-tawada-dystopian-novel-the-emissary-is-a-bitingly-smart-satire-japan.

Matthew, Robert. *Japanese Science Fiction: A View of a Changing Society.* London: Routledge, 1989.

McCaffery, Larry, and Takayuki Tatsumi. "Keeping Not Writing: An Interview with Yasutaka Tsutsui." *Review of Contemporary Fiction* 22, no. 2 (2002): 202–7.

Nicoll, James. "Party in the Sun." *James Nicoll Reviews* (May 2018). https://jamesdavisnicoll.com/review/party-in-the-sun.

Orthofer, M. A. "*Parasite Eve.*" *Complete Review* (n.d.). http://www.complete-review.com/reviews/japannew/senah.htm.

———. "*Salmonella Men on Planet Porno.*" *Complete Review* (n.d.). http://www.complete-review.com/reviews/japannew/tsutsui.htm.

———. "*Ten Billion Days and One Hundred Billion Nights.*" *Complete Review* (December 2012). http://www.complete-review.com/reviews/trscifi/mitsuser.htm.

Rao, Mythili G. "Yoko Ogawa's *Revenge.*" *Words without Borders* (March 2013). https://www.wordswithoutborders.org/book-review/yoko-ogawas-revenge.

Rubin, Jay. *Haruki Murakami and the Music of Words.* London: Vintage, 2005.

Tatsumi, Takayuki. "Generations and Controversies: An Overview of Japanese Science Fiction, 1957–1997." *Science Fiction Studies* 27 (March 2000). https://www.depauw.edu/sfs/backissues/80/current%20trends.html.

———. "Sakyo Komatsu's Planetary Imagination: Reading *Virus* and *The Day of Resurrection.*" In *Lingua Cosmica: Science Fiction from around the World*, edited by Dale Knickerbocker, 95–106. Urbana: University of Illinois Press, 2018.

Tatsumi, Takayuki, Christopher Bolton, and Istvan Csicsery-Ronay Jr., eds. "Japanese Science Fiction." Special issue, *Science Fiction Studies* 29, pt. 3 (2002). https://www.depauw.edu/sfs/covers/cov88.htm.

Tensor Posadas, Baryon. *Double Visions, Double Fictions: The Doppelganger in Japanese Film and Literature.* Minneapolis: University of Minnesota Press, 2018.

Yamano, Koichi. "Japanese SF, Its Originality and Orientation." Translated by Kazuko Behrens. Edited by Darko Suvin and Takayuki Tatsumi. *Science-Fiction Studies* 21 (March 1994). https://www.depauw.edu/sfs/backissues/62/yamano62art.htm.

Yu, Charles. "World-Shifting: Murakami Haruki's *1Q84.*" *Los Angeles Review of Books*, December 12, 2011. https://lareviewofbooks.org/article/world-shifting-haruki-murakamis-1q84/.

Korean-Language SFT

Introduction

Speculative imagination has a long history in Korea. Its earliest surviving historical texts—*Historical Records of the Three Kingdoms* (1146) and *Memorabilia of the
Three Kingdoms* (1285)—contain marvelous stories about royals, Buddhist monks,
and other important historical figures experiencing or performing supernatural
phenomena. These stories drew their inspiration not only from *chuanqi* (tales of
wonder), an ancient literary genre from Tang China, but also from local myths,
legends, and folktales. In Chosŏn Korea (1392–1910), the speculative imagination further developed in the vernacular novels that flourished after the 1443
introduction of *han'gŭl*, the Korean alphabet. Among the best-known titles are
Kim Man-jung's *The Nine Cloud Dream*, a refined dream-adventure novel that
critiques Confucian society from a Buddhist perspective, and *The Tale of Hong
Kiltong*, a work of epic fiction with a Taoist bandit and wizard as the protagonist.

Inheriting some tropes from premodern literary tradition, the genre of science
fiction came to Korea in the early twentieth century through the translation of
Western writers like Jules Verne, H. G. Wells, and Karel Čapek. Despite making
early inroads as a literature of mass enlightenment, however, the genre failed
to take root in Korean culture during the era of Japan's colonial rule (1910–45).
Among the reasons were the primacy of realism in modern Korean literature, the
scarcity of science education in the colony, and a pervasive sense of alienation,
among Koreans, from imperial technoindustrial modernity.

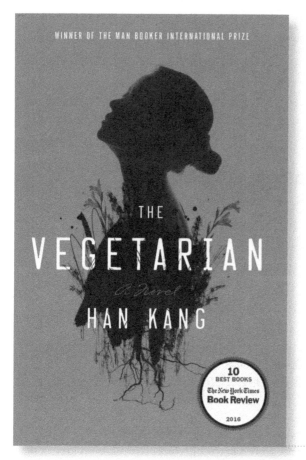

The Vegetarian (2016)

The decisive formation of a science fiction culture in South Korea occurred between the late 1950s and late 1960s. It was then that, under American and Japanese influence, the genre was popularized by works such as Kim Sanho's superhero comic *Ryphie* (1959) and Han Nagwŏn's space race–themed novels for young adults, including *The Venus Expedition* (1964). Also from this era was Mun Yunsŏng's *Perfect Society* (1967), the first SF novel for adults, which partly owed its inspiration to Robert Heinlein's *Stranger in a Strange Land*. The novel projected some of the anxieties of postwar male Korean society onto the dystopian vision of a futuristic Earth that is inhabited only by women.[1] Despite the presence of an ambivalence toward modernization, this first wave of science fiction had an overall techno-utopian tenor, reflective of the period's general aspiration for national development.

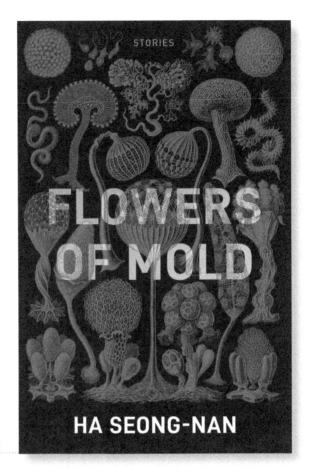

Flowers of Mold (2019)

In contrast with previous eras, in the 1970s and 1980s science fiction took a dystopian turn under the cloud of dictatorship. In particular, the "National Science Campaign" both stimulated science fiction culture and caused a rejection of technoindustrial modernity among South Korean writers, directors, and comic artists. The science fiction from this period indeed formed a minor but important part of the democratization movement that reached its climax in 1987. Significantly, socially and politically engaged works like Sin Ki-hwal's postapocalyptic antinuclear comic satire *Here Come Nuclear Bugs* (1985–89) and Bok Geo-il's alternate history novel *In Search of an Epitaph* (1987) lent critical legitimacy in South Korea to a genre that had hitherto been regarded mostly as juvenile and escapist.[2]

The advent of the Internet in the 1990s brought something like a cyberrevolution to South Korea. It was in cyberspace that a new, experimental, and distinctly cosmopolitan wave of speculative fiction started to thrive under the critical influence of postmodernism. In this period, South Korean SF writers and artists (re)discovered the works of Octavia Butler, Stanisław Lem, Ursula Le Guin, and Philip K. Dick, as well as the visual arts of Ridley Scott, Jean Giraud, and Miyazaki Hayao, in their endeavor to create new aesthetic visions. Two anthologies in particular—*The Creative Machine* (1994) and *Cyberpunk* (1995)—signaled a shift to a more liberal and techno-utopian brand of science fiction. Among the contributors was Djuna, an anonymous queer feminist writer and critic, who would exert much influence on the succeeding generation of science fiction writers with a prodigious knowledge of Western science fiction and radically subversive thought experiments.

Alongside the resurgence of science fiction, other speculative fiction genres also prospered in the 1990s. Among the decade's best sellers, for instance, was Yi Uhyŏk's *Record of Exorcism* (1994), a horror novel mixed with *wuxia* (martial art) fiction. Marked by genre hybridization and reevaluation, this postmodern boom in speculative imagination contributed to contesting the critical hegemony of literary realism, which had been preferred by local cultural intellectuals during the struggle for democracy due to its powerful truth claim and its reportage-like potential to represent the marginalized and the oppressed.

Over the past twenty years, science fiction has become more of a transmedia and transgenre cultural mode in a highly technological South Korea. The trauma of the 1997 Asian financial crisis and its social aftermaths have contributed to a resurgence of countercultural, socially conscious science fiction that is epitomized by the films of Bong Joon-ho (*Snowpiercer* [2013]) and the literature of Kim Bo-Young (*Evolution Myths* [2010]), Jeong Soyeon (*Iutchip Yŏnghŭi* [2015]), and Kim Changgyu (*Our Banished World* [2016]). At the core of these works lies an aspiration for an alternative to the neoliberal capitalist status quo and its alienating consequences along with a penchant for formal experimentation. In these and other works, science fiction is increasingly exploring the dynamic intersections between posthuman imagination and queer and crip sensibilities, raising epistemological questions about our bodily and sexual norms. Along with these developments, authors have also found inspiration in the treatment of environmental and ecological themes, leading to the recent rise of a politically poignant subgenre of "climate science fiction" or "cli-fi."

Today, a new generation of authors, visual artists, and fandom leaders is once again expanding and renewing the field of South Korean science fiction. More resources and translations mean that non-Korean audiences are increasingly able to access the speculative imaginations of South Korean authors. The following pages present a list of the titles that are currently available in English translation. Reflective of the relatively recent development of science fiction and its adjacent speculative genres in the country, the list is short but also points to exciting opportunities for exchange and cultural communication in the years to come.

Sunyoung Park

The Texts

Korean-language speculative fiction has only been available in English translation since the mid-2000s, partly because of how the genre has historically been received in Korea and partly because the SFT scene only started to blossom worldwide around that same time.[3] Korea has a long tradition of fantastic literature—myths, fairy tales, and the like—though only some of it has been translated into English as of this printing. As Haerin Shin points out in his study of Korean science fiction, "The incongruity between the high level of technological immersion seen in South Korea's contemporary lifestyle and its surprisingly sparse representation in the literary realm can be traced back to the deeply engraved tradition of realism that held sway throughout the past century."[4] Korea's colonization by Japan (1910–45), the Korean War (1950–53), and subsequent efforts toward democratization and industrialization, Shin argues, favored the development of a "realistic" literature that dealt with the trauma of the twentieth century. Speculative fiction, however, was deemed too frivolous to address those issues.

Nonetheless, several novels, one collection, one anthology, and a wealth of short stories have been translated into English from Korean since 2006. Thanks to translators like Deborah Smith, Sora Kim-Russell, Anton Hur, Gord Sellar, and Jihyun Park, Korean SFT is taking its place as one of the most exciting areas of international speculative fiction. And because of a grant from the Literature Translation Institute of Korea, the major American science fiction magazine *Clarkesworld* published nine short works of Korean SFT in 2019.

The diversity of subjects taken up by Korean speculative fiction authors suggests that the genre there is quickly developing an audience and a character all its own. While the short stories that have been translated and published in the Anglophone world tend to be works of science fiction, the novels are hard-to-classify stories of loneliness and despair in the city.[5] Novels and collections by Korean women in translation, in particular, have seen a sharp rise in recent years.

SCIENCE FICTION

Anglophone awareness of Korean SFT received a major boost in 2018 with the publication of *Readymade Bodhisattva: The Kaya Anthology of South Korean Science Fiction*, which offers readers an introduction to the SF scene in Korea and its fandom, as well as thirteen stories by some of the nation's most accomplished SF authors. Yet two novel-length works of Korean science fiction in translation were already available by 2014: a work of surrealist social protest and a collection of far-future aphorisms and observations by Ganymedean settlers.

Cho Se-Hui's linked novel *The Dwarf* (1978; 2006) is a modernist novel with science fictional elements, though it might just as easily be classified as "magical realism" or even "fabulation."[6] Originally published in Korean in 1978, Cho's novel is a stylistically experimental renunciation of the "realism" that was encouraged in Korean literary circles. Here, metaphors are made tangible and class divisions are heightened in a kind of hyperrealism to underscore the social divisions and exploitation in Korean society during the period of military dictatorship in the 1960s and '70s. While the eponymous character is a literal dwarf whose family toils unceasingly as part of the working class, one of the people that exploits their labor is a giant, who represents the large financial conglomerates. This contrast between oppressor and oppressed, upper class and working class, and capital and labor foregrounds the tensions running through a country that is rocketing toward industrialization after decades of foreign rule.

More recognizable as "science fiction" in the modern Anglophone world is Bok Geo-il's *The Jovian Sayings* (2002; 2014), which offers an intriguing and unique approach to telling the stories of colonial societies in the Jovian system between the twenty-seventh and thirtieth centuries.[7] Presented as a collection of recovered fragments edited by a historian who focuses on that period, Bok's text foregrounds the complexities of written history and the human drive to record and narrativize in order to explain itself to itself. What we're given are the fragments (sayings, maxims, poems) that survived the Ganymedean Catastrophe, in which the human colonies were destroyed in 2998 by a stray piece of Comet Rashid. These bits and pieces offer a window into the difficulties and privations of frontier life and the wonders of human adaptability in a literally alien environment.

SURREALISM

Of the five genre-bending texts from Korea published in English between 2016 and 2019, four are by women, two are novels, two are linked novels, and one is a collection. All five resolutely defy classification but share themes of loneliness and dislocation, alienation in the city, estrangement from human relationships, and (especially in *The Vegetarian* and *The Hole*) a preoccupation with the literal Earth.

These texts have variously been described in terms of "magical realism," "surrealism," "psychological horror," and "offbeat fantasy." One could also call them works of "fabulation," a term that applies to "a tale whose telling is *foregrounded* in a way which emphasizes the inherent arbitrariness of the words we use, the stories we tell."[8] Indeed, the novel-length Korean SFT that has taken Anglophone audiences by storm and won multiple awards eschews spaceships and time travel; instead, it investigates people's dark and intense physical and sexual desires, their despair upon realizing that their lives have been built on illusions, and their attempts to find meaning and keep on living in the face of these crises.

Han Kang's novel of three linked stories, *The Vegetarian* (2007; 2016), based on her 1997 story "The Fruit of My Woman,"[9] is a disturbing, nightmarish portrait of a woman, Yeong-hye, as she physically wastes away and imagines that she's turning into a tree. Originally giving up meat because she's started having violent and blood-soaked dreams, Yeong-hye eventually stops eating completely and shrivels into a figure that looks, ironically, like a sapling. Her vegetarianism causes grief and rage in several of her family members, who try to force-feed her. Yet Yeong-hye is not alone in her painful metamorphosis: her passive resistance to social norms and behavior radiates out to multiple other characters, who themselves begin to question their lives (as husbands, artists, mothers, sisters).[10]

This focus on the natural world, and the soil in particular, lies at the heart of Pyun Hye-young's *The Hole* (2016; 2017), which grew out of the author's earlier short story "Caring for Plants."[11] Variously described as a dystopia and a psychological thriller, *The Hole* could just as easily be called a work of horror for its slowly building crescendo of threatening acts and dark pronouncements. The protagonist, a professor named Oghi who was badly injured in a car accident that killed his wife, winds up in the care of his mother-in-law, who is methodically pulling up all of the plants that his wife had lovingly cultivated and has started digging large holes around the garden, claiming that she is finishing her daughter's work. The professor's memories of his troubled marriage and his wife's disappointment with her own life weigh on Oghi as he lies trapped in his own body, picking up terrifying hints of his mother-in-law's plans for him.[12] Similarly, Pyun's *City of Ash and Red* (2010; 2018), an apocalyptic mystery, focuses on one man's attempt to escape a paranoid and grotesque city, even as he finds out that he is the suspect in his own wife's murder.[13]

A sense of creeping uneasiness also haunts *One Hundred Shadows* (2010; 2016) by Hwang Jungeun, described by the publisher, Tilted Axis Press, as a "mix of oblique fantasy, hard-edged social critique, and offbeat romance" that has won several awards in Korea.[14] *One Hundred Shadows* takes place in a downtrodden electronics market in central Seoul.[15] Because this slum is deemed an eyesore against the backdrop of vibrant new buildings and K-pop in a rapidly industrializing Korea, it is slated for demolition. Eking out a living in this environment are Eungyo and Mujae, repair-shop assistants whose shy friendship gradually blossoms into love. Hwang builds up this world layer by layer, asking us to reconsider words that we take for granted, street scenes that we might look at but never really see, people's shadows (and why they might detach themselves from their owners), and much more.

Set in a similar slum-like environment, Hwang Sok-yong's *Familiar Things* (2011; 2017) takes place on the outskirts of the capital city, in an area ironically called "Flower Island."[16] When thirteen-year-old Bugeye and his mother move to this landfill area after his father's confinement in a "reeducation" camp, they're given the opportunity to make a small living by scavenging for reusable things that are later collected and sold. The landfill area itself, though, is teeming with ghosts and memories that refuse to be completely buried. Set during the early 1980s, when Korea was undergoing rapid economic development under the shadow of a dictatorship, *Familiar Things* foregrounds the clash between a long past and a future that arrived much too quickly.

Ha Seong-nan further explores this clash in her collection *Flowers of Mold* (1999; 2019), lingering in every story on the line between reality and illusion.[17] Here, city life is marked by paranoia, obsession, disturbing moments of déjà vu, and ghosts that may or may not be products of a character's hallucinations. As in *The Vegetarian*, "The Woman Next Door," for instance, slowly builds up uncertainty about the main character's perspective on her own life, leaving us wondering if she is imagining that the next-door neighbor is sucking up her life like a bloodless vampire or if it is really happening. None of these stories offers us firm footing, making us question our conclusions immediately after they form.

The English publication in 2018 of *Readymade Bodhisattva: The Kaya Anthology of South Korean Science Fiction* signaled a new chapter in Anglophone interest in Korean speculative fiction. This anthology introduces Anglophone readers to some of the most exciting Korean speculative fiction authors working today, including Kim Bo-young, Djuna, and Park Min-gyu. According to editor Sunyoung Park, the genre evolving in Korea includes "a strong sense of the apocalypse having already happened, whether through war, colonization, dictatorship, or the corporate monopolization of resources."[18] The mix of novel excerpts and standalone stories offers readers a more complex portrait of the texts that have been written over the past few decades. Alternate histories about colonialism, far-future explorations of cryogenics, robots achieving enlightenment and becoming an integral part of people's lives, alien invasions, time travel, and virtual reality: all of these stories reveal how Korean authors have taken some of the genre mainstays and transformed them into commentary on their own society in the traumatic twentieth century.

The Korean speculative fiction finding its way into English at the start of this century is encouraging Anglophone readers to expand their understanding of what speculative fiction looks like and how it can be used to comment both on historical traumas and on contemporary sociopolitical issues. Experimental and bold, these books contribute to the exciting global evolution of the genre.

Primary Sources

1978:   Cho Se-Hui. *The Dwarf.* Translated by Bruce Fulton and Ju-Chan Fulton. University of Hawaii Press, 2006.
1999:   Ha Seong-nan. *Flowers of Mold.* Translated by Janet Hong. Open Letter, 2019.
2002:   Bok Geo-il. *The Jovian Sayings.* Translated by the author. Stallion Press, 2014.
2007:   Han Kang. *The Vegetarian.* Translated by Deborah Smith. Hogarth Press, 2016.
2010:   Hwang Jungeun. *One Hundred Shadows.* Translated by Jung Yewon. Tilted Axis Press, 2016.
        Pyun Hye-young. *City of Ash and Red.* Translated by Sora Kim-Russell. Arcade, 2018.
2011:   Hwang Sok-yong. *Familiar Things.* Translated by Sora Kim-Russell. Scribe UK, 2017.
2016:   Pyun Hye-young. *The Hole.* Translated by Sora Kim-Russell. Arcade, 2017.
2018:   Park, Sunyoung, and Sang Joon Park, eds. *Readymade Bodhisattva: The Kaya Anthology of South Korean Science Fiction.* Various translators. Kaya Press.

Notes

1. See Park, "Between Science and Politics," 350–52.

2. Park, "Reciprocal Assets."

3. I will use the term "Korean" throughout this chapter but will generally refer to literature coming out of South Korea.

4. H. Shin, "Curious Case of South Korean Science Fiction."

5. Translators Deborah Smith, Anton Hur, and Sora Kim-Russell have suggested to me in conversation that "magical realism" might be the best way to describe these novels because of their sense of dislocation, bizarre circumstances, and unsettling dream imagery.

6. S. Shin review.

7. See Hyun, "Interview."

8. Clute, "Fabulation."

9. Translated by Deborah Smith, published in *Granta* in 2016.

10. *The Vegetarian* won the 2016 Man Booker International Prize. See also Alexandrescu's "Korean Daphne," for a discussion of Yeong-hye as a mythological Daphne figure.

11. Published in English translation in the *New Yorker*.

12. "Hye-young Pyun's surreal, violent novels reject stereotypes about Korean women's writing, taking up global themes of environmental collapse and the loneliness of city life." Chung, "Dystopia Is Everywhere."

13. Orthofer review.

14. Tilted Axis was started by Deborah Smith, Han Kang's translator into English.

15. Cordasco review.

16. Ntrouka and Mallon reviews.

17. Gordon review.

18. Park, introduction to *Readymade Bodhisattva*, 13.

Secondary Sources

Alexandrescu, Ioana. "Korean Daphne: Becoming a Plant in Han Kang's *The Vegetarian*." *Annals of the University of Oradea Romanian Language and Literature* 1 (2016): 125–32.

Chung, Jae Won. "Dystopia Is Everywhere." *Boston Review* (February 14, 2019). http://bostonreview.net/literature-culture-arts-society/jae-won-chung-dystopia-everywhere/.

Clute, John. "Fabulation." In *The Encyclopedia of Science Fiction*, edited by John Clute, David Langford, Peter Nicholls, and Graham Sleight. London: Gollancz, updated January 23, 2018. http://www.sf-encyclopedia.com/entry/fabulation.

Cordasco, Rachel. "Review: *One Hundred Shadows* by Hwang Jungeun." *SfinTranslation.com* (September 2016). https://www.sfintranslation.com/?p=981.

Gordon, Peter. "*Flowers of Mold*, Stories by Ha Seong-nan." *Asian Review of Books* (March 2019). https://asianreviewofbooks.com/content/flowers-of-mold-stories-by-ha-seong-nan/.

Hyun, Ko Doo. "Interview: The Journey of a Science Fiction Writer: Novelist Bok Geo-il." *Korean Literature Now* (November 2014). https://koreanliteraturenow.com/interviews/journey-science-fiction-writer-novelist-bok-geo-il.

Mallon, Fionn. "Does Capitalism Make Good Compost? *Familiar Things*, Hwang Sok-yong's Novel of Waste and Reclamation." *Los Angeles Review of Books*, October 7, 2018. https://lareviewofbooks.org/article/does-capitalism-make-good-compost-familiar-things-hwang-sok-yongs-novel-of-waste-and-reclamation.

Ntrouka, Anna. "Guest Post: Review: *Familiar Things* by Hwang Sok-Yong." *SfinTranslation.com* (September 2017). https://www.sfintranslation.com/?p=2751.

Orthofer, M. A. "*City of Ash and Red*." *Complete Review* (December 2018). http://www.complete-review.com/reviews/korea/pyunhy2.htm.

Park, Sunyoung. "Between Science and Politics: Science Fiction as a Critical Discourse in South Korea, 1960s–1990s." In "Science and Literature," special issue edited by Christopher Hanscom and Dafna Zur, *Journal of Korean Studies* 23, no. 2 (2018): 347–67.

———. Introduction to *Readymade Bodhisattva: The Kaya Anthology of South Korean Science Fiction*, edited by Sunyoung Park and Sang Joon Park, 9–18. Los Angeles: Kaya Press, 2019.

———. "Reciprocal Assets: Science Fiction and Democratization in 1980s South Korea." In *Revisiting Minjung: New Perspectives on the Cultural History of 1980s South Korea*, edited by Sunyoung Park, 247–73. Ann Arbor: University of Michigan Press, 2019.

Pyun, Hye-young. "Caring for Plants." Translated by Sora Kim-Russell. *New Yorker* (July 2017). https://www.newyorker.com/magazine/2017/07/10/caring-for-plants.

Shin, Haerin. "The Curious Case of South Korean Science Fiction: A Hyper-technological Society's Call for Speculative Imagination." *Azalea: Journal of Korean Literature and Culture* 6 (2013): 81–82.

Shin, Soojeong. "The Story of a Dwarf Family, the Urban Poor: *The Dwarf* by Cho Se-Hui." *Korean Literature Now* (November 2014). https://koreanliteraturenow.com/fiction/reviews/cho-se-hui-story-dwarf-family-urban-poor-dwarf-cho-se-hui.

Polish-Language SFT

Introduction

Rachel Cordasco opens her discussion of Polish SFT with an interesting observation that Slavic languages are equipped with a handy umbrella term covering all kinds of speculative fiction: *fantastyka*. It covers not just the traditional pop genres, such as science fiction, fantasy, and horror, but also all future kinds of *fantastyka* that haven't been invented yet. I think there's a reason we need this word so badly, at least in Poland. *Fantastyka* is present at the very core of our cultural DNA.

Let's do a thought experiment: suppose we have a panel of experts on American literature and we ask them to compile a list of the "Top 10 Great American Novels." We will probably end up with titles like *East of Eden, The Great Gatsby,* or *Moby-Dick,* all offering different flavors of realism. The experts would probably not even consider any book we might call *fantastyka.* We would get a similar list from a panel on poetry or drama. Edgar Allan Poe could get some recognition for his love poems, but not for his *Tales of Mystery & Imagination.* No *fantastyka* there, either. In another room we would have a panel of experts on Polish literature, compiling similar lists of Polish novels, poems, and dramas. They would end up with some works that were never translated into English, so you have to take my word on this: the Polish list would be full of *fantastyka.*

Our literary canon, which includes the most cherished novels, plays, and poems, written by people who have marble statues on city squares named in their honor, surprisingly often deals with such topics as zombies, vampires, witchcraft, necromancy, utopias and dystopias, nymphs luring unfaithful lovers to drown them in an enchanted lake, and engineers inventing alloys lighter than air or a new way of using ultraresistant glass as a construction material for futuristic cities. We continue this tradition to this very day. Our latest Nobel Prize laureate, Olga Tokarczuk, frequently uses elements of *fantastyka* in her fiction. If you analyze the fiction of our masters of science fiction and fantasy—Stanisław Lem, Andrzej Sapkowski, Jacek Dukaj—you will discover that they draw their inspiration largely from the nineteenth-century masterpieces from our literary canon: Mickiewicz, Słowacki, Wyspiański, Sienkiewicz.

I would go as far as to say that without some basic knowledge of Polish *fantastyka*, you cannot understand Polish culture, or even properly speak the Polish language. The Polish school system requires everyone pursuing any degree to pass a test of knowledge of the literary canon (this is a rough equivalent of British A-levels or German *Abitur*). Everyone assumes that you know this canon, or at least that you will pretend to know it, and therefore you will understand references to it in our vernacular language. Take one example. Sooner or later, you will hear that someone is "dancing the straw-man dance." A sports commentator can say it about some athletic team or a political pundit about the government or the opposition. What does it mean?

This metaphor comes from a drama that would definitely make it onto any list of "the greatest Polish plays"—Stanisław Wyspiański's *Wesele* (*The Wedding Party*). It was inspired by an actual wedding that happened in Krakow in 1900. An affluent urban writer marries a peasant girl. The party guests represent almost all social strata, and since it happens right after an election, people want to talk politics, just like in the present day. Initially, the guests try to be friendly to each other, but as they drink more vodka, their personal, economical, political, and sexual frustrations spiral out of control. As the party goes on, there are some fistfights, bribery, extortion, blackmail, adultery, and possibly rape.

In front of the building there is a rose bush, covered with straw to protect it from the cold. In the dark of the night, people mistake it for a human. Eventually, the groom invites this "straw man" to the party, asking him to bring his friends. Now the *fantastyka* begins! The guests are haunted by spectral "visitors," representing their subconscious dreams and memories. Note how similar this is to Stanisław Lem's *Solaris*!

At the break of dawn, the ghosts finally disappear. The party guests return to painful sobriety. But the straw man is still there, even in broad daylight. He starts to play the fiddle, singing a ghastly song, telling the party guests (and probably the theater audience as well) that they are all pathetic failures. Everyone seems to be under his spell; they dance and sing along with the straw man the song of failure. The end: the curtain falls. Quite a metaphor!

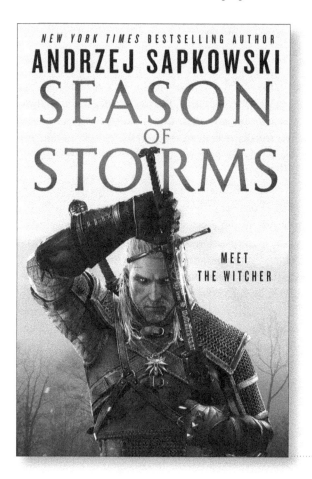

Season of Storms
(2018)

This is just a single example. There's a treasure trove of similar ones in the Polish literary canon. But I hope this can explain that *fantastyka* for us is much more than a collection of campfire stories. You have to learn Polish *fantastyka* if you want to learn Polish. And the following chapter is a great way to begin![1]

Wojciech Orliński

The Texts

When it comes to Polish-language SFT, Anglophone readers inevitably point to the novels and stories of the brilliant and prolific Stanisław Lem. And while his influence on authors in Poland and beyond is significant, Lem is not the only

Solaris (2014)

Polish speculative fiction writer of note available in English. Since the 1990s, Anglophone readers have had access to Polish science fiction from such award-winning writers as Marek Huberath and Jacek Dukaj and fantasy from Stefan Grabiński and Andrzej Sapkowski. Thanks to translators Michael Kandel, David French, Stanley Bill, Antonia Lloyd-Jones, Sean Bye, Miroslaw Lipinski, and many others, Anglophone readers can learn more about the development of science fiction, high fantasy, and expressionism in a nation plagued by war and political upheaval during the twentieth century.

The Polish-language SFT discussed in this chapter is grouped under either "science fiction" or "fantasy," but a discussion of the term *fantastyka* is in order here.[2] A word that has been used for decades in eastern Europe and Russia to refer to speculative fiction in all of its various manifestations (both Bulgaria and Poland have had genre magazines called *Fantastyka*), it has more recently been used by author and critic John Clute (of *The Encyclopedia of Science Fiction*).[3] Like the Italian *fantascienza*, *fantastyka* represents a particular source language's attempt to describe a kind of fiction that is notoriously slippery and prone to mutation. Its focus on the fantastic (again, as with the Italian term) privileges the nonscientific aspects of genre texts without dismissing the Anglo-American and French branches of the genre concerned with technological breakthroughs and scientific theories. And while Lem, for instance, is usually referred to as a "science fiction" author, his stories often range far beyond the subgenre, one that he explored himself in essays about what science fiction should ultimately do.

SCIENCE FICTION

Thanks in large part to translator Michael Kandel and publishers Seabury and Harcourt, Anglophone readers have access to nineteen texts by Stanisław Lem, including novels, story collections, and even a collection of introductions to nonexistent novels.[4] Published between 1970 and 1994, these translations together demonstrate the depth and breadth of Lem's ideas about everything from genetic manipulation to encounters with alien civilizations. As several scholars of Lem's work have argued, the author's traumatic experiences as a Jew during the Holocaust shaped his sardonic, unvarnished depiction of human brutality and the questionable future of human civilization. It is through science fiction that Lem, according to scholar Agnieszka Gajewska, was able to explore his grotesque visions of the future: "Beneath Lem's splendid, bold and often grotesque visions of the future, the writer buried traces of his own traumatic past—a series of terrifying experiences, which included having escaped death in a pogrom and having lost most of his relatives in the Holocaust."[5]

While Lem does range widely across topics in his novels and stories, the absurdity of the human condition remains a constant theme. *The Science Fiction Encyclopedia*'s entry on Lem offers an illuminating reading of several of his most well-known texts, in terms of that theme:

> *Eden, Solaris, The Invincible, Tales of Pirx the Pilot,* and *More Tales of Pirx the Pilot* use the mystery of strange beings, events and localities to educate their protagonists into understanding the limitations and strengths of humanity. These parables for our age are fittingly open-ended: their tenor is that no closed reference system is viable in the age of Cybernetics and rival political absolutisms; the protagonists are redeemed by ethical and aesthetic insight rather than by hardware, abstract cognition or power—thence Lem's strong, at times oversimplifying but salutary critique of English-language sf in his ... *Microworlds: Writings on Science Fiction and Fantasy* (1985) for abusing the potentials of the new in gimmicks and disguised fairytales.[6]

Lem's Earth-bound stories, as well, imagine, for instance, how individuals might react to absurd situations (*Memoirs Found in a Bathtub*) and the potentially disturbing outcomes of human progress (*Return from the Stars*).

Lem's novels and stories tend to fall into three distinct categories: several take place on other planets, some are set on Earth, and two collections focus exclusively on robots of one kind or another. In the first category fall stories about Lem's most well-known characters: astronaut-explorers (and sometime detectives) Ijon Tichy and Pirx the Pilot.[7] Through these individuals, Lem is able to turn a critical mirror on human nature by putting his astronauts in often absurd or dangerous situations, or both. And while these stories tend toward black humor, those novels that are set on Earth are all sober, even bleak, depictions of dystopian futures. Lem's robot-centered stories (*The Cyberiad* and *Mortal Engines*), like several of Italo Calvino's texts, meet at the intersection between fable and science fiction. These jaunty cybernetic scenarios enable Lem to explore not so much the technology itself so much as humans' perceptions of artificial intelligence.

Lem's best-known work in English remains *Solaris* (1961; 1970), which was also the first of his texts to be translated into English. This haunting off-Earth psychological thriller perhaps retains this position because of its many film adaptations.[8] *Solaris* has also been (and continues to be) the focus of much critical attention and debate, with scholars reading the novel in terms of its commentary on psychology, technology, and memory.[9] Set on an alien planet covered by a mysterious ocean, *Solaris* follows astronaut Kris Kelvin and his crew as they explore the planet and realize that the ocean is able to produce physical manifestations of unconscious memories. Without knowing how or why the manifestations occur, the crew is forced to reconsider its own existence in relation to the Alien and how the human mind may or may not be able to interact with it.

Both *The Invincible* (1964; 1973) and *Fiasco* (1987; 1987) are also set on inscrutable alien worlds with human explorers trying (unsuccessfully) to make contact with an intelligence they cannot understand. When the *Invincible* (an interstellar cruiser) lands on Regis III in search of its lost sister ship, *Condor*, the crew at first believes that the planet is uninhabited. However, they eventually realize that life *does* exist on Regis III in the form of autonomous, self-replicating micromachines. Having likely evolved over aeons after being left there by an alien civilization, the swarm is able to repulse any hostile maneuvers by the human crew via a surge of electromagnetic interference. The crew of the *Invincible* eventually realizes that the swarm is deeply embedded in the planet's ecology and that nothing short of the planet's total obliteration would destroy it. *Fiasco*, reminiscent of US efforts to force Japan to open up to the West in 1854 and the latter years of the Cold War, chronicles the work of the crew of the spaceship *Eurydika* to make contact with the alien intelligence on the surface of the planet Quinta. These efforts escalate quickly into increasingly destructive attempts to establish contact, resulting in the fiery obliteration of the alien world.

Similarly critical of human efforts to discover, communicate with, and potentially colonize alien worlds, Lem's *Eden* (1959; 1989) offers readers a description of a planet so surreal and strange that it could have come from the brush of Bosch or Dalí. After a ship manned by human scientists and explorers crashes on a mysterious planet, the crew starts going out on expeditions, building up their own complex, highly speculative theory about the life on Eden and its history. *Eden* asks us to consider it on its own terms: as a cautionary tale about misinterpretation, authoritarianism, and the human urge to interpret that which cannot ever be fully explained. Lem similarly explores this idea in *His Master's Voice* (1968; 1983), in which scientists unsuccessfully try to decode a signal from space that may be from an alien intelligence. Despite their multitude of theories as to the message's content and purpose, the scientists never actually discover the true nature of the signal.

Lem's most well-known character, the galactic explorer Ijon Tichy, first appeared in Polish in 1957, those stories ultimately being collected in English as *The Star Diaries* (1957; 1976) and *Memoirs of a Space Traveler* (1957; 1982). Described by Seabury as "the Candide of the Cosmos" on the cover of *The Star Diaries*, Lem's Tichy flies all over the universe in his beat-up rocket, encountering strange civilizations and even stranger practices (like reducing oneself to atoms at night and reconstituting oneself during the day), and even moving back and forth through time. In reality, Tichy tells us more about our own species than any other. After all, *The Star Diaries* can be read as one long, entertaining diatribe against the human race: its penchant for brutality and cruelty, its obsession with the "new," and its naively arrogant belief that it knows best how to shape its own destiny and change history "for the better." And did I mention the predatory potatoes? *Memoirs of a Space Traveler* collects all of those stories that were left out of the publication of *The Star Diaries* and includes accounts of Tichy going back in time to create the universe, a well-intentioned robot reducing the world to a place of authoritarian bleakness, and the discovery of how to place human consciousness in a box.

The Futurological Congress (1971; 1974) and *Peace on Earth* (1986; 1994) offer us novel-length windows into Tichy's life and times. When Tichy is sent to the Eighth World Futurological Congress in Costa Rica (the focus of which is solutions to overpopulation), he falls victim to the hallucinogenic drugs that the government has dropped into the water supply to pacify the population. When the government then bombs his hotel, Tichy seeks shelter in the sewers and here follows a series of bizarre hallucinations, which make up the bulk of the novel. These involve Tichy waking up from cryogenic sleep in 2039 to find that Earth's population is controlled by drugs that mask a horrifyingly grim and disgusting reality. Only with other drugs can one break through the illusion and see the world for what it is. In *Peace on Earth*, Tichy is called upon to help solve an unexpected problem with lunar robots. When the world powers decide to place all of their weapons factories on the moon in order to demilitarize Earth while also establishing a scenario of mutually assured destruction, the increasingly autonomous factory robots begin warring with one another (ironically), ultimately severing communication with Earth. It's up to Tichy to assess the danger that this situation poses to Earth.

Lem's other recurring astronaut character, Pirx, appears in stories written between 1958 and 1971 and collected in English in *Tales of Pirx the Pilot* (1968; 1979) and *More Tales of Pirx the Pilot* (1968; 1982). Here we see Pirx dealing with complicated technical malfunctions, flying to the moon, trying (and failing) to intercept an alien ship adrift in space, confronting an out-of-control mining robot, and much more. As with Tichy, Lem uses Pirx to probe the nature of artificial intelligence, human-alien communication (and its impossibility), and a whole host of other issues that explorers and scientists might need to confront in the future. And while Pirx is not as fully realized as a character, he nonetheless offers insight into the evolution of Lem's ideas and distinctive style.

Lem's five novels set on Earth range from the absurdist maze of *Memoirs Found in a Bathtub* to the mystery–science fiction hybrids of *The Investigation* and *The Chain of Chance*. Written between 1959 and 1975, and published in English between 1973 and 1983, these texts demonstrate Lem's virtuosity when it comes to exploring ideas about human nature, chance, and the expected dystopian far future. His *Memoirs Found in a Bathtub* (1961; 1973) can be read either as simply a black comedy about the absurdity and meaninglessness of human existence or as a thinly veiled autobiography depicting the violence and brutality of the Holocaust.[10] The "memoirs," presented as the only manuscript to survive mysterious microbes that destroyed all paper and brought down civilization, are introduced by a historian living sometime in the thirty-second century. The author of these memoirs describes being trapped in a "Building" and wandering around trying to carry out an unexplained mission. Along the way he comes up against senseless bureaucracy, random violence, suicides, endless corridors, and a realization that there may not be any meaning in life.

Both *The Investigation* (1959; 1974) and *The Chain of Chance* (1975; 1978) read like detective novels, but the crimes here are ultimately the work not of people but of random chance.[11] Set in London during a rash of apparent corpse resurrections, *The Investigation* follows a lieutenant from Scotland Yard as he consults scientific, philosophical, and theological experts in order to find out how and why certain bodies in the morgue are being moved around and ultimately disappearing.

"Reality," Lem argues in *The Investigation*, is shaped by the very people trying to understand it, and it is this that has somehow resulted in what normally seems like an impossible situation. Similarly, in *The Chain of Chance*, an investigation by a former astronaut into why several wealthy businessmen have suddenly died reveals that the laws of nature, and not a twisted criminal, are to blame. Apparently, the unintentional mixture of certain harmless chemicals has resulted in a chemical weapon, and only the most random events could have triggered these deaths. Once again, Lem argues that humans understand the world much less than they think they do and that this ignorance is actually lethal.

As in much of Lem's work, **Return from the Stars** (1961; 1980) imagines what humanity might be like in the future, especially in response to medical or pharmacological advances.[12] While in *The Futurological Congress* people take drugs in order to live in a world too grotesque to accept in its true form, in *Return from the Stars* people submit to a procedure called "betrization," by which people no longer have the ability or inclination to kill. Seen through the eyes of an astronaut who has returned to Earth after 127 years (though the astronaut himself aged only 10 years), this future human civilization has lost its interest in risk, exploration, and discovery along with its ability to kill.

Lem's robot fables, collected in *The Cyberiad: Fables for the Cybernetic Age* (1965; 1974) and *Mortal Engines* (1977), encourage readers to consider the ways in which science fiction (specifically about robots and artificial intelligence) is really a new twist on an old storytelling technique. Indeed, Lem is not interested here in exploring robotics and the nature of AI as much as he is using twentieth-century approaches to those topics in order to turn a mirror on human nature. In the stories of *The Cyberiad* (whose primary characters are the partially robotic inventors Klapaucius and Trurl), we learn about how these two avert a war by bringing warring armies into a collective consciousness, how they tire of studying that which *does* exist and thus turn to studying dragons and other nonexistent phenomena, and their encounter with a machine that threatens to kill anyone who doesn't agree that two plus two equals seven. The robot fables of *Mortal Engines* are also cautionary allegories.[13] Here we read about extraterrestrial robots that take over entire planets, computers that fight moon dragons, robots that go off on galactic expeditions for their robot king, and similar tales that are surreal and strange because they're unexpected.

Among the last Lem texts brought into English are those collected in *The Cosmic Carnival of Stanisław Lem* (1981).[14] The latter, edited and translated by Kandel, brings together some of Lem's best stories as well as excerpts from *The Invincible*, *Return from the Stars*, *Solaris*, and *The Futurological Congress*. And while Lem's *Imaginary Magnitude* (1984) and *A Perfect Vacuum* (1999) may not be considered "speculative fiction" per se, these collections of introductions to nonexistent books and reviews of other such books, respectively, underscore Lem's linguistic playfulness and the kind of sardonic humor that runs throughout his oeuvre.

Nearly twenty years passed before Anglophone readers were treated to a new work of Polish SFT. This time it wasn't by Lem but by Bruno Jasienski (pseudonym of Wiktor Zysman), one of the founders of the Polish futurist movement (1919–24).[15] In Jasienski's only work of speculative fiction, *I Burn Paris* (1928–29; 2012), a disgruntled factory worker poisons Paris's water supply with a plague bacillus. When the people of Paris realize what has happened, they isolate themselves in ethnic and political enclaves, though they are nevertheless wiped out. Only thirty thousand members of the proletariat, who have been holed away in prisons, survive the contamination and form a socialist commune.

Following Jasienski's novel was the first translation of a living Polish speculative author: Marek Huberath, a professor of biophysics and biological physics in Krakow. Huberath's disorientingly strange metafictional novel *Nest of Worlds* (1998; 2014) tackles nothing less than life, death, and literature.[16] Centered around a man named Gavein as he sets out on a journey, the novel reveals a world in which everyone must take that same journey every thirty-five years. Eventually, we learn that bodies pile up wherever Gavein goes, and everyone seems to be reading a book called ... *Nest of Worlds*. And that's just the first metafictional level: there are many others. These deaths and the nested books ask us to consider not our own consciousness as it consumes the characters and events in a narrative, but the existences of the characters themselves and whether they "die" when we put down a book. Huberath's (post)modern take on George Barclay's theory of immaterialism and subjective idealism will undoubtedly make Anglophone readers demand more Huberath in English.

The following year brought us the translation of Jacek Dukaj's *The Old Axolotl* (2015; 2015), the first novel brought into English by Poland's most famous living science fiction author.[17] A story about transhumanism and how the digital experience shapes our identity, *The Old Axolotl* imagines a scenario in which a "neutron wave" wipes out every living thing on Earth, except those people who are able to upload their consciousnesses into mecha bodies via an old virtual-reality game. Unable to move past their devastation over the death of humanity, a group of transformers decides to reboot organic life on Earth by drawing on the work done by biochemists before the catastrophe and the DNA maps from the Human Genome Project. Throughout, we're asked to consider the "point" of evolution, if organic life should even be brought back, and if the transformers are still human or just performing humanness.

Yale University Press's publication a few years later of Czesław Miłosz's unfinished science fiction novel *The Mountains of Parnassus* (2012; 2017) has broadened our understanding of the Nobel Prize–winning poet's beliefs about how literature intersects with and acts on reality and why he would turn to a genre and form in which he rarely worked.[18] Originally written in the 1970s and published posthumously in Polish in 2012, the novel is set in a dystopian future devoid of hierarchy, patriarchy, and religion. Through four main characters—a rebel, an astronaut, a cardinal, and a prophet—Milosz imagines what technological progress and a decline in the arts and religion will do to the human spirit. As Stanley Bill writes in an introduction to his translation, Milosz further explored "the refinement of state techniques for totalitarian control . . . and the dangers inherent in the fantasy of human existence without death." The science fiction setting itself enabled the author "to take these familiar themes in new directions, presenting the future as accomplished fact in a descriptive realist style, and thus bringing prophecy to life in an act of dystopian world creation."[19]

Science fiction from Poland thus seems to have entered a period of revival, especially with the recent news that Dukaj's massive novel *Ice* is currently being translated into English and is under contract with a UK publisher.

FANTASY

Of the Polish fantasists writing in the early to mid-twentieth century, only Bruno Schulz, Witold Gombrowicz, and Stefan Grabiński have been translated into English. Their fascination with a world behind, beyond, and beneath everyday reality enabled them to produce stories and novels of dark fantasy verging on horror that explore the occult, hypnosis, the grotesque, and identity formation. Writing under the influence of decadence, surrealism, and expressionism, Schulz, Gombrowicz, and Grabiński transformed these styles and approaches into uniquely Polish tales.

Schulz published only two volumes of short fiction in his lifetime, a life cut short by a Nazi officer in German-occupied Drohobycz in 1942. Michael Cisco describes his short stories as "atmospheric" and "phantasmagorical" and a kind of early form of magical realism; Schulz was "more interested in mystery, wonder, and the play of the grotesque than he was in terror, although much of his fiction does involve a kind of intense emotion of expectancy, if not dread."[20] Schulz also assisted in translating Franz Kafka's *The Trial* into Polish. In his collection *The Street of Crocodiles* (1934; 1963), Schulz tells the story of a merchant family living in a small Galician town (similar to his own Drohobycz), only the father, who runs a textile shop, is a kind of mad scientist with superhuman abilities, while his son, Jacob (the narrator), describes life in the town from his uniquely perceptive point of view. Through Jacob Schulz uses metaphors, obscure words, scientific terms, and Latin words to destabilize what would otherwise seem like a "normal" world. In stories like "The Comet," the impending destruction of Earth sparks celebration in the town's inhabitants, who are psychologically lifted out of their daily boring routine and forced to consider larger cosmic questions. "Tailors'

Dummies" invites us to see inanimate objects as participating in the world as living things do, just by different means.

Gombrowicz, too, was interested in flux and transformation, exploring them through a variety of genres, including the gothic novel. Writing within and against the strictures of Polish society, Gombrowicz invites readers to question the ways in which people perform the Self for others and for what purpose. His first novel, *Ferdydurke* (1937; 1961), received high praise from Bruno Schulz, who called the book "a new and revolutionary form of novel" and "an annexation of a new field of spiritual phenomena."[21] Deemed scandalous when it was first released in Polish, *Ferdydurke* tells the story of a thirty-year-old man named Joey Kowalski as he attempts to live a life free from constraints. Nonetheless, Joey's experiences reveal how he is shaped by his circumstances and surroundings and that he can never truly banish the ghosts of tradition and social mores.

In Gombrowicz's *Possessed; or, The Secret of Myslotch* (1939; 1980), all of the elements of a gothic novel are present, including an old castle, a dark family secret, and ghosts. The author then explores and pushes the boundaries of the genre in his depiction of the castle's inexplicable psychological and supernatural effect on two people staying at a pension nearby. As this couple falls in love, their identities start to merge, and the outcome is a dangerous and destructive creature that reflects the secrets and dark forces emanating from the castle. Here, Gombrowicz further explores ideas of impersonation, evil, duality, and immaturity.[22] His only collection of stories in English, *Bacacay* (1957; 2004) continues to explore the absurdities that linger just under the surface of everyday life. In these tales, recluses turn into stalkers, a civil servant flouts respectability by running after plain housemaids, and what might be the flesh of a murdered child winds up in a stew served to jaded aristocrats.

Writing slightly earlier than Schulz and Gombrowicz but similarly interested in exploring the opportunities offered by *fantastyka*, Stefan Grabiński coined the terms "psychofantasy" and "metafantastica" to explain his own approach to fantastic fiction.[23] Grabiński believed that literature could offer readers a view beyond reality that science couldn't access in order to reveal otherwise obscured psychological and metaphysical phenomena. His "expressionist extremism," characterized by intensity and sexual explicitness, was influenced by the horrors of World War I, but also by the haunting work of Edgar Allan Poe (Grabiński has often been called the "Polish Poe"). In his later work, Grabiński focused more on the occult, writing about demonology and magic rituals.

That Grabiński's first appearance in English was via a Dedalus Books collection should come as no surprise, since it is in keeping with that press's interest (like Wakefield's) in publishing English translations of avant-garde fantastic and horror fiction. *The Dark Domain* (1993), which brings together some of Grabiński's most horrifying tales, includes pieces like "Fumes," which explores the crossroads of eroticism and insanity, and "The Wandering Train," a ghost story born of the inscrutable nature of certain then-modern technology. Both "The Motion Demon" and "In the Compartment" were originally published in Grabiński's *The Motion Demon* (1919; 2005), a collection originally published in 1919 that explored the fantastic inherent in rampant technological progress. A series of fantastic railway stories, those pieces in *The Motion Demon* feature ghost trains from other dimensions, orgies, and doppelgängers, suggesting both that modern technology serves as a gateway for the supernatural and bizarre and that progress cannot and never will suppress these elements.

The stories in Grabiński's collection *In Sarah's House* (2007) continue the author's unflinching exploration of horror and sexuality. In the title story, a noblewoman absorbs the life out of each of her lovers, "White Virak" depicts a creature who lives in a chimney and preys on chimney sweeps, and stories such as "The Grey Room" and "The Dead Run" offer readers the kind of psychological horror that authors like Poe and Walpole explored before. *On the Hill of Roses* (2012) collects even more such stories in which evil spirits possess the inhabitants of a farmhouse, characters engage in sadomasochistic behavior, and synesthesia (à la the decadent movement) helps uncover a tragedy.

The large gap in translated Polish fantasy that exists between Schulz, Gombrowicz, and Grabiński, on the one hand, and Andrzej Sapkowski, on the other, suggests the wealth of Polish *fantastyka* to which Anglophone readers don't yet have access. Nonetheless, Sapkowski's international best-selling **Witcher** series (1994–99; 2007–18) has influenced how fantasy is written and marketed around the world since the start of the twenty-first century.[24] With his prizewinning debut novella, *The Witcher* (1986), Sapkowski inaugurated what would become a nine-book series, including novels and collections, that explores the life and times of monster-hunter Geralt of Rivia and a war between humans, dwarves, gnomes, and elves, as well as the birth of a prophesied and powerful child that promises to change the world. The Witcher books have been translated into more than twenty languages, and Sapkowski was given the World Fantasy Award for lifetime achievement in 2016.[25] The Witcher narrative was briefly interrupted by the publication in English of *The Malady, and Other Stories: An Andrzej Sapkowski Sampler* (2013), which includes pieces from *The Last Wish* and *Blood of Elves*, a non-Witcher story ("The Malady").

The only magical realist Polish fiction in English today is by Nobel Prize–winning author Olga Tokarczuk. Both *House of Day, House of Night* (1998; 2003) and *Primeval and Other Times* (1996; 2010) are amalgams of myth, fairy tale, and fable, portraying Polish villages filled with characters who are at once unique and timeless.[26] While *Primeval* depicts the life and customs of one particular village over the course of the twentieth century, with its universal joys and sorrows, violence and redemption, *House of Day* offers us a mix of genre types (straightforward fictional plot, essay, observational note) that gives us an unconventional window into the author's own backyard and its religious and natural history.

ANTHOLOGIES

With the publication of *The Dedalus Book of Polish Fantasy* in 1996 and *A Polish Book of Monsters* in 2010, Anglophone audiences were introduced to a wider variety of Polish speculative fiction authors, including Stanisław Mrożek, Jan Barszczewski, and Tomasz Kołodziejczak. In both anthologies, though, readers will recognize authors of both science fiction and fantasy: Huberath, Grabiński, Schulz, Jasienski, Dukaj, and Sapkowski. In his introduction to *The Dedalus Book of Polish Fantasy*, Wiesiek Powaga points to the centrality of the "devil" figure in Polish storytelling: "Polish tradition abounds in stories about the devil, which were collected when the interest in the native folklore was first awakened during the Romantic era."[27] This fascination, together with the turn toward the supernatural and the occult during the early twentieth century, has allowed contemporary Polish authors to draw on a rich tradition of *fantastyka* that is at once diverse and vibrant. *A Polish Book of Monsters* also demonstrates the richness of Polish *fantastyka*, albeit in just five stories, each by a well-known author.[28] Huberath's "Yoo Retoont, Sneogg. Ay Noo" explores what it means to be human in the aftermath of a nuclear holocaust, while Jacek Dukaj's "The Iron General" explores the concept of the monstrous in an alternate world ruled by both technology and magic.

The continued popularity of Sapkowski's Witcher books and the growing interest in Dukaj's work in the Anglophone world bode well for the future of Polish-language SFT. As in several other speculative fiction traditions around the world, it is Poland's fantasy (rather than science fiction, horror, or other subgenres) that is finding its way into the hands of Anglophone readers.

Primary Sources

1919: Grabiński, Stefan. *The Motion Demon.* Translated by Miroslaw Lipinski. Ash-Tree Press, 2005.

1928–29 (serialized): Jasienski, Bruno [Wiktor Zysman]. *I Burn Paris.* Translated by Soren A. Gauger and Marcin Piekoszewski. Twisted Spoon Press, 2012.

1934: Schulz, Bruno. *The Street of Crocodiles.* Translated by Celina Wieniewska. Walker, 1963.

1937: Gombrowicz, Witold. *Ferdydurke.* Translated from the French, German, and Spanish editions by Eric Mosbacher. Harcourt, Brace, and World, 1961. First direct Polish-to-English translation by Danuta Borchardt. Yale University Press, 2000.

Schulz, Bruno. *Sanatorium under the Sign of the Hourglass.* Translated by Celina Wieniewska. Walker, 1978. *The Complete Fiction of Bruno Schulz* (Walker, 1989) is a combination of the stories from *The Street of Crocodiles* and *Sanatorium.* Madeline G. Levine published a new translation of this collection, *Collected Stories,* with Northwestern University Press in 2018.

1939: Niewieski, Zdisław [Witold Gombrowicz]. *Possessed; or, The Secret of Myslotch.* Translated by J. A. Underwood from the French translation. Marion Boyars, 1980.

1957: Gombrowicz, Witold. *Bacacay.* Translated by Bill Johnston. Archipelago Books, 2004.

Lem, Stanisław. *Memoirs of a Space Traveler.* Translated by Joel Stern and Maria Swiecicka-Ziemianek. Secker & Warburg, 1982.

———. *The Star Diaries.* Translated by Michael Kandel. Seabury Press, 1976.

1959: Lem, Stanisław. *Eden.* Translated by Marc E. Heine. Harcourt Brace Jovanovich, 1989.

———. *The Investigation.* Translated by Adele Milch. Seabury Press, 1974.

1961: Lem, Stanisław. *Memoirs Found in a Bathtub.* Translated by Christine Rose. Seabury Press, 1973.

———. *Return from the Stars.* Translated by Barbara Marszal and Frank Simpson. Secker & Warburg, 1980.

1962: Lem, Stanisław. *Solaris.* Translated from the 1964 French edition by Joanna Kilmartin and Steve Cox. Walker, 1970. First direct Polish-to-English translation by Bill Johnson. Amazon Kindle Edition, 2014.

1964: Lem, Stanisław. *The Invincible.* Translated by Wendayne Ackerman from the 1967 German edition. Seabury Press, 1973. First direct Polish-to-English translation by Bill Johnston. Pro Auctore Wojciech Zemek, 2006.

1965: Lem, Stanisław. *The Cyberiad: Fables for the Cybernetic Age.* Translated by Michael Kandel. Seabury Press, 1974.

1968: Lem, Stanisław. *His Master's Voice.* Translated by Michael Kandel. Harcourt Brace Jovanovich, 1983.

———. *More Tales of Pirx the Pilot.* Translated by Louis Iribarne and Magdalena Majcherczyk. Harcourt Brace Jovanovich, 1982.

———. *Peace on Earth.* Translated by Elinor Ford and Michael Kandel. Harcourt Brace, 1994.

———. *Tales of Pirx the Pilot.* Translated by Louis Iribarne. Harcourt Brace Jovanovich, 1979.

1971: Lem, Stanisław. *The Futurological Congress (from the Memoirs of Ijon Tichy).* Translated by Michael Kandel. Seabury Press, 1974.

1975: Lem, Stanisław. *The Chain of Chance.* Translated by Louis Iribarne. Harcourt Brace Jovanovich, 1978.

1977: Lem, Stanisław. *Mortal Engines*. Translated by Michael Kandel. Seabury Press.

1981: Kandel, Michael, ed. *The Cosmic Carnival of Stanisław Lem: An Anthology of Entertaining Stories by the Modern Master of Science Fiction*. Continuum.

1987: Lem, Stanisław. *Fiasco*. Translated by Michael Kandel. Harcourt Brace Jovanovich.

1992: Sapkowski, Andrzej. *The Sword of Destiny*. Translated by David French. Orbit, 2015.

1993: Grabiński, Stefan. *The Dark Domain*. Translated by Miroslaw Lipinski. Dedalus.

1994: Sapkowski, Andrzej. *Blood of Elves (Witcher #1)*. Translated by Danusia Stok. Gollancz, 2008.

1995: Sapkowski, Andrzej. *Time of Contempt (Witcher #2)*. Translated by David French. Gollancz, 2013.

1996: Powaga, Wiesiek, ed. and trans. *The Dedalus Book of Polish Fantasy*. Dedalus.

Sapkowski, Andrzej. *Baptism of Fire (Witcher #3)*. Translated by David French. Gollancz, 2014.

Tokarczuk, Olga. *Primeval and Other Times*. Translated by Antonia Lloyd-Jones. Twisted Spoon Press, 2010.

1997: Sapkowski, Andrzej. *The Tower of Swallows (Witcher #4)*. Translated by David French. Orbit, 2016.

1998: Huberath, Marek S. *Nest of Worlds*. Translated by Michael Kandel. Restless Books, 2014.

Tokarczuk, Olga. *House of Day, House of Night*. Translated by Antonia Lloyd-Jones. Northwestern University Press, 2003.

1999: Sapkowski, Andrzej. *The Lady of the Lake (Witcher #5)*. Translated by David French. Orbit, 2017.

2007: Grabiński, Stefan. *In Sarah's House*. Translated by Wiesiek Powaga. CB Editions.

Sapkowski, Andrzej. *The Last Wish*. Translated by David French. Gollancz.

2010: Kandel, Michael, ed. and trans. A Polish Book of Monsters: Five Dark Tales from Contemporary Poland. PIASA Books.

2012: Grabiński, Stefan. *On the Hill of Roses*. Translated by Miroslaw Lipinski. Hieroglyphic Press.

Miłosz, Czesław. *The Mountains of Parnassus*. Translated by Stanley Bill. Yale University Press, 2017.

2013: Sapkowski, Andrzej. *The Malady, and Other Stories: An Andrzej Sapkowski Sampler*. Unknown translator. Gollancz.

———. *Season of Storms*. Translated by David French. Orbit, 2018.

2015: Dukaj, Jacek. *The Old Axolotl*. Translated by Stanley Bill. Allegro.

Notes

1. Classic Polish *fantastyka* on film is also available online, including the movie adaptation of *Wesele* by Andrzej Wajda.

2. Also spelled *fantastika*.

3. Clute and Langford, "Fantastika."

4. See the special issues of *Science Fiction Studies* on Lem: Csicsery-Ronay, "Stanislaw Lem"; "Special Section on Stanislaw Lem"; and Latham, "Special Section on Stanislaw Lem's *Summa Technologiae*."

5. Gliński, "Stanislaw Lem."

6. Suvin and Clute, "Lem, Stanislaw."

7. See Klapcsik, *Liminality in Fantastic Fiction*.

8. By Boris Nirenburg in 1968, Andrei Tarkovsky in 1972, and Steven Soderbergh in 2002.

9. See Csicsery-Ronay, "The Book Is the Alien."

10. Cordasco review.

11. See Seed, "Investigating the Investigation."

12. Cordasco review.

13. Cordasco review.

14. See also Pa and Raczynska, *Lemistry*, which includes stories by Lem translated by Antonia Lloyd-Jones.

15. For discussions of Polish futurism, see Kolesnikoff, "Polish Futurism"; and Kremer, "Polish Futurism Revisited."

16. Cordasco review.

17. Cordasco review. For more on Dukaj's oeuvre, see Frelik, "Jacek Dukaj's Science Fiction as Philosophy." *The Old Axolotl* was only released as a hypertextual e-book with digital elements that can be rendered by three-dimensional printers.

18. Florczyk review. See also Bill, "Translator's Introduction."

19. Bill, "Translator's Introduction," xxiii.

20. Cisco, "Schulz, Bruno."

21. *Culture.pl*, "Witold Gombrowicz."

22. Mandolessi, "Gombrowicz and the Monster."

23. Stanisław Lem became very interested in Grabiński's work and edited a collection of the latter's stories in Polish.

24. See Piven, "Threats or Victims."

25. The series has also been turned into a highly popular video game (starting with *The Witcher* in 2007) and has been adapted into an English-language television series for Netflix (beginning in 2019).

26. See a profile of her at https://culture.pl/en/artist/olga-tokarczuk.

27. Powaga, "Introduction: Dialogue with the Devil," 8.

28. Wodzynski review.

Secondary Sources

Bill, Stanley. "Translator's Introduction: Science Fiction as Scripture." In *The Mountains of Parnassus*, by Czesław Miłosz, translated by Stanley Bill, vii–xxv. New Haven, CT: Yale University Press, 2017.

Cisco, Michael. "Schulz, Bruno." In *Horror Literature throughout History: An Encyclopedia of the Stories That Speak to Our Deepest Fears*, edited by Matt Cardin, 734–35. Westport, CT: Greenwood Press, 2017.

Clute, John, and David Langford. "Fantastika." In *The Encyclopedia of Science Fiction*, edited by John Clute, David Langford, Peter Nicholls, and Graham Sleight. London: Gollancz, updated October 30, 2018. http://www.sf-encyclopedia.com/entry/fantastika.

Cordasco, Rachel. "Review: *Memoirs Found in a Bathtub* by Stanislaw Lem." *SFinTranslation. com* (March 2018). https://www.sfintranslation.com/?p=3919.

———. "Review: *Mortal Engines* by Stanislaw Lem." *SFinTranslation.com* (March 2019). https://www.sfintranslation.com/?p=6516.

———. "Review: *Nest of Worlds* by Marek Huberath." *SFinTranslation.com* (May 2016). https://www.sfintranslation.com/?p=77.

———. "Review: *The Old Axolotl: Hardware Dreams* by Jacek Dukaj." *SFinTranslation.com* (May 2016). https://www.sfintranslation.com/?p=201.

———. "Review: *Return from the Stars* by Stanislaw Lem." *SfinTranslation.com* (December 2017). https://www.sfintranslation.com/?p=3413.

Csicsery-Ronay, Istvan, Jr. "The Book Is the Alien: On Certain and Uncertain Readings of Lem's *Solaris*." *Science-Fiction Studies* 12, no. 1 (1985): 6–21.

———, ed. "Stanislaw Lem." Special issue, *Science Fiction Studies* 13, pt. 3 (1986). https://www.depauw.edu/sfs/covers/cov40.htm.

Culture.pl. "Witold Gombrowicz." https://culture.pl/en/artist/witold-gombrowicz.

Florczyk, Piotr. "*The Mountains of Parnassus* by Czesław Miłosz." *World Literature Today* (January 2017). https://www.worldliteraturetoday.org/2017/january/mountains-parnassus-czeslaw-milosz.

Frelik, Pawel. "Jacek Dukaj's Science Fiction as Philosophy." In *Lingua Cosmica: Science Fiction from around the World*, edited by Dale Knickerbocker, 22–38. Urbana: University of Illinois Press, 2018.

Gliński, Mikołaj. "Stanisław Lem: Did the Holocaust Shape His Sci-Fi World?" *Culture. pl* (September 2017). https://culture.pl/en/article/stanislaw-lem-did-the-holocaust-shape-his-sci-fi-world.

Klapcsik, Sandor. *Liminality in Fantastic Fiction: A Poststructuralist Approach*. Jefferson, NC: McFarland, 2012.

Kolesnikoff, Nina. "Polish Futurism: Its Origin and the Aesthetic Program." *Canadian Slavonic Papers* 18, no. 3 (1976): 301–11.

Kremer, Aleksandra. "Polish Futurism Revisited: Anatol Stern and His Post-war Poetry Recording." *Modern Language Review* 111, no. 1 (2016): 208–26.

Latham, Rob, ed. "Essays on Stanislaw Lem's *Summa Technologiae*." Special issue, *Science Fiction Studies* 40, pt. 3 (2013). https://www.depauw.edu/sfs/covers/cov121.htm.

Mandolessi, Silvana. "Gombrowicz and the Monster." *Polish Review* 60, no. 2 (2015): 53.

Pa, Rage, and Magda Raczynska, eds. *Lemistry: A Celebration of the Work of Stanislaw Lem*. Manchester: Comma Press, 2012.

Piven, Sviatoslav. "Threats or Victims: The Ambiguous Nature of Supernatural Creatures in Andrzej Sapkowski's and George R. R. Martin's Fantasy." *A/R/T Journal* 3, no. 1 (2015): 20–28.

Powaga, Wiesiek. "Introduction: Dialogue with the Devil." In *The Dedalus Book of Polish Fantasy*, edited by Wiesiek Powaga, 7–10. Sawtry, Cambridgeshire: Dedalus, 1996.

Seed, David. "Investigating the Investigation: Mystery Narratives in *The Investigation* and *The Chain of Chance.*" In *Lemography: Stanislaw Lem in the Eyes of the World,* edited by Waclaw M. Osadnik and Peter Swirski, 43–64. Liverpool: Liverpool University Press, 2014.

"Special Section on Stanislaw Lem." *Science Fiction Studies* 19, pt. 2 (July 1992). https://www.depauw.edu/sfs/covers/cov57.htm.

Suvin, Darko, and John Clute. "Lem, Stanislaw." In *The Encyclopedia of Science Fiction,* edited by John Clute, David Langford, Peter Nicholls, and Graham Sleight. London: Gollancz, updated April 3, 2020. http://www.sf-encyclopedia.com/entry/lem_stanislaw.

Wodzynski, Lukasz. "A Polish Book of Monsters: Five Dark Tales from Contemporary Poland." *Cosmopolitan Review* 3, no. 2 (2011). http://cosmopolitanreview.com/a-polish-book-of-monsters/.

Russian-Language SFT

Introduction[1]

The word for "speculative fiction" in Russian (as it is in many eastern European countries) is *fantastika* (*фантастика*), a term that doesn't distinguish between what readers in the Anglosphere call "science fiction" and "fantasy." With a literary heritage rich in fairy tales and a focus on excellence in math and science, Russia has produced a significant number of speculative fiction writers who have frequently moved between and combined subgenres, including Arkady and Boris Strugatsky and Victor Pelevin. Indeed, science fiction appeared in Russia not too long after Jules Verne and H. G. Wells were gaining in popularity in France and England at the end of the nineteenth century, with scientist and author Konstantin Tsiolkovsky (who explored the possibility of space flight in 1878) writing novels about the construction of space habitats and future planetary colonization. However, one must also not forget Mikhail Bulgakov's and Nikolai Gogol's satirical fantasies, Sigizmund Krzhizhanovsky's stories of the absurd, and Mikhail Saltykov-Shchedrin's dystopias just before the turn of the twentieth century.[2]

Russian speculative fiction in the early twentieth century (following the Bolshevik Revolution) took two divergent paths in response to censorship and ideological pressures. According to Alex Shvartsman, while writers like Alexander Belyaev (*Professor Dowell's Head*, *The Amphibian Man*) and Aleksei Tolstoy (*Aelita*, *The Hyperboloid of Engineer Garin*) wrote procommunist science fiction, others, such as Evgeny Zamyatin (*We*) and Mikhail Bulgakov (*The Fatal Eggs*,

Vita Nostra (2018)

Heart of a Dog, The Master and Margarita) criticized the Soviet regime via dystopian narratives.[3] These latter works were not published in the Soviet Union until
decades after they were originally written.

By the 1970s and '80s, Kir Bulychev was bringing in more young readers to the
world of science fiction, but it was Arkady and Boris Strugatsky who made Russian speculative fiction famous around the globe, especially in the Anglosphere.
Despite censorship and the threat of political denunciation, these remarkable
brothers produced a diverse array of speculative fiction that included everything
from detective to thriller tropes and ultimately, according to Russian scholar
John Givens, "shaped a whole generation of Soviet readers."[4]

With the fall of the Soviet Union in the late 1980s, translated and original speculative fiction exploded in popularity. Once more, writers produced dystopias that

Roadside Picnic (2012)

reflected the economic, social, and political instabilities that inevitably followed the collapse of a decades-long regime. This time, though, modern fantasy began to compete with science fiction. The 1990s saw the rise of Sergei Lukyanenko and the massive popularity of his urban fantasy *Nightwatch* series. Fantasy mixed with dystopia, horror, and magical realism as well thrived at the end of the twentieth century, especially in texts by Pelevin, Max Frei, and Marina and Sergey Dyachenko. Science fiction, too, has adapted to new sociopolitical conditions; Dmitry Glukhovsky, for his part, has described the books in his *Metro* series as "postnuclear novel[s]," with their setting in a post–World War III apocalyptic world.[5]

The wealth of speculative fiction written by those who grew up in the post-Soviet era, with access to the Internet and stories from around the world, is in keeping with the dynamic and expressive texts that were written and translated throughout the twentieth century. With authors such as Mariam Petrosyan, K. A. Teryna, Anna Starobinets, and many others, the future of Russian speculative fiction is bright indeed.

Rachel S. Cordasco

The Texts

Russian-language SFT, like its French-language counterpart, has been available to Anglophone readers in large numbers since the 1960s. This veritable flood of (mostly) science fiction from the USSR into the United States reflected both the former's long speculative fiction history as well as its intensive space program during that time. In the United States at the time, the appetite for science fiction and fantasy was growing, and thus it turned to the USSR—out of curiosity and perhaps a mix of fear and jealousy—to find out what Russian-language science fiction authors were exploring in their stories and novels.[6]

Much has been written about the differences in style and theme in the science fiction of the two nations during the Cold War, with the focus usually on Soviet writers either toeing the party line or attempting to avoid the literary censors. Rafail Nudelman explores this in detail, arguing in part that because "Russian social thought and, accordingly, Russian literature have always displayed a heightened sense of their ideological potentiality," it was inevitable that Russian-language science fiction would be influenced by such constraints. Russian writers turned to science fiction in the 1920s, Nudelman explains, because they needed "to assume a distinct position toward this social upheaval and to represent it in adequate—i.e., global—terms." Characterized by "the expansion of space and the contraction of time," these stories often reflected the Cold War reality, often featuring powerful groups locked in conflict.[7]

The flood of Russian-to-English translations of science fiction in the 1960s and '70s can also be explained by the USSR's political and social liberalization at that time, as well as the rise in English-to-Russian translations of Anglo-American science fiction. The Moscow-based Foreign Languages Publishing House (which would be split later into Progress and Mir) enabled authors such as Ivan Yefremov, Sever Gansovsky, and Arkady and Boris Strugatsky to be read by millions of Anglophone science fiction fans. Magazines specializing in science fiction also provided markets for authors that hadn't existed before.

The end of the Cold War and the dissolution of the Soviet Union have not, however, slowed the pace of Russian-language SFT. Indeed, between 1960 and 1989, fifty works of Russian speculative fiction were translated and published in

200

the Anglophone world; between 1990 and the present, the number jumped to fifty-seven. What's interesting about these two numbers is that their similarity conceals an important shift, namely, from the domination of science fiction to the ascendance of fantasy. Of the fifty texts published prior to 1989, forty-five were classified as science fiction, while just twenty of the fifty-seven texts published after 1989 were so classified. As in several other source languages, fantasy has started to surpass science fiction as the dominant subgenre. This is the case specifically with Russian-language fantasy because the subgenre was basically discouraged until the fall of the Soviet Union.[8]

And while horror and the gothic account for just a fraction of the Russian-language SFT up until now, they reveal the energy and experimentation that Russian authors bring to a genre that has been around for centuries in various forms.

SCIENCE FICTION

Anthologies have been the major source of Russian-language science fiction in English since 1961, with twenty out of the twenty-three anthologies published before 1989. The remaining three anthologies (published between 1990 and the present) contain works of fantasy or both fantasy and science fiction. No other source-language SFT has brought Anglophone readers such a large number of anthologies and with such a famous cast of introduction writers (Theodore Sturgeon, Isaac Asimov, and others).[9] Macmillan's Best of Soviet Science Fiction series, which ran from 1977 to 1986, came in hardback and trade paperback editions, with the latter published by Collier and called "Theodore Sturgeon Introduces New Science Fiction from Russia." These texts included anthologies, collections, and novels, including those by Arkady and Boris Strugatsky as well as Kir Bulychev.[10]

These anthologies, with titles such as *Destination: Amaltheia* (1963), *Last Door to Aiya: A Selection of the Best New Science Fiction from the Soviet Union* (1968), and *The Ultimate Threshold: A Collection of the Finest in Soviet Science Fiction* (1970), introduced Anglophone audiences to the stories of Valentina Zhuravleva, Gennady Gor, Ilya Varshavsky, the Strugatskys, and many others.[11] In the 1960s, editor Robert Magidoff and translators Doris Johnson and Helen Saltz Jacobson brought readers *Russian Science Fiction* (1963), *Russian Science Fiction, 1968*, and *Russian Science Fiction, 1969* with Anglophone publishers, including Macmillan, Ardis, and UK-based MacGibbon and Kee, capitalizing on the Russian-language SFT wave.[12]

For Theodore Sturgeon, whose reputation as an American speculative fiction author was ensured by the 1960s, Soviet science fiction offered a fascinating glimpse into a world only partially exposed to American eyes through stories in the national news. Having already written introductions to four Strugatsky texts (three novels and one collection) by the time he wrote his remarks for *New Soviet Science Fiction* in 1979, Sturgeon notes that, despite the inevitable examples of "national and cultural difference," "one is struck by the similarities herein of the people and places we know, the problems and issues we face."[13] Theorizing that "boundaries and ethnic and cultural and political differences tend to blur in this metier," Sturgeon offers a different title for the anthology: *New Terran Science Fiction.*

Despite the sharp drop-off in anthologies of Russian-language science fiction in English after the 1980s, Anglophone readers can still find such texts even into the twenty-first century. *Worlds Apart: An Anthology of Russian Fantasy and Science Fiction* (2007) ranges across the centuries, offering Anglophone readers stories from the eighteenth century down through the 1950s, with only a few familiar authors included. *Red Star Tales: A Century of Russian and Soviet Science Fiction* (2015) includes only stories that hadn't been translated before. Like *Worlds Apart*, *Red Star* helps us situate Soviet and Russian science fiction in its historical and political contexts. Early stories about the rise of autonomous machines mix with later tales of animated heads, the future of nuclear research, and portals to other dimensions.

Amid the avalanche of anthologies and collections from Russia during the 1960s, only two novels made their way into Anglophone readers' hands around this time: Ivan Yefremov's *Andromeda: A Space-Age Tale* (1957; 1959) and Konstantin Tsiolkovsky's *Beyond the Planet Earth* (1920; 1960). Both prominent scientists and authors, Yefremov (a paleontologist and leading figure in the growth of Soviet science fiction) and Tsiolkovsky (who explored the possibility of space flight in 1878) offer readers visions of a far future that includes global weather control and an ideal socialist state (Yefremov) and the construction of space habitats in high Earth orbit with a view to future planetary colonization (Tsiolkovsky). Tsiolkovsky's story, originally published in Russian in 1920, predates Yefremov's by nearly forty years, but like the Anglophone science fiction and SFT published at the height of the Cold War, these novels imagine an Earth radically changed by technology and the human race poised to explore beyond the solar system.

The 1970s and '80s witnessed the near-complete domination of Russian-language SFT by Arkady and Boris Strugatsky, who are often regarded as the greatest Russian science fiction authors of the twentieth century. Fourteen Strugatsky novels and collections were published in English between 1973 and 1986.[14] In a recent study of the Strugatskys' fiction, scholar and translator Kevin Reese argues that the brothers' early traumatic experience in the Siege of Leningrad, the constant anti-Semitic threat, and their decision to walk a fine line between expression and anti-Soviet sedition are integral to an understanding of their fictional worlds—what Reese terms their "celestial hellscapes."[15] In terms of their overall career, the brothers' more optimistic stories that include the possibility of a near-future utopia eventually give way to more somber, pessimistic tales in which utopia is impossible in the face of human nature and history.[16] Recurring themes include humans dealing with radically different alien societies, the suspicion that Earth's destiny is being directed by aliens, and the belief that science is inadequate in its attempt to explain the workings of the universe. Several of their books can easily be read as searing critiques of the Soviet system, though the brothers were careful to disguise such a critique in science fictional scenarios. We can also attribute the success of their work to their deft handling of multiple subgenres (for example, some stories are a mix of mystery and science fiction or of picaresque and science fiction) and their talent for building worlds in which alien presences are felt but not necessarily seen or consciously recognized.

Of the Strugatskys' sixteen texts in English, ten are set in the "Noon universe," with recurring characters who act out humanity's urge to explore and grow beyond the species' dependence on Earth. Several of these novels or novellas involve one or two human explorers trying to make sense of an alien planet and coming up against their own imaginative and psychological shortcomings. In *Hard to Be a God* (1964; 1973), an undercover agent from the future planet Earth named Anton travels to another planet that nonetheless is home to a human population.[17] This civilization, however, is still in the Middle Ages, and Anton witnesses the brutality of human progress and how religion has been used to justify power. An opposite problem exists in *Noon, 22nd Century* (1962; 1978), in which two explorers find themselves on a planet similar to Earth but a century in the future, where they find automated farms supporting large populations, conveyor-belt roads that erase distances, and a drive to discover that promises the inhabitants knowledge that will allow them to leap to unimaginable scientific and artistic heights.

Like *Hard to be a God*, *Prisoners of Power* (1971; 1977) features a gifted human explorer (Maxim Kammerer) who works for a security agency; he must struggle with whether to intervene in what he sees as a troubled civilization on another planet. The first of the Kammerer subsection of Noon-universe books, *Prisoners* portrays a civilization that is technologically advanced (they have atomic bombs) but socially oppressive. Frustrated by the brutality and bureaucracy around him, Kammerer joins an underground resistance and becomes embroiled in the planet's political affairs. Similarly, *Escape Attempt* (1982), which included the title novella plus two other Noon-universe stories (*Space Mowgli* and *The Kid from Hell*), is the story of two adventurers eager to learn about life on other planets. This time, though, the Strugatskys' characters happen upon a planet governed by a brutal feudalism that features extermination camps and strange alien machines with which prisoners are forced to interact.

With *Beetle in the Anthill* (1979; 1980) and *The Time Wanderers* (1986; 1986), the Strugatskys continue their Maxim Kammerer subplot. In *Beetle*, Kammerer's mission is to locate a certain "Progressor" who has returned to Earth without permission (Progressors are scouts who make first contact with alien civilizations). Part science fiction, part thriller, part mystery, *Beetle* ultimately asks us to consider who this rogue Progressor might be and why he poses a danger to Earth. By *The Time Wanderers*, Kammerer has become the head of the Department of Unusual Events (and this novel functions as his fictional memoir). Having realized that an alien species' version of Progressors might be interfering with humanity, Kammerer tasks one of his agents with discovering the truth. While not part of the Noon universe, *Definitely Maybe* (1976–77; 1978) takes up this theme of Progressors and Wanderers from the perspective of an astrophysicist bent on winning the Nobel Prize. Despite sending his family to his mother's house and holing himself up in his office, Dmitri Malianov keeps being interrupted, as if someone or something is deliberately interfering with his work and a leap forward in human understanding.

Far Rainbow and *The Second Invasion from Mars* (1964, 1968; 1979), published together, offer readers further alien and alien-planet scenarios. In the former novella, a thousand people, mostly scientists, live on planet Rainbow and conduct experiments in instant teleportation. And while this research regularly produces potentially destructive shock waves, the scientists have figured out how to neutralize them . . . for the most part. The day eventually comes when a new kind of wave threatens the entire planet, and just a small portion of its inhabitants and research can squeeze into the only spaceship available. In the face of this catastrophe, the inhabitants must decide who should live and how much of their research they can save from destruction. Unlike *Far Rainbow*, *The Second Invasion* is set on Earth and acts as a kind of sequel to H. G. Wells's *The War of the Worlds*. Having learned their lesson from that first attempted invasion of Earth, the Martians have returned with a much more sinister and subtle plan—namely, to weave themselves into the fabric of human society and then change it from within.

Set hundreds of years before the other Noon-universe novels, *Space Apprentice* (1962; 1981) follows a young space welder (on probation) named Yuri Borodin as he attempts to catch up with the spaceship that is transporting his fellow workers to their next site. A kind of space picaresque, the novel features giant Martian slugs, gravitational wave experiments, space pearls, and even capitalist-communist quarrels. The Strugatskys followed up on this story with *The Final Circle of Paradise* (1965; 1976), set ten years after the events of *Space Apprentice* and after the World Council has been established on Earth to unify the planet. A utopian vision of a future world, *The Final Circle* imagines how advanced technology and political thought might bring about a better world.

The brothers' surrealist *Snail on the Slope* (1972; 1980) is made up of two inter-locking stories ("Kandid" [1966] and "Pepper" [1968]) set on an alien planet in which reality itself is called into question.[18] While both Kandid and Pepper are trapped in a kind of nightmarish void, they have diametrically opposed perspec-tives on the "alien" space that is at the heart of the book: the Forest. It is this Forest and "the Directorate" that form two poles of human experience in the book: while the former encompasses many forms of constantly evolving and fluctuating life that is mystical in its mysteriousness, the former reveals a hyperbureaucratized state filled with people who have become like robots.

The Strugatskys returned to (various versions of) Earth in five of their books, four of which were originally written in the 1970s. *Roadside Picnic* (1972; 1977), the most famous of these, tells the story of a "stalker" named Red Schuhart who illegally enters his local "Zone" to pick up alien artifacts to sell on the black mar-ket.[19] At some point, these strange artifacts were scattered all over the planet, as if members of an alien race had made a brief stop on Earth and left their trash laying around when they continued on their journey. These objects somehow disturb the laws of physics wherever they are found, which is why it's so danger-ous for people like Red to enter these Zones. Nonetheless, he keeps going back, even when one of his expeditions turns out to be more dangerous than ever. An unseen but definitely felt alien presence also hangs over *The Dead Mountaineer's Inn* (1970; 2015), in which a police inspector goes to a mountain inn for vacation and becomes caught up in a maelstrom of intrigue, deception, mystery, mur-der, ghosts, vampires, alien robots, and an avalanche that cuts the inn off from the outside world.[20] Once again, the Strugatskys deftly combine multiple genres (country-house murder or Poirot mystery, science fiction, and horror) to produce a surreal text that keeps the reader guessing.

In *The Doomed City* (1989; 2016), which the Strugatskys couldn't publish in Russian until 1989 because of censorship, people from different points in the twentieth century have been plucked from their time lines and dropped into a strange (alien?) place in which the traditional laws of physics don't seem to apply.[21] Each of these people may be taking part in an alien experiment, and they spend much of the novel trying to figure out its purpose. And while we never find out what that purpose is, the book's commentary on unknown forces driving human behavior invites us to read *The Doomed City* in the context of the Soviet Union's oppressive and mazelike bureaucracy.

Even with their impressive output and internationally recognized talent, the Strugatskys weren't the only Russian-language speculative fiction authors being translated into English in stand-alone editions during the 1970s, '80s, and beyond. Indeed, work by Kir Bulychev, Mikahil Emtsev and Eremei Parnov (who always wrote as a team), Dmitri Bilenkin, Vladimir Savchenko, Alexander Beliaev, Vadim

Shefner, Chingiz Aitmatov, Alexei Nikolaevich Tolstoy, Vladimir Voinovich, Alexander Kabakov, and Tatyana Tolstaya has been made available to Anglophone readers between 1977 and 2003.[22] Several of these authors have also had multiple short pieces included in the anthologies discussed above.

Bulychev's novel and two collections in English translation are filled with stories about (often benign) aliens, broken-down spaceships, and human acclimation to alien life and even to robots.[23] In the title story of *Half a Life, and Other Stories* (1975; 1977), cosmonauts discover a dead automated alien spacecraft and learn about the woman who was kidnapped by it in the days after World War II. The only human on board, she kept a journal of her experiences and tried to establish a relationship with the other specimens that the ship had collected on its journey. Other stories feature temporal distortion ("I Was the First to Find You," "May I Please Speak to Nina"), interplanetary Olympic Games, an alternate Earth, and an alien snow maiden. *Gusliar Wonders* (1972; 1983), made up of eight tales all dealing with the inhabitants of the Russian town of Great Gusliar, offers readers a more lighthearted perspective on science fiction and fantasy themes. Here, tripodal aliens apologize to the town's residence for crashing their spaceship nearby, an alien uses dreams to determine if humans should join a galactic union, and a flower in one woman's window box might be the key to saving the galaxy.

In his only translated novel, *Those Who Survive* (1988; 2000), Bulychev tells the story of the starship *PolarStar*, which crashed on an unnamed planet during an exploratory mission. Those who survived the crash had to then find a way to survive on the hostile world, with its poisonous and carnivorous plants, dangerous animals, and extreme climate. Twenty years later, those living in the small human settlement start making plans to return home to Earth and their loved ones, but the effort might make them lose what they've worked so hard to build.

The translations of work by Chinghiz Aitmatov, Vladimir Voinovich, and Alexander Kabakov in the 1980s and '90s reveal a distinct pessimism about the future of the Soviet political system. Aitmatov's *The Day Lasts More than a Hundred Years* (1980; 1983) stands out from the era's Soviet science fiction in part because it was written by a Kyrgyz and set partly in Kyrgyzstan. A story about the clash between the old and the new, as well as humanity's responsibility toward alien species in need of help, Aitmatov's book offers us a glimpse into Brezhnev-era politics and concerns near the end of the Cold War. Voinovich's *Moscow 2042* (1986; 1987) follows a time traveler (via Lufthansa Airlines) sixty years into the future, where the communist "Utopia" in Moscow is actually an oppressive network made up of the KGB, the Communist Party, and the Russian Orthodox Church. Ultimately, a parodic version of Aleksandr Solzhenitsyn rides into liberate Moscow. Finally, in Kabakov's novella *No Return* (1990; 1990), a time-traveling physicist jumps three years into the future to witness the chaos and brutality resulting from a strong resistance to perestroika.

The Russian-language SFT of the post–Soviet Union era is much darker and more pessimistic than its predecessors. It is also more gender diverse, with authors like Tatyana Tolstaya, Anna Starobinets, and Olga Slavnikova publishing multiple genre-bending texts that both skewer and satirize what Russia was and has become. Vladimir Sorokin, Dmitri Glukhovsky, and Sergei Lukyanenko (the most popular speculative fiction author in post–Soviet Russia)[24] also use a postapocalyptic perspective to explore the ruins of what was the Soviet Union.

Sorokin, known for his postmodernist satires and the controversies he has generated, has five books in English translation, three of which constitute the mashup of science fiction, fantasy, and absurdity that is the *Ice* trilogy.[25] In *Ice* (2002; 2007), *Bro* (2004; 2011), and *23,000* (2005; 2011), Sorokin imagines an alternate history in which people realize that the ice from the Tunguska meteorite that struck Siberia in 1908 can be shaped into hammers that will awaken twenty-three thousand (blue-eyed, blond-haired) people who are destined to destroy the world. Like Sorokin himself, the *Ice* trilogy has generated enough controversy and polarized opinion to keep it on the Anglophone reader's radar for a long time to come.

Sorkin's other two novels in English, *Day of the Oprichnik* (2006; 2011) and *The Blizzard* (2010; 2015), share with the *Ice* trilogy an interest in apocalyptic scenarios. A near-future tale about a resurrected czarist regime and its Oprichniki (formed centuries before by Ivan the Terrible to torture and murder his enemies), *Day of the Oprichnik* is a response to Russia's slide back into authoritarianism under Putin and reads like a carnivalesque horror story. *The Blizzard*, however, is smaller in scope and ambition, focusing on a doctor trying to make his way to a village that has been struck by a strange illness that transforms people into zombies. The trip shouldn't take long, and the doctor has a vaccine that should be able to combat the disease, but an intense storm seems to block him at every turn. The doctor experiences all kinds of strange and unexplained things and meets fascinating people, all of which turns the journey into more of an internal one than otherwise.

Dmitri Glukhovsky's *Metro* trilogy, like Sorokin's, is a bleak work of postapocalyptic fiction, though Glukhovsky's centered around the aftermath of a nuclear World War III. The first book in the trilogy, *Metro 2033* (2002; 2009), first appeared online in 2002 and expanded into an interactive reading experience, ultimately becoming a printed book and a video game.[26] Set in the near future after nuclear war has wiped out most of humanity, the novel follows the few survivors who have made it to the Moscow Metro—the largest air-raid shelter in the world and now a refuge for the last people on Earth. Each station of the Metro has become its own mini state, replicating the divisions and resentments that had existed before the war. As described in *Metro 2034* (2009; 2014) and *Metro 2035* (2015; 2016), it is ultimately the survivors' desire to find out if any other survivors exist around the world, and their desperate fight against a mysterious disease making its way from station to station, that drives the protagonists to team up across station lines and risk their lives.

In this male-dominated milieu of Russian-language SFT, a few female voices have leaped onto Anglophone readers' radar, namely, Tatyana Tolstaya, Anna Starobinets, and Olga Slavnikova. Each of these writers creates worlds that exist somewhere between science fiction and fantasy, encouraging us to think more about the fluidity of genre "boundaries." Tolstaya's satirical and disturbing novel *The Slynx* (2000; 2003) is a dystopia with many twists.[27] Set two hundred years in the future after an unspecified nuclear disaster, the novel offers us a picture of downtrodden people with scales on their bodies and claws instead of toes, relying on mice for food and clothing. Benedikt, the protagonist, slowly learns about the books that have been hidden in people's homes and confiscated by the authorities, but despite reading them and even agreeing to carve a statue of Pushkin for a friend, he remains unable to think beyond the literal. Here Tolstaya signals the futility (and nobility) of attempting to resurrect a world long since reduced to ashes.

Dystopia and satire also characterize Starobinets's work, though her books and stories often defy genre boundaries. While **An Awkward Age** (2005; 2010) has been classified as horror, **The Living** (2011; 2012) and **The Icarus Gland** (2013; 2014) read more like dystopian science fiction. The title story in *An Awkward Age* focuses on a young boy whose body is apparently taken over by an ant colony. As the boy matures and continues to write in his diary, the reader realizes that the young man's voice has been taken over by the ruler of the anthill. In *The Living*, Starobinets, like Emtsev and Parnov in *World Soul* and Sorokin in the *Ice* trilogy, explores the concept of collectivism in the context of postapocalyptic life. After a catastrophe has whittled the world's population down to an unchanging three billion, death no longer exists. Instead, via a kind of reincarnation, people are reborn with an "in-code" that keeps track of their previous selves. When one child is born without a code, he threatens to upset the balance of the entire world. The stories in *The Icarus Gland*, as well, imagine a bleak near future in which technology rules people's lives to the extreme.[28]

Olga Slavnikova's **2017** (2006; 2010) and **Light Headed** (2010; 2015) also partake in the bleak dystopian literary turn in Russian speculative fiction. The novel *2017*, a near-future satire, is set a century after the Russian Revolution and focuses on the extremes of capitalism, environmental disaster, and paranoid conspiracies.[29] Even more disturbing is her novel *Light Headed*, a story about a child, Maxim, who is born with an empty space above his brain. His literal light-headedness gives him unexpected powers, like allowing him to ingest information from the air. Yet like the unfortunate "extra" person in Starobinets's *The Living*, Maxim finds out that his very existence threatens the world and is responsible for natural disasters, terrorist attacks, and other catastrophes. When he's encouraged to commit suicide in order to save the world, though, Maxim refuses, thus beginning his rebellion against the state.

Unlike the dystopian novels that have marked the first two decades of the twenty-first century in Russian SFT, Sergei Lukyanenko's *The Genome* (1999; 2014) harks back to earlier science fiction in its exploration of humans in space.[30] Known best in the Anglophone world for his six-part *Night Watch* fantasy series, Lukyanenko's far-future science fiction thriller focuses on humans being divided into "naturals" and "speshes" (people who have been genetically modified to serve a single purpose). One pilot in particular has been modified to navigate the dangers of space by communication telepathically with his ship, but when he meets a teenage girl with a secret, his willingness to help her threatens his own world and many others. Lukyanenko's other work of science fiction in English, *Labyrinth of Reflections* (1996; 2016), takes on the physiological and psychological dangers of immersive VR.

FANTASY

As with many other literary traditions, modern Russian fantasy has evolved from centuries-old folklore and fairy tales. The two strains in Russia in particular— romantic and folkloric—first emerged in the work of Nikolai Gogol and then in Alexei Nikolayevich Tolstoy, with the latter becoming the dominant form by the end of the nineteenth century. According to the entry on Russia in *The Encyclopedia of Fantasy*, the subgenre developed haltingly over the past century and a half because "in a properly functioning materialistic and atheistic society, there could be no place for demons, wizards, goblins, and so on."[31] Yet Russian fantasy has branched off into fascinatingly varied streams, from the absurdist stories of Sigizmund Krzhizhanovsky to the black satire of Bulgakov and Zamyatin, and from Lukyanenko's urban fantasy to Victor Pelevin's surrealist satires. In a study of Lukyanenko's fantasy fiction, critic Stephanie Dreier argues that the "two moral paradigms that dominate recent Russian fantasy fiction and film [are] individualism and collectivism": a dichotomy that is especially relevant to the linguistically and ethnically diverse post-Soviet Russia.[32]

Perhaps the most well-known Russian-language fantasy author in translation is Mikhail Bulgakov, a physician, playwright, and author who served in World War I. Highly controversial in the Soviet Union before his death in 1940, works like *The Master and Margarita* (1967; 1967) and *The Heart of a Dog* (1969; 1968) were published only posthumously. The former, considered by many to be one of the classics of modern Russian literature, offers readers a perspective on 1930s Soviet life via the story of the devil and his companions: a naked witch and a large chess-playing, vodka-drinking, talking black cat. As one critic has pointed out about *The Master and Margarita*, "Written during the Stalinist purges in the 1930s, [the novel] expresses the criticism of dictatorship, bureaucracy, and corruption in society under Stalin through an allegory of good and evil, raising questions about human nature, atheism, and totalitarianism."[33] So too *The Heart of a Dog* criticizes the Soviet social structure, with a scientist implanting human testicles into the body of a dog (read: "peasant") in order to "civilize" him. Ultimately, though, the experiment fails, and the dog-man must be changed back.

The fantasy fiction of Zamyatin, Osip Senkovsky, and Krzhizhanovsky emerges from a similar vein as Bulgakov's: all darkly satirize Russian culture and politics via stories that veer often into the surreal. Best known for his anti-utopian novel *We*, Zamyatin also wrote a few dozen collections of stories, plays, and essays, as well as a second (nonspeculative) novel. Reminiscent at times of the brief, fable-like absurdist tales of American naturalist author Stephen Crane, the pieces in *The Dragon: Fifteen Stories* (1967) focus on, among other things, the sordid and grotesque in daily life, the hypocrisies of organized religion, and the futility and tragedy of war. In the title story, the "dragon" is nothing more than a single trigger-happy soldier in an oversize uniform that echoes the size of his ego.

Thanks to NYRB Classics, the absurdist, surreal stories of Krzhizhanovsky are being published in beautiful editions that help contextualize the work of a man often discussed in relation to Karel Čapek, Witold Gombrowicz, and even Jorge Luis Borges.[34] In Krzhizhanovsky's tales (collected in *7 Stories* [2006], *Memories of the Future* [2009], and *Autobiography of a Corpse* [2013]), the Eiffel Tower stomps across Paris, human bile becomes the world's best clean alternative-energy source, a wrong train leads to a nightmarish alternate reality, and a corpse misses his own funeral. What sets Krzhizhanovsky apart, according to Leiderman, is his talent for writing "quasi-scientific anti-utopias," such as those included in the linked narratives of *The Letter Killers Club* (2012). Here the members of a secret society come together to imagine the most fantastical scenarios without committing any of their ideas to paper (and thus "tainting" them). The backdrop of this society is 1920s Moscow, where suspicion and an increasingly oppressive political and social system have infiltrated even this group. Krzhizhanovsky's only novel, *The Return of Munchausen* (1928; 2017) picks up the legend surrounding the real-life eighteenth-century cavalry officer Hieronymus von Münchhausen and reimagines him as a two-hundred-year-old secret agent for Lenin.

A turn toward fantasy becomes apparent in Russian-language SFT starting in the 1990s. Both Vladimir Orlov's *Danilov, the Violist* (1980; 1987) and Nikolai

Dezhnev's *In Concert Performance* (1995; 1999) employ the figure of a benign demon sent to Earth to accomplish a specific task (and getting sidetracked). In Orlov's novel, a viola player in a professional orchestra is actually a demon in disguise who is supposed to be wreaking havoc around the world but would rather visit his girlfriends and do *good* deeds. When he falls in love with a human woman, Danilov is eventually recalled from Earth and put on trial by his fellow demons, who ultimately send him back to Earth forever with the added bonus of forever hearing the heartbeats of those suffering around the world. In Dezhnev's novel, Earth is also a punishment for a wayward demon. Sent to atone for his past sins, the demon (Lukary) arrives as a middle-aged man and quickly falls in love, though the demon sent to watch his every move begins to plot against Lukary with his beloved's physicist husband. Soon after, the chaos that Lukary has been causing in the woman's apartment (to drive the husband away) breaks out of the confines of that single household.

Victor Pelevin has taken fantasy to a whole new level since the early 1990s with his Zamyatin- and Krzhizhanovsky-esque absurdist satires of modern Russia. Populating his texts are werewolves, vampires, insects that are also human, and many other bizarre and grotesque characters.[35] The werewolf figure features prominently in his collection *A Werewolf Problem in Central Russia* (1998) and novel *The Sacred Book of the Werewolf* (2004; 2008), functioning as a liminal character that offers multiple and simultaneous possibilities.[36] Certain stories in the collection portray people and animals that are both one thing *and* another: black swans are enchanted KGB agents, werewolves are businessmen, and video games are reality (and vice versa). Winner of the Russian Booker Prize, this collection serves as an absurdist and philosophically fascinating panorama of post-Soviet thought and art. *The Sacred Book*, too, includes a paradoxical figure—a fox-werewolf who is also a two-centuries-old prostitute in a fifteen-year-old's body. Awakening desire wherever she goes, this fox-werewolf enables Pelevin to explore themes of desire, consumerism, and human nature in modern Russia.

With *Empire V: The Prince of Hamlet* (2006; 2016), Pelevin pivots from werewolves to vampires, suggesting that civilization, culture, human values, and desires are all nothing more than the side effects of vampiric domestication.[37] Pelevin's protagonist is transformed from a human into a vampire before our very eyes, initiated into the elite group of vampires, and told a completely different story about the rise of human civilization, which he can accept only following his transformation. In *Omon Ra* (1992; 1998), Pelevin suggests that the entire Soviet space program was a badly engineered hoax: for example, robot-guided spacecraft are actually manned by humans (who have no hope of returning to Earth) and don't really work anyway. Thus, Pelevin sends up the Soviet Union's space race with the United States in the 1950s and '60s. Pelevin turns to deconstructing myths in *The*

Helmet of Horror: The Myth of Theseus and the Minotaur (2005; 2006), where the Labyrinth becomes a twenty-first-century Internet chat room controlled by some mysterious "master" or "monitor." While the characters try to find their way out of the maze, readers are invited to consider how our perceptions and understanding of fantasy versus reality change depending on our situations both on- and offline.

Like Starobinets, Pelevin also explores the human connections to insects, imagining in *The Life of Insects* (1993; 1999) what would happen if businessmen, fathers and sons, drug dealers, and artists were simultaneously human and mosquito, fly, cicada, and so on. All of these characters are connected in unexpected ways, and all are trying to understand one another's motivations in a society that is still struggling with what it wants to become. The same is true, too, in *The Clay Machine-Gun* (1996; 1999), in which one man believes that he is both alive during the civil war of 1919 and the counterrevolutionary chaos of 1991. His fear that literature will be reduced to ashes doesn't change at all between those two dates, reflecting Pelevin's own complicated relationship with modern literature.

In *Homo Zapiens* (1999; 2000), Pelevin tells the story of a shop assistant who was once a failed poet and eventually joins an ad agency to sell Western products to Russian consumers (following the collapse of the Soviet Union).[38] Despite trying to convince himself that nothing has changed, Pelevin's protagonist is forced to adapt to shifting circumstances, developing advertising concepts for US companies that will, in the *future*, wish to market to Russians. His increasingly bizarre and hallucinogenic ad scripts are accepted enthusiastically by his bosses, who are out to make as much money as possible as quickly as possible. Pelevin takes this idea of imagining what post-Soviet Russia will look like in the future even further in *S.N.U.F.F.: Special Newsreel Universal Feature Film: A Utøpia* (2011; 2015), where the rich live in flying cities and wage war from time to time on the Earthbound poor. From their perch, the oligarchs and other elites manipulate (for their own amusement) the media that the less fortunate consume, blurring the line between the dying Earth of their reality and the virtual reality that keeps them going.

Like Pelevin's *Empire V*, Lukyanenko's *Night Watch* series (1998–2014; 2006–16) imagines that our world is not at all as it seems, with individuals known as "Others" monitoring the forces of Light and Darkness in order to keep the reality that humans perceive in check. This urban fantasy meets spy thriller reimagines the Cold War in terms of the two groups of Others who are locked in a political rivalry: Lukyanenko's characters continually discuss the moral questions inherent in supporting the "Light" or the "Dark," which is connected to the parallel Twilight dimension that exists in conjunction with our own reality. As the series develops, this delicate balance of power between the Light and Dark is threatened by the prophesied coming of a new kind of Other, one that can perhaps see the future and that threatens the Night Watchers and Day Watchers themselves.

More high fantasy from Russia comes to readers from Alexey Pehov, whose *Chronicles of Siala* series (2002–3; 2010–12) (published by Tor) focuses on a mysterious entity that is gathering giants, ogres, and others into a menacing army, threatening the city of Avendoom. Only Shadow Harold, a master thief, can save it—but first he must capture the magic horn that restores the world's peace and balance. Tor has also published the translation of the first book (*Chasers of the Wind* [2005; 2014]) in Pehov's next series, *The Cycle of Wind and Sparks*, a story of evil necromancers, master thieves, and magical weapons.

A lighter kind of fantasy can be found in the novels of "Max Frei," the pen name of Ukrainian-born author Svetlana Yuryevna Martynchik. In the four books of *The Labyrinths of Echo* series (1996–97; 2009–13), Frei (who is also the main character) wanders among alternate universes, rooting out criminals and facing down dangerous magicians. An unusual combination of humor and fantasy, the *Labyrinths* series offers readers a wide variety of adventures involving, for instance, a palace coup, attempted murder, and various international intrigues. Mix together Sherlock Holmes, Harry Potter, Doctor Who, and various Douglas Adams characters, and you'll get a better picture of Max Frei.

The psychological horror/fantasy written by Marina and Sergei Dyachenko makes these authors unique in the general field of Russian-language SFT. Indeed, their superb mixture of subgenres makes their work especially inviting. In their first two translated books—*The Burned Tower* (1998; 2012) and *The Scar* (2012; 2012)—the Dyachenkos give modern fantasy a new twist. *The Burned Tower* tells the story of a truck driver on a lonely stretch of road tasked with delivering caged animals to someone on the other side of the forest. Picking up a mysterious hitchhiker, he is unexpectedly drawn into the world of an ancient curse by what turns out to be a Piper from ancient folklore. Ancient curses come up once more in *The Scar*, the story of an arrogant member of the elite guards who kills an innocent man in a duel and then must embark on a dangerous journey to undo the damage he has caused.

It is with *Vita Nostra* (2007; 2018), however, that the Dyachenkos have gained the most attention in the Anglophone world.[39] A remarkable example of dark philosophical fantasy and psychological horror, the novel operates on multiple levels: it is at once a bildungsroman, a philosophical meditation on the nature of language and reality, and an exploration of the mysteries and possible demonic presences lying latent in everyday life.

Several other works of Russian-language fantasy have been published in English since 2007, ranging from sword-and-sorcery adventure to magical realism. Nick Permov's *Godsdoom* (1994; 2007) falls into the former category and tells the story of Hedin (Sage of Darkness), who has been sent into exile for a thousand years as punishment for misuse of his powers. Hedin has used that time to hone his skills and learn new types of magic in order to exact revenge on the magi who sentenced him. Moving from high fantasy to an intriguing mix of time travel and mythical civilizations, Mariia Galina's *Iramifications* (2004; 2008) highlights the seeming rift between East and West that continues to this day. When a trader from present-day Odessa embarks on a trip to Istanbul with his new partner, the two wind up chasing a robber and then getting bound up in the theft of a stele from a local museum. They are then transported back in time to the mythical city of Iram and its political and court intrigues.

Along the lines of the Dyachenkos' psychological fantasy, Armenian author Mariam Petrosyan's *The Gray House* (2009; 2017) explores how an isolated boarding school for disabled young people on the outskirts of town turns out to be a force in and of itself, shaping the inhabitants' lives in subtle ways. Only when several students die in a short amount of time does the school bring in an outsider to try to understand the House's power over the students and staff. This sense of mystery also informs Tatyana Tolstaya's collection *Aetherial Worlds* (2014; 2018), a much different kind of literature from her novel *The Slynx*. In these stories, Tolstaya blends memory and the imagination to explore how the two come together to color and even alter how we narrate our own lives. What seems like a normal day, for instance, can suddenly be swept aside by cursed amulets, murder, and second sight. Like several other works of Russian fantasy, *Aetherial Worlds* asks readers what might happen if we thought harder about the nature of what we call "reality."

HORROR

While only a few works of Russian-language horror and the gothic have come to Anglophone readers since the 1960s, those examples give us a glimpse of how the subgenre has developed in a country that has undergone significant social and cultural change. Three out of the four texts that are discussed in this section are associated with gothic horror, a subgenre that has a particularly interesting position in Russian speculative fiction. In the introduction to a multiessay study on the history of the Russian gothic, Kevin Platt, Caryl Emerson, and Dina Khapaeva explain that while gothic literature developed much later in Russia than in the rest of Europe, it found particularly fertile ground in postrevolutionary literature. After all, "the Gothic is a mode ideally suited to register and critique historical and social experience in Russia, which for the past century has been among the world's greatest laboratories of failed revolution." Fearing that capitalism would continue to erupt into the developing and solidifying communist order, revolutionary figures "found in the Gothic a striking and highly marketable emblem of this threatening reanimation of prerevolutionary ills."[40]

Russian-language gothic texts have only sporadically appeared in English since the height of the Cold War, however. The first was Alexei Constantinovich Tolstoy's collection *Vampires: Stories of the Supernatural* (1969), which includes an 1841 pre-Dracula novella that explores an ancient family legend, a cursed Italian villa, Russian vampires, and a young woman's ghost. Thus, the figure of the vampire, though only intermittently used in Russian horror, continues to fascinate modern Russian authors. Indeed, fifteen years after this Tolstoy collection, Anglophone readers were treated to an anthology of such tales, *Russian 19th-Century Gothic Tales* (1984), which ranges across the past two centuries and offers readers a fascinating peek into the development of this subgenre in Russia and the Soviet Union.

A further anthology of the Russian gothic came out more recently, titled *Red Spectres: Russian Gothic Tales from the Twentieth Century* (2013). Including nine stories that have never before been translated into English, this anthology includes pieces by such internationally known authors as Ivan Bunin, Zamyatin, and Bulgakov, who used the gothic to explore the decay of imperial Russia and the conflicting and confusing alliances that formed and dissolved as the communists gained power.

Finally, there's Ludmilla Petrushevskaya's disturbing horror collection *There Once Lived a Woman Who Tried to Kill Her Neighbor's Baby: Scary Fairy Tales* (2011; 2009).[41] Here are stories of a woman driven by jealousy to try to sabotage her neighbor's pregnancy, a young hitchhiker who learns to strike matches that take her to an alternate reality, and encounters with old acquaintants that are later discovered to have been impossible. Strange dreams, unexplained occurrences, grim situations: Petrushevskaya's stories tap into the subtle horrors that lurk below everyday life and give them a fable-like stylistic veneer to make them seem almost timeless.

✳ ✳ ✳

Due to its longtime existence and robust variety, Russian-language SFT offers Anglophone readers one of the most exciting libraries of speculative fiction from a non-Anglophone tradition. The breadth of science fiction, fantasy, and horror tales reveals that authors writing in Russian have grappled in fascinating ways with massive social and political transitions, even as they look inward to the realm of dreams and the soul, as well as outward toward European and Anglo-American literary styles and genres.

Primary Sources

Titles are arranged by date of first English-language publication.

1833: Senkovsky, Osip. *The Fantastic Journeys of Baron Brambeus.* Translated by Louis Pedrotti. Peter Lang, 1993.

1920: Tsiolkovsky, Konstantin. *Beyond the Planet Earth.* Translated by Kenneth Syers. Pergamon Press, 1960.

1925: Bulgakov, Mikhail. *Diaboliad, and Other Stories.* Translated by Carl R. Proffer. Indiana University Press, 1972.

Ginsburg, Mirra, ed. and trans. *The Fatal Eggs, and Other Soviet Satire.* Macmillan, 1965.

1928: Krzhizhanovsky, Sigizmund. *The Return of Munchausen.* Translated by Joanne Turnbull and Nikolai Formozov. New York Review of Books, 2017.

1937: Beliaev, Alexander. *Professor Dowell's Head.* Translated by Antonina W. Bouis. *Best of Soviet Science Fiction.* Macmillan, 1980.

1950: Tolstoy, Alexei Nikolaevich. *Aelita.* Translated by Leland Fetzer. Ardis, 1985.

1957: Yefremov, Ivan. Andromeda: *A Space-Age Tale.* Translated by George Hanna Foreign Languages Publishing House, 1959.

1961: *The Heart of the Serpent.* Editor uncredited. Translated by R. Prokofieva. Foreign Languages Publishing House, 1961. Reprinted under the title *More Soviet Science Fiction,* with an added introduction by Isaac Asimov. Editor uncredited. Translated by R. Prokofieva. Collier Books, 1962.

A Visitor from Outer Space. Editor uncredited. Translated by Violet L. Dutt. Foreign Languages Publishing House, 1961. Reprinted as *Soviet Science Fiction,* with an added introduction by Isaac Asimov. Editor uncredited. Translated by Violet L. Dutt. Collier Books, 1962.

1962: Strugatsky, Arkady, and Boris Strugatsky. *Noon, 22nd Century (Noon Universe).* Translated by Patrick L. McGuire. Macmillan, 1978.

———. *Space Apprentice (Noon Universe).* Translated by Antonina W. Bouis. Macmillan, 1981.

1963: Dixon, Richard, ed. *Destination: Amaltheia.* Translated by Leonid Kolesnikov. Foreign Languages Publishing House.

Magidoff, Robert, ed. *Russian Science Fiction: An Anthology.* Translated by Doris Johnson. Ryerson Press.

1964: Emtsev, Mikhail, Eremei Parnov. *World Soul.* Translated by Antonina W. Bouis. *Best of Soviet Science Fiction.* Macmillan, 1978.

Strugatsky, Arkady, and Boris Strugatsky. *Hard to Be a God.* Translated from the German edition by Wendayne Ackerman. Seabury Press, 1973. First direct Russian-to-English translation by Olena Bormashenko. Chicago Review Press, 2014.

1964, 1968: Strugatsky, Arkady, and Boris Strugatsky. *Far Rainbow / The Second Invasion from Mars.* Translated by Antonina W. Bouis. Macmillan, 1979. Far Rainbow was originally published in English in 1967 by Mir, translated by A. G. Myers.

216

1965:   Strugatsky, Arkady, and Boris Strugatsky. *The Final Circle of Paradise*. Translated by Leonid Renen. DAW Books, 1976.

      ———. *Monday Begins on Saturday*. Translated by Leonid Renen. DAW Books, 1977. New translation: *Monday Starts on Saturday*. Translated by Andrew Bromfield. Seagull Books, 2005.

1966:   Obukhova, Lydia. *Daughter of the Night: A Tale of Three Worlds*. Translated by Mirra Ginsburg. Macmillan, 1974.

1967:   Bulgakov, Mikhail. *The Master and Margarita*. Translated by Mirra Ginsburg. Grove Press. Translated by Michael Glenny. Harper & Row, Signet, and Collins editions, 1967.

      Savchenko, Vladimir. *Self-Discovery*. Translated by Antonina W. Bouis. Best of Soviet Science Fiction. Macmillan, 1979.

      Zamyatin, Yevgeny. *The Dragon: Fifteen Stories*. Translated by Mirra Ginsburg. Random House.

1967, 1964:   Shefner, Vadim. *The Unman / Kovrigin's Chronicles*. *The Unman* translated by Alice Stone Nakhimovsky and Alexander Nakhimovsky. *Kovrigin's Chronicles* translated by Antonina W. Bouis. Best of Soviet Science Fiction. Macmillan, 1980.

1968:   Ginsburg, Mirra, ed. and trans. *Last Door to Aiya: A Selection of the Best New Science Fiction from the Soviet Union*. S. G. Phillips.

      Magidoff, Robert, ed. *Russian Science Fiction, 1968: An Anthology*. Translated by Helen Saltz Jacobson. New York University Press/ University of London Press.

      The Molecular Café. Editor uncredited. Unknown translator. Mir.

      Path into the Unknown: The Best Soviet SF. Editor uncredited. Unknown translator. MacGibbon and Kee.

1969:   Bulgakov, Mikhail. *The Heart of a Dog* (written 1925). Translated by Michael Glenny. Collins and Harvill Press, 1968. Translated by Mirra Ginsburg. Grove Press, 1968.

      Magidoff, Robert, ed. *Russian Science Fiction, 1969: An Anthology*. Translated by Helen Saltz Jacobson. New York University Press.

      Tolstoy, Alexei Constantinovich. *Vampires: Stories of the Supernatural*. Edited by Linda Kuehl. Translated by Fedor Nikanov. Hawthorn Books.

1970:   Bearne, C. G., ed. *Vortex: New Soviet Science Fiction*. Unknown translator. MacGibbon and Kee.

      Ginsburg, Mirra, ed. and trans. *The Ultimate Threshold: A Collection of the Finest in Soviet Science Fiction*. Holt, Rinehart, and Winston.

      Strugatsky, Arkady, and Boris Strugatsky. *The Dead Mountaineer's Inn: One More Last Rite for the Detective Genre*. Translated by Josh Billings. Melville House, 2015.

1971:   Strugatsky, Arkady, and Boris Strugatsky. *Prisoners of Power (Noon Universe: Maxim Kammerer)*. Translated by Helen Saltz Jacobson. Macmillan, 1977. New edition—based on a noncensored version—translated as *The Inhabited Island* by Andrew Bromfield. Chicago Review Press, 2020.

1972:   Bulychev, Kir. *Gusliar Wonders*. Translated by Roger DeGaris. Macmillan, 1983.

Strugatsky, Arkady, and Boris Strugatsky. *Roadside Picnic / Tale of the Troika*. Translated by Antonina W. Bouis. Macmillan, 1977. New translation: *Roadside Picnic*. Translated by Olena Bormashenko. Chicago Review Press, 2012.

————. *The Snail on the Slope*. Translated by Alan Myers. Bantam Books, 1980. New translation by Olena Bormashenko. Chicago Review Press, 2018.

————. *The Ugly Swans*. Translated by Alice Stone Nakhimovsky and Alexander Nakhimovsky. Macmillan, 1979.

1973: *Everything but Love*. Editor uncredited. Translated by Arthur Shkarovsky. Mir.
Journey across Three Worlds: Science-Fiction Stories. Editor uncredited. Translated by Gladys Evans. Mir.

1975: Bulychev, Kirill. *Half a Life, and Other Stories*. Translated by Helen Saltz Jacobson. Macmillan, 1977.

1976: Ginsburg, Mirra, ed. and trans. *The Air of Mars, and Other Stories of Time and Space*. Macmillan.

1976–77: Strugatsky, Arkady, and Boris Strugatsky. *Definitely Maybe: A Manuscript Discovered under Unusual Circumstances*. Translated by Antonina W. Bouis. Macmillan, 1978.

1978: Bilenkin, Dmitri. *The Uncertainty Principle*. Translated by Antonina W. Bouis. Best of Soviet Science Fiction. Macmillan.

1979: *New Soviet Science Fiction*. Editor uncredited. Best of Soviet Science Fiction. Macmillan. Reprinted with the same title, editor uncredited, and translated by Violet L. Dutt. Collier Books, 1980.
Strugatsky, Arkady, and Boris Strugatsky. *Beetle in the Anthill (Noon Universe: Maxim Kammerer)*. Translated by Antonina W. Bouis. Macmillan, 1980.

1980: Aitmatov, Chinghiz. *The Day Lasts More than a Hundred Years*. Translated by John French. Indiana University Press, 1983.
Orlov, Vladimir. *Danilov, the Violist*. Translated by Antonina W. Bouis. William Morrow, 1987.

1981: Gakov, Vladimir, ed. *World's Spring: Macmillan Best of Soviet Science Fiction*. Translated by Roger DeGaris. Macmillan.

1982: Altov, Genrikh, and Valentina Zhuravleva. *Ballad of the Stars*. Translated by Roger DeGaris. Best of Soviet Science Fiction. Macmillan.
Fetzer, Leland, ed. and trans. *Pre-Revolutionary Russian Science Fiction: An Anthology (Seven Utopias and a Dream)*. Ardis.
Strugatsky, Arkady, and Boris Strugatsky. *Escape Attempt*. Translated by Roger DeGaris. Macmillan.

1984: Korovin, Valentin, ed. *Russian 19th-Century Gothic Tales*. Raduga.
Strugatsky, Arkady, Boris Strugatsky, and Roger DeGaris, eds. *Aliens, Travelers, and Other Strangers*. Translated by Roger DeGaris. Best of Soviet Science Fiction. Macmillan.

1986: Strugatsky, Arkady, and Boris Strugatsky. *The Time Wanderers (Noon Universe: Maxim Kammerer)*. Translated by Antonina W. Bouis. Richardson and Steirman.
Voinovich, Vladimir. *Moscow 2042*. Translated by Richard Lourie. Harcourt Brace Jovanovich, 1987.

1988: Bulychev, Kir. *Those Who Survive*. Translated by John H. Costello. Xlibris / Fossicker Press, 2000.

1989: Strugatsky, Arkady, and Boris Strugatsky. *The Doomed City*. Translated by Andrew Bromfield. Chicago Review Press, 2016.

1990: Kabakov, Alexander. *No Return*. Translated by Thomas Whitney. William Morrow.

1992: Pelevin, Victor. *Omon Ra*. Translated by Andrew Bromfield. New Directions, 1998.

1993: Pelevin, Victor. *The Life of Insects*. Translated by Andrew Bromfield. Faber and Faber, 1999.

1994: Perumov, Nick. *Godsdoom*. Translated by Liv Bliss. Zumaya Otherworlds / Zumaya, 2007.

1995: Dezhnev, Nikolai. *In Concert Performance*. Translated by Mary Ann Szporluk. Nan A. Talese, 1999.

1996: Dyachenko, Marina, and Sergey Dyachenko. *The Scar*. Translated by Elinor Huntington. Tor Books, 2012.

Frei, Max. *The Stranger (The Labyrinths of Echo #1)*. Translated by Polly Gannon. Overlook Press, 2009.

Lukyanenko, Sergei. *Labyrinth of Reflections*. Translated by Liv Bliss. Independently published, 2016.

Pelevin, Victor. *The Clay Machine-Gun*. Translated by Andrew Bromfield. Faber and Faber, 1999.

1997: Frei, Max. *The Stranger's Magic (The Labyrinths of Echo #3)*. Translated by Polly Gannon and Ast A. Moore. Overlook Press, 2012.

———. *The Stranger's Shadow (The Labyrinths of Echo #4)*. Translated by Polly Gannon and Ast A. Moore. Overlook Press, 2013.

———. *The Stranger's Woes (The Labyrinths of Echo #2)*. Translated by Polly Gannon and Ast A. Moore. Overlook Press, 2011.

1998: Dyachenko, Marina, and Sergey Dyachenko. *The Burned Tower*. Translated by the authors. Tor Books, 2012.

Lukyanenko, Sergei. *Nightwatch (Night Watch #1)*. Translated by Andrew Bromfield. Anchor Canada, 2006.

Pelevin, Victor. *A Werewolf Problem in Central Russia, and Other Stories*. Translated by Andrew Bromfield. New Directions.

1999: Lukyanenko, Sergei. *The Genome*. Translated by Liv Bliss. Open Road Media, 2014.

Pelevin, Victor. *Homo Zapiens* (UK title: *Babylon*). Translated by Andrew Bromfield. Faber and Faber, 2000.

2000: Lukyanenko, Sergei. *Day Watch (Night Watch #2)*. Translated by Andrew Bromfield. Miramax Books, 2007.

Tolstaya, Tatyana. *The Slynx*. Translated by Jamey Gambrell. Houghton Mifflin, 2003.

2002: Glukhovsky, Dmitry. *Metro 2033 (Metro #1)*. Unknown translator. Gollancz, 2009.

Pehov, Alexey. *Shadow Chaser (Chronicles of Siala #2)*. Translated by Andrew Bromfield. Tor, 2011.

———. *Shadow Prowler (Chronicles of Siala #1)*. Translated by Andrew Bromfield. Tor, 2010.

Sorokin, Vladimir. *Ice (Ice #1)*. Translated by Jamey Gambrell. New York Review of Books, 2007.

2003: Pehov, Alexei. *Shadow Blizzard (Chronicles of Siala #3)*. Translated by Andrew Bromfield. Simon & Schuster UK, 2012.

2004: Galina, Mariia. *Iramifications*. Translated by Amanda Love Darragh. Glas New Russian Writing, no. 43. Glas, 2008.

Lukyanenko, Sergei. *Twilight Watch (Night Watch #3)*. Translated by Andrew Bromfield. Miramax Books, 2007.

Pelevin, Victor. *The Sacred Book of the Werewolf*. Translated by Andrew Bromfield. Faber and Faber, 2008.

Sorokin, Vladimir. *Bro (Ice #2)*. Translated by Jamey Gambrell. New York Review of Books, 2011.

2005: Lukyanenko, Sergei. *Last Watch (Night Watch #4)*. Translated by Andrew Bromfield. Miramax Books, 2009.

Pehov, Alexei. *Chasers of the Wind (The Cycle of Wind and Sparks #1)*. Translated by Elinor Huntington. Tor Books, 2014.

Pelevin, Victor. *The Helmet of Horror: The Myth of Theseus and the Minotaur*. Translated by Andrew Bromfield. Canongate Books, 2006.

Sorokin, Vladimir. *23,000 (Ice #3)*. Translated by Jamey Gambrell. New York Review of Books, 2011. Published as *The Ice Trilogy*. New York Review of Books, 2011.

Starobinets, Anna. *An Awkward Age*. Translated by Hugh Aplin. Hesperus Press, 2010.

2006: Krzhizhanovsky, Sigizmund. *7 Stories*. Translated by Joanne Turnbull. Glas.

Pelevin, Victor. *Empire V: The Prince of Hamlet*. Translated by Anthony Phillips. Gollancz, 2016.

Slavnikova, Olga. *2017*. Translated by Marian Schwartz. Overlook Duckworth, 2010.

Sorokin, Vladimir. *Day of the Oprichnik*. Translated by Jamey Gambrell. FSG, 2011.

2007: Dyachenko, Marina, and Sergey Dyachenko. *Vita Nostra*. Translated by Julia Meitov Hersey. Harper Voyager, 2018.

Levitsky, Alexander. *Worlds Apart: An Anthology of Russian Fantasy and Science Fiction*. Overlook Press.

2009: Glukhovsky, Dmitry. *Metro 2034 (Metro #2)*. Translated by Andrew Bromfield. Gollancz, 2014.

Krzhizhanovsky, Sigizmund. *Memories of the Future*. Translated by Joanne Turnbull with Nikolai Formozov. NYRB Classics.

Petrosyan, Mariam. *The Gray House*. Translated by Yuri Machkasov. AmazonCrossing, 2017.

2010: Slavnikova, Olga. *Light Headed*. Translated by Andrew Bromfield. Dedalus, 2015.

Sorokin, Vladimir. *The Blizzard*. Translated by Jamey Gambrell. FSG, 2015.

2011: Pelevin, Victor. *S.N.U.F.F.: Special Newsreel Universal Feature Film: A Utøpia*. Translated by Andrew Bromfield. Gollancz, 2015.

Petrushevskaya, Ludmilla. *There Once Lived a Woman Who Tried to Kill Her Neighbor's Baby: Scary Fairy Tales*. Translated by Keith Gessen and Anna Summers. Penguin Books, 2009.

Starobinets, Anna. *The Living*. Translated by James Rann. Hesperus Press, 2012.

2012: Krzhizhanovsky, Sigizmund. *The Letter Killers Club*. Translated by Joanne Turnbull. NYRB Classics.

Lukyanenko, Sergei. *New Watch (Night Watch #5)*. Translated by Andrew Bromfield. Harper, 2014.

2013: Krzhizhanovsky, Sigizmund. *Autobiography of a Corpse*. Translated by Joanne Turnbull with Nikolai Formozov. NYRB Classics.

Maguire, Muireann, ed. and trans. *Red Spectres: Russian Gothic Tales from the Twentieth Century*. Overlook Press.

Starobinets, Anna. *The Icarus Gland, and Other Stories of Metamorphosis*. Translated by James Rann. Skyscraper, 2014.

2014: Lukyanenko, Sergei. *Sixth Watch (Night Watch #6)*. Translated by Andrew Bromfield. Harper, 2016.

Tolstaya, Tatyana. *Aetherial Worlds*. Translated by Anya Migdal. Alfred A. Knopf, 2018.

2015: Glukhovsky, Dmitry. *Metro 2035 (Metro #3)*. Translated by Andrew Bromfield. Future, 2016.

Howell, Yvonne, ed. *Red Star Tales: A Century of Russian and Soviet Science Fiction*. Translation editor Anne O. Fisher. Russian Life Books.

Notes

1. Thank you to Alex Shvartsman for his input and assistance with this introduction.

2. "Russia," in *The Science Fiction Encyclopedia*.

3. See Alex Shvartsman's forthcoming essay about the history of Russian speculative fiction, "A Brief History of Russian SF in the 20th Century."

4. Givens, "Strugatsky Brothers and Russian Science Fiction," 4.

5. Sirotin, "Russian Science Fiction," 88.

6. Several works of Russian-language SFT were published in English prior to 1960, including Ivan Turgenev's *Knock, Knock, Knock, and Other Stories* (translated in 1922), Yevgeny Zamyatin's *We* (first translation 1924), and Alexei Nikolaevich Tolstoy's *The Death Box* (translated in 1936). See also Csicsery-Ronay and Simon, "Soviet SF."

7. Nudelman, "Soviet Science Fiction and the Ideology of Soviet Society," 38, 40.

8. Shvartsman, note to the author.

9. For a detailed listing of these anthologies and collections, see Terra and Philmus, "Russian and Soviet Science Fiction in English Translation."

10. In his *New York Review of Science Fiction* essay on the Strugatskys, Patrick L. McGuire explains that "in the mid-1980s, [he] was told by a former low-level Macmillan employee that the publisher had not particularly wanted the science fiction but had agreed to take it as part of a package deal in order to get the rights for an English translation of the new edition (1969–78) of *The Great Soviet Encyclopedia* (an English edition of selected articles was marketed mostly to large libraries, such as at universities). Macmillan made a genuine effort once they did have the sf series, getting Theodore Sturgeon to provide introductions to many

of the volumes, having the popular sf artist Richard Powers paint the covers, and paying decent rates to translators." McGuire, "Strugatskys' Traditional Science Fiction Revisited."

11. As translator Mirra Ginsburg writes in her preface to *The Ultimate Threshold*, "Perhaps because the authors are scientists, and thus are accustomed to greater freedom in their work, or because the science fiction form has not received as much attention from the political censorship as the rest of Soviet literature, the writers in this field can often say much more than those working in more realistic and conventional areas. Whatever the cause, the best of Soviet science fiction is far removed from the dreary mainstream of the standardized, made-to-order, didactic writing that still dominates the Soviet literary scene" (viii).

12. See also Isaac Asimov's introduction to *Soviet Science Fiction* (1962).

13. Sturgeon, introduction to *New Soviet Science Fiction*, ix.

14. While most of the Strugatskys' novels and collections were translated into English in the 1970s and '80s, new translations are being published as of this writing, mostly by Chicago Review Press.

15. Reese, *Celestial Hellscapes*. See also Howell, "Arkady and Boris Strugatsky."

16. In order to get published at all early in their career, the Strugatskys needed to write Soviet utopias. (Thanks to Alex Shvartsman for this point.)

17. Bhatia review.

18. Cordasco review.

19. See Reese, "Exceptions to the Laws of Thermodynamics: Roadside Picnic," in *Celestial Hellscapes*, 77–97.

20. Cordasco review.

21. Grinberg review.

22. Tatyana Tolstaya is the granddaughter of Alexei Nikolaevich Tolstoy.

23. Bulychev was primarily known in Russia as a writer of juvenile fiction.

24. Shvartsman, note to the author.

25. See Toymentsev, "Retro-Future in Post-Soviet Dystopia," 21–25. This essay also discusses Tolstaya's *The Slynx*, Slavnikova's *2017*, and Dmitry Bykov's *Zhd*.

26. Froggatt review.

27. Cordasco review.

28. Aslanyan review.

29. See Tretiakova, "Urban Spaces in Olga Slavnikova's Novel *2017*."

30. "Book Review: *The Genome*."

31. Gakov et al., "Russia."

32. Dreier, "Ethics of Urban and Epic Russian Fantasy," 73, 83.

33. Leshcheva, "Rediscovering *The Master and Margarita*," 1.

34. Clute, "Krzhizhanovsky, Sigizmund." See also Leiderman, "Intellectual Worlds of Sigizmund Krzhizhanovsky"; and Spektor, "Timely Discovery."

35. See Berlina, "Russian Magical Realism and Pelevin as Its Exponent," 11–15.

36. Le Guin review.

37. Cordasco and Gubasci reviews.

38. "Victor Pelevin."

39. Cordasco review.

40. Platt, Emerson, and Khapaeva, "Introduction: The Russian Gothic," 4.

41. These stories were translated and published in English first, then published in Russian later.

Secondary Sources

Asimov, Isaac. Introduction to *Soviet Science Fiction*. New York: Collier Books, 1962.

Aslanyan, Anna. "*The Icarus Gland*: A Book of Metamorphoses." *TLS* (April 2015): 21.

Berlina, Alexandra. "Russian Magical Realism and Pelevin as Its Exponent." *Comparative Literature and Culture* 11, no. 4 (2009).

Bhatia, Gautam. "*Hard to Be a God* by Arkady and Boris Strugatsky." *Strange Horizons* (2015). http://strangehorizons.com/non-fiction/reviews/hard-to-be-a-god-by-arkady -and-boris-strugatsky/.

"Book Review: *The Genome* by Sergei Lukyanenko (Translated by Liv Bliss)." *Skiffy and Fanty* (January 2015). https://skiffyandfanty.com/blogposts/reviews/bookreviews /book-review-the-genome-by-sergei-lukyanenko-translated-by-liv-bliss/.

Clute, John. "Krzhizhanovsky, Sigizmund." In *The Encyclopedia of Science Fiction*, edited by John Clute, David Langford, Peter Nicholls, and Graham Sleight. London: Gollancz, updated March 30, 2020. http://www.sf-encyclopedia.com/entry /krzhizhanovsky_sigizmund.

Cordasco, Rachel. "Marina and Sergey Dyachenko, *Vita Nostra*." *Foundation* (October 2019). https://www.sf-foundation.org/cordasco-dyachenko-liu.

———. "Review: *The Dead Mountaineer's Inn* by Arkady & Boris Strugatsky." *SFinTranslation.com* (May 2016). https://www.sfintranslation.com/?p=157.

———. "Review: *Empire V: The Prince of Hamlet* by Victor Pelevin." *SFinTranslation.com* (May 2016). https://www.sfintranslation.com/?p=291.

———. "Review: *The Slynx* by Tatyana Tolstaya." *SfinTranslation.com* (May 2017). https:// www.sfintranslation.com/?p=2018.

———. "Review: *The Snail on the Slope* by Arkady and Boris Strugatsky." *SFinTranslation. com* (October 2017). https://www.sfintranslation.com/?p=2931.

Csicsery-Ronay, Istvan, Jr., and Erik Simon. "Soviet SF: The Thaw and After." Special issue, *Science Fiction Studies* 31, pt. 3 (2004). https://www.depauw.edu/sfs/covers/cov94.htm.

Dreier, Stephanie. "The Ethics of Urban and Epic Russian Fantasy." *Canadian Slavonic Papers* 60, nos. 1–2 (2018): 72–86.

Froggatt, Michael. "*Metro 2033* by Dmitry Glukhovsky." *Strange Horizons* (May 2010). http:// strangehorizons.com/non-fiction/reviews/metro-2033-by-dmitry-glukhovsky/.

Gakov, Vladimir, Alan Myers, Igor Tolokonnikov, Peter Nicholls, and David Langford. "Russia." In *The Encyclopedia of Science Fiction*, edited by John Clute, David Langford, Peter Nicholls, and Graham Sleight. London: Gollancz, updated June 28, 2019. http://www. sf-encyclopedia.com/entry/russia.

Ginsburg, Mirra. Preface to *The Ultimate Threshold: A Collection of the Finest in Soviet Science Fiction*, edited and translated by Mirra Ginsburg. New York: Holt, Rinehart, and Winston, 1970.

Givens, John. "The Strugatsky Brothers and Russian Science Fiction, Editor's Introduction." *Russian Studies in Literature* 47, no. 4 (2011).

Grinberg, Marat. "The Soviet Matrix: On the Strugatsky Brothers' *The Doomed City*." *Los Angeles Review of Books*, November 5, 2016. https://lareviewofbooks.org/article/the-soviet-matrix-on-the-strugatsky-brothers-the-doomed-city/.

Gubasci, Beata. "Victor Pelevin, *Empire V: The Prince of Hamlet*." *Foundation* 46.1, no. 126 (2017): 109–11.

Howell, Yvonne. "Arkady and Boris Strugatsky: The Science-Fictionality of Russian Culture." In *Lingua Cosmica: Science Fiction from around the World*, edited by Dale Knickerbocker, 202–20. Urbana: University of Illinois Press, 2018.

Le Guin, Ursula. Review of *The Sacred Book of the Werewolf*, by Victor Pelevin. *Guardian*, February 15, 2008. https://www.theguardian.com/books/2008/feb/16/features reviews.guardianreview21.

Leiderman, N. L. "The Intellectual Worlds of Sigizmund Krzhizhanovsky." *Slavic and East European Journal* 56, no. 4 (2012): 507–35.

Leshcheva, Olga. "Rediscovering *The Master and Margarita*: From Creation to Adaptation." PhD diss., University of Alberta, 2013.

McGuire, Patrick L. "The Strugatskys' Traditional Science Fiction Revisited, Part 1." *NYRSF* (2013). https://www.nyrsf.com/2013/11/patrick-l-mcguire-the-strugatskys-traditional-science-fiction-revisited-part-1.html.

Nudelman, Rafail. "Soviet Science Fiction and the Ideology of Soviet Society." *Science-Fiction Studies* 16, no. 1 (1989): 38.

Platt, Kevin M. F., Caryl Emerson, and Dina Khapaeva. "Introduction: The Russian Gothic." *Russian Literature* 106 (May–June 2019): 1–9.

Reese, Kevin. *Celestial Hellscapes: Cosmology as the Key to the Strugatskiis' Science Fictions*. Boston: Academic Studies Press, 2019.

Shvartsman, Alex. "A Brief History of Russian SF in the 20th Century." Forthcoming.

Sirotin, Sergei. "Russian Science Fiction." *Russian Studies in Literature* 47, no. 4 (2011).

Spektor, Alexander. "A Timely Discovery: Experimental Realism of Sigizmund Krzhizhanovsky." *Slavic and East European Journal* 59, no. 1 (2015): 110–15.

Sturgeon, Theodore. Introduction to *New Soviet Science Fiction*. Best of Soviet Science Fiction. Macmillan, 1979.

Terra, Richard P., and Robert M. Philmus. "Russian and Soviet Science Fiction in English Translation: A Bibliography." *Science-Fiction Studies* 18, no. 2 (1991): 210.

Toymentsev, Sergey. "Retro-Future in Post-Soviet Dystopia." *CLCWeb: Comparative Literature and Culture* 21, no. 4 (2019). https://doi.org/10.7771/1481-4374.3179.

Tretiakova, Evgeniya. "Urban Spaces in Olga Slavnikova's Novel *2017*." PhD diss., University of Alberta, 2013.

"Victor Pelevin: Поколение «П»" (UK: *Babylon*; US: *Homo Zapiens*)." *Modern Novel* (n.d.). https://www.themodernnovel.org/europe/europe/russia/victor-pelevin/babylon/.

Spanish-Language SFT

Introduction

Speculative fiction in the twenty-one Spanish-language (SL) nations is as hetero-
geneous as one would expect in a vast geographical area with an ethnically diverse
population. Historically, when romanticism and the gothic were flourishing in
most of Europe, they were never really prominent in Spain or its then colonies.
It is not surprising, then, that much of Latin America's tradition of fantastic or
supernatural narratives has its roots in indigenous mythologies and folklores or,
in the Caribbean Basin, in those of African slaves. The European tradition would
be introduced there only as a result of the independence movements fought in the
nineteenth century, when it became fashionable for the liberal elite to be educated
in northern Europe and waves of Irish, German, and Italian immigrants arrived
to settle, particularly in Argentina. Once independence was won, science fiction,
based on post-Enlightenment interest in scientific advances, was able to take root.

With respect to much of the rest of the non-Anglophone world, Latin America enjoys a warranted reputation for having a long tradition of first-rate fantasy, and, while less well known in the Anglophone world, it has also produced
much fine science fiction. Examples of figures whose fame extends outside SL
countries include Horacio Quiroga (Uruguay, 1878–1937), Leopoldo Lugones
(Argentina, 1874–1938), and Clemente Palma (1872–1946), Peru's first writer of
science fiction. Furthermore, many of the major mainstream figures of the midcentury "boom" also published genre fiction, including Argentine authors Jorge

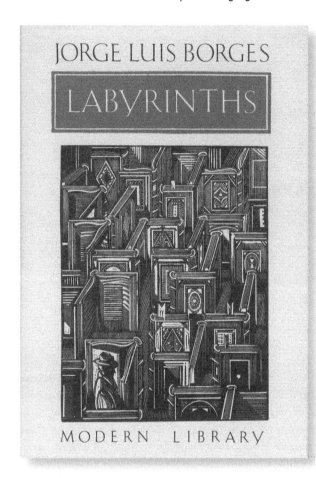

Labyrinths (1984)

Luis Borges (1899–1986), Julio Cortázar (1914–84), and Adolfo Bioy Casares (1914–99); Guatemalan Nobel Prize winner Miguel Ángel Asturias (1899–1974), who published political novels and was a precursor of Colombian Gabriel García Márquez and magical realism; and even Mexico's Carlos Fuentes, who ventured into the fantastic with his 1987 *Christopher Unborn*. The financial success of their translations smoothed the road for future SF practitioners. And, of course, Ursula K. Le Guin's promotion and translation of Angélica Gorodischer's *Imperial Kalpa* (1983, trans. 2003) were a shot in the arm to Latin American SF in general.

Comparing contemporary SF production between SL nations, it is not surprising to find that the more prosperous countries enjoy a more developed publishing infrastructure and therefore also see the highest production of SF: Spain, Argentina, and Mexico. Indeed, many Latin American authors of genre fiction

A Planet for Rent (2014)

go to publishing houses in Spain to publish their work. The greatest challenge faced by SF authors, however, is that competition from well-known English-language genre writers translated into Spanish dominates the market and suppresses demand for autochthonous writing, a situation that has occasioned the rise of Internet SF portals as venues for publication. Given this situation, most Anglophone publishers have not shown much interest in translating SL genre fiction. Fortunately, this has been changing, albeit slowly, since the events of the mid-twentieth century described above—and this change accelerated greatly in the second decade of the twenty-first.

This acceleration is due to a conjunction of factors from all sectors: fans, writers, publishers, bloggers, and critics. Fans are beginning to utilize social media effectively to share information, organize themselves into groups, and stage successful conventions where they can mingle with authors and where publishers can recruit, such as Spain's Celsius 232 and Hispacon. Respected Anglophone journals such as *World Literature Today* have begun to review more works published in translation; genre journals such as *Science Fiction Studies* have published numerous country- and area-focused special issues. Multilingual journals such as *Alambique* (United States) and *Brumal* (Spain) are springing up. In 2019 prestigious academic publisher Routledge established a new series, Studies in Global Genre Fiction. There are well-established academic conferences on SL SF in Lima, Peru, and León and Barcelona, Spain; one dedicated exclusively to SL Caribbean Basin SF is held in Puerto Rico. Small publishing houses such as Small Beer Press and Apex Publications, and genre-focused houses such as Tor, have begun to invest in this area. Publishers are beginning to send representatives to academic conferences to see what is out there. Two new online magazines have recently been founded: *Samovar* (United Kingdom) is a quarterly of and about speculative fiction translated from many languages, while the Spain-based *SuperSonic* publishes SF in English and Spanish as well as translations from and into both.

Bloggers, such as Rachel Cordasco (the editor of this book), help popularize translated SF. There now exists a stable core of excellent professional Spanish-to-English translators such as Sue Burke, Lawrence Schimel, and Steve Redwood. Perhaps the most important work done in recent years has been the anthologizing of translated SL speculative fictions, beginning with the wildly successful *Cosmos Latinos: An Anthology of Science Fiction from Latin America and Spain* (2003), edited by Andrea Bell and Yolanda Molina-Gavilán, who also did the first-rate translations. *Three Messages and a Warning*, an anthology of short SF from Mexico, was published in 2012, and several anthologies of short stories from the Pan-Hispanic world have appeared: Sportula, a small author-run purveyor of publishing-on-demand and electronic books, has translated a number of its titles since 2013 and launched the well-received anthologies *Terra Nova: An Anthology of Contemporary Spanish Science Fiction* (2015) and *Castles in Spain: 25 Years of Spanish Fantasy and Science Fiction* (2016). Also worthy of mention are Nevsky Books' *The Best of Spanish Steampunk* (2015) and Palabrista Press's *Spanish Women of Wonder* (2016).

It is impossible to identify even a majority of trends in SL SF over recent years. The 1990s and early 2000s saw an unsurprising surge in apocalyptically themed SF throughout SL countries, accompanied by an interest in cyborgs and hybridity that, in keeping with trends in other parts of the world, seems to have evolved into an interest in genetic manipulation and mutation. It is interesting to note that the (nearly) worldwide postmillennial zombie revival was not apparent in Latin America but was quite present in Spain.

At the risk of being proved wrong over time, I would identify two current trends that should soon be reflected in translations: the surge in the number of women authors being published and an explosion in their readership as well as the increasing popularity of the use of the fantastic or the Weird in the horror genre—particularly by women, some of whom are winning prizes and being translated into English, such as Mexico's Guadalupe Nettel or Argentina's Mariana Enriquez and Samanta Schweblin. This bodes well for the future of SF written in Spanish.

Dale Knickerbocker

The Texts

The Spanish-language speculative fiction that has been translated into English since the 1960s comes from a multitude of countries in the Americas and the Caribbean, as well as, of course, from Spain. And while Spain and Argentina together account for 75 percent of the translated fantasy, science fiction, and horror from Spanish-speaking countries, nations such as Chile, Cuba, and Mexico have shown Anglophone audiences the sheer variety of style and theme that Spanish-language authors have explored over time.[1]

Of course, Anglophone readers tend to associate "nonrealistic" literature from South America with magical realism, though that subgenre is only one of many that has been employed by Spanish-speaking South American authors in the twentieth and twenty-first centuries. Nonetheless, the work of Jorge Luis Borges and Gabriel García Márquez continues to captivate Anglophone readers, leading to translations of many of their novels and stories to the exclusion of other lesser-known voices. Only recently have Anglophone publishers "rediscovered" Borges's sometime collaborators, Adolfo Bioy Casares and Silvina Ocampo.

More Spanish-language SFT has been published in the 2010s than in the five preceding decades put together. Part of this likely reflects the fact that SFT itself is enjoying a kind of golden age, but also that Anglophone publishers realize that their readers want more from the Spanish-speaking speculative world than the familiar works of magical realism. What's particularly interesting is that, unlike with French or Russian (where translated science fiction dominated the 1960s and '70s), Spanish SFT meant *just* fantasy and magical realism between 1962 and 1990. Only with the publication in 2001 of Spanish neuroscientist and author Santiago Ramón y Cajal's *Vacation Stories* (originally published in Spanish in 1905) did Spanish science fiction start making its way into the hands of Anglophone readers. Since then, Spanish SFT has meant a steady mix of science fiction, fantasy and magical realism, and horror, with the latter constituting more than

10 percent of the total book-length titles (which is relatively high compared to other source languages). Several titles, especially those by Rodolfo Martinez, Liliana Colanzi, and Cristina Jurado, refuse easy categorization, effortlessly moving between fantasy and science fiction.

THE AMERICAS

Argentina and Colombia

Fantasy and Magical Realism   As noted earlier, Spanish-language SFT is most often associated in the Anglophone world with the "magical realism" of the midtwentieth century and its most well-known practitioners: Borges, Bioy Casares, Ocampo, and García Márquez.[2] The SFE characterizes the subgenre as "a technique of interpretation... [and] a way of telling the story of reality.... [I]ts deep popularity in Latin America reflects the fact that old European modes had failed to capture the complex, interwoven, fabulous history of that vast region."[3] Thus, magical realism is firmly situated in actual events, histories, and traditions, but it offers readers an alternative method of interpretation. Here absurdity mingles with surreality, resulting in a funhouse mirror–like style that destabilizes our belief in our perception of the world and of reality.

It is Borges who first showed Anglophone readers what magical realism could do to literature.[4] His highly acclaimed collection *Ficciones* (1944; 1962) (which includes the famous stories "Tlön, Uqbar, Orbis Tertius," "Pierre Menard, Author of Don Quixote," and "The Library of Babel") has been described by many as one of the most important books of the twentieth century, if not *the* most. In "Tlön," Borges uses the mise en abyme technique of the double-mirroring effect: an imaginary encyclopedia somehow creates the nation of Uqbar, which in turn creates a literature of the fantastic. The eponymous protagonist of "Pierre Menard" insists that he has created a "new" *Don Quixote* merely by rewriting it word for word. The other stories in *Ficciones* explore similarly dizzying and unsettling themes, including a library with infinitely recursive corridors and a game of chance that sounds a lot like what we would call "reality."

Borges's other collections of more overtly fantastic or magical realist stories, *Labyrinths* (1962) and *The Aleph* (1949; 1970), include tales of magical objects that contain the entire universe, the Labyrinth from the perspective of the Minotaur, and a reality in which the belief *in* reality has crumbled away.

Borges's close friends Adolfo Bioy Casares and Silvina Ocampo also produced some of the most accomplished magical realist texts of the twentieth century. Bioy Casares, best known now for his 1940 science fiction and fantasy novella *The Invention of Morel* (1940; 1964), had one collection and four novels translated into English between 1964 and 1987. *The Invention of Morel* centers on an unnamed island populated with high-society people who seem to exist in an eternal resort. Eventually, the protagonist realizes that these people are three-dimensional projections that may be what's left after the real models were killed by a mysterious film projector attempting to give them immortality. Bioy Casares's *A Plan for Escape* (1975; 1975) also features a fictional island as the setting for mysterious occurrences, bizarre brain surgeries, and one mad scientist (see Wells's *The Island of Doctor Moreau* [1896]).

Diary of the War of the Pig (1969; 1972) uses allegory and dream to explore mob terror and group mania a decade before the Dirty War (1976–83), when tens of thousands of Argentineans were disappeared under state terrorism (the Dirty War also has a central place in Rodrigo Fresán's science fictional trilogy). In *Asleep in the Sun* (1973; 1978), Bioy Casares uses the concept of "soul transplantation" to tell the story of a hospital in which doctors place dog souls into humans and vice versa. Madness, once again, is a central theme, and the soul transplants invite readers to think more deeply about how people are manipulated and controlled by powerful (sometimes medical) forces in an oppressive political atmosphere. Bioy Casares's last novel to be translated, *The Dream of the Heroes* (1954; 1987), described by critics as a "metaphysical mystery novel," tells the story of a man rescued from death by a mysterious person and the same events happening again years later. The concept of "destiny" plays a major role in the novel, with a sorcerer telling the protagonist that it is ultimately how people explain their lives to themselves.

Writing at the same time as Borges and Bioy Casares, Silvina Ocampo also collaborated with the two men on multiple projects, including *The Book of Fantasy* (1940, translated into English in 1988), which includes stories of the fantastic from writers around the world. Ocampo's two novels and one collection in English reveal her important contribution to the development of magical realism in Argentina.[5] Only in the twenty-first century, however, has her work become available to Anglophone readers. In *The Topless Tower* (1986; 2010), Ocampo combines fantasy and horror in a story about one man meeting a stranger carrying eerie paintings, only to then realize that he is trapped in one of those very paintings. A profound reorientation is also at the heart of *The Promise* (2011; 2019), in which a woman who has fallen off a transatlantic ship imagines how she will write her life story if she is rescued. As she considers what she'll include, the protagonist begins to blend real-life events with imaginary occurrences, literalizing the shift in narrative approach that is inherent in magical realism itself. Ocampo's work of collected stories, *Thus Were Their Faces* (2015), features tales about doppelgängers, talking winged-horse statues, and a house made of sugar that is the site of a mysterious kind of possession. Grotesque, magical, and absurd, these tales offer readers a new take on the preoccupations of magical realism as it developed over the course of the twentieth century and into the twenty-first.

Contemporary with the Argentinian Borges, Bioy Casares, and Ocampo, García Márquez was experimenting with the same kind of style in his native Colombia. The winner of the Nobel Prize in Literature in 1982, García Márquez's best-known work among Anglophone readers, *One Hundred Years of Solitude* (1967), was first published in English in 1970 and reprinted many times since. On the surface a chronicle of several generations of a family in the fictional town of Macondo, *One Hundred Years* ultimately is a story about how we narrativize our world and our lives. The plague of amnesia, which forces the inhabitants of Macondo to look to a special book that will teach them who they are, winds up pulling the reader into a complicated narrative about books and labyrinths and mirrors à la Borges. Classifying García Márquez's work is necessarily difficult because of the ways in which he plays with how reality can be perceived and what constitutes reality itself.

The kinds of fantasy being written and translated in contemporary Argentina, however, explore the limits of fantasy and magical realism in new and varied ways, despite the long shadow of magical realism. The translated books and stories by César Aira, Ana María Shua, and Liliana Bodoc reveal a kind of fantasy-surreality influenced by the deaths and disappearances during the Dirty War. Aira's novel and two novellas, in particular, use ghosts, dreams, and violence to comment on an Argentina still dealing with trauma. In *Ghosts* (1990; 2009), Aira tells the story of a migrant Chilean family squatting in a ghost-infested house under construction in Buenos Aires.[6] Only the mother and her oldest child, Elisa, can really see the ghosts, to whom the latter flees when her mother starts lecturing her about finding a husband. *The Little Buddhist Monk* (2005) and *The Proof* (1992) (published together in 2017) further explore the fundamental uncertainty of reality and the violence that lies just beneath the surface.

This eruption of violence is at the heart of Ana María Shua's *Death as a Side Effect* (1997; 2010), set in a version of Argentina in which crime is rampant and people are numb to the death and brutality literally playing out in the streets. Older residents are forced into convalescent homes, and when a makeup artist named Ernesto tries to break his father out of one, he must go to great lengths to keep his father hidden from the authorities. A near-future dystopia originally published in Spanish in 1997, *Death as a Side Effect* functions as a memory of trauma and a warning for the future.

Liliana Bodoc similarly inscribes the threat of violence and a crumbling old order in her high fantasy trilogy, *The Saga of the Borderlands*, of which only the first book, *The Days of the Deer* (2000; 2013), has been translated. Admired by Ursula Le Guin, who in turn influenced Bodoc, this first novel in the series takes the usual high fantasy tropes and recontextualizes them within the history of colonization and oppression in Latin America by Old World invaders.

Science Fiction   When it comes to science fiction in Argentina, award-winning author Angélica Gorodischer instantly comes to mind, having published a multitude of novels and stories that bring a sophisticated literary style to her treatment of alien societies, strange technologies, and alternate universes.[7] And while only three of her texts have been translated into English so far, we can expect many more in the coming years due to her popularity in the Anglophone world and also the fact that Ursula Le Guin herself has translated one of those books. Gorodischer, however, is not the only science fiction author from Argentina to be translated over the past several years. From Teresa P. Mira de Echeverría, we have a novella about family, genetic engineering, and Martian terraforming; from Rodrigo Fresán, we have a brilliant trilogy about the nature of reality, narrative, and dreams; and from Martín Felipe Castagnet and Pola Oloixarac we've gotten novels that get to the heart of how modern technology is changing humanity's ethical and social mores (and often not for the better). Thus, Argentina stands as one of the most vibrant sites of speculative writing in the early twenty-first century, and hopefully more of it will be translated into English soon.

Often described as literary science fiction, Gorodischer's stories unfold leisurely and carefully, building upon themselves until entire worlds are created before the reader even realizes it. Indeed, *Trafalgar* and *Prodigies* bring together groups of people to hear stories (the main narrative of the novels), highlighting the importance of communities to the creation of imaginary worlds. Gorodischer's first translated text, ***Kalpa Imperial: The Greatest Empire That Never Was*** (2001; 2003), is told from multiple perspectives and in varying styles (fairy tale, political commentary, and so forth), with each narrator relating stories of a nameless empire that has risen and fallen multiple times.[8] At once a novel and a collection of stories, *Kalpa* offers multiple and fascinating windows into an empire in which technologies emerge and wither (and not in the order that they have in our reality).[9]

Trafalgar (1979; 2013), unlike *Kalpa*, focuses on an individual's perspective on the universe that he's explored over many years. Narrated by Trafalgar Medrano to a rapt audience at a café, the stories in this book often waver between the plausible and the unbelievable. Medrano, having traveled to many planets as a businessman, tells his audience about, for instance, an alternate Earth from 1492 (complete with Isabella and Ferdinand as well as Columbus), a planet where time is concrete, a world where the dead don't actually stay dead, and much more. *Prodigies* (1994; 2015), too, is about how stories circulate in a particular community, though this small novel hovers more in the fantastic realm than in that of science fiction. Set in a boardinghouse that was once the home of nineteenth-century German romantic poet Novalis, the residents of *Prodigies* are all locked in a kind of personal stasis, lingering on their past triumphs and failures and uncertain about how to move forward into the future.

Carrying on Gorodischer's work of producing lyrical, scintillating prose about alternate universes and other planets, Teresa P. Mira de Echeverría is one of Argentina's next generation of science fiction writers for Anglophone readers to keep an eye on. Besides her novella *Memory* (2012; 2015),[10] several of Mira de Echeverría's stories have been translated and published in Anglophone magazines such as *Strange Horizons* and the *Dark*. In *Memory* Mira de Echeverría describes a Mars that has been terraformed by humans who were genetically altered in order to live in the harsh Martian environment. Hundreds of years later, those original humans have become "native" Martians who feel neglected by Earth and humans who no longer recognize them. A novella about how love transcends time and species, *Memory* is a powerful short text that makes readers rethink ideas about Martian colonization.

Focused decidedly on Earth and the next iteration of human development, Castagnet's *Bodies of Summer* (2012; 2017)[11] and Oloixarac's *Dark Constellations* (2015; 2019)[12] take up the long science fictional tradition of exploring what humanity might become in the face of new technologies and relationship to the environment. Castagnet's novel is specifically interested in the intersection of human consciousness, the Internet, and a kind of reincarnation, while Oloixarac explores similar ideas but through large questions about evolution (both biological and technological) and interspecies hybridization.

Standing in intriguing contrast to Gorodischer, Mira de Echeverría, Castagnet, and Oloixarac's style of science fiction is that of Rodrigo Fresán, whose texts are really *about* science fiction rather than *of* science fiction. Fresán's trilogy (*The Invented Part* [2014; 2017],[13] *The Dreamed Part* [2017; 2019],[14] and *The Remembered Part* [forthcoming]) explores the nature of authorship (with long digressive passages on the literary biographies of writers such as F. Scott Fitzgerald and Vladimir Nabokov), the ways in which stories are shaped by and in turn shape reality, and the ways in which books, television, music, and film draw on social and political anxieties and turn them into something entirely new. Sprawling, demanding, and magnetic, Fresán's books invite readers to think about *why* science fiction is uniquely suited to telling certain kinds of stories about our reality.

Fresán's most overtly science fictional novel, *The Bottom of the Sky* (2009; 2018), is, like Mira de Echeverría's *Memory*, a story about the triumph of love over the impossible.[15] At first glance a novel about three young people during the early years of American science fiction fandom, *The Bottom of the Sky* quickly turns into a science fiction story about telepathic aliens and the malleability of reality. This is a novel about perspective, people as pawns in the hands of a greater power, and the place of humanity in the larger universe and across infinite realities. It is about the tragedy of 9/11 and rewriting life and the stories about life.

Horror   Horror fiction comes in myriad different forms, but the horror from Argentina that's making its way into English is among the most disturbing. Eschewing supernatural creatures and large quantities of blood and gore, Argentinian horror in translation is dominated by the uncanny, the eerie, and the weirdly grotesque. The novels and stories of Samanta Schweblin, Mariana Enriques, and Roque Larraquy, all translated and published in English since 2017, push the horror genre to new heights of visceral terror.

Told as a conversation between Amanda (a grown woman) and David (a child, but not hers), *Fever Dream* (2014; 2017) is about a summer vacation that turns into a nightmare centered around "soul transplantation."[16] Something is obviously wrong with many of the children in this particular seaside town, and one woman who is rumored to have special powers "heals" one particular boy by transplanting his soul into another child's body. The dialogue, set in an unnamed hospital, gives the story a kind of clinical creepiness that lingers long after the novella ends. Schweblin's second translated text, the collection *Mouthful of Birds* (2009; 2019), further tests the limits of literary surrealism and the uncanny. The title story follows a bewildered father as he tries to understand why his daughter, on the cusp of womanhood, has taken to eating only live sparrows, while in "Irman" the narrator is confronted with inexplicable brutality and violence when they and a traveling companion stop at a roadside diner.

Mariana Enriques's collection *Things We Lost in the Fire* (2016; 2017) also focuses on the horror that emerges from decay and violence, only Enriques situates her stories more specifically in the political. Having grown up in Argentina during the Dirty War, Enriques evokes the fragility of existence and the illusion of safety in a world where the well-off are distinguished from the impoverished only by what the former allow themselves to see. In "Under the Black Bridge," an attorney enters a slum and thus learns about police murdering children and mutants created out of the filth of the environment. The title story focuses on women countering domestic violence with a different kind of violence, one that splinters off into the unexpected and horrifying.

Finally, Larraquy's *Comemadre* (2010; 2018) departs from Schweblin's and Enriques's texts by veering off into body horror.[17] Split between Buenos Aires in 1907 and 2009, the novel begins with doctors at a sanatorium severing patients' heads via a contraption that can then allow the severed heads to talk. Perhaps, the doctors think, the patients can tell them about the afterlife. A century later, a performance artist and his doppelgänger stage shows that include their severed body parts. It turns out that the artist, who is actually related to the doctor-narrator of the first part, wants to create a system of guillotines based on those created by the doctors in 1907. Larraquy explores how quickly certain kinds of scientific inquiry can lead to the decay of ethical considerations.

Bolivia

While only two works of Bolivian speculative fiction have been translated into English, they reveal to Anglophone readers the sophistication and creativity of the authors living in this small South American country. Together, Edmundo Paz Soldán's technothriller *Turing's Delirium* (2004; 2007) and Liliana Colanzi's genre-bending collection *Our Dead World* (2016; 2017) demonstrate the ways in which these authors are simultaneously drawing on the science fiction and surrealism of Latin America and that being published abroad. Paz Soldán's novel imagines a near-future dystopia that has definitely not improved with increasingly sophisticated technology. Paz Soldán pits grassroots hackers against powerful transnational corporations to demonstrate how new technologies can foment revolutions that look nothing like those that have plagued Bolivia over the past century. In contrast, Colanzi's *Our Dead World* weaves its way among subgenres, with science fiction, fantasy, magical realism, and horror mingling freely within and between the eight stories.[18] From a lonely colony on Mars and a psychopathic cannibal in Paris to a girl pushed into a nervous breakdown by her fanatical mother, Colanzi's stories hold up a warped mirror to reality.

Chile

As with Bolivian speculative fiction, only a couple of texts from Chile have been translated into English. One of the authors, however, is Roberto Bolaño, whose nongenre texts have found a prominent place in the Anglophone cannon. Bolaño's *Nazi Literature in the Americas* (1996; 2008), a prime example of fabulation in the style of Borges and Poland's Stanisław Lem, is the author's most speculative text: a completely fictional encyclopedia of fascist authors.[19] Including lengthy bibliographies, scandals, literary feuds, and references that reach far into the twenty-first century, *Nazi Literature* offers readers a horrifying yet nonexistent artifact that implies a chilling alternate ending to World War II.

From the Chilean French author and filmmaker Alejandro Jodorowsky we have *Albina and the Dog-Men* (2000; 2016), a mythic novel that defies categorization. Set in Peru and Chile, it tells the story of Crabby (a Lithuanian recluse) and Albina (a goddess who is saved from attacking monks by Crabby). With no memory of her origins but still astoundingly beautiful, Albina settles with Crabby in a town in Chile until her beauty drives the men insane. After turning one of them into a dog-man, Albina flees with Crabby (via bicycle) north to find a rare cactus plant that may reverse the goddess's transformation into a man-eating monster. A heady mix of the magical and the grotesque, *Albina* is ultimately the story of love between two unlikely individuals.

Mexico

The majority of the translated speculative fiction that has come from Mexico since 1960 is more fantastic than science fictional. Through the stories in the anthology *Three Messages and a Warning*, the collection by Amparo Dávila, and the novels by Carlos Fuentes,[20] Joan Pablo Villalobos, and Carmen Boullosa, Anglophone readers can see how easily these writers move between and among such subgenres as fantasy, magical realism, surrealism, and horror. Those novels by José Zaidenweber and Rodrigo Márquez Tizano, however, fall more clearly into the science fiction category, with their foci on cloning and a devastating virus, respectively.

Known internationally for both his genre and nongenre books, Panamanianborn writer Carlos Fuentes has had six of the former translated into English.[21] Ranging from ghost stories to magical realism dreamscapes to political thrillers, Fuentes's stories are ultimately bound up in the diversity and complexity of Mexican culture and history. Both the first and the last of his novels that were translated into English—*Aura* (1962; 1965) and *Vlad* (2010; 2012)—are works of gothic horror featuring vampires. In *Aura* a young man applies for an unusual job, that of preparing for publication the memoirs of a man who died sixty years before. The work, he learns, must take place only in the (very dark) home of the deceased's ancient wife and her disturbing niece (named Aura). It doesn't take long for the young man to fall under Aura's spell. *Vlad*, on the other hand, is more obviously a vampire tale from the outset, with an émigré count from eastern Europe moving into a house in Mexico. It falls to a middle-aged lawyer to assist the count in preparing the house, which includes blacking out all of the windows.

Mexico's turbulent history serves as the setting for another two Fuentes novels, written in the 1970s and '80s, this time from a magical realist approach. An alternate history that jumps between the past and the future (the sections are titled "The Old World," "The New World," and "The Next World"), *Terra Nostra* (1975; 1976) juxtaposes severe climate change in a dying Paris in 1999 with Spain descending into bloodshed and madness just before the "discovery" of the New World. This meeting of the Old and the New Worlds comes up once again in *Christopher Unborn* (1987; 1989), only this time the narrative is told from the point of view of an unborn child who will eventually become the most powerful man in Mexico (because his surname is closest to "Columbus"). Set in 1992 on the five-hundredth anniversary of Columbus's arrival in America, the novel portrays Mexico as a slave to American corporate interests and the tourism industry.

Like Fuentes, Villalobos in **Quesadillas** (2012; 2014) tells a story about Mexico via satire and the absurd.[22] Via characters with classical Greek names, Villalobos takes readers on an adventure across the Mexican countryside as the protagonist, Orestes ("Oreo"), goes in search of his brothers, who may or may not have been kidnapped by aliens. At one point, he acquires a device that can fix any broken machine with the push of a single button. A crowded and dilapidated house, scarce quesadillas, and political violence characterize this roller-coaster ride of a novel.

From the prolific and award-winning author Carmen Boullosa come two very different novels that both use memory and consciousness to drop readers into the fascinating worlds of her characters. **Before** (1989; 2016) is narrated by a ghost, one who feels compelled to share the multitude of strange occurrences that led to her current situation: trees actively avoid her, ink marks turn into spiders under her gaze, and the sound of footsteps apparently heralds the approach of death.[23] An intensely personal narrative, *Before* is ultimately about one girl's fight against fear and frustration. Broader in scope but still focused on the central role that memory plays in human consciousness, **Heavens on Earth** (1997; 2017) is told via three different voices: a sixteenth-century Franciscan monk named Hernando, a present-day translator named Estela, and an archaeologist named Learo who lives in a postapocalyptic future. Even as Estela translates Hernando's memoirs of the destruction visited upon indigenous Mexican peoples by Spain, she can sense the political and social collapse of her own world. This translation is then found by Learo, who is living Estela's nightmare.

Originally written between the 1950s and the 2010s, the stories collected in **Three Messages and a Warning: Contemporary Mexican Stories of the Fantastic** (2011) introduce Anglophone readers to some of the most important voices in Mexican speculative fiction today, including Pepe Rojo, Gabriela Damián Miravete,[24] and Alberto Chimal. Ranging from the humorous to the gruesome, these tales ask us to imagine, for instance, a nation and media obsessed with its leader's bizarre illness ("The President without Organs"), the existence of "pocket apocalypses" ("Photophobia"), and a metatextual romance ("Nereid Future").

Like Boullosa, Amparo Dávila is one of just a few Mexican women to have their speculative fiction published in English translation. Dávila's collection **The Houseguest, and Other Stories** (2018) includes stories of the surreal and strange, even horrifying. In the title story, a man brings home a stranger and demands that his wife accept him into their home; the stranger, though, stalks her and her children and generally terrorizes them. "Moses and Gaspar" is told from an animal's perspective, while other stories ask us to delve deep into the seemingly placid lives of ordinary people.

The book-length science fiction that has emerged from Mexico is tantalizing in its rarity and approach to such issues as cloning and the spread of disease.

In José Zaidenweber's near-future thriller *Feast of Egos* (1985; 1993), a scientist attempts to influence public policy and the world government via his cloning research.[25] Viewing cloning as a major step forward in achieving immortality, the scientist catalyzes a conversation about the ethical, psychological, and religious implications of the process. In contrast to this rather utopian vision of the future is Rodrigo Márquez Tizano's novel *Jakarta* (2016; 2019), which focuses on those humans who have survived a viral epidemic called the Ź-Bug.[26] Tizano's protagonist works as a member of a team (the Ź-Brigade) tasked with clearing out rats and other vermin from the sewers to prevent another outbreak. Questions about identity and community in the aftermath of devastation and fear thus run throughout *Jakarta*.

The Caribbean

Cuba   In contrast to Mexico, Cuba's speculative fiction in English falls overwhelmingly into the science fiction subgenre. All five of the novels (two from Agustín de Rojas and three from Yoss) come to Anglophone readers from Restless Books. The exception to this is the work of Daína Chaviano, an award-winning and versatile author who stands as one of Cuba's most acclaimed writers of both genre and nongenre fiction. Her novel *The Island of Eternal Love* (2006; 2008) is a supernaturally infused work of historical fiction about a ghost house that appears at various points around Miami. When a Cuban-born journalists tries to investigate, she winds up being pulled into a world of clairvoyants and eccentric people in touch with another dimension.[27]

Cuba's "patron saint" of science fiction, Agustín de Rojas, wrote novels of a decidedly political bent. His work has had a major influence on subsequent Cuban science fiction authors, and his stories bring together the possibilities of the future and the stagnation and despair of a society under a repressive regime.[28] Rojas's trilogy comprises *Spiral*, *A Legend of the Future* (1985; 2015),[29] and *The Year 200* (1990; 2016),[30] each of which functions as a window into specific concerns about what the future might bring in terms of everything from space exploration to political clashes. While *Legend* centers on a doomed space mission and the crew's desperate efforts to return to Earth, *The Year 200* is a hyperbolic story about communism and capitalism battling it out centuries from now via the transplantation of consciousnesses.

Part of the next generation of Cuban science fiction writers, Yoss (José Miguel Sánchez Gómez) stands out with his unique blend of satire and science fiction and his hard-rock persona (he is the lead singer for the heavy metal band Tenaz). His three novels in English—*A Planet for Rent* (2001; 2015),[31] *Super Extra Grande* (2012; 2016),[32] and *Condomnauts* (2013; 2018)[33] (all translated by David Frye)— pulse with energy and curiosity. Like Rojas, Yoss focuses in his work on Cuba's position as a pawn of the Cold War superpowers and its uncertain position after the collapse of the Soviet Union. All of his books in English posit a world in which humans have been overwhelmed and marginalized by powerful and indifferent alien species, and it is this depiction of a humbled and sometimes disgraced humanity that most keenly demonstrates his view of Cuban and world politics in the late twentieth and early twenty-first centuries.

In *Planet* Yoss asks the reader to imagine what it would be like if several powerful alien species decided to colonize and degrade Earth. *Condomnauts*, too, imagines an Earth transformed for the worse. The protagonist, Josué Valdés, had grown up an orphan in twenty-second-century Havana following nuclear war, but his lot improves when he becomes a "sexual ambassador" ("condomnaut") who conducts trade negotiations with alien species. *Super Extra Grande*, which also involves faster-than-light travel and human-alien contact, depicts humans and aliens as more equals than anything else. Here we meet Dr. Jan Amos Sangan Dongo, "Veterinarian to the Giants" (that is, the man who treats the galaxy's largest organisms, like titanic amoebas from the planet Brobdingnag). His usual "house calls" involve removing obstructions or dispensing medication, but then a ship carrying two human diplomats is swallowed by two-hundred-kilometer-wide amoeba and it's up to the doctor to save them.

Dominican Republic   While we have only two SFT novels from the Dominican Republic, both offer exciting glimpses into the kinds of science fiction being written there. From Pedro Cabiya we have **Wicked Weeds** (2011; 2016), a self-styled "zombie novel" that is about so much more.[34] It is a complex and carefully plotted exploration of the intersection of the human mind, body, and soul. Drawing on the concept of the zombie in Caribbean history and culture, Cabiya creates a gentleman/scientist/zombie who is searching for a cure for his situation via his job with a pharmaceutical giant. Cabiya makes us think beyond the physicality of reviving a corpse and asks us to consider zombification in multiple dimensions: What does it feel like to try to pass as someone you're not? What *is* that specific spark that turns "animated" into "alive"? How is a zombie different from an AI or a wooden doll, and why are these differences important?

Also from the Dominican Republic is a novel by musician and writer Rita Indiana called **Tentacle** (2015; 2018), a near-future novel about ecological catastrophe, imperialism, and gender identity.[35] After a series of disasters that have devastated the Caribbean Sea, with effects spreading to the Atlantic, a former sex worker named Acilde uses an anemone with magical properties to take on a male body and then fulfill a prophecy. Traveling back in time, she is ultimately able to save the Caribbean Sea from devastation. Indiana draws on issues like Haitian-Dominican political and social conflicts, racism, immigration, and the history of the Caribbean going back to the Spanish arrival to warn readers about a potentially devastating future.

SPAIN

Spain offers a particularly interesting picture of the state of SFT in the twenty-first century. Starting in 2001, translated speculative fiction from that country exploded onto the Anglophone scene, with forty-two novels, collections, and anthologies in just nineteen years. The stories coming out of Spain are also a vibrant mix of fantasy, science fiction, and horror (with several books falling somewhere between science fiction and fantasy). And while Spanish SFT comes from a diverse array of (trade and university) presses, publishers such as the feminist science fiction–focused Aqueduct and the Spain-based Sportula (started by internationally known author Rodolfo Martínez) have injected fresh, exciting stories into the mix. Readers will find plenty of subgenres in Spanish SFT, including surrealism, Lovecraftian horror, space opera, steampunk, and much more.

Fantasy

Carlos Ruiz Zafón's thousand-plus-page tetralogy, *The Cemetery of Forgotten Books*, is the story of a special library in Barcelona that houses and protects threatened texts. Comprising *The Shadow of the Wind* (2001; 2004), *The Angel's Game* (2008; 2009), *The Prisoner of Heaven* (2011; 2012), and *The Labyrinth of the Spirits* (2016; 2018), the tetralogy is filled with interlocking fictional authors and titles, political intrigues, and the threat of censorship. Drawing on the history of Spanish literature's conflicts with state and religious oppression over the centuries, Zafón's novels celebrate the power of literature to create alternate worlds and open up new perspectives. A mix of fantasy, police procedural, mystery, and metafiction, *Cemetery* is a major work by an internationally beloved author.

From Elia Barceló we have two books about love transcending time and space. Set in the present and in 1920s Buenos Aires, *Heart of Tango* (2007; 2010) weaves together a story about a mysterious woman who is dancing the tango with a man and then disappears and a love story in which Natalia in turn tangos with the mysterious Diego a couple of days before her wedding to a much older man. Through the passionate dance, both couples are transported to another time and life. Like *Heart of Tango*, *The Goldsmith's Secret* (2003; 2011) involves the dizzying conjunction of the past and the present. When a goldsmith decides to leave New York to return to Spain in the hopes of reconnecting with a lost love, he instead meets a young woman and begins an affair with her. Strangely, though, this relationship echoes his earlier affair, as if the goldsmith is reliving his past.

The most recent works of Spanish fantasy in English translation demonstrate an intriguing variety of approaches and subgenres. Tamara Romero's novel *Her*

241

Fingers (2012), published as part of Eraserhead's New Bizarro Author Series, involves witches whose persecution has led them to flee to the forest and merge with the trees there. Sergio Llanes's epic fantasy *The Twilight of the Normidons (Tears of Gea #1)* (2016; 2016) depicts an alternate world in which a Rome-like empire is deteriorating from within after three centuries of Sforza rule. It is up to the emperor's Normidon Guard to put down the rebellion along the empire's borders before it's too late. Ángel Luis Sucasas's collection *Moon Scars* (2017), in contrast, offers readers four different worlds within a single slender volume.[36] Werewolves, technologically sophisticated gadgets, underwater worlds, and people who vanish only to reappear as monsters are part of the fabric of these stories that invite readers to think deeper about alienation, assimilation, the natural world, our understanding of physics, and the nature of reality.

Science Fiction

It's fitting that the first publication of Spanish science fiction in English was of Santiago Ramón y Cajal's 1905 collection *Vacation Stories: Five Science Fiction Tales* (2001). A neurobiologist whose research into the structure of the micron led to a Nobel Prize in Medicine in 1906, Ramón y Cajal was also a medical artist whose depictions of the microstructures of the brain continue to teach neuroscience students in the twenty-first century. Originally published in Spanish under the pseudonym "Dr. Bacteria," the tales in *Vacation Stories* involve science and technology on the fringes, including one story of a paranoid husband and scientist who invents a machine to measure the seismic activity in his wife's bed and infect her lovers with tuberculosis ("For a Secret Offence, Secret Revenge"). In "The Fabricator of Honor," another scientist claims to have invented a serum that forces people to be ethical at all times.

One of Spain's first works of science fiction published in Spanish—Enrique Gaspar's *The Time Ship: A Chrononautical Journey* (1887)—wasn't published in English until 2012. The author, who was also a diplomat and playwright, may have been the first to describe a time machine (and a protagonist's subsequent adventures in the past) in literature.[37] When the device's builder returns to the past to seek immortality, he first returns to 1860 and a battle that Spain won against Morocco (though it's seen in reverse). Subsequent adventures involve the time machine becoming a part of the fabric of history (becoming Noah's Ark during the Flood, for instance). Ultimately, the reader is told that the adventures were all a dream, but the ideas Gaspar elaborates in *The Time Ship* reach all the way down to the *Star Trek* and *Doctor Who* franchises.

The modern Spanish science fiction that's being translated since the start of the new millennium resists easy classification, with authors such as José Carlos Somoza, Ray Loriga, Rafael Reig, Félix J. Palma, Rosa Montero, Lola Robles,

Sofia Rhei, Rodolfo Martínez, Carlos Maleno, and Cristina Jurado writing about everything from time travel to memory-erasing chemicals. Some, like Somoza and Reig, mix dystopia and science fiction with noir or even the western. It is from this exciting mix that Anglophone readers can get a sense of Spain's contemporary science fiction environment.

Somoza, born in Cuba but raised in Spain, blends ideas about the art and philosophy of the past with present-day concerns about new technologies and scientific discoveries. His first novel in English, *The Athenian Murders* (2000; 2002), is a cross between a murder mystery and metafiction. Somoza's text is presented as an ancient Greek story that is being translated; the translator, however, finds that the characters in the story begin addressing *him* from the text. The book itself (in all of its layers) is a meditation on the tension between Plato's theory of Ideas and his *Allegory of the Cave* (the original title in Spanish is *The Cave of Ideas*) and the tangible world. In *Zig Zag* (2006; 2007), Somoza plays with recent ideas in physics—specifically, superstring theory—and the idea that "time strings" can be manipulated in order to let people get a glimpse of the past. When scientists and philosophers are brought together on a remote island to do just that, what they see winds up haunting them for years, and even leads to death for some of them.

Both Loriga and Reig write about the deleterious effects of new kinds of drugs developed for seemingly positive purposes. Loriga's *Tokyo Doesn't Love Us Anymore* (1999; 2004) is a bleak dystopia featuring a traveling salesman who peddles a drug that can erode short-term memory. Bored with his life and work, the salesman eventually samples his own wares and spirals into confusion and eventual brain damage. In Reig's two novels *Blood on the Saddle* (2002; 2007) and *A Pretty Face* (2003; 2007), Spain has deteriorated (whether technologically or politically), and a private eye named Carlos Clot is called in to investigate some suspicious murders. *Blood on the Saddle* evokes the western in its depiction of Clot as a lone lawman out to solve cases, some of which involve a major genetic engineering company and its underhanded dealings. And then there's the case of one missing person who turns out to be a fictional character that wandered off the pages of a novel called . . . *Blood on the Saddle*. In *A Pretty Face*, the narrator is a murdered woman who was carrying sensitive papers belonging to her estranged neuroscientist husband. His breakthrough, involving a neuroprotein that can reconstruct brain tissue, is so coveted that those who want it will do anything to get it.

In Félix J. Palma's *Victorian* trilogy (2008–14; 2011–15), time travel, H. G. Wells, Jack the Ripper, aliens, and more mingle to produce a unique thriller, science fiction, and fantasy mashup. Here Palma meditates on the role of the writer in society, whether time travel is possible, and how narratives circulate among other narratives (for example, Palma turning the real-life Wells into a character involved in conspiracies he himself had written about at the turn of the twentieth century). Throughout, Wells learns to accept the existence of the supernatural, and he is assisted in his uncovering of conspiracies by none other than Arthur Conan Doyle and Lewis Carroll. Thus, the Victorian trilogy is, like several other texts in this chapter, a story about stories.

Mextatextuality informs both Robles's and Rhei's books, which are both science fictional explorations of how language circulates among human and alien societies and how it has a unique power to shape the world and reality as we know it. Robles's *Monteverde: Memoirs of an Interstellar Linguist* (2005; 2016) declares this in its very title.[38] By calling this fictional text a "memoir," Robles asks us to consider the fine line between "fiction" and "nonfiction" and how writing about events from memory is always a narrative act.

Like Robles, Rhei is concerned with how writing, translation, and even the tangible nature of texts influences how we see the world. Her collection *Everything Is Made of Letters* (2019) brings together some of her best stories that approach these issues from a multitude of directions. Both "Techt" and "Secret Stories of Doors" demonstrate how language refuses to be trapped and put to use by the authorities to pacify the population.[39] In "The BubbleLon Cyclotech," words have become literal objects in the service of an extreme "print on demand" machine. If a word is damaged or lost, though, that word drops out of the language itself, making each one precious. Other stories involve humans turning an alien species into an educational toy for language learning ("Learning Report") and an extreme kind of fan-fiction writing factory ("You Cannot Kill Frownyflute!").

Inspired by *Blade Runner* and its cyberpunk, dystopian aesthetic, Rosa Montero's "Bruna Husky" novels (only two of which have been translated) raise issues of human-replicant relationships, government conspiracies, and a future that is as grim as Philip K. Dick imagined. In *Tears in Rain* (2011; 2012) (the title comes from the famous quote at the end of *Blade Runner*), a former soldier turned detective replicant named Bruna Husky reflects on the certainty of her death (via a cancer with which all replicants are produced) and seeks answers to who is threatening the leader of a replicant's rights organization. What she uncovers is an antireplicant conspiracy that is as insidious as it is sinister. Husky is back at it again in *Weight of the Heart* (2015; 2016), investigating a stolen diamond that leads her to a conspiracy involving nuclear power that could destroy every living thing.

One of Spain's most internationally acclaimed, virtuosic writers, Rodolfo Martínez has also worked to bring more SFT from Spain to Anglophone audiences via his press, Sportula. Martínez's five books in English fall all along the subgenre spectrum: Lovecraftian horror, cyberpunk, and a unique blend of fantasy, spy thriller, and science fiction. His *Queen's Adept* trilogy (of which the first and third have been published in English) evokes an alternate universe of age-old traditions, sophisticated technologies, and warring empires. *The Queen's Adept* (2009; 2012) offers a unique take on religious conflict, our perception of reality, and the manipulation of memory, while *Faces from the Past* (2018) focuses on the age-old conflict between the pain of remembering and the balm of forgetfulness.[40]

Martínez is also known for writing Spain's first cyberpunk novel, ***Cat's Whirld*** (1995; 2015). A heady mix of malevolent AIs, vast political conspiracies, and *Babylon-5*-type space-station machinations, *Cat's Whirld* imagines how one place can maintain an uneasy truce while functioning as a free zone for developing advanced technology and engaging in all kinds of otherwise unlawful or barely lawful activities. When some stranger-than-usual characters show up on the Whirld, it's up to the aptly named Arthur Conan Chandler and his band of "Irregulars" to put a stop to a plan that threatens to destroy the entire space station. Moving from cyberpunk-noir to Lovecraftian horror in ***The Wisdom of the Dead*** (2019), Martínez engages in metafictional speculation, calling our attention to the act of writing and translating, suggesting the power of language to bring into being not just characters and plots, but also belief systems and communities built around particular stories. Here, detective fiction, Lovecraft's Cthulhu mythos, and occultism blend in a story about Sherlock Holmes investigating why someone is posing as him and what certain members of an occult society plan to do with the grimoire in their hands.[41] Readers can find even more stories about humankind's relationship to technology, AI, alien planets, and more in Martínez's collection ***The Road to Nowhere*** (2018).

Two of the most recent Spanish-language speculative fiction collections in English offer Anglophone readers a tantalizing glimpse of the future of science fiction coming out of this part of Europe. Carlos Maleno's ***The Irish Sea*** (2014; 2017) includes stories of a postmortem way station on another planet (and reincarnation?), a breed of American cattle that is physically identical to human women, and Christ as the lead singer in a punk band. Tending more toward the surrealistic horror end of the spectrum, Cristina Jurado's ***Alphaland*** (2018) features dead fathers returning to haunt their tortured daughters; prostitutes turning out to be horrifying, human-devouring alien intelligences; and spaceships that function as nurturing mothers.[42]

An important anthology that has contributed to this explosion of SFT from Spain since 2000, ***Castles in Spain: 25 Years of Spanish Fantasy and Science Fiction*** (2016) brings award-winning classics of the genre to Anglophone readers, often for the first time.[43] Edited by Mariano Villareal, these stories take up everything from sentient AI satellites to human cloning, asking us to consider a wide range of thought-provoking alternate realities, including what would happen if human cloning was accessible to anyone who could pay ("My Wife, My Daughter") and what might happen if humans were wiped out and only machines and animals

245

were left ("The Flock"). Written by award-winning authors such as Elia Barceló, César Mallorquí, Rodolfo Martínez, Rafael Marín, Félix J. Palma, and others, *Castles in Spain* introduces Anglophone readers to ideas and styles that Spanish readers have long enjoyed.

Horror

Horror from Spain, as is the case with many other countries, is hard to come by but does indeed exist. Several such texts are even available in English, including those by Carlos Sisi, Tamara Romero, and Manel Loureiro. It is Loureiro, however, who has the most name recognition, since he has both a zombie trilogy and two stand-alone novels in English. Both Sisi and Loureiro have capitalized on the rise of interest in zombie stories over the past couple of decades.

Though part of a trilogy, Sisi's *The Wanderers* (2009; 2011) is the only book to have been translated so far. A postapocalyptic thriller, it follows thirty survivors of a pandemic as they attempt to keep out the zombies that the illness created. Loureiro's books, too, begin with a mysterious virus turning anyone it infects into a zombie. *This Apocalypse Z* trilogy, which began as a blog, consists of *The Beginning of the End* (2008; 2012), *Dark Days* (2010; 2013), and *The Wrath of the Just* (2011; 2014). Focusing on an unnamed (an non-zombified) lawyer fighting to survive in a world increasingly chaotic and deadly, these novels are in large part about how an individual can cope with severe social and political disruption without also falling victim to it. With a few other survivors, the lawyer tries to find a safe haven from the virus and the chaos that it has unleashed.

Loureiro's two other novels in English, *The Last Passenger* (2013; 2015) and *Only She Sees* (2017; 2017), deal not with zombies but with mysterious German ships and shattered memories, respectively. In the former, a reporter has been assigned to look into the story of a German ship called the *Valkyrie* after it was found adrift in 1939 with only a baby boy onboard. When that boy grows up and spends his fortune attempting to re-create its final voyage, both he and the reporter realize that something horrible is about to be unleashed. *Only She Sees* is a work of psychological horror in which a woman's body and mind are severely damaged by a car accident. Unsure about whether she is actually being stalked, Cassandra simultaneously becomes involved in her husband's work investigating a series of murders. With her reality seemingly slipping away and a murderer on the loose, Cassandra must decide what to believe in order to save her family.

Anthologies

Six anthologies of Spanish-language speculative fiction in English have been published since 1991, opening up for Anglophone readers a wealth of fantasy and science fiction from all over the Spanish-speaking world. The first two such books, both published in the '90s, focus on the fantastic: *The Secret Weavers: Stories of the Fantastic by Women of Argentina and Chile* (1991) and *The Dedalus Book of Spanish Fantasy* (1999). The former concentrates on the work of women fantasists of the early to mid-twentieth century and includes stories by Ocampo, Shua, Gorodischer, Isabel Allende, and many others, while *The Dedalus Book of Spanish Fantasy* casts a wider net, including stories that stretch from the mid-nineteenth to the late twentieth centuries, written not just in Spanish but also in the other languages of Spain: Castilian, Basque, Catalan, and Gallego. Stories about bird people, doppelgängers, transmigration of souls, and humans turning into animals fill this volume, by Spanish-language writers such as Pilar Diaz-Mas, Javier Marias, and Alonso Zamora Vicente.

Science fiction takes center stage in the next two translated anthologies: *Cosmos Latinos: An Anthology of Science Fiction from Latin America and Spain* (2003) and *Terra Nova: An Anthology of Contemporary Spanish Science Fiction* (2012; 2013),[44] though the two volumes differ in their focus. While *Cosmos Latinos* is a more academic compendium of Spanish-language science fiction since the late nineteenth century, *Terra Nova* features fewer and more contemporary authors. In the former, we have stories by some of the best-known Spanish-language speculative authors, including Eduardo Goligorsky, Angélica Gorodischer, Daína Chaviano, Elia Barceló, and Pepe Rojo, who write a kind of science fiction that, in contrast to its Anglophone version, "downplay[s] scientific plausibility . . . [and] show[s] the influence of the region's celebrated literary fantastic."[45] In contrast, *Terra Nova*'s tighter focus and spotlight on authors writing at the beginning of the twenty-first century allow Anglophone readers to get a sense of what's happening in more recent times in Spanish-language speculative fiction. Spanish author Felicidad Martínez's "The Texture of Words" imagines a world in which women live as the blind dependents of men but actually exercise the real power behind the scenes. From Cuban author Erick J. Mota, we get a story about the zombification of Cuba via a mysterious alien virus, a serum that renders those zombies harmless and passive, and the government's subsequent use of the virus and serum to intentionally zombify the populace. This anthology is also the original home of Argentinian author Mira de Echeverría's *Memory*.

James Womack and Marian Womack's collection *The Best of Spanish Steampunk* (2015) offers readers yet another fascinating perspective on Spanish-language speculative fiction, revealing how authors in Latin America, Spain, and the Caribbean have used and transformed the relatively young steampunk subgenre.[46] The writers represented in this anthology reimagine a world in which European colonial forces often failed to subjugate native populations and where those populations developed steam-driven technology designed with their particular and unique environments and cultures in mind.

Like *The Secret Weavers*, **Spanish Women of Wonder** (2016) highlights women writers and the work they do to move speculative fiction forward into this young century.[47] As editors Cristina Jurado and Leticia Lara point out, women are writing excellent speculative fiction in Cuba, Spain, Argentina, Mexico, and beyond, "reflecting a wide spectrum of interests, a large portion concerning the effects of technology and scientific advances on the lives of future generations."[48] Included are many names already mentioned in previous anthologies, such as Mira de Echeverría, Felicidad Martínez, Lola Robles, Sofia Rhei, and Angélica Gorodischer. From technology that bends time and space ("Terpsichore") to a planet's indigenous species rising up against human "infestation" ("The Infestation"), *Spanish Women of Wonder* is an invaluable resource for anyone interested in great contemporary Spanish-language speculative fiction available in English.

Primary Sources

ARGENTINA

1935: Borges, Jorge Luis. *A Universal History of Infamy*. Translated Norman Thomas di Giovanni. E. P. Dutton, 1972.

1940: Casares, Adolfo Bioy. *The Invention of Morel, and Other Stories from "La trama celeste."* Translated by Ruth L. C. Simms. University of Texas Press, 1964. *The Invention of Morel* published alone in 2003 by the New York Review of Books.

1941: Borges, Jorge Luis, with Adolfo Bioy Casares. *Six Problems for Don Isidro Parodi*. Translated by Norman Thomas di Giovanni. E. P. Dutton, 1981.

1944: Borges, Jorge Luis. *Ficciones*. Translated by Anthony Kerrigan et al. Weidenfeld and Nicolson, 1962.

1949: Borges, Jorge Luis. *The Aleph, and Other Stories*, 1933–1969. Translated by Norman Thomas di Giovanni. E. P. Dutton, 1970.

1954: Casares, Adolfo Bioy. *The Dream of the Heroes*. Translated by Diana Thorold. Quartet Books, 1987.

1962: Borges, Jorge Luis. *Labyrinths: Selected Stories and Other Writings*. Translated by Norman Thomas di Giovanni, edited by Donald A. Yates and James E. Irby. New Directions, 1964.

1969: Casares, Adolfo Bioy. *Diary of the War of the Pig*. Translated by Gregory Woodruff and Donald A. Yates. McGraw-Hill, 1972.

1973: Casares, Adolfo Bioy. *Asleep in the Sun*. Translated by Suzanne Jill Levine. Persea, 1978.

1975: Casares, Adolfo Bioy. *A Plan for Escape.* Translated by Suzanne Jill Levine. E. P. Dutton, 1975.

1979: Gorodischer, Angélica. *Trafalgar.* Translated by Amalia Gladhart. Small Beer Press, 2013.

1986: Ocampo, Silvino. *The Topless Tower.* Translated by James Womack. Hesperus Press, 2010.

1990: Aira, César. *Ghosts.* Translated by Chris Andrews. New Directions, 2009.

1992: Aira, César. *The Proof.* Translated by Nick Caistor. And Other Stories, 2017.

1994: Gorodischer, Angélica. *Prodigies* (1994). Translated by Sue Burke. Small Beer Press, 2015.

1997: Shua, Ana María. *Death as a Side Effect.* Translated by Andrea G. Labinger. University of Nebraska Press, 2010.

2000: Bodoc, Liliana. *The Days of the Deer (Saga of the Borderlands #1).* Translated by Nick Caistor and Lucia Caistor Arenda. Corvus, 2013.

2001: Gorodischer, Angélica. *Kalpa Imperial: The Greatest Empire That Never Was.* Translated by Ursula K. Le Guin. Small Beer Press, 2003.

2005: Aira, César. *The Little Buddhist Monk.* Translated by Nick Caistor. And Other Stories, 2017.

2009: Fresán, Rodrigo. *The Bottom of the Sky.* Translated by Will Vanderhyden. Open Letter, 2018.

Schweblin, Samanta. *Mouthful of Birds.* Translated by Megan McDowell. Riverhead Books, 2019.

2010: Larraquy, Roque. *Comemadre.* Translated by Heather Cleary. Coffee House Press, 2018.

2011: Ocampo, Silvina. *The Promise.* Translated by Suzanne Jill Levine and Jessica Powell. City Lights, 2019.

2012: Castagnet, Martín Felipe. *Bodies of Summer.* Translated by Frances Riddle. Dalkey Archive Press, 2017.

Mira de Echeverría, Teresa P. *Memory.* Translated by Lawrence Schimel. Upper Rubber Boot Books, 2015. Novella first published in *Terra Nova*, 2013.

2014: Fresán, Rodrigo. *The Invented Part.* Translated by Will Vanderhyden. Open Letter, 2017.

Schweblin, Samanta. *Fever Dream.* Translated by Megan McDowell. Riverhead Books, 2017.

2015: Ocampo, Silvina. *Thus Were Their Faces.* Translated by Daniel Balderston. NYRB Classics, 2015.

Oloixarac, Pola. *Dark Constellations.* Translated by Roy Kesey. Soho Press, 2019.

2016: Enriques, Mariana. *Things We Lost in the Fire.* Translated by Megan McDowell. Hogarth Press, 2017.

2017: Fresán, Rodrigo. *The Dreamed Part.* Translated by Will Vanderhyden. Open Letter, 2019.

BOLIVIA

2004: Paz Soldán, Edmundo. *Turing's Delirium.* Translated by Lisa Carter. Mariner Books, 2007.

2016: Colanzi, Liliana. *Our Dead World.* Translated by Jessica Sequeira. Dalkey Archive Press, 2017.

CHILE

1996: Bolaño, Roberto. *Nazi Literature in the Americas.* Translated by Chris Andrews. New Directions, 2008.

2000: Jodorowsky, Alejandro. *Albina and the Dog-Men.* Translated by Adam MacAdam. Restless Books, 2016.

COLOMBIA

1962: Márquez, Gabriel García. *In Evil Hour.* Translated by Gregory Rabassa. Harper & Row, 1979.

1967: Márquez, Gabriel García. *One Hundred Years of Solitude.* Translated by Gregory Rabassa. Harper & Row, 1970.

CUBA

1985: Rojas, Agustín de. *A Legend of the Future.* Translated by Nick Caistor. Restless Books, 2015.

1990: Rojas, Agustín de. *The Year 200.* Translated by Nick Caistor. Restless Books, 2016.

2001: Yoss. *A Planet for Rent.* Translated by David Frye. Restless Books, 2015.

2006: Chaviano, Daína. *The Island of Eternal Love.* Translated by Andrea Labinger. Riverhead Books, 2008.

2012: Yoss. *Super Extra Grande.* Translated by David Frye. Restless Books, 2016.

2013: Yoss. *Condomnauts.* Translated by David Frye. Restless Books, 2018.

DOMINICAN REPUBLIC

2011: Cabiya, Pedro. *Wicked Weeds.* Translated by Jessica Powell. Mandel Vilar Press, 2016.

2015: Indiana, Rita. *Tentacle.* Translated by Achy Obejas. And Other Stories, 2018.

MEXICO

1962: Fuentes, Carlos. *Aura.* Translated by Lysander Kemp. FSG, 1965.

1975: Fuentes, Carlos. *Terra Nostra.* Translated by Margaret Sayers Peden. FSG, 1976.

1978: Fuentes, Carlos. *The Hydra Head.* Translated by Margaret Sayers Peden. FSG.

1985: Zaidenweber, José. *Feast of Egos.* Translated by the author. Dorrance, 1993.

1987: Fuentes, Carlos. *Christopher Unborn.* Translated by Alfred MacAdam and the author. FSG, 1989.

1989: Boullosa, Carmen. *Before.* Translated by Peter Bush. Deep Vellum, 2016.

1997: Boullosa, Carmen. *Heavens on Earth.* Translated by Shelby Vincent. Deep Vellum, 2017.

2002: Fuentes, Carlos. *The Eagle's Throne*. Translated by Kristina Cordero. Bloomsbury, 2006.

2010: Fuentes, Carlos. *Vlad*. Translated by Alejandro Branger and Ethan Shaskan Bumas. Dalkey Archive, 2012.

2011: Mayo, Eduardo Jiménez, and Chris N. Brown, eds. *Three Messages and a Warning: Contemporary Mexican Stories of the Fantastic*. Small Beer Press.

2012: Villalobos, Juan Pablo. *Quesadillas*. Translated by Rosalind Harvey. FSG Originals, 2014.

2016: Tizano, Rodrigo, Márquez. *Jakarta*. Translated by Thomas Bunstead. Coffee House Press, 2019.

2018: Dávila, Amparo. *The Houseguest, and Other Stories*. Translated by Matthew Gleeson and Audrey Harris. New Directions.

MULTIPLE COUNTRIES

1991: Agosin, Marjorie, ed. *The Secret Weavers: Stories of the Fantastic by Women of Argentina and Chile*. Various translators. White Pine Press.

1999: Costa, Margaret Jull, and Annella McDermott, eds. and trans. *The Dedalus Book of Spanish Fantasy*. Dedalus.

2003: Bell, Andrea L., and Yolanda Molina-Gavilán, eds. and trans. *Cosmos Latinos: An Anthology of Science Fiction from Latin America and Spain*. Wesleyan.

2016: Jurado, Cristina, and Leticia Lara, eds. *Spanish Women of Wonder*. Translated by Sue Burke, Lawrence Schimel, and Amalia Gladhart. Palabaristas Press, Eurocon.

SPAIN

1887: Gaspar, Enrique. *The Time Ship: A Chrononautical Journey*. Translated by Yolanda Molina-Gavilán and Andrea Bell. Wesleyan University Press, 2012.

1905: Ramón y Cajal, Santiago. *Vacation Stories: Five Science Fiction Tales*. Translated by Laura Otis. University of Illinois Press, 2001.

1995: Martínez, Rodolfo. *Cat's Whirld*. Translated by Steve Redwood. Sportula, 2015.

1998: Sierra, Javier. *The Lady in Blue*. Translated by James Graham. Simon and Schuster / Atria Books, 2007.

1999: Loriga, Ray. *Tokyo Doesn't Love Us Anymore*. Translated by John King. Grove / Atlantic, 2004.

2000: Somoza, José Carlos. *The Athenian Murders*. Translated by Sonia Soto. FSG, 2002.

2001: Montero, Rosa. *Tears in Rain (Bruna Husky #1)*. Translated by Lilit Zekulin Thwaites. AmazonCrossing, 2012.

Zafón, Carlos Ruiz. *The Shadow of the Wind (Cemetery of Forgotten Books #1)*. Translated by Lucia Graves. Penguin Press, 2004.

2002: Reig, Rafael. *Blood on the Saddle*. Translated by Paul Hammond. Serpent's Tail, 2007.

2003: Barceló, Elia. *The Goldsmith's Secret*. Translated by David Frye. MacLehose Press, 2011.

Reig, Rafael. *A Pretty Face*. Translated by Paul Hammond. Serpent's Tail, 2007.

2005: Robles, Lola. *Monteverde: Memoirs of an Interstellar Linguist.* Translated by Lawrence Schimel. Aqueduct Press, 2016.

2006: Somoza, José Carlos. *Zig Zag.* Translated by Lisa Dillman. Rayo, 2007.

2007: Barceló, Elia. *Heart of Tango.* Translated by David Frye. MacLehose Press, 2010.

2008: Palma, Félix J. *The Map of Time (Victorian #1)* (2008) by Translated by Nick Caistor. Atria Books, 2011.

    Zafón, Carlos Ruiz. *The Angel's Game (Cemetery of Forgotten Books #2).* Translated by Lucia Graves. Doubleday, 2009.

2009: Martínez, Rodolfo. *The Queen's Adept (The Queen's Adept Book #1).* Translated by the author. Sportula, 2012.

    Sisi, Carlos. *The Wanderers.* Unknown translator. Permuted Press, 2011.

2010: Loureiro, Manel. *Dark Days (Apocalypse Z #2).* Translated by Pamela Carmell. AmazonCrossing, 2013.

    Sierra, Javier. *The Lost Angel.* Translated by Carlos Frias. Simon and Schuster / Atria Books, 2011.

2011: Loureiro, Manel. *The Wrath of the Just (Apocalypse Z #3).* Translated by Pamela Carmell. AmazonCrossing, 2014.

    Zafón, Carlos Ruiz. *The Prisoner of Heaven (Cemetery of Forgotten Books #3).* Translated by Lucia Graves. Weidenfeld & Nicolson, 2012.

2012: Loureiro, Manel. *The Beginning of the End (Apocalypse Z #1).* Translated by Pamela Carmell. AmazonCrossing.

    Palma, Félix J. *The Map of the Sky (Victorian #2).* Translated by Nick Caistor. Atria Books.

    Romero, Tamara. *Her Fingers.* Translated by the author (?). Eraserhead Press.

    Villarreal, Mariano, ed. *Terra Nova: An Anthology of Contemporary Spanish Science Fiction.* Coselected by Mariano Villareal and Luis Pestarini. Sportula, 2013.

2013: Loureiro, Manel. *The Last Passenger.* Translated by Andrés Alfaro. AmazonCrossing, 2015.

2014: Maleno, Carlos. *The Irish Sea.* Translated by Eric Kurtzke. Dalkey Archive Press, 2017.

    Palma, Félix J. *The Map of Chaos (Victorian #3).* Translated by Nick Caistor. Atria Books, 2015.

2015: Montero, Rosa. *Weight of the Heart (Bruna Husky #2).* Translated by Lilit Zekulin Thwaites. AmazonCrossing, 2016.

    Womack, James, and Marian Womack, eds. and trans. *The Best of Spanish Steampunk.* Cheeky Frawg Books + Ediciones Nevsky.

2016: Llanes, Sergio. *The Twilight of the Normidons (Tears of Gea #1).* Translated by Sue Burke. Ediciones Dokusou.

    Villareal, Mariano, *Castles in Spain: 25 Years of Spanish Fantasy and Science Fiction.* Various translators. Sportula.

2017: Loureiro, Manel. *Only She Sees.* Translated by Andrés Alfaro. AmazonCrossing.

    Sucasas, Ángel Luis. *Moon Scars.* Translated by James Womack. Nevsky Books.

2018: Jurado, Cristina. *Alphaland*. Translated by James Womack. Nevsky Books.

Martínez, Rodolfo. *The Road to Nowhere*. NewCon Press.

Martínez, Rodolfo, and Felicidad Martínez. *Faces from the Past (The Queen's Adept Book #2)*. Translated by Rodolfo Martínez. Sportula.

Zafón, Carlos Ruiz. *The Labyrinth of the Spirits (Cemetery of Forgotten Books #4)*. Translated by Lucia Graves. Harper.

2019: Martínez, Rodolfo. *The Wisdom of the Dead (The Lost Files of Sherlock Holmes)*. Translated by the author with assistance from Rachel Cordasco. Sportula.

Rhei, Sofia. *Everything Is Made of Letters*. Translated by Sue Burke, James Womack, and the author, with assistance from Ian Whates, Arrate Hidalgo, and Sue Burke. Aqueduct Press.

Notes

1. See Martín and Moreno, "Spanish SF."

2. See the introduction to this volume for a more in-depth discussion of magical realism and its relationship to fantasy. See also "On Latin American SF."

3. Scott Bradfield and Clute, "Magic Realism,"

4. Much has been written about Borges. See, for instance, Frisch, *You Might Be Able to Get There from Here*; Fiddian, *Postcolonial Borges*; and Stabb, *Borges Revisited*.

5. See Klingenberg and Zullo-Ruiz, *New Readings of Silvina Ocampo*.

6. Hachard review.

7. See Mesa, "20 Questions "https://smallbeerpress.com/20-questions-with-angelica-gorodischer/; and Molina-Gavilán, "Angélica Gorodischer."

8. Samatar review.

9. Mesa, "20 Questions." The fact that this text was translated into English by Ursula Le Guin necessarily lends *Kalpa* an extra degree of interest for Anglophone science fiction fans. Having met Le Guin at the International Writing Program at Iowa in 1988, Gorodischer has said that the two became friends, which led to the translation project.

10. *Memory* first appeared in the anthology *Terra Nova* in 2013.

11. Cordasco review.

12. Cordasco review.

13. Cordasco review.

14. Cordasco review.

15. Cordasco and Massot reviews.

16. Barker review. *Fever Dream* was shortlisted for the Man Booker International Prize in 2017 and went on to win the Shirley Jackson Award for best novella in the same year.

17. Osborne review.

18. Cordasco review.

19. See Williams, "Sovereignty and Melancholic Paralysis in Roberto Bolaño."

20. Although Fuentes was born in Panama, he is considered a Mexican writer.

21. See Gyurko, *Lifting the Obsidian Mask*.

22. Dixon review.

23. Henson review.

24. Damián Miravete won the 2018 Tiptree Award for her short story "They Will Dream in the Garden" (*Latin American Literature Today*, 2018).

25. In 1994 Zaidenweber "founded and directed the magazine *Asimov, ciencia ficcion* (Asimov, science fiction) with the goal of creating an outlet and source of distribution for science fictioon in Mexico." Lockhart, *Latin American Science Fiction Writers*, 210.

26. Mond review.

27. For more on Chaviano's work, see Toledano Redondo, "Daína Chaviano's Science-Fiction Oeuvre."

28. "By creating a moral universe in which the principles of socialism, exemplified by the ubiquitous figure of Che Guevara, are followed to the letter, Rojas forces the reader to compare and contrast the optimistic fictional reality of his novels with the crude reality of everyday Cuba." Toledano Redondo, "Rojas, Agustín de," http://www.sf-encyclopedia.com/entry/rojas_agustin_de.

29. Hernandez review.

30. Cordasco review.

31. Cordasco review.

32. Cordasco review.

33. Guynes-Vishniac review.

34. Cordasco review.

35. Jones review.

36. Cordasco review.

37. Clute, "Gaspar, Enrique."

38. Cordasco review.

39. "Techt" was first published in English in Jurado and Lara, *Spanish Women of Wonder*.

40. Cordasco review.

41. A grimoire is a book of magic spells or incantations.

42. Cordasco review.

43. Cordasco review.

44. Cordasco review.

45. Publisher's copy.

46. Cordasco review.

47. Cordasco review.

48. Jurado and Lara, introduction to *Spanish Women of Wonder*.

Secondary Sources

Barker, Ray. "Samanta Schweblin's *Fever Dream*." *Music and Literature* (January 2017). https://www.musicandliterature.org/reviews/2017/1/6/samanta-schweblins-fever-dream.

Bradfield, Scott, and John Clute. "Magic Realism." In *The Encyclopedia of Science Fiction*, edited by John Clute, David Langford, Peter Nicholls, and Graham Sleight. London: Gollancz, updated April 9, 2015. http://www.sf-encyclopedia.com/entry/magic_realism.

Clute, John. "Gaspar, Enrique." In *The Encyclopedia of Science Fiction*, edited by John Clute, David Langford, Peter Nicholls, and Graham Sleight. London: Gollancz, updated January 25, 2019. http://www.sf-encyclopedia.com/entry/gaspar_enrique.

Cordasco, Rachel. "*Bodies of Summer* by Martin Felipe Castagnet, Translated by Frances Riddle." *Strange Horizons* (April 2017). http://strangehorizons.com/non-fiction/reviews /bodies-of-summer-by-martin-felipe-castagnet-translated-by-frances-riddle/.

———. "Book Review: *Alphaland* by Cristina Jurado, Translated by James Womack." *Skiffy and Fanty* (October 2018). https://skiffyandfanty.com/blogposts/reviews/bookreviews /reviewalphalandbyjuradotransbywomack/.

———. "*Dark Constellations* by Pola Oloixarac." *World Literature Today* (2019). https:// www.worldliteraturetoday.org/2019/summer/dark-constellations-pola-oloixarac.

———. "*A Planet for Rent* by Yoss." *SFinTranslation.com* (May 2016). https://www .sfintranslation.com/?p=43.

———. "Review: *The Best of Spanish Steampunk.*" *SFinTranslation.com* (May 2016). https:// www.sfintranslation.com/?p=282.

———. "Review: *The Bottom of the Sky* by Rodrigo Fresán." *SFinTranslation.com* (April 2018). https://www.sfintranslation.com/?p=4136.

———. "Review: *Castles in Spain: 25 Years of Spanish Fantasy and Science Fiction*, edited by Mariano Villarreal." *SFinTranslation.com* (May 2016). https://www.sfintranslation .com/?p=80.

———. "Review: *The Dreamed Part* by Rodrigo Fresán." *SFinTranslation.com* (October 2019). https://www.sfintranslation.com/?p=7328.

———. "Review: *The Invented Part* by Rodrigo Fresán." *SFinTranslation.com* (June 2017). https://www.sfintranslation.com/?p=2236.

———. "Review: *Monteverde: Memoirs of an Interstellar Linguist* by Lola Robles." *SFinTrans- lation.com* (October 2016). https://www.sfintranslation.com/?p=1210.

———. "Review: *Moon Scars* by Ángel Luis Sucasas." *SFinTranslation.com* (February 2017). https://www.sfintranslation.com/?p=1728.

———. "Review: *Our Dead World* by Liliana Colanzi." *SFinTranslation.com* (June 2017). https://www.sfintranslation.com/?p=2256.

———. "Review: *The Queen's Adept* by Rodolfo Martínez." *SFinTranslation.com* (April 2017). https://www.sfintranslation.com/?p=1913.

———. "Review: *Spanish Women of Wonder*, Ed. Cristina Jurado and Leticia Lara." *SFin- Translation.com* (November 2016). https://www.sfintranslation.com/?p=1279.

———. "Review: *Super Extra Grande* by Yoss." *SFinTranslation.com* (May 2016). https:// www.sfintranslation.com/?p=186.

———. "Review: *Terra Nova: An Anthology of Contemporary Spanish Science Fiction*, Ed. Mariano Villareal." *SFinTranslation.com* (November 2016). https://www.sfintranslation .com/?p=1299.

———. "Review: *Wicked Weeds* by Pedro Cabiya." *SFinTranslation.com* (September 2016). https://www.sfintranslation.com/?p=1020.

———. "Review: *The Year 200* by Agustín de Rojas." *SFinTranslation.com* (June 2016). https://www.sfintranslation.com/?p=449.

Dixon, Arthur. "*Quesadillas* by Juan Pablo Villalobos." *World Literature Today* (March 2014). https://www.worldliteraturetoday.org/2014/march/quesadillas-juan-pablo -villalobos.

Fiddian, Robin W. *Postcolonial Borges: Argument and Artistry.* Oxford: Oxford University Press, 2017.

Frisch, Mark F. *You Might Be Able to Get There from Here: Reconsidering Borges and the Postmodern.* Madison, NJ: Fairleigh Dickinson University Press, 2004.

Guynes-Vishniac, Sean. "*Condomnauts* by Yoss." *World Literature Today* (July 2018). https://www.worldliteraturetoday.org/2018/july/condomnauts-yoss.

Gyurko, Lanin A. *Lifting the Obsidian Mask: The Artistic Vision of Carlos Fuentes.* N.p.: Digitalia, 2007.

Hachard, Tomas. "Chasing Ghosts: On Argentinian Author César Aira." *Los Angeles Review of Books*, October 27, 2013. https://lareviewofbooks.org/article/chasing-ghosts-on-argentinian-author-cesar-aira/.

Henson, George. "*Before* by Carmen Boullosa." *World Literature Today* (January 2017). https://www.worldliteraturetoday.org/2017/january/carmen-boullos a.

Hernandez, Carlos. "Agustín de Rojas, *A Legend of the Future* and Yoss, *A Planet for Rent.*" *Foundation* 45.2, no. 124 (2016): 121–23.

Jones, Ellen. "Little Book with Big Ambitions: Rita Indiana's *Tentacle.*" *Los Angeles Review of Books*, December 13, 2018. https://lareviewofbooks.org/article/little-book-with-big-ambitions-rita-indianas-tentacle.

Jurado, Cristina, and Leticia Lara. Introduction to *Spanish Women of Wonder*, edited by Cristina Jurado and Leticia Lara, translated by Sue Burke, Lawrence Schimel, and Amalia Gladhart. N.p.: Palabaristas Press, Eurocon 2016.

Klingenberg, Patricia N., and Fernanda Zullo-Ruiz. *New Readings of Silvina Ocampo: Beyond Fantasy.* Woodbridge, Suffolk: Boydell & Brewer, 2016.

Lockhart, Darrell B. *Latin American Science Fiction Writers: An A-to-Z Guide.* Westport, CT: Greenwood Press, 2004.

Martín, Sara, and Fernando Ángel Moreno. "Spanish SF." Special issue, *Science Fiction Studies* 44, pt. 2 (2017). https://www.depauw.edu/sfs/covers/cov132.htm.

Massot, Josefina. "Space Oddity: Rodrigo Fresán and the Dawn of the Psy-Fi Heroine." *Asymptote* (August 2018). https://www.asymptotejournal.com/blog/2018/08/23/space-oddity-rodrigo-fresan-and-the-dawn-of-the-psy-fi-heroine/.

Mesa, Gabriel. "20 Questions with Angélica Gorodischer." *Small Beer Press* (2003). https://smallbeerpress.com/20-questions-with-angelica-gorodischer/.

Molina-Gavilán, Yolanda. "Angélica Gorodischer: Only a Storyteller." In *Lingua Cosmica: Science Fiction from around the World*, edited by Dale Knickerbocker, 73–94. Urbana: University of Illinois Press, 2018.

Mond, Ian. "Ian Mond Reviews *Jakarta* by Rodrigo Márquez Tizano." *Locus Magazine* (2020). https://locusmag.com/2020/02/ian-mond-reviews-jakarta-by-rodrigo-marquez-tizano/.

"On Latin American SF." Special section, *Science Fiction Studies* 34, pt. 3 (2007). https://www.depauw.edu/sfs/covers/cov103.htm.

Osborne, J. David. "*Comemadre* by Roque Larraquy." *World Literature Today* (September 2018). https://www.worldliteraturetoday.org/2018/september/comemadre-roque-larraquy.

Samatar, Sofia. "Entanglement: Angélica Gorodischer's *Kalpa Imperial.*" *Tor.com* (June 2014). https://www.tor.com/2014/06/04/entanglement-angelica-gorodischers-kalpa -imperial/.

Stabb, Martin S. *Borges Revisited*. Boston: Twayne, 1991.

Toledano Redondo, Juan Carlos. "Daína Chaviano's Science-Fiction Oeuvre: Fables of an Extraterrestrial Grandmother." In *Lingua Cosmica: Science Fiction from around the World*, edited by Dale Knickerbocker, 1–21. Urbana: University of Illinois Press, 2018.

———. "Rojas, Agustín de." In *The Encyclopedia of Science Fiction*, edited by John Clute, David Langford, Peter Nicholls, and Graham Sleight. London: Gollancz, updated January 14, 2019. http://www.sf-encyclopedia.com/entry/rojas_agustin_de.

Williams, Gareth. "Sovereignty and Melancholic Paralysis in Roberto Bolaño." *Journal of Latin American Cultural Studies* 18 (2009): 125–40.

Swedish-Language SFT

Introduction

Genre literature—whether science fiction, fantasy, or horror—has a somewhat contradictory history in Sweden. Several famous, even world-famous, Swedish authors have written works that can certainly be classified as genre fiction. Also, many Swedish mainstream authors incorporate some degree of folklore-inspired fantasy and more or less obvious genre tropes into their work. Even so, Sweden's literary establishment has often treated genre fiction with disdain, or neglected its existence altogether. This may be changing, though, with a new crop of Swedish authors who are not afraid to proclaim their love for genre fiction and whose works are available in translation across the world.

Two early examples of genre works by Swedish writers that received international attention are Nobel laureate Harry Martinson's spaceship poem *Aniara* and Karin Boye's dystopic novel *Kallocain*. Both works showcase some oft-recurring themes in Swedish genre fiction: a penchant for dystopic futures, a literary bent, and a focus on the future of people and societies, rather than the specs of future technology.

Aniara (1956, trans. 1963) is arguably the most famous and influential work of Swedish science fiction ever published. The poem has been adapted into musicals, plays, and movies, and it has inspired other writers and creators, including Vernor Vinge and Poul Anderson. The poem tells the story of a spaceship bound for Mars carrying colonists who are leaving a ravaged future Earth. After an accident, the ship is thrown off course and set on a trajectory out of the solar system.

Kallocain, by Karin Boye, was published in 1940 and is often compared to both Orwell's *1984* and Huxley's *A Brave New World*. When writing her tale of a totalitarian state that uses drugs to ensure the loyalty and subservience of its citizens, Boye was influenced by what was occurring in both Nazi Germany and the Soviet Union at the time. *Kallocain* has continued to receive international attention long after its original release, and new English translations were published in 2002 (by Gustaf Lannestock) and 2019 (by David McDuff). It is interesting to note that while both Martinson and Boye mostly wrote literary fiction and poetry, their forays into genre fiction are probably what has made the biggest and most lasting impression outside Sweden.

The main Swedish publishing houses largely withdrew from publishing genre literature from the 1950s onward, and this made the Swedish literary landscape a challenging one for genre fiction. This division and tension between genre fiction and literary fiction, and its resulting marginalization, are present in many countries, but the effect is more widespread in a small country such as Sweden, where the number of publishers, writers, critics, and readers is limited.

One literary area where Swedish genre fiction has thrived, when it comes to both sales and the reception from critics and readers, is children's literature. Astrid Lindgren, a prime example of a "kidlit" author who has been embraced for her genre fiction work both in Sweden and internationally, is one of the most popular Swedish authors of all time. Not all of Lindgren's books are genre fiction, but some of her most internationally successful works—including *Mio, My Son*; *The Brothers Lionheart*; and *Ronia, the Robber's Daughter*—are classic secondary-world fantasy novels.

Lindgren's work has been translated into numerous languages, as well as adapted into plays and movies. *Mio, My Son* as well as *The Brothers Lionheart* have both been compared to the works of J. R. R. Tolkien and C. S. Lewis, but her most original fantasy novel is probably *Ronia, the Robber's Daughter*, which features various creatures inspired by Swedish folklore, as well as a forest setting that feels decidedly Scandinavian.

In recent years, as genre fiction has become more commercially viable across the world, a new generation of Swedish writers has embraced genre fiction more wholeheartedly, and several of them have received wide acclaim and international recognition for their work. For example, writers like John Ajvide Lindqvist (*Let the Right One In*), Karin Tidbeck (*Jagannath* and *Amatka*), as well as Mats Strandberg and Sara Bergmark Elfgren (cowriters of *The Engelsfors* trilogy) have published works that have been well received both in Sweden and elsewhere.

Let the Right One In
(2007)

Lindqvist's horror fiction includes his best-selling debut novel, *Let the Right One In*, a romantic vampire horror tale set in the present day, and *Handling the Undead*, a zombie novel set in Stockholm. Strandberg and Elfgren's *Engelsfors* trilogy—*The Circle*, *Fire*, and *The Key*—straddles the line between horror and fantasy. The trilogy takes place in Engelsfors, a fictional rural town, where a group of teenage girls discover that they are witches, destined to save the world from an approaching apocalypse. Strandberg has embraced the horror genre, with his acclaimed horror novel *Blood Cruise* (2016), while Elfgren has delved into the fantasy genre, penning a series of graphic novels called *Vei*, described as "*Hunger Games* meets Norse mythology."

Karin Tidbeck is one of the most internationally lauded genre fiction writers to emerge in Sweden in recent years. She debuted with the Swedish short-story

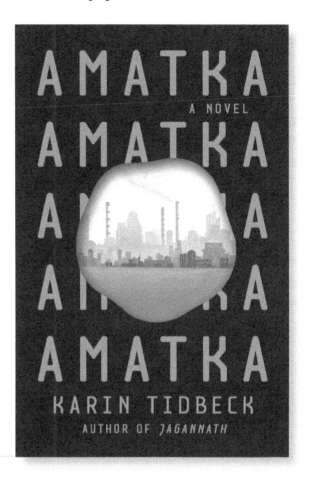

Amatka (2017)

collection *Vem är Arvid Pekon?* in 2010, followed by her surreal novel *Amatka* in 2012. *Jagannath*, her first short-story collection in English, was published in 2012 and made the short list for the 2012 James Tiptree Jr. Award. It was also nominated for the World Fantasy Award. Tidbeck's short story "Augusta Prima," originally written in Swedish, was translated into English by Tidbeck and won the 2013 Science Fiction and Fantasy Translation Award in the Short Form category. *Amatka* was published in English in 2017, translated by the author herself, and was a Locus Award finalist. The book was also short-listed for the Compton Crook Award 2018 and Prix Utopiales 2018.

Looking at the work by these newer authors, it is hard to discern any overarching theme in current Swedish genre fiction, but writers often seem to lean into the surreal, uncanny, and Weird, regardless of genre. Like Martinson and Boye before them, they also often deal with dystopian themes, as Tidbeck does in her novel *Amatka*. These are interesting times for Swedish genre fiction, with the work of several authors receiving increasing interest from readers and publishers inside and outside Sweden. One can only hope that, perhaps, Swedish genre fiction will finally receive the respect and attention it deserves.

Maria Haskins

The Texts

A surprising amount of Swedish SFT is available in Anglophone countries, given the relatively small amount of Swedish literature generally available in translation. While no one press can take credit for the bulk of these published translations, the UK-based Quercus Books has made several works by horror writer John Ajvide Lindqvist available to Anglophone readers in recent years, as well as one novel by Mats Strandberg, another horror writer. Thanks to these horror titles, the amount of Swedish SFT published in the 2010s equals that of all of the titles published between 1960 and 2009 combined. Besides the obvious explanation that a rising tide floats all boats (more SFT from many source languages was published in the 2010s than in any previous decade), we can point to the sudden worldwide popularity of Swedish journalist Stieg Larsson's *Millennium* series (also published by Quercus), which initiated a wave of interest in crime fiction, especially from Scandinavia, in the mid-2000s.

This recent dominance of horror in Swedish SFT, though, obscures the rich tradition of science fiction and fantasy that has been translated from that source language in previous decades. Indeed, the most important work of speculative fiction in Sweden isn't even a novel but a science fictional epic poem.[1] Dystopias, alternate futures, magical dimensions: all of these and more make up the Swedish SFT that Anglophone readers have access to today.

SCIENCE FICTION

Two main strands run through the Swedish SFT available in English: the dystopian future and space travel. The former isn't confined to any particular decade but includes novels from the 1960s (Karin Boye's *Kallocain*), 1970s (Sam Lundwall's *2018 AD*), 2000s (Ninni Holmqvist's *The Unit*), and 2010s (Åsa Avdic's *The Dying Game*). And while the circumstances and settings necessarily change from novel to novel over the decades, their uniformly bleak outlook and focus on entrapment suggest a continuing concern in parts of Swedish culture with independence (something the nation gained politically centuries before).

Boye's **Kallocain** (1940; 1966), the earliest work of Swedish SFT available in English (but only the second to be translated), takes its place alongside George

Orwell's *1984* and Yevgeny Zamyatin's *We* in its depiction of a repressive society characterized by total government surveillance and social conformity. Boye, who witnessed the fall of Weimar Germany and the rise of Nazism in the 1930s,[2] drew on these experiences to imagine a world ruled by terror and organized into two eternally warring nations. More than thirty years later, prominent Swedish science fiction author, editor, and publisher Sam Lundwall would write *2018 AD; or, The King Kong Blues* (1974; 1975), in which governments have ceded their power to multinational corporations that are themselves owned by a bedouin prince who controls vast oil fields. By turns satirical and despairing, *2018 AD* uses an ad executive's search for a young woman (whose face he wants on a product campaign) as a way to examine how power is used and abused in this system.

In Ninni Holmqvist's *The Unit* (2006; 2009), the totalitarian trap has become tangible: here it is a literal prison (albeit a generally comfortable one) in which people who have reached a certain age must relinquish their organs one by one to younger citizens.[3] These women (fifty and over) and men (sixty and over) must also submit themselves to tests and experiments in order to give researchers information that can be used to treat ill or dying people in the outside world. Told from the point of view of a middle-aged childless writer imprisoned in the Unit, Holmqvist's novel raises timely and difficult ethical, legal, economic, and social issues and asks us what we "owe" to our communities and what we're willing to give or ask others to give up.

A remote island, rather than a compound, provides the setting for Åsa Avdic's near-future novel *The Dying Game* (2016; 2017), where seven people are brought to compete in a two-day test for a top-secret totalitarian-government intelligence position. One of the seven, Anna Francis, is not actually a test subject but the focus of the test itself—she must stage her own death and then observe the others from a secret position as they react to the revelation that one of them is a murderer. The test is undermined by an unexpected storm that changes the rules of the test in unexpected ways.

Simultaneous with this dystopian strand has been a focus on the future of space travel and its impact on human culture and community. This is the subject of the first work of Swedish SFT published since 1960—the epic poem *Aniara: A Review of Man in Time and Space* (1956; 1963) by author, poet, and Nobel Prize winner Harry Martinson.[4] His only work of science fiction, *Aniara* tells the story of the doomed eponymous spaceship in 103 cantos. Destined for another planet that will offer the passengers a better life (since the Earth of the novel has become a wasteland), *Aniara* is knocked off course by an asteroid and sent into interstellar space. Since the passengers were not prepared to live on the ship indefinitely, they quickly realize that their ship has become their coffin. And though Mima, the ship's sentient communications network, at first tries to keep up the crew's and passengers' morale with images of Earth, it ultimately terminates itself because of the knowledge that its crew is doomed. The crew and passengers, too, commit suicide. The impact of this poem has been felt in other areas of Swedish culture, resulting in its adaptation into an opera (1959) and a film (2018).

A twenty-thousand-mile-long spaceship (named *Refanut*) is featured in Lundwall's ***Bernhard the Conqueror*** (1973; 1973), on which people, robots, and sentient machines mingle in a timeless community. The product of a long-dead galactic empire, this ship is merely passing through the galaxy in an aimless journey. When it passes over a prison planet, former private Bernhard manages to escape his sentence and stow away on the *Refanut*, where he discovers that certain machines there "love" him and want to protect him from the people who wish him gone. In a similarly jocular vein, Mikael Niemi's ***AstroTruckers*** (2004; 2007) is a collection of humorous space adventures à la Lem's *Memoirs of a Space Traveler*. Through the eyes of one particular astrotrucker, we meet "ponorists" (people who travel into space beyond the point of no return), learn about the oldest writing in the universe, and discover the consequences of turning an android's personality setting to "humor."

Olof Johannesson's *The Great Computer: A Vision*, the only work of Swedish SFT to take up computers specifically, came out in Swedish and then in English in the 1960s (1966; 1968). Winner of the 1970 Nobel Prize in Physics, Johannesson imagines a future Earth where prosperity has given way to disaster, due to human actions, and out of the ashes rises a world run by highly advanced computers. Written thirty years before the rise of the worldwide Internet, *The Great Computer* suggests that the trajectory of evolution on Earth is toward sentient machines.

FANTASY

As with Swedish science fiction in English, Swedish fantasy comes in a variety of styles. From Lars Gustafsson's collage-like *Sigismund* and Gabi Gleichmann's tale of immortality to Stefan Spjut's shape-shifting trolls and Karin Tidbeck's surrealist genre-bending tales, there is something for every reader. Gustafsson's ***Sigismund*** (1976; 1984) offers readers a semiautobiographical perspective on 1970s West Berlin, but it is narrated by a man who can remove himself from the world while still being a part of it. Thus, he depicts reality via stylistically diverse vignettes about the seventeenth-century Sigismund III of Poland, a young painter who sells his soul to the devil in exchange for wealth, fame, and a different identity for one day. Gustafsson includes everything from Dante and the Faust legend to intergalactic travel in a colorful snapshot of a particular time and place.

Likewise, Gleichmann blends fantasy and history in *The Elixir of Immortality* (2012; 2013), a tale of several generations of the Spinoza family and the secret recipe for immortality that they have passed down from father to son since the eleventh century.[5] Narrated by the last man to hold the family name (he is on his deathbed and has no children), the novel is a chronicle of the Spinoza family's involvement in Europe's most important religious, social, cultural, and political movements and revolutions over the past several centuries. Gleichmann asks readers to consider the ways in which memory and storytelling offer their own kind of immortality.

In contrast to the Gustafsson and Gleichman style of fantasy meets history, Stefan Spjut's *The Shapeshifters* (2012; 2015) is genre fantasy meets mystery. When a four-year-old boy is kidnapped, Susso Myrén puts herself on the case. Having spent her life trying to prove to people that trolls are real, and after capturing the kidnapper (a small, strange-looking man) on camera, Myrén tries to get the truth out. She thus becomes a target for those who protect the shape-shifting trolls and other such creatures (called the "stallo").

Karin Tidbeck, who also takes her cue from Swedish legend, became the most recognizable fantasy author in the Anglophone world in the 2010s. Her collection *Jagannath* (2012)[6] and novel *Amatka* (2012; 2017)[7] reveal a nimbleness of imagination that moves easily among fantasy subgenres. Influenced by Borges, Le Guin, Lovecraft, and other giants from the speculative fiction world, Tidbeck has published widely both in Sweden and in US and UK magazines. The stories in *Jagannath* range from depictions of a far-future biological ark to academic papers about creatures called the Pyret that live in rural Sweden. In *Amatka*, Tidbeck ambitiously takes on the concept of language itself. Set in a world in which words literally have the power to change reality, *Amatka* is ultimately a story about how one young woman rebels against authority and tradition to forge her own *new* reality. Her growing insistence that the world can be other than it is pushes her to ultimately embrace dematerialization (writing or pronouncing a word wrong) and then use it to her advantage.

HORROR

Swedish horror has become quite popular with Anglophone reading audiences—specifically the horror fiction of John Ajvide Lindqvist. A former magician, Lindquist has been likened to Stephen King in that both cultivate a kind of psychological horror that goes beyond blood and gore.[8] With his first novel, *Let the Right One In* (2004; 2007), Lindqvist became an internationally best-selling author (*Let the Right One In* was eventually adapted for film).[9] A modern-day vampire tale, the book details the budding friendship between a lonely preteen boy named Oskar and Eli, the strange new girl who moves into his apartment building. As the story goes on, we find out that Eli is an androgynous vampire who can produce claws and wings when feeding on human blood. Along with these horrors is the fact that her "guardian" turns out to be a pedophile. Lindqvist deftly explores the classic vampire subgenre in terms of the loss of childhood, the pain of loneliness, and helplessness in the face of the unknown.

Handling the Undead (2005; 2009) is about zombies, rather than vampires, and follows various characters as they try to deal with the fact that their dead loved ones are inexplicably returning to them. As with *Let the Right One In*, Lindqvist invites readers into his characters' worlds and personal struggles in order to focus the horror and make it more intense. Lindqvist returns to this novel and *Let the Right One In* in his subsequent story collection *Let the Old Dreams Die, and Other Stories* (2006; 2012). While the title story follows Oskar and Eli after they leave Blackeberg (a suburb of Stockholm) behind, other stories examine the fallout from *Handling the Undead* ("Final Processing") and follow yet another person who dies but then mysteriously returns ("Eternal/Love").

Lindqvist turns to the sea in *Harbor* (2008; 2010), a psychological thriller about a young girl who goes missing and her father's desperate attempt to find her. Set on an island not far from Stockholm, the story includes ghosts, possessions, and strange wormlike creatures. A mysterious baby found in the forest is the starting point of *Little Star* (2010; 2011), and when that baby grows into a dissatisfied teenage girl with supernatural vocal powers, what follows is a strange story involving a cult, wolves, Eurovision, and senseless murder.

In his *Platserna* ("Place") series, Lindqvist invents a kind of nonspace that brings out the worst in anyone unfortunate enough to find themselves in it. Only the first two novels have been translated into English: *I Am Behind You* (2014; 2017) and *I Always Find You* (2015; 2018).[10] Though *I Am Behind You* came out first, it can be better understood if read after *I Always Find You*. The latter reads like a depressing coming-of-age story about an aspiring and poor magician living in a rundown suburb of Stockholm in the 1980s. Pretty quickly, though, it shifts into a bloody, nightmarish tale that encompasses not only the author and his neighbors but also the prime minister of Sweden at the time, Olof Palme. When this magician (named John Lindqvist) and his neighbors discover a kind of sludge in the laundry-room bathroom, they realize that it isn't like anything known on Earth. All the characters have to do is cut themselves and then dip the cut finger or limb into the sludge to be transported to another "place" where they are truly themselves. Such a sense of fulfillment and euphoria is addictive, of course, but after a while the sludge starts to lose its potency.

I Am Behind You takes *I Always Find You* as a starting point, as it is set entirely within the "field" that the characters in the former novel only visited. The characters in *I Am Behind You*, however, don't choose to enter this "field"; rather, they just wake up one day in their camping caravans and find themselves there. They can't figure out exactly *where* they are, or even if they're still on Earth. The grass seems to drink up blood, the sun is nowhere to be seen, and there aren't any landmarks or other people around. Each character sees different figures based on their individual traumas or deepest desires. Lindqvist weaves together these characters' past experiences to show how their traumas share certain features, as if the author is trying to find a way to capture just *how* trauma is internalized and influences the rest of a person's life.

Joining Lindqvist on the Swedish horror scene is Mats Strandberg, whose vampire/zombie novel ***Blood Cruise*** (2017) came out in English in 2018. Set on a cruise ship filled with drunken partiers, this novel follows a vampiric mother and her son as they make their way through the passengers, biting and gnawing as they go. Adding to the horror of these murders and transformations is that readers learn much about some of the passengers before any of this carnage takes place. Like Lindqvist, Strandberg is interested in exploring how ordinary, often depressed, people react in unnatural and horrifying situations.

✳ ✳ ✳

As the next decade unfolds, we can expect more Swedish speculative fiction in English, especially from authors like Tidbeck and Lindqvist. If what we already have in English is any indication, the next wave of Swedish SFT will be as diverse and interesting as ever.

Primary Sources

1940: Boye, Karin. *Kallocain.* Translated by Gustaf Lannestock. University of Wisconsin Press, 1966.

1956: Martinson, Harry. *Aniara: A Review of Man in Time and Space.* Translated by Hugh MacDiarmid and Elspeth Harley Schubert. Hutchinson, 1963.

1966: Johannesson, Olof. *The Great Computer: A Vision.* Translated by Naomi Walford. Victor Gollancz, 1968.

1973: Lundwall, Sam. *Bernhard the Conqueror.* Translated by the author. DAW.

1974: Lundwall, Sam. *2018 AD; or, The King Kong Blues.* Translated by the author. DAW, 1975.

1976: Gustafsson, Lars. *Sigismund.* Translated by John Weinstock. New Directions, 1984.

2004: Lindqvist, John Ajvide. *Let the Right One In.* Translated by Ebba Segerberg. Quercus, 2007.

Niemi, Mikael. *AstroTruckers.* Translated by Laurie Thompson. Harvill Secker, 2007.

2005: Lindqvist, John Ajvide. *Handling the Undead.* Translated by Ebba Segerberg. Quercus, 2009.

2006: Holmqvist, Ninni. *The Unit.* Translated by Marlaine Delargy. Other Press, 2009.

Lindqvist, John Ajvide. *Let the Old Dreams Die, and Other Stories.* Translated by Ebba Segerberg. Quercus, 2012.

2008: Lindqvist, John Ajvide. *Harbor.* Translated by Marlaine Delargy. Quercus, 2010.

2010: Lindqvist, John Ajvide. *Little Star.* Translated by Marlaine Delargy. Riverrun, 2011.

2011: Tidbeck, Karin. *Jagannath.* Translated by the author. Cheeky Frawg Books, 2012.

2012: Gleichmann, Gabi. *The Elixir of Immortality.* Translated by Michael Meigs. Other Press, 2013.

Spjut, Stefan. *The Shapeshifters.* Translated by Susan Beard. Mariner Books, 2015.

Tidbeck, Karin. *Amatka.* Translated by the author. Vintage, 2017.

2014: Lindqvist, John Ajvide. *I Am behind You (Platserna #1).* Translated by Marlaine Delargy. Riverrun, 2017.

2015: Lindqvist, John Ajvide. *I Always Find You (Platserna #2).* Translated by Marlaine Delargy. Riverrun, 2018.

2016: Avdic, Åsa. *The Dying Game.* Translated by Rachel Willson-Broyles. Penguin Books, 2017.

2017: Strandberg, Mats. *Blood Cruise.* Translated by Agnes Broome. Quercus, 2018.

Notes

1. While *Out of This World* focuses on adult book-length prose fiction, *Aniara* is such an important work in the context of Swedish science fiction and falls within the temporal constraints of this volume, which is why it is included here.

2. Clute, "Boye, Karin."

3. Cordasco review.

4. Martinson won the 1974 Nobel Prize for Literature. See Smith, "Role of the Emersonian 'Poet.'"

5. Cheuk review.

6. Petrie review.

7. Cordasco review.

8. See Aldana Reyes, "John Ajvide Lindqvist."

9. Johnson review.

10. Cordasco review.

Secondary Sources

Aldana Reyes, Xavier. "John Ajvide Lindqvist." In *Horror Literature through History: An Encyclopedia of the Stories That Speak to Our Deepest Fears,* edited by Matt Cardin, 181–82. Westport, CT: Greenwood, 2017.

Cheuk, Leland. "*The Elixir of Immortality* by Gabi Gleichmann." *Rumpus* (November 2013). https://therumpus.net/2013/11/the-elixir-of-immortality-by-gabi-gleichmann/.

Clute, John. "Boye, Karin." In *The Encyclopedia of Science Fiction,* edited by John Clute, David Langford, Peter Nicholls, and Graham Sleight. London: Gollancz, updated August 11, 2018. http://www.sf-encyclopedia.com/entry/boye_karin.

Cordasco, Rachel. "*I Am behind You* and *I Always Find You* by John Ajvide Lindqvist." *Strange Horizons* (December 2018). http://strangehorizons.com/non-fiction/reviews/i-am-behind-you-and-i-always-find-you-by-john-ajvide-lindqvist/.

———. "Review: *Amatka* by Karin Tidbeck." *SFinTranslation.com* (November 2017). https://www.sfintranslation.com/?p=3123.

———. "*The Unit* by Ninni Holmqvist." *Necessary Fiction* (January 2018). http://necessary fiction.com/reviews/TheUnitbyNinniHolmqvisttranslatedbyMarlaineDelargy.

Johnson, Andrea. "*Let the Right One In,* by John Ajvide Lindqvist." *Little Red Reviewer* (November 2014). https://littleredreviewer.wordpress.com/2014/11/07/let-the-right-one -in-by-john-ajvide-lindqvist/.

Petrie, Simon. "Book Review: *Jagannath,* by Karin Tidbeck." *Simon Petrie* (December 2017). https://simonpetrie.wordpress.com/2017/12/28/book-review-jagannath-by-karin -tidbeck/.

Smith, Scott Andrew. "The Role of the Emersonian 'Poet' in Harry Martinson's *Aniara*: A Review of Man in Time and Space." *Extrapolation* 39 (1998): 324–37.

Resources

Web Resources

Arielle Saiber's World Science Fiction Course website: https://courses.bowdoin.edu
/ital-2500-spring-2015/
The Encyclopedia of Fantasy: http://sf-encyclopedia.uk/fe.php
The Encyclopedia of Science Fiction: http://www.sf-encyclopedia.com/
Europa SF: The European Speculative Fiction Portal: http://scifiportal.eu/
Internet Speculative Fiction Database: http://www.isfdb.org/cgi-bin/index.cgi
Locus Magazine: https://locusmag.com/
Speculative Fiction in Translation website: https://www.sfintranslation.com/

SFT-Friendly Presses and Magazines

Alfred A. Knopf
Asymptote Journal
Black Coat Press
Clarkesworld Magazine
Comma Press
DAW (especially 1972–1985)
Dedalus Books
Future Science Fiction Digest
Gollancz
Haikasoru (on hiatus)
Harcourt (Brace Jovanovich)

Macmillan
New Directions
Open Letter
Orbit
Samovar Magazine
Seabury (especially 1973–1977) (now defunct)
Tor Books (especially since 1999)
Vertical
Wakefield Press
Words without Borders
World Literature Today

Acknowledgments

Completing *any* kind of project is difficult when you have young kids and a part-time job. Thus, this book wouldn't exist if it weren't for my patient husband, Jared, who on weekends watched the kids while I wrote at a nearby café and on weeknights tucked them into bed (multiple times).

Thank you also to my extended family, who supported me in this endeavor, and especially to my mom, who kindly listened to me drone on about this project many times.

Guidance and support also came from my boss, Kate Thompson, who answered my many questions about publishing and editing with patience and keen insight. Thank you also to my colleague Diane Drexler for her advice, support, and enthusiasm for this project.

This book has been mightily enriched by those translators, editors, authors, and scholars who so kindly agreed to write the chapter introductions, read drafts, connected me to other scholars, and offered helpful revisions: Emad El-Din Aysha, Pawel Frelik, Sonja Fritzsche, Edward Gauvin, Sean Guynes, Maria Haskins, Elisabeth Jaquette, Dale Knickerbocker, Ken Liu, Antonia Lloyd-Jones, J. Pekka Mäkelä, Jenny McPhee, Julie Nováková, Keren Omry, Wojciech Orliński, Sunyoung Park, Chad Post, M. Lynx Qualey, Lola Rogers, Arielle Saiber, Alex Shvartsman, Mingwei Song, Jonathan Strahan, Takayuki Tatsumi, and Francesco Verso.

A big thank-you to Dale, in particular, whose *Lingua Cosmica* inspired me to embark on this project and who connected me to the University of Illinois Press.

One person cannot possibly keep track of the multitude of long- and short-form SFT that comes out each year, so I am particularly grateful to Joachim Boaz, Anton Hur, Andrea Johnson, Cristina Jurado, and Lawrence Schimel for sending me titles and links to add to the SFT site. A major thank-you also goes to Daniel Haeusser for contributing reviews of short SFT to the site and joining me on the SFT podcast, which ran for sixteen episodes in 2018–19. We are grateful to *Skiffy and Fanty*'s Jen Zink and Shaun Duke for making that podcast happen.

Sue Burke, Adrian Demopulos, Kristy Eagar, Jaymee Goh, Arrate Hidalgo, Crystal Huff, and S. Qiouyi Lu brought insight and extensive knowledge to the SFT panels at Wiscon over the past several years and helped me think more critically about SFT and its role in the publishing industry—thank you! And thank you to the very talented translators Anatoly Belilovsky, Jennifer Delare, Julia Meitov Hersey, Ken Liu, and Alex Shvartsman for the great discussions about translation.

Thank you to to the editors at *SFRA Review, Locus Magazine, World Literature Today, Words without Borders, Strange Horizons, Samovar Magazine, Future Science Fiction Digest*, and others for featuring my reviews and essays on SFT and for sending me SFT that wasn't previously on my radar.

Of course, this book would never have been written had John DeNardo of *SF Signal* not sent me SFT to review for his site back in 2014. Neil Clarke's, Cheryl Morgan's, Lavie Tidhar's, and Francesco Verso's work promoting and publishing SFT inspired me to start the SFinTranslation.com and build it into the resource that it has become.

And finally, thank you to the University of Illinois Press for taking on this project, to editors Marika Christofedes, James Engelhardt, Alison Syring Bassford, and Jennifer Argo for their help and guidance throughout this process, and to copyeditor Annette Wenda for her painstaking attention to detail.

Contributors

Each of the following contributors wrote an introduction about the source-language speculative fiction in translation for which they have expertise. Their introductions and comments on chapter drafts have proved invaluable to this volume.

Emad El-Din Aysha is a Cairo-based academic, journalist, translator, and author of science fiction. He is a member of the Egyptian Society for Science Fiction and, to date, has one SF anthology in print (Arabic) and one unpublished novel in English. He has translated several novels from Arabic into English, one in print and another in preparation, and has published articles and designed courses on SF.

Sonja Fritzsche is a professor of German studies and associate dean for academic personnel and administration in the College of Arts and Letters at Michigan State University. Her publications include *Science Fiction Literature in East Germany* (2006), *The Liverpool Companion to World Science Fiction Film* (2014), and *Science Fiction Circuits of the South and East* (2018), with Anindita Banerjee.

Award-winning translator **Edward Gauvin** has made a living almost exclusively in various creative fields from film to fiction, with a personal focus on contemporary comics (specifically, bandes dessinées) and postsurrealist literatures of the fantastic. His work has appeared in the *New York Times*, *Harper's*, and *World Literature Today*. The translator of more than 350 graphic novels, he is a contributing editor for comics at *Words without Borders*.

Maria Haskins is a Swedish Canadian writer and reviewer of speculative fiction. Her work has appeared in *Black Static, Fireside, Beneath Ceaseless Skies,* and elsewhere. She grew up in Sweden and debuted as a writer there, but currently lives outside Vancouver with her husband, two kids, several birds, a snake, and a very large black dog.

Dale Knickerbocker is McMahon Distinguished Professor of Foreign Languages and Literatures at East Carolina University, where he teaches Hispanic literatures and cultures.

As a son of two journalists, **J. Pekka Mäkelä** (b. 1962) knew early on that writing is what a normal human being does. It just took a few decades, two different unfinished majors, and miscellaneous other studies and jobs to figure out how, when, why, and about what.

Julie Nováková is a scientist, educator, and award-winning Czech author and translator whose work has appeared in *Asimov's, Analog, Clarkesworld Magazine,* and elsewhere and been translated into eight languages so far. She edited an anthology of Czech speculative fiction in translation, *Dreams from Beyond*; coedited a book of European SF in Filipino translation, *Haka*; and created an outreach anthology of astrobiological SF, *Strangest of All*. Her newest book is a story collection titled *The Ship Whisperer* (2020).

Keren Omry is a senior (research) lecturer in the Department of English at the University of Haifa. Her main fields of scholarly interest include alternate histories, contemporaneity, and Israeli speculative fiction.

Wojciech Orliński (born in 1969 in Warsaw) trained as a chemist but has devoted most of his professional life to writing about science fiction, as a journalist, writer, and blogger. Since 1997 he has been a regular columnist for *Gazeta Wyborcza*. He has published science fiction stories and opinion pieces in *Nowa Fantastyka*, and his books include *What Are Sepulki?, All about Lem* (2010), and *America Does Not Exist* (2010).

Sunyoung Park is an associate professor in the Departments of East Asian Languages and Cultures and Gender and Sexuality Studies at the University of Southern California. Her publications include the monograph *The Proletarian Wave: Literature and Leftist Culture in Colonial Korea, 1910–1945* (2015), a collected volume titled *Revisiting Minjung: New Perspectives on the Cultural History of 1980s South Korea* (2019), and a translation anthology titled *On the Eve of the Uprising, and Other Stories from Colonial Korea* (2010).

Mingwei Song is an associate professor of Chinese literature at Wellesley College. He is the author of *Young China: National Rejuvenation and the Bildungsroman, 1900–1959* (2015) and the coeditor of *The Reincarnated Giant: An Anthology of Twenty-First-Century Chinese Science Fiction* (2018).

Takayuki Tatsumi, a science fiction critic, has taught American literature and critical theory at Keio University, Tokyo, for thirty years. He has been on the board of several journals: *Science Fiction Eye, Science Fiction Studies, Paradoxa, Journal of Transnational American Studies*, and others. His monograph *Full Metal Apache: Transactions between Cyberpunk Japan and Avant-Pop America* (2006) received the 2010 IAFA Distinguished Scholarship Award.

Francesco Verso is a multiple-award-winning Italian science fiction writer and editor. He has published *Antidoti umani, e-Doll, Nexhuman, Bloodbusters*, and *I camminatori* (includes *The Pulldogs* and *No/Mad/Land*). *Nexhuman* and *Bloodbusters*—translated by Sally McCorry—have been published in the United States and United Kingdom and soon in China. He also works as editor of *Future Fiction*, a multicultural project dedicated to scouting and publishing the best SF in translation from around the world. He may be found at www.futurefiction.org.

Index

Page numbers in italic refer to figures.

RACHEL S. CORDASCO has a PhD in literary studies and currently works as a developmental editor. She founded the website SFinTranslation.com in 2016, writes reviews for *World Literature Today* and *Strange Horizons*, and translates Italian speculative fiction, some of which has been published in magazines such as *Clarkesworld Magazine* and *Future Science Fiction Digest*. Her translation, with Jennifer Delare, of Clelia Farris's collection *Creative Surgery* is out from Rosarium Publishing. Links to her reviews, essays, and translations as well as SFT news can be found at https://www .sfintranslation.com/, https://www.facebook.com/sfintranslation, and https://twitter.com/Rcordas.

The University of Illinois Press
is a founding member of the
Association of University Presses.

—————————————————————

University of Illinois Press
1325 South Oak Street
Champaign, IL 61820-6903
www.press.uillinois.edu